Digital Transformation and Innovation

This book series is an in-depth exploration of the multifaceted nature of modern business and societal transformations driven by digital technologies. It delves into the complex interactions among technological advancements, process innovations, infrastructural requirements, and the evolving roles and skills of participants in the digital marketplace. It is a pioneering series that integrates the 'soft factors' of digitization with technological advancements in the context of structured change management. The series emphasizes the human aspect at the center of digitalization and innovation, highlighting the roles of change management, leadership, innovation, and communication as key factors for successful corporate innovation management. Covering all socially relevant fields and sectors, this series serves as a comprehensive guide for effective digitization and innovation processes.

Key Focus Areas

Technological and Process Innovations: The series examines how cutting-edge technological innovations and evolving processes are reshaping industries and organizations. It provides insights into the integration of new technologies in various business processes and how these adaptations are driving efficiency, productivity, and growth.

Infrastructural Prerequisites: A critical examination of the infrastructure needed to support the digital transformation is also a focus. This includes an exploration of both the physical (like hardware and network capabilities) and the intangible (such as digital literacy and policy frameworks) infrastructures that underpin successful digital transitions.

Media and Communication Skills: Understanding the transformation in media and the requisite communication skills in the digital age is vital. The series delves into how digital media has altered communication channels and strategies, impacting everything from customer engagement to internal corporate communications.

Business Innovation: Central to the proposed series is our focus on business innovation. This encompasses a study of how traditional business models are being reinvented through digital means, leading to new market opportunities, and competitive advantages.

Networked Management: The book series explores the concept of networked management, highlighting how digital networks facilitate new forms of collaboration, decision-making, and organizational structures. It addresses the challenges and opportunities of managing in an interconnected world where boundaries between industries, markets, and geographies are increasingly blurred.

Digital Transformation of the Media: A closer look at how the media industry is evolving in response to digital technologies. This includes changes in content creation, distribution, consumption, and monetization models, as well as the implications for privacy, ethics, and regulation.

Customer Behavior in the Digital Age: The series provides an analysis of how digital technologies have transformed customer behaviors, expectations, and engagement patterns. It offers insights into creating customer-centric strategies and experiences in a digitally-driven marketplace.

Kristina Bodrožić-Brnić · André Lucenti Estevam ·
Thomas Thiessen
Editors

AI and the Ethics of Innovation

Responsibility in Practice

Springer

Editors
Kristina Bodrožić-Brnić
Programm Management Creative AI
Mittelstand-Digital Zentrum Zukunftskultur
Potsdam, Germany

André Lucenti Estevam
Huck Otranto Camargo
São Paulo, Brazil

Thomas Thiessen
Head of Institute for Digital Transformation and Innovation
BSP Business and Law School
Berlin, Germany

ISSN 3005-1053 ISSN 3005-1061 (electronic)
Digital Transformation and Innovation
ISBN 978-3-032-20637-4 ISBN 978-3-032-20638-1 (eBook)
https://doi.org/10.1007/978-3-032-20638-1

This Springer imprint is published by the registered company Springer Nature Switzerland AG
The registered company address is: Gewerbestrasse 11, 6330 Cham, Switzerland

Preface

With the third volume in the *Digital Transformation and Innovation* series, we continue our exploration of the profound changes shaping our technological age. *AI and the Ethics of Innovation—Responsibility in Practice* arises from the growing recognition that the rapid development of Artificial Intelligence (AI) and automation demands not only technological creativity but also ethical reflection and social responsibility. Building on the foundations laid in previous volumes, this title expands the discourse to include one of the most pressing questions of our time: How can innovation remain genuinely human-centred, responsible, and value-oriented in a constantly evolving digital world shaped by economic pressures?

This third volume therefore brings together interdisciplinary contributions that examine the multifaceted relationship between ethics, innovation, and responsibility in societal, organisational, and normative contexts. The first part, *Responsibility in Society and Organisations*, is dedicated to the cultural, educational, and communicative dimensions of ethical reflection. Our authors explore how AI reshapes human relationships, democratic discourse, and artistic expression, while questioning the limits of moral agency in human–machine interaction. The contributions highlight ethical education, critical AI literacy, and cultural awareness as key foundations for an inclusive and reflective digital society.

The second part, *Governance and Normative Frameworks*, focuses on structure, law, and accountability. Here, the authors discuss how ethical principles can be translated into practice, from regulatory models and sustainability frameworks to fairness in algorithms and corporate responsibility. These reflections highlight the need to integrate ethics into the operational and strategic levels of innovation, especially as AI is increasingly embedded in decision-making processes, thereby fostering new ways of generating trust and transparency within digital ecosystems. The contributions gathered here demonstrate that responsibility in the age of AI a task that requires collaboration between technologists, educators, policymakers, and citizen.

May this book inspire our readers to see Artificial Intelligence not only as a technological challenge, but as a space for conscious ethical action and learning.

Potsdam, Germany — Kristina Bodrožić-Brnić
São Paulo,Brazil — André Lucenti Estevam
Berlin, Germany — Thomas Thiessen

AI and the Ethics of Innovation: Responsibility in Practice

In recent years, societal engagement with digital transformation has shifted significantly, with the rapid development of Artificial Intelligence playing a decisive role. Where innovation was once understood mainly in technical or economic terms, current debates increasingly address the normative standards that should guide a digitally shaped world and the question of how responsibility can be meaningfully exercised within complex technological environments. The swift and widespread integration of algorithmic systems into entrepreneurial practice, political decision-making, public communication, educational settings, and everyday social interactions makes clear that existing ethical and legal frameworks are being challenged in terms of their scope, applicability, and enforcement.

The title *AI and the Ethics of Innovation: Responsibility in Practice* responds to these developments. It understands innovation not as a purely technical process of advancement but as a societal phenomenon that requires new forms of judgement, evaluation, and responsibility. The contributions gathered here examine, from diverse disciplinary perspectives, how normative orders are being renegotiated under the influence of digital technologies, how decision-making spaces are shifting, and what roles individual, institutional, and collective forms of responsibility play within these transformations.

In this sense, the volume addresses a central diagnosis of the present: the introduction of algorithmic systems generates not only new possibilities for action but also new uncertainties, such as those arising in the context of disinformation, democratic culture, educational and competency requirements, organisational governance, and the evolving relationship between law, regulation, and technological dynamics. This constellation makes clear that ethical and legal reflection cannot occur retrospectively; it must instead be an integral component of innovation processes. The structure of the book, comprising two parts directly reflects this dual challenge.

While the first part *Responsibility in Society and Organisations* analyses how digital technologies are reshaping social practices, cultural perceptions, educational concepts, and organisational realities, the second part *Governance and Normative Frameworks* examines the normative and legal orders that accompany, constrain, or enable these transformations. This division makes clear that responsible innovation must be grounded both in social practice and in institutional and regulatory structures, and that these levels are closely interconnected and mutually reinforcing.

As the third volume in the *Digital Transformation and Innovation* series published by the Institute for Digital Transformation and Innovation (IDTI) at BSP Business and Law School, this book brings together scholarly insights and practice-oriented perspectives. Building on the first volume, *Leadership for Digital Transformation*, and the second, *Digital Transformation in Knowledge Transfer: Shaping the Future*, it continues the series' commitment to exploring how digital transformation can be shaped to enhance societal participation, safeguard democratic principles, and promote responsible forms of organisation and leadership.

Part I—*Responsibility in Society and Organisations* opens with an article whose question-form title captures the complexity of the section's central theme: "Can Ethics Be Programmed? On the Algorithmic Simulation of Moral Judgement and the Impossibility of Delegating Ethical Responsibility to Artificial Intelligence", by Thomas Thiessen and Martin Scheiber. Drawing on practical case studies from fields as diverse as economics and medicine, the authors show that while AI can organise and support decision-making processes, ethical responsibility ultimately remains with human agents.

This is followed by an article that introduces several of the book's core themes from a philosophical perspective. In "Technology, Artificial Intelligence, Disinformation, and Democratic Culture", São Paulo–based scholar Eugênio Bucci builds on the concept of *artificial ignorance*. He argues that today ignorance is no longer defined by absence, but by an overproduction of manufactured, saturating signs strategically engineered by the disinformation industry. Through clear examples, Bucci demonstrates why artificial ignorance cannot be countered by didactic knowledge, just as disinformation cannot be "treated" with additional information.

The following article by Lucas Fucci Amato, Laurindo Dias Minhoto, and Pedro de Almeida Pires Camargos develops a case study that directly illustrates Bucci's preceding analysis. The authors show how social media platforms such as Facebook and WhatsApp have contributed to the rise of the far right in Brazil in recent years. Entitled "From analogue to digital communication: economic and moral pressures on functional differentiation in the Brazilian context", the article draws on Luhmann's systems theory to examine how the digitalisation of communication—shaped by monetised information and moral binarism—is reshaping functional differentiation itself. Still on the topic of disinformation, the analysis by researchers Jan Doria and David Klotz builds on the previous discussion and introduces an essential shift in perspective. In "Detecting disinformation with AI? Escaping the Technology Solutionist Trap by Enabling AI Literacy," the authors highlight the risks of relying on AI to detect fake news and redirect the debate by proposing AI literacy as a more responsible alternative. To continue the conversation about AI literacy, moving from a *technosolutionism* review to a rather normative proposal, Eva Gengler and Marco Wedel present an evaluation of the aspects of the European Union's AI Act related to AI readiness. In "AI Literacy as a Shared Responsibility: Balancing Corporate Roles, Societal Goals, and Inclusive Education", they propose a shared-responsibility model to promote AI awareness, including a feminist-informed framework that supports inclusive education.

The next step shifts from conceptual debate to the everyday experiences of young people who take part in an extensive study of their relationship with the algorithm-driven video app TikTok. Susan Hinterding and Nicole Hanisch bring these results to the discussion in "Generation Alpha and the Power of Algorithms: TikTok Knows You Better Than You Know Yourself". Their research points out that media literacy encompasses both the critical evaluation of information and the capacity to situate oneself in digital environments emotionally. In the subsequent article "Can You Love ChatGPT? A Philosophical, Socio-Psychoanalytical, and Sociological Discussion on Relationships with Artificial Intelligence", by Sünje Lorenzen and Susan Hinterding, the authors observe the development of another mainstream app: ChatGPT. The discussion revolves around socio-psychoanalytical questions, placing the central inquiry: Are humans capable of forming loving relationships with AI?

Kristina Bodrožić-Brnić closes the first part of the book with a contribution that also encompasses artistic expressions, extending the questions of social, ecological, and technological responsibility. Her article "Ethical Resonance Worlds: Digital Art between People, Responsibility and Technology" investigates the intersection of digital art, emerging technologies, and ethical responsibility, particularly in relation to environmental degradation, societal challenges, and the affective power of immersive media. She shows how artistic practice can serve as an ethical case study by creating "resonance spaces" that invite audiences to sense and reflect on responsibility. Her analysis reinforces a central message of Part I: that human–technology relations are shaped not only by systems and infrastructures but also by meaning-making, perception, and cultural imagination.

Part II—*Governance and Normative Frameworks* opens with André Lucenti Estevam's paper, "Law, Technology and Structural Transformations: The Reconfiguration of Legal Thought", which puts forward the debate by assessing how rapid technological change compels a rethinking of foundational legal categories, interpretative methods, and institutional functions. His argument provides a conceptual anchor for the articles that follow, each of which considers a distinct dimension of the rapidly evolving governance landscape in the AI age.

In the following study, Maria Cristina De Cicco, a law scholar based in Italy, deals with the responsibilities involved in balancing ethics, the market, and new technologies from a civil law perspective. In "The Duty of Self-Protection and the Culture of Responsibility: A Reflection on Ethics, Market, and New Technologies from a Civil Law Perspective", De Cicco explains the difference between the "vulnerable" and the "responsible consumer" and nurtures the idea that a culture of responsibility is essential to assure democratic principles. After establishing who the responsible subject is and where legal rationality derives, the volume returns to the field of governance models with the study by Juliano Souza de Albuquerque Maranhão and Bernardo de Souza Dantas Fico, "Governance Frameworks for High-Risk Artificial Intelligence: Balancing Ethical Principles and Technological Innovation". Here they examine approaches and identify convergences and differences in existing (or proposed) governance models. They provide strategic guidance for advancing adaptive, inclusive, and rights-respecting regulatory frameworks that integrate innovation and accountability.

Building on this discussion, the following essay, "The Ethical Blind Spot: How AI Perpetuates Intersectional Bias", argues that, despite ongoing efforts, current ethical and compliance frameworks remain insufficient to prevent oppression arising at the intersection of multiple social categories. Fernanda Santana de Souza, the author, demonstrates through experiments with AI models the complexity of achieving ethically sound behaviour.

Shifting the focus to the corporate realm, the paper by Andreas Braun, Patricia Graf, and Anna Lejpras draws on the Douhnut Model, which provides a methodology for balancing human needs with the planet's ecological boundaries, and further provides an insightful perspective for assessing and shaping entrepreneurial practices. "Integrating Sustainability, Ethics, and Digital Transformation: A Doughnut-Inspired Framework for Responsible Entrepreneurship" introduces a new method that integrates sustainability, ethical considerations, and digital transformation within the broader field of responsible entrepreneurship. Continuing this examination of business responsibility, the article "From Digital Laggard to Responsible Leader? Why the German *Mittelstand* Turns Out to Be an Unexpected Role-Model for the Digital Age", by Ninette Florschütz and Philipp Garra, unveils how the German Mittelstand challenges dominant narratives of digital transformation by embodying a value-driven approach rooted in trust, long-term orientation, and clear communicative alignment, in an era where digitalisation prioritises speed over substance.

The book then turns to a concrete case with significant legal implications, examining recent developments in São Paulo's metropolitan rail system. In their study, "Legal and Ethical Implications of AI in Urban Transportation: A Case Study from São Paulo", the authors Cristina Godoy B. de Oliveira, Otavio de P. Albuquerque, Emily L. Belotti, Isabella F. Lopes, Tiago Augustini, and João Victor P. Gianecchini analyse the legal and ethical dimensions of AI-driven urban transportation.

The volume concludes with the paper "Civil Liability of Digital Platforms: The Imaginary Conflict Between Freedom of Expression and the Protection of Democracy—Brazilian Experiences and Guidelines" by Anderson Schreiber. He addresses the ethical dimensions of digital transformation at the constitutional level. By analysing the Court's emerging stance, the author explores the broader implications for freedom of expression and democratic resilience in the digital age, offering a well-founded perspective on the evolving relationship between technology, law, and constitutional rights, using Brazil as a paradigm.

Our editorial team consists of Thomas Thiessen, Head of the Institute for Digital Transformation and Innovation and an experienced facilitator of digital transformation processes in German small and medium-sized enterprises; Kristina Bodrožić-Brnić, a specialist in AI transfer, with a focus on creative approaches to fostering AI acceptance; and André Lucenti Estevam, our guest editor, lawyer at Huck Otranto Camargo in São Paulo and a scholar of legal theory specialising in the ethical, normative, and regulatory challenges of emerging technologies.

Besides the editors' own contributions, *AI and the Ethics of Innovation—Responsibility in Practice* brings together twenty-eight authors representing a wide range of scientific and professional backgrounds. This diversity is deliberate and reflects the understanding that questions of responsibility in the digital age can only be addressed through sustained dialogue across disciplines, professions, and societal perspectives. Accordingly, this book positions responsibility as a guiding principle for shaping AI and innovation, economic and social practices, as well as institutional and legal frameworks.

Dr. Caroline Menezes
BSP Business and Law School
Institute for Digital Transformation and Innovation
Project and Publication Management

Contents

About the Editors

Kristina Bodrožić-Brnić is an AI trainer, researcher, and university lecturer who focuses on the intersection of creativity and Artificial Intelligence. Her work explores how AI can support creative processes, strengthen human potential in SMEs, and foster technology acceptance among staff. As Program Manager at the *Mittelstand-Digital Zentrum Zukunftskultur* and Co-Manager of the Institute for Digital Transformation and Innovation at the BSP Business and Law School, she supports SMEs and academic partners in developing and applying AI-driven innovation in practice.

André Lucenti Estevam is a legal scholar specialised in the intersection of law, technology, and innovation. He holds a Ph.D. in Theory and Philosophy of Law from the University of São Paulo (USP) and a Master of Law and Business (MLB) from Bucerius Law School and WHU—Otto Beisheim School of Management. His postdoctoral research, conducted at the Max Planck Institute for Comparative and International Private Law (Hamburg), the Università Mediterranea di Reggio Calabria, and the USP, examine how emerging technologies are transforming legal approaches.

Thomas Thiessen chairs the Scientific Advisory Board at BSP Business and Law School, serves as Head of its Institute for Digital Transformation and Innovation, and is a member of the university's Senate. He also leads the consortium of the *Mittelstand-Digital Zentrum Zukunftskultur*, funded by the German Federal Ministry for Economic Affairs and Energy, which supports SMEs in navigating digital transformation. Thiessen holds a professorship in Communication and Media Management and served as Rector of BSP from 2010 to 2023, during which he played and still plays a formative role in the university's establishment and development.

Part I
Responsibility in Society and Organisations

Can Ethics Be Programmed? On the Algorithmic Simulation of Moral Judgement and the Impossibility of Delegating Ethical Responsibility to Artificial Intelligence

Martin Scheiber and Thomas Thiessen

Abstract Can machines make moral judgements, and if so, who bears responsibility for their decisions? This article explores the algorithmic representability of moral judgement and the implications for ethical accountability in the age of Artificial Intelligence (AI). Drawing from classical ethical theories (deontology, utilitarianism, virtue ethics), contemporary responsibility ethics, and sociotechnical systems analysis, it investigates the extent to which AI systems are capable of simulating moral evaluations without becoming moral agents themselves. Through practical case studies in the fields of economics, medicine, law, and the military, it is shown that while AI can structure and support decision-making processes, ethical responsibility ultimately and inescapably remains with human actors. The article advocates for an ethics of ambiguity–one that bridges technological rationality and normative reflection, while fostering ethical maturity within organisations and society.

Keywords Moral judgement · Ethical accountability · Responsibility ethics · Human agency

1 Introduction: Artificial Intelligence as a Moral Authority? A Philosophical-Ethical Assessment

Within a matter of years, Artificial Intelligence (AI) has evolved from an abstract field of research into a structural force shaping modern societies. Whether in medical diagnostics, crime prevention, recruitment, or autonomous driving, algorithmically assisted systems are now making decisions that have far-reaching consequences for

M. Scheiber (✉)
Philosophical-Theological University of Münster (PTH Münster), Münster, Germany
e-mail: martin.scheiber@web.de

T. Thiessen
BSP Business and Law School, Berlin, Germany
e-mail: thomas.thiessen@businessschool-berlin.de

K. Bodrožić-Brnić et al. (eds.), *AI and the Ethics of Innovation*, Digital Transformation and Innovation, https://doi.org/10.1007/978-3-032-20638-1_1

individuals and communities alike. No longer confined to functioning as background tools under human control, AI increasingly takes on tasks previously reserved for human judgement alone. Precisely because AI is being deployed in contexts requiring normatively charged decisions, the question arises as to whether and in what sense, AI is capable of "moral" judgement, and who ultimately bears responsibility for such judgements.

The urgency of this question becomes evident when algorithmic systems are not merely improving operational efficiency but determining what counts as just, legitimate, preferable, or worthy of protection. Consider, for instance, the selection of applicants by recruitment algorithms, triage decisions in emergency medicine based on automated risk assessments, or the identification of military targets through algorithmic image analysis. In such cases, the issues at stake are not merely technical; they involve value judgements. Machines, even if configured and steered by humans, operate in a mode that only resembles moral evaluation. This necessitates an ethical reflection on the role of AI.

At the core of this inquiry lies a question with both philosophical and practical implications: can moral and ethical judgement be algorithmically represented—and can Artificial Intelligence thereby engage in moral reasoning or assume ethical responsibility?

This question is not abstractly theoretical. It touches politics, business ethics, medicine, and security policy.

Why This Question Matters

There are three main reasons why it is crucial to address this question in a nuanced and interdisciplinary manner:

First, AI systems are increasingly being embedded in domains of public life where the stakes go beyond efficiency and functionality, where justice, equality, human dignity, and even the protection of life are concerned. Normative weight is shifting towards technical systems, often without adequate transparency or reflection regarding their normative assumptions.

Second, the public and political discourse surrounding AI tends to oscillate between two extremes: techno-utopian visions of "objectively fair" AI on the one hand, and dystopian warnings of uncontrollable machines on the other. A philosophically grounded, sober analysis can help mediate between these poles and generate more robust and nuanced assessments.

Third, institutions that implement AI, including corporations, public agencies, and governmental bodies, are increasingly under pressure to justify the ethical legitimacy of their systems. "Ethical AI" has become a popular slogan, but it often remains unclear which ethical standards are being invoked, how sustainable they are, and who ultimately bears responsibility—or legal liability—when these systems fail or cause harm.

This article therefore aims to examine the algorithmic representability of moral judgement and the possibility of delegating ethical responsibility to AI. It does so through philosophical and interdisciplinary analysis, with the ultimate goal of clarifying whether moral or ethical reasoning can, even in principle, be a domain of Artificial Intelligence. The primary focus lies at the intersection of normative theory, especially classical and modern ethics, and technological practice, particularly machine learning and automated decision systems.

Methodological Approach
Although grounded in philosophy, this investigation adopts an explicitly interdisciplinary approach. It is not based on empirical research in the narrow sense, but on theoretical-systematic analysis. The method involves conceptual clarification, argumentative differentiation, and theory-led reflection. The article draws upon the fields of normative ethics, philosophy of technology, and applied systems ethics.

Specifically, it will proceed as follows:

- clarifying the key terms: "morality", "ethics", and "algorithm";
- examining classical and modern ethical theories for their algorithmic compatibility;
- analysing real-world case studies in application domains (e.g. medicine, law, business, military) while focusing on their ethical structure;
- concluding with a comparative matrix indicating which ethical theories are compatible with which AI functionalities and where the boundary lies between moral judgement and ethical responsibility.

2 Ethics, Morality, and Algorithms—A Conceptual Clarification

On normative reflection, social rules and technical formalisation.

The concepts of "ethics", "morality" and "algorithm" are not only central to the argument of this paper but are also often used ambiguously or inconsistently in public discourse and in interdisciplinary academic contexts. This section, therefore, aims to provide terminological precision and to explore the fundamental tension between normative judgement and algorithmic formalisation.

2.1 Morality: Social Rules and Cultural Conditioning

The term *morality* refers to the set of value convictions, behavioural norms and expectations that are regarded as binding within a specific social group, society or culture. Morality manifests in rules such as "You shall not lie", "Help those in need", or "Treat all people equally". In the first instance, morality is descriptive: it describes what people in a given context regard as right or wrong, regardless of whether those beliefs are philosophically justifiable (Gert & Gert, 2025)

However, morality is also normative, typically expressed through its claim to binding validity. Moral norms do not merely describe how people act, but also prescribe how they ought to act. Morality, therefore, serves as a compass for normative orientation both in everyday life and in extreme situations. These may include conflicts involving fairness, justice or compassion. The observance of prevailing moral principles can be expected and demanded, which gives morality a regulatory function within social relations (Väyrynen, 2025).

Nonetheless, morality is always embedded in cultural narratives or religious traditions, making it historically contingent. What may be considered "moral" in one epoch or culture might be perceived as highly problematic in another. This makes morality well-suited for collective practice, but also vulnerable to blind spots and group-specific biases. Since most people perceive the moral norms of their own community not only as "commonplace" but as "right", significant conflict may arise when these norms are imposed on members of other groups, in which quite different moral standards prevail. This dynamic poses a particular challenge for contemporary pluralistic societies striving to balance cultural diversity with shared ethical frameworks (Wong, 2006; Rachels & Rachels, 2019).

2.2 Ethics: Normative Reflection and Philosophical Justification

Ethics, by contrast, refers to the philosophical reflection on morality. It does not simply ask what people regard as right but investigates why they hold such beliefs. It examines moral norms and judgements in terms of their internal coherence, universal validity, rational justification, and practical consequences (Chaddha, 2023). As Immanuel Kant in the 1785 *Groundwork of the Metaphysics of Morals* succinctly framed it, the guiding question of ethics is: "What ought I to do?" [*Was soll ich tun?*] (Kant, 1996).

Ethics is thus normative, argumentative and theory driven. While morality often operates spontaneously and contextually, ethics requires systematic analysis and critical distance. It is not bound to a particular culture or society but, at least in many of its classical forms, aspires to universality or at least to trans-cultural plausibility (Singer, 2025).

This distinction becomes practically relevant, for instance, when a hospital considers a triage decision to be morally "necessary" (e.g. based on the principle "first come, first served"), but must then examine, from an ethical standpoint, whether such a rule remains justifiable under conditions of scarcity and distributive justice.

2.3 Algorithm: Technical Form and Decision Automation

Technically speaking, an algorithm is a finite, well-defined sequence of instructions for solving a problem or computing a value. In computer science, algorithms form the basis of all software, from simple sorting procedures to complex neural networks (Rapaport, 2023). Yet algorithms are not limited to computing environments. An everyday example would be: "If it rains, take an umbrella". This already reveals an "if–then" structure—a rule that is common in many algorithms, although not universal.

An example of an algorithm without an if–then structure, translated into an everyday situation, would be:

1) Boil water.
2) Place teabag in cup.
3) Pour in the water.
4) Let steep.
5) Remove teabag.
6) Drink.

There are three basic types of algorithmic instructions.

1) Sequential instructions (step by step):
   "Pick up the toothbrush." → "Apply toothpaste." → "Brush teeth."
2) Conditional instructions (if–then):
   "If the account balance is negative, send an alert."
3) Repetitive instructions (loops):
   "Stir the dough until smooth.

Each instruction should meet the following criteria.

- Definiteness: It must be clearly formulated, leaving no room for interpretation.
- Effectiveness: It must be implementable by an agent (person, machine, or programme).
- Finiteness: It is part of a finite sequence—every algorithm must reach an end.

In the context of AI, learning algorithms are of particular relevance—especially those used in machine learning (ML) and deep learning systems. These go far beyond the basic examples above in terms of complexity. Such systems construct models that detect patterns, perform classifications, or make predictions based on large data sets. The "decisions" produced by these systems are formally unambiguous, even if they are probabilistic in nature.

Yet, regardless of their complexity, algorithmic decision processes in AI differ fundamentally from human judgement because they are:

- non-intentional (the algorithm does not "want" anything),
- non-normative (it does not derive its judgement from moral principles),
- non-reflective (it does not question its own criteria),

- non-responsible (it cannot take responsibility for outcomes or experience guilt) (Binns, 2020; Spaulding, 2020; Stader, 2024).

This makes algorithmic decision-making highly powerful, but also inherently limited.

2.4 The Central Tension: Moral Judgement vs Algorithmic Form

At this juncture, the central philosophical challenge becomes fully apparent: Can an algorithmic process achieve something that has traditionally been reserved for human, normative, context-sensitive judgement?

More concretely: If an AI system determines which patient receives priority treatment, who is eligible for a loan, or how a self-driving car should act in a dilemma, is this a moral or an ethical judgement?

This question cannot be answered simply. On a functional level, many AI systems simulate moral judgement—that is, they reproduce certain external features of human moral reasoning by evaluating data, weighing alternatives, classifying inputs, and selecting among outcomes. However, this simulation remains purely operational: the system follows programmed rules or learned statistical patterns without conscious awareness, normative reflection, or the capacity for moral accountability.

The comparison presented in the following table is not merely descriptive but analytically foundational for the argument that follows (Table 1). It highlights that algorithmic systems may replicate certain structural features of decision-making-such as consistency, rule application, and pattern recognition-while lacking the core conditions that constitute moral judgement in the full sense. In particular, intentionality, normative justification, and responsibility are not incidental attributes but essential components of moral agency. Their absence in algorithmic systems therefore marks not just a quantitative limitation, but a qualitative difference. This distinction provides the conceptual basis for the subsequent examination of whether and to what extent different ethical theories can be translated into algorithmic form.

Explanation of Evaluative Terms and Their Scope

Table 1 A comparison of human moral judgement and algorithmic decision

Feature	Human moral judgement	Algorithmic decision
Intentionality	Present (awareness, volition)	Absent
Context sensitivity	High (situational, empathetic)	Limited (model-based)
Normative justification	Possible (ethical principles)	Absent (formal, statistical)
Responsibility	Present (accountability, guilt)	Absent (technical execution)

- *Intentionality* refers to the presence of conscious purpose or volition behind an action. In human moral judgement, decisions are typically guided by deliberate intentions, informed by values, beliefs, and goals. By contrast, algorithmic processes lack any form of awareness or purpose. They execute operations based on inputs and instructions without "wanting" or "meaning" anything.
- *Context sensitivity* describes the ability to adapt decisions to the nuances of a particular situation. Human beings can respond flexibly to social cues, emotional subtleties, and ethical ambiguity. Algorithmic systems, on the other hand, operate within predefined models and datasets; their understanding of context is restricted to what has been explicitly encoded or statistically learned.
- *Normative justification* concerns the ability to ground decisions in ethical reasoning or moral principles. Humans can provide arguments for their actions, referencing duties, rights, or values. Algorithms may generate outputs that appear ethically relevant, but these are based on formal criteria or statistical optimisation—not on any genuine normative reasoning.
- *Responsibility* addresses the capacity to be held morally and legally accountable. Humans can be praised, blamed, or punished for their actions; they experience emotions like guilt and can engage in moral repair. By contrast, algorithmic systems cannot assume responsibility, as they have no agency, conscience, or moral identity. Responsibility in such cases ultimately rests with the humans and institutions that design, deploy, and oversee these systems.

2.5 Transition: From Conceptual Analysis to Theoretical Testing

This conceptual groundwork paves the way for further analysis: If ethics is more than the mere application of rules namely, a reflective engagement with questions of moral value and normative justification—we must now ask whether particular ethical theories are at all compatible with algorithmic structures.

The next section therefore turns to classical theories of ethics, deontology, utilitarianism, and virtue ethics, and assesses whether and how their fundamental principles can be modelled or simulated through technical systems.

3 Classical Ethical Theories and Algorithmic Representability

What Ethical Theories Reveal About Technical Responsibility.

For millennia, classical ethical theories have provided systematic interpretative frameworks for justifying, evaluating, and guiding moral action. Each of these theories centres on different aspects of morality: rules, consequences, or character. In the context of algorithmic systems, we must now ask: which of these theories can, in principle, be transferred to algorithmic decision-making structures, and where are their limits?

This section examines three paradigmatic approaches to ethics:

1. Deontology (Immanuel Kant)
2. Utilitarianism (Jeremy Bentham, John Stuart Mill)
3. Virtue ethics (Aristotle, Alasdair MacIntyre)

Each theory is first outlined in its core tenets and then assessed regarding its algorithmic compatibility. The goal is not merely to explore technical feasibility, but also to critically examine the normative and anthropological assumptions of each ethical model.

3.1 Deontology: Morality from Duty

Core Assumptions of the Theory

Immanuel Kant's (1724–1804) deontological ethics is based on the principle of duty: an action is morally good if it is performed out of respect for the moral law—regardless of its consequences. Central to this is the categorical imperative, especially in its universalisation formula: "Act only according to that maxim whereby you can at the same time will that it should become a universal law". (Kant, 1785/1996, p. 31)

Kant attributes to human beings a special dignity, as they are capable of giving themselves moral law through reason, which is an expression of their autonomy. From this follows a fundamental claim: only autonomous beings, who are ends in themselves, can be bearers of moral responsibility.

Algorithmic Implementation

A machine could, in principle, test whether certain rules are logically consistent and universally applicable. One could simulate the categorical imperative technically, for example by having a system evaluate proposed maxims and exclude those that cannot be generalised. Some research in "machine ethics" pursues precisely this approach (Anderson & Anderson, 2011).

However, Kant's ethics is not merely rule-based; it is an ethics of intention. Moral action, for him, presupposes the inner capacity to consent to the law out of reverence. A machine may follow rules, but it does not "respect" them. It possesses neither consciousness nor self-legislation nor moral insight.

Critical Assessment

To clarify these distinctions, the following table summarises the central evaluative criteria of Kantian ethics and assesses their respective potential for algorithmic implementation (Table 2). It highlights a crucial asymmetry: while certain formal aspects of deontological reasoning-most notably the logical testing of rules for universalisability-can be approximated in computational terms, the core moral dimensions of Kant's framework remain beyond the reach of technical systems. In

Table 2 Critical assessment of core ethical evaluation criteria, highlighting their potential and limitations for algorithmic simulation

Evaluation criterion	Potential for algorithmic implementation
Rule evaluation (universalisability)	Suitable for algorithmic simulation
Autonomy and self-legislation	Not machine achievable
Intention (respect for the law)	Not representable
Responsibility and dignity	Bound to human subjects

particular, autonomy, intention understood as respect for the moral law, and the attribution of responsibility are irreducibly tied to human subjectivity and cannot be meaningfully replicated by algorithmic processes.

Conclusion
While deontology allows for formal approximations—such as universal rule testing, the core ethical dimension lies in the subjective capacity of the rational agent. AI systems cannot act "out of duty". Morality here is inseparable from consciousness and human dignity.

3.2 Utilitarianism: Morality from Consequences

Core Assumptions of the Theory
Utilitarianism (Bentham, 1789; Mill, 1863) is based on the principle of the greatest happiness: an action is morally right if it produces the greatest amount of happiness (or utility) for the greatest number. This is a consequentialist approach: it is the outcome, not the intention, that counts.

Utilitarian reasoning lends itself to quantification: units of happiness (Bentham's "hedons") could, at least hypothetically, be measured and used to calculate and compare possible courses of action. In practice, this often means maximising efficiency, minimising risk, and aggregating utility.

Algorithmic Implementation
Precisely because utilitarianism is grounded in calculating consequences, it appears particularly compatible with algorithmic logic:

- Machine learning systems can simulate decision scenarios, predict probabilities, and optimise for certain utility metrics.
- In decision trees and AI-controlled agent systems, utilitarian principles are frequently applied, for example, in medical triage or autonomous driving scenarios.

However, fundamental challenges remain:

- What exactly constitutes "utility"? How should we weigh values such as freedom, justice, or human dignity against safety or time-saving?

Table 3 Overview of utilitarian evaluation criteria and their feasibility and limits in algorithmic systems

Evaluation criterion	Potential for algorithmic implementation
Utility calculation	Feasible in principle
Scenario modelling	Technically simulable
Value weighting	Normatively demanding
Inclusion of intangible goods	Limited representability

- For whom is the happiness calculated? How are minorities, future generations, or non-human entities taken into account?
- How are instrumentalising decisions avoided? If the benefit to the many justifies the suffering of a few, severe moral conflicts may arise.

Critical Assessment

The following table summarises the central evaluative criteria of utilitarian ethics and assesses their respective suitability for algorithmic implementation (Table 3). At first glance, utilitarianism appears particularly compatible with computational systems, as it relies on the aggregation and optimisation of outcomes. Indeed, functions such as utility calculation and scenario modelling can be operationalised within algorithmic frameworks. However, the table also makes clear that this apparent compatibility is conditional: it depends on prior normative decisions regarding what counts as "utility", how different values are to be weighted, and whether non-quantifiable goods-such as dignity, rights, or justice-can be adequately represented. These unresolved normative assumptions mark the limits of any straightforward translation of utilitarian reasoning into machine-based decision-making.

Conclusion

Utilitarianism is technically compatible, but philosophically fragile. Its algorithmisation depends on prior normative assumptions about what counts as "utility" and how it is to be measured. Without well-defined ethical foundations, moral judgement risks becoming arbitrary or blind to non-quantifiable values.

3.3 *Virtue Ethics: Morality from Character*

Core Assumptions of the Theory

Virtue ethics originates in Aristotle (2009) and has been modernised by thinkers such as Alasdair MacIntyre (1981). It does not primarily ask about rules or consequences, but about moral character and the good life (*eudaimonia*). Actions are morally good when they arise from virtuous dispositions, shaped by practical wisdom (*phronesis*), justice, courage, temperance, and the like.

Virtues are not rules but habituated dispositions, formed through experience, practice, and social interaction. Moral judgement here expresses itself in situational appropriateness, empathy, sensitivity to context, and moderation.

Table 4 Critical assessment of virtue-ethical evaluation criteria and their incompatibility with algorithmic implementation

Evaluation criterion	Potential for algorithmic implementation
Development of virtues	Not possible
Context-sensitive action	Highly limited
Practical wisdom (*phronesis*)	Not formalisable
Social embeddedness	Not present

Algorithmic Implementation

The limitations of technical modelling become especially evident here:

- AI has no character—it does not form habits or dispositions.
- AI does not experience the world—it does not live, suffer, or err in the human sense.
- AI is not embedded in social practices—it is externally programmed or trained.

Even if a system arrives at excellent decisions, it does not do so *out of virtue* but by executing code. It lacks subjectivity, social embeddedness, and affective resonance.

Critical Assessment

The following table systematises this fundamental limitation by outlining the core evaluative criteria of virtue ethics and assessing their compatibility with algorithmic systems (Table 4). Unlike deontological or utilitarian approaches, which at least partially lend themselves to formalisation, virtue ethics is grounded in the development of character, practical wisdom, and socially embedded forms of judgement. As the table illustrates, these elements resist computational modelling in a more radical sense: they are not merely difficult to implement, but conceptually incommensurable with algorithmic structures. What is at stake here is not a deficit of technical sophistication, but a categorical difference between embodied, experience-based moral agency and rule-based or data-driven processing.

Conclusion

Virtue ethics makes it unmistakably clear why moral action is more than rule compliance or outcome optimisation. It is an expression of a mature character; it means something that cannot be programmed. AI may simulate rule-based decision-making or calculate consequences, but it can neither develop a moral character nor embody virtue.

4 Modern Ethics of Responsibility and Socio-Technical Networks

From the Principle of Responsibility to an Ethics of Distributed Systems

Classical ethical theories tend to focus on individual agents, conceived as rational subjects, utility maximisers or bearers of virtue. In contrast, modern approaches increasingly emphasise the complex contexts, in which technological action unfolds. These approaches not only ask whether a decision is morally "right", but also examine who can be held responsible in the technologically networked and distributed structures of contemporary systems.

This section examines two influential concepts that precisely address these issues:

1. Hans Jonas's *Principle of Responsibility* as a future-oriented ethics of technological power, and
2. Bruno Latour's *Actor-Network Theory* as a model of distributed agency and responsibility.

Both perspectives foreground dimensions that are central to the ethical discussion of AI systems: long-range effects, uncertainty, interdependencies, and institutional responsibility.

4.1 Hans Jonas: Responsibility in the Face of Technological Power

Core assumptions of the theory
In his seminal work *The Imperative of Responsibility* (1978), Hans Jonas formulates an ethics for the age of technological civilisation. His core thesis is as follows: the greater the power of human action, the greater the ethical responsibility for its consequences. Technology, according to Jonas, is not merely a neutral tool, it is a power amplifier, capable of producing irreversible effects on future life.

Because technological interventions often entail long-term, unforeseeable consequences (e.g. in ecology, medicine, or AI), Jonas calls for an ethics that does not solely rely on existing rights and duties but instead prioritises the preservation of the conditions of human life for future generations. His famous imperative reads: "Act so that the effects of your action are not destructive of the future possibility of such life". (Jonas, 1984, p. 11.)

Relevance for AI
AI systems are paradigmatic examples of technological power whose consequences are difficult to predict:

- They influence decision-making structures in business, law, and politics.
- They may exacerbate structural discrimination or improve fairness.
- They can give rise to new forms of dependency, loss of control, or alienation.

Jonas's approach therefore demands a heightened ethical awareness of potential long-range effects, whether through unintended side effects, social polarisation, or technological path dependency.

Algorithmic Implementation
AI may support risk modelling, scenario planning, or the forecasting of long-term impacts–such as through ethical impact assessments. However, Jonas's ethics is more

than risk calculus: it calls for an existential relationship to the future. Responsibility, for Jonas, is not a numerical variable, but a moral attitude, shaped by care, humility, and anticipation.

Conclusion

Jonas provides a dimension of ethical depth that AI systems themselves cannot deliver—though they may be guided by it. His ethics calls on human actors to bear responsibility for the power that AI places in their hands. Responsibility can be delegated but never offloaded.

4.2 *Bruno Latour: Actor-Network Theory (ANT)*

Foundational Assumptions of the Theory

The French sociologist and science theorist Bruno Latour (2005) proposed a radically different view of technical agency. In his *Actor-Network Theory* (ANT), the traditional distinction between subjects (humans) and objects (technologies) is dissolved. Instead, both human and non-human entities form socio-technical networks in which actions emerge in a distributed and relational way.

Within these networks, non-human entities, such as algorithms, platforms, or sensors, are regarded as *actants* because they actively participate in shaping decisions. This participation can take the form of filtering, pre-selecting options, structuring interaction flows, or generating automated responses.

Responsibility, according to ANT, is not localised but distributed. It arises from the way networks are configured, governed, and maintained. Whoever designs, trains, deploys, or regulates a system becomes co-responsible for its effects, even when no single decision can be attributed to a specific actor.

Relevance for AI

Latour's model proves particularly useful for analysing contemporary AI infrastructures, which are rarely reducible to singular decisions made by isolated systems:

- In credit scoring, it is not "the AI" alone that determines outcomes, but a network comprising training data, IT architecture, algorithmic models, user inputs, regulatory standards, and market incentives.
- In medicine or law, decisions emerge from the interplay between clinicians or legal professionals, AI tools, software vendors, institutional frameworks, and client or patient data.

In these complex constellations, the traditional model of individual accountability becomes insufficient. Instead, a new ethic of networked responsibility is needed: Who is shaping the system? Who has the capacity to intervene? Who bears ethical responsibility for emergent outcomes?

Table 5 Assessment of Actor–Network Theory (ANT) in relation to algorithmic implementation and ethical AI.

Assessment criterion	Potential for algorithmic implementation
Concept of distributed responsibility	Not machine-executable, but institutionally applicable
Systemic transparency	Can be supported through governance design
Collective ethics of design	Human-led, not automatable
Technological agency	Recognised as part of social configurations

Algorithmic Implementation

ANT is not a normative theory and therefore not programmable. It does not tell us what *should* be done but reveals *how* agency is distributed and mediated. Nonetheless, ANT can substantially inform our ethical understanding of AI systems by shifting focus away from isolated actors towards systemic relations.

Algorithmic decision-making, from this perspective, is not interpreted as autonomous agency but as the activation of nodes within a relational and socio-technical web. The following table clarifies this shift in perspective by outlining the central analytical dimensions of Actor-Network Theory and their relevance for the assessment of algorithmic systems (Table 5). Rather than asking whether ethical principles can be encoded into machines, ANT reframes the problem by examining how agency and responsibility are distributed across socio-technical networks. As the table demonstrates, this approach does not lend itself to direct algorithmic implementation, since it is not a normative framework prescribing action. However, it offers valuable conceptual tools for understanding and governing AI systems: by highlighting the roles of institutional design, systemic transparency, and collective responsibility, it enables a more nuanced account of how ethically relevant outcomes emerge within complex technological environments.

Conclusion

Latour's perspective demands a fundamental shift in thinking: it is not *the AI* that morally judges, but the *network* of humans and technologies that jointly produces morally relevant outcomes. Responsibility, in this model, becomes a matter of design power, not of computational capability. It must be anchored in governance structures and shared accountability, rather than in the illusion of neutral or autonomous machines.

5 The Limits of the Machine: Judgement and Responsibility

A Critical Reflection on Machine Ethics and the Anthropological Boundary.

Following the analysis of classical and modern ethical theories, we arrive at a central question: Can AI not only simulate decisions but also morally judge and act with ethical responsibility in the full sense of the term?

This question is not merely speculative. It lies at the core of the emerging field of *machine ethics* and touches on deep anthropological, epistemological, and philosophy-of-technology issues.

5.1 What Does It Mean to "Judge Morally"?

Before evaluating whether AI can engage in moral judgement, we must clarify what such judgement entails. Philosophical accounts vary but converge on several key conditions:

- Capacity for reflection: Moral judgement presupposes the ability to weigh and consider reasons.
- Context sensitivity: Judgement is not purely formal but attuned to situations and specificities.
- Intentionality: Moral acts are purposeful and value-laden.
- Accountability: Whoever judges morally can be held ethically responsible for the consequences of that judgement.

AI systems may partially fulfil some of these conditions (e.g. through statistical context analysis), but others, particularly those involving subjectivity, are fundamentally out of reach.

5.2 Research Perspectives in Machine Ethics

James Moor (2006) offers a widely adopted classification of ethical machines by distinguishing three types. The following table provides a systematic overview of Moor's influential classification and serves to differentiate levels of ethical functionality in artificial systems (Table 6). It makes clear that what is often loosely described as "ethical AI" in fact encompasses fundamentally distinct categories: from systems that merely constrain harmful behaviour to those that are designed to simulate ethical reasoning, and finally to hypothetical agents that would possess full moral agency. This differentiation is crucial, as it prevents a conceptual conflation of technical capabilities with genuine moral agency. While current AI systems may approximate elements of implicit or explicit ethical behaviour, the notion of a fully ethical agent presupposes capacities-such as consciousness, free will, and accountability-that remain beyond the scope of contemporary technology. The table thus situates current developments within a broader conceptual landscape and underscores the gap between functional simulation and authentic moral agency.

Table 6 James Moor's (2006) classification of ethical machines

Type	Description
Implicit ethical agents	Systems designed to avoid harmful behaviour (e.g. emergency shut-off mechanisms)
Explicit ethical agents	Systems that incorporate coded ethical rules and respond to moral dilemmas
Full ethical agents	Hypothetical entities with consciousness, free will, and moral responsibility

While the first two categories are already being realised (e.g. in medical assistance systems or autonomous vehicles), the third remains entirely speculative, requiring a form of artificial consciousness that does not currently exist.

Recent contributions (e.g. Gunkel, 2018) reinforce the point: Ethical standards for machines cannot be fulfilled by technical means alone. A machine may apply rules, however, it does not *understand* them. It may pass a moral dilemma test, but it cannot *justify* its choice beyond statistical or symbolic reference.

5.3 Anthropological Difference: Why AIs Are Not Moral Subjects

The defining limit lies in the anthropological difference between humans and machines. Moral action is not just a functional output—it is an inner act involving:

- self-relation and conscience,
- empathy, compassion, emotional resonance (which AI may convincingly simulate but not *experience*),
- existential concern for one's own life and the lives of others (again, simulable but not lived),
- the capacity to endure and reflect on normative tension.

Vallor (2016) argues that while AI can assess possible options, it cannot assume moral responsibility. And Gunkel (2018) contends that AI systems may simulate moral decision-making processes but lack the capacity for moral judgement.

5.4 Ethical Responsibility: A Non-transferable Dimension?

Even when AI systems appear precise, consistent, and fair, the crucial question remains: Who bears ethical responsibility for the decisions they enable?

Several principles follow:

- Responsibility may be delegated—but it cannot be eliminated.

Table 7 Overview of AI capabilities and their limitations in moral judgement and responsibility

Question	AI systems are capable of...	But...
Can they morally judge?	Rule application, simulation	No true comprehension or justification
Can they assume ethical responsibility?	No	Lacking subjectivity, conscience, accountability
What is their proper role?	Decision support, modelling of scenarios	Not ethical agents or moral subjects

- Technical attribution is not equivalent to moral accountability.
- Developers, institutions, policymakers, and users remain the true moral agents.

This has tangible consequences for governance, law, and ethics:

- Whoever deploys AI must integrate ethical expertise alongside technical skill.
- Organisations need formal mechanisms of ethical reflection: ethics boards, impact assessments, and transparent audit procedures.

Responsibility Remains Human

The following table synthesises the preceding argument by systematically contrasting the functional capacities of AI systems with the normative requirements of moral judgement and ethical responsibility (Table 7). It illustrates that, while AI can replicate certain procedural aspects of decision-making-such as rule application or scenario modelling-it does not fulfil the conditions necessary for moral agency. In particular, the absence of subjectivity, understanding, and accountability marks a decisive boundary that cannot be overcome through increasing technical sophistication alone. The table therefore makes explicit that the role of AI must remain instrumental: it can inform and support human judgement, but it cannot replace the human capacity to assume responsibility. This distinction is not merely practical but conceptual, and it underpins the normative conclusion of this chapter.

Conclusion

AI can simulate moral judgements, but it cannot bear ethical responsibility. The distinction between ethical output and moral agency is fundamental and no technical advancement can bridge it.

6 AI and Morality: Simulation or Genuine Moral Judgement?

The previous sections have shown that AI systems are capable of simulating moral evaluation, for example, by applying rules, calculating utility, or recognising patterns. But does this already imply that AI systems are capable of moral judgement in the proper sense? And if they issue such judgements, a follow-up question inevitably arises: who is responsible for them? This section differentiates between various notions of machine "moral behaviour" and highlights the limits of ethical attribution.

6.1 Simulation ≠ Moral Judgement

The crucial difference between human and algorithmic judgement lies in the capacity for self-reflection, intentionality, and the assumption of responsibility. AI can apply rules, but it does not understand why. It can deliver outputs, however, it has no awareness of norms, no empathy, and no integrity.

Thus, the moral status of algorithmic decisions remains instrumental: they are tools for decision-making, not morally accountable agents. They do not act on reasons, nonetheless, execute computations.

6.2 Responsibility in Organisations

Ethical responsibility for algorithmically supported judgements remains with the human agents and organisations that:

- develop the systems (e.g. engineers, developers, companies),
- deploy them (e.g. public authorities, hospitals, businesses),
- oversee them (e.g. regulatory bodies, ethics boards),
- legitimise them (e.g. political institutions, the public).

This responsibility cannot be delegated, even when decision-making processes are automated. What is needed are procedural safeguards that clearly anchor accountability: including well-defined responsibility structures, auditable decisions-making processes, and institutionalised spaces for ethical reflection.

Conclusion

AI can simulate certain aspects of moral judgement, particularly where structured rules or quantifiable utilities are involved. However, moral judgement in the proper sense, that is, the reflective engagement with normative conflicts, taking into account context, meaning, values, and consequences, remains a fundamentally human faculty. Responsibility for the moral implications of algorithmic systems does not lie within the machine, but with those who design, implement, and apply them.

7 Practical Domains: Business, Medicine, Law, and the Military. How AI issues moral judgements—and who bears ethical responsibility

Theory and ethical debate only gain real traction when tested against concrete practice. The question of whether AI can engage in moral judgement is no mere speculation, it pertains directly to real, often highly sensitive and dramatic decision-making scenarios across key sectors of society. This section examines four such domains: business, medicine, law, and the military. In each case, we ask whether AI makes moral judgements, what form these take, and who ultimately bears ethical responsibility.

7.1 Business: Algorithmic Fairness in Recruitment and Credit Assessment

In economic contexts, AI is increasingly used for decision support and in some cases, even decision automation. This is particularly evident in recruitment, where tools such as HireVue, Pymetrics, or CV-Parsers employing natural language processing analyse and rank applicant profiles.

Similarly, automated scoring systems have long been used in the credit sector. They assess creditworthiness based on past payment data, residence, employment, and purchasing behaviour, often without transparency regarding how criteria are weighted or decisions justified.

Moral Judgements by AI

In these cases, AI in effect issues moral judgements, for example, in deciding who is deemed "trustworthy" or who deserves a fair chance in an application process. Such decisions go beyond operational efficiency; they touch on social conceptions of justice, access, and equal opportunity.

Ethical Responsibility

Given that decisions are based on complex, often opaque models, assigning ethical responsibility becomes difficult. Yet ultimately it rests with:

- the developers of the models,
- the organisations that deploy them,
- the regulatory authorities that oversee standards of fairness.

In such cases, an ethics audit is imperative: Are certain groups systematically disadvantaged? Are the criteria justifiable? Are there mechanisms for appeal?

7.2 Medicine: AI-Supported Triage Systems

In emergency medicine, critical decisions must often be made within seconds, for instance, in the case of mass casualties or resource scarcity. Increasingly, algorithmic triage systems are used to prioritise patients based on vital signs, medical history, and comparative data.

An example of a well-established triage protocol is the *Rapid Emergency Triage and Treatment System for Adults* (RETTS-A), used in Scandinavian emergency departments (Kauppi et al., 2025). Although not a learning AI system, RETTS-A is often benchmarked against—or augmented by—modern AI tools. A recent study tested an AI tool designed to predict severe complications in patients and found that it outperformed RETTS-A in accuracy, demonstrating the potential for intelligent decision-support in future emergency contexts (Kauppi et al., 2025).

Moral Judgements by AI

Suppose a system determines that Patient A should receive priority over Patient B. In this case, it is making a moral judgement. It is not only about medical urgency but, implicitly, about the situational relevance of one life over another in times of scarcity.

Ethical Responsibility

Although final decisions typically remain with medical professionals, there is a growing risk of automatic deference to algorithmic recommendations. Ethics demands the following:

- transparency in the system's decision criteria,
- continuous review and calibration of the models,
- clear attribution of responsibility: physicians must retain moral agency and cannot abdicate judgement to machines.

7.3 Law: Risk Assessment and Algorithmic Justice

One of the most controversial application areas lies in criminal justice. In the United States, the COMPAS system is used to calculate the likelihood of reoffending. These risk scores inform decisions regarding bail, sentencing, and probation (Potts, 2020).

Moral Judgements by AI

The algorithm classifies individuals as "high-risk" or "low-risk", with real consequences for their liberty. This classification amounts to a moral assessment of whether a person is likely to harm others. The issue is particularly fraught because studies have shown that COMPAS yields significantly higher false-positive rates for Black defendants (Angwin et al., 2016).

Ethical Responsibility
Responsibility lies with the legal system as a whole:

- Is the score treated as advisory or determinative?
- How are biases identified and mitigated?
- Are affected persons given the opportunity to challenge algorithmic decisions?

This case illustrates a recurring pattern: while the algorithm delivers a moral evaluation, ethical responsibility remains with the institution that implements it.

7.4 Military: Target Identification by AI

In military contexts, the Israeli armed forces have deployed AI systems such as *Lavender* and *The Gospel* in Gaza to merge aerial imagery, intercepted communications, and behavioural data into target recommendations for human analysts. According to *The Guardian*, the system known as *Lavender* compiled a database of approximately 37,000 potential targets, which were then reviewed and approved by human intelligence officers (McKernan & Davies, 2024). This reportedly accelerated the pace of targeting but raised ethical concerns about automation, proportionality, and diminished human oversight.

While military officials claim that such systems aim to reduce civilian harm, critics, including analysts featured in the *Financial Times* podcast *Tech Tonic*, warn that overreliance on AI can lead to a loss of moral accountability and increased detachment from the consequences of lethal decisions (Financial Times, 2025).

Moral Judgements by AI
The identification of a target is a decision about legitimacy—and thus about life and death. It constitutes one of the gravest forms of moral evaluation imaginable.

Ethical Responsibility
According to the Geneva Conventions, all military strikes must comply with principles of proportionality and distinction. Ethical responsibility, therefore remains unequivocally human:

- Who authorised the strike?
- Were the underlying data verified?
- Was human judgement involved in the final decision?

Fully automated targeting without human oversight would violate international humanitarian law and is ethically indefensible.

Responsibility Remains Human
The following table extends this analysis beyond the military domain and synthesises the findings across all examined application areas (Table 8). It provides a comparative overview of how AI systems operate in different sectors and clarifies a consistent

Table 8 Allocation of ethical responsibility in AI-supported decision-making across sectors

Sector	Does AI make moral judgements?	Can it assume responsibility?	Who bears ethical responsibility?
Business	Yes (e.g. applicant selection)	No	Developers, companies, regulators
Medicine	Yes (e.g. triage systems)	No	Medical professionals, hospital leadership
Law	Yes (e.g. risk assessments)	No	Judiciary, legislators, legal institutions
Military	Yes (e.g. target selection)	No	Military command, government, armed forces

pattern: although such systems are capable of generating outputs that resemble moral judgements, they lack the capacity to assume ethical responsibility. Across domains as diverse as business, medicine, law, and military operations, responsibility remains anchored in human actors and institutional frameworks. The table thus makes explicit that the ethical implications of AI are not confined to isolated cases but reflect a structural feature of algorithmic decision-making in contemporary societies.

8 Conclusion and Outlook

Why AI Can Assist in Moral Judgement, but Can Never Assume Ethical Responsibility

Following the theoretical analysis and the practical exploration of diverse fields of application, a clear conclusion emerges: Artificial intelligence can assist humans in making moral judgements, but it cannot replace them, nor can it assume ethical responsibility.

This insight is neither technophobic nor culturally pessimistic. On the contrary, it acknowledges the capabilities of modern algorithmic systems while also addressing their fundamental limitations. The strength of AI lies in its ability to:

- process large volumes of data,
- detect patterns,
- apply rules consistently, and
- relieve human actors of cognitive bottlenecks.

All these functions can contribute to making human decision-making more precise, fairer, and more efficient.

However, at the threshold of the ethical, it becomes apparent what machines cannot do—and arguably never will:

- They do not reflect on norms; they merely apply them.
- They do not understand meaning; they process probabilities and symbols.
- They do not assume responsibility; they remain technically attributable systems.

- They do not judge with conscience, but with calculation.

Ethical Judgement Means

- enduring ambiguity,
- weighing perspectives,
- reasoning through normative conflicts, and
- taking responsibility for consequences.

No algorithm can do this, because it lacks intentionality, subjectivity, and moral awareness.

AI as a Challenge to Ethical Maturity

The central challenge of the coming years is therefore not primarily to develop "ethical AI", but rather to foster ethically mature human beings and responsible organisations capable of handling AI in sensitive domains.

This entails:

- Embedding ethics in education, not only in the humanities, but also in technology development, medicine, and management.
- Institutionalising ethical deliberation within organisations, through ethics boards, impact assessments, and transparent accountability structures.
- Establishing normative frameworks in politics that go beyond risk mitigation to actively safeguard human values.

This also calls for a critical engagement with existing ethical frameworks, such as the EU AI Act or the AI ethics guidelines of major technology firms, which often oscillate between minimal technical standards and far-reaching moral aspirations.

Outlook: Towards an Ethics of Ambiguity

Following the reflections of Simone de Beauvoir (*Pour une morale de l'ambiguïté*, 1947) and Zygmunt Bauman (*Postmodern Ethics*, 1993), one could argue: A mature ethics for the age of AI is not an ethics of clarity, but an ethics of ambiguity.

Such an ethics acknowledges that:

- There are no simple answers.
- Moral conflicts are often irresolvable.
- Responsibility must always be borne concretely, situationally, and through dialogue.

It demands:

- Resistance to the seduction of algorithmic simplification,
- Responsibility in the face of uncertainty, and
- A culture of ethics that not only shapes technology but also interrogates it.

Final Thesis

AI can support us in moral judgement, but it can never replace our ethical responsibility. It is a tool, not a moral subject—a guide, not a conscience. The responsibility for acting rightly, justly, and with dignity remains—inescapably—human.

References

Anderson, M., & Anderson, S. L. (2011). *Machine ethics*. Cambridge University Press. https://doi.org/10.1017/CBO9780511978036

Angwin, J., Larson, J., Mattu, S., & Kirchner, L. (2016, May 23). *Machine bias: There's software used across the country to predict future criminals. ProPublica*. https://www.propublica.org/article/machine-bias-risk-assessments-in-criminal-sentencing

Aristotle. (2009). *Nicomachean ethics* (W. D. Ross & L. Brown, Trans. & Eds.). Oxford University Press. (Original work published 350 BCE).

Bauman, Z. (1993). *Postmodern ethics*. Blackwell.

Beauvoir, S. de. (1947). *Pour une morale de l'ambiguïté*. Gallimard.

Bentham, J. (1789). *An introduction to the principles of morals and legislation*. T. Payne.

Binns, R. (2020). Human judgment in algorithmic loops: Individual justice and automated decision-making. *Regulation & Governance, 14*(1), 100–116. https://doi.org/10.1111/rego.12358

Chaddha, R. (2023). Ethics and morality. *International Journal of Ethics and Governance*. Advance online publication. https://www.ncbi.nlm.nih.gov/pmc/articles/PMC10593668/

Financial Times. (2025, April 29). Future weapons—Battlefield AI [Audio podcast episode]. In Tech Tonic. https://www.ft.com/content/802864cb-a680-48ea-837b-32cb31ad09e4

Gert, J., & Gert, B. (2025). The definition of morality. In E. N. Zalta & U. Nodelman (Eds.), *The stanford encyclopedia of philosophy* (Spring 2025 ed.). Metaphysics Research Lab, Stanford University. https://plato.stanford.edu/archives/spr2025/entries/morality-definition/

Gunkel, D. J. (2018). *Robot rights*. MIT Press.

Jonas, H. (1978). Technology and responsibility: Reflections on the new tasks of ethics. *Social Research, 40*(1), 31–54.

Jonas, H. (1984). *The imperative of responsibility: In search of an ethics for the technological age*. University of Chicago Press. (Original work published 1979).

Kant, I. (1996). *Groundwork of the metaphysics of morals* (M. Gregor, Trans. & Ed.). Cambridge University Press. (Original work published 1785).

Kauppi, W., Imberg, H., Herlitz, J., Molin, O., Axelsson, C., & Magnusson, C. (2025). Advancing a machine learning-based decision support tool for pre-hospital assessment of dyspnoea by emergency medical service clinicians: A retrospective observational study. *BMC Emergency Medicine, 25*(1), Article 2. https://doi.org/10.1186/s12873-024-00999-8

Latour, B. (2005). *Reassembling the social: An introduction to actor-network-theory*. Oxford University Press.

MacIntyre, A. (1981). *After virtue: A study in moral theory*. University of Notre Dame Press.

McKernan, B., & Davies, H. (2024, April 3). 'The machine did it coldly': Israel used AI to identify 37,000 Hamas targets. *The Guardian*. https://www.theguardian.com/world/2024/apr/03/israel-gaza-ai-database-hamas-airstrikes

Mill, J. S. (1863). *Utilitarianism*. Parker, Son, and Bourn.

Moor, J. H. (2006). The nature, importance, and difficulty of machine ethics. *IEEE Intelligent Systems, 21*(4), 18–21. https://doi.org/10.1109/MIS.2006.76

Potts, A. (2020, October 30). *Implementation of risk assessment tools in the criminal justice system: What is a fair approach?* Roosevelt Institute. https://rooseveltinstitute.org/publications/implementation-of-risk-assessment-tools-in-the-criminal-justice-system/

Rachels, J., & Rachels, S. (2019). *The elements of moral philosophy* (9th ed.). McGraw-Hill Education.

Rapaport, W. J. (2023). Philosophy of computer science. In E. N. Zalta & F. Beck (Eds.), *The stanford encyclopedia of philosophy* (Winter 2023 ed.). Metaphysics Research Lab. https://plato.stanford.edu/archives/win2023/entries/computer-science/

Singer, P. (2025, December 29). Ethics. In *Encyclopaedia britannica*. Retrieved March 25, 2026, from https://www.britannica.com/topic/ethics-philosophy

Spaulding, N. W. (2020). Is human judgment necessary? Artificial intelligence, algorithmic governance, and the law. In M. D. Dubber, F. Pasquale, & S. Das (Eds.), *The Oxford handbook of ethics of AI* (pp. 259–282). Oxford University Press. https://doi.org/10.1093/oxfordhb/9780190067397.013.25

Stader, D. (2024). Algorithms don't have a future: On the relation of judgement and calculation. *Philosophy & Technology*. Advance online publication. https://doi.org/10.1007/s13347-024-00705-3

Vallor, S. (2016). *Technology and the virtues: A philosophical guide to a future worth wanting*. Oxford University Press.

Väyrynen, P. (2025). Thick ethical concepts. In E. N. Zalta & U. Nodelman (Eds.), *The stanford encyclopedia of philosophy* (Winter 2025 ed.). Metaphysics Research Lab. https://plato.stanford.edu/entries/thick-ethical-concepts/

Wong, D. B. (2006). *Natural moralities: A defense of pluralistic relativism*. Oxford University Press.

Martin Scheiber studied Philosophy, Psychology, and German Literature at Ludwig Maximilian University in Munich. After graduating, he worked in Munich and Berlin in various strategy and management consulting roles, focusing on change management, leadership, digital transformation, organisational culture, mission development, and communication. His recent work includes playing a leading role in the strategic and organisational development of the Philosophical-Theological University of Münster and driving the establishment of the Campus for Theology and Spirituality in Berlin, where he contributed to the design of academic programs, research initiatives, and professional training formats.

Thomas Thiessen chairs the Scientific Advisory Board at BSP Business and Law School, serves as Head of its Institute for Digital Transformation and Innovation, and is a member of the university's Senate. He also leads the consortium of the Mittelstand-Digital Zentrum Zukunftskultur, funded by the German Federal Ministry for Economic Affairs and Energy, which supports SMEs in navigating digital transformation. Thiessen holds a professorship in Communication and Media Management and served as Rector of BSP from 2010 to 2023, during which he played and still plays a formative role in the university's establishment and development.

Technology, Artificial Intelligence, Disinformation, and Democratic Culture

Eugênio Bucci

Abstract This article offers reflections on the complex interplay between Artificial Intelligence, disinformation, and democratic culture. Instead of treating disinformation solely as a collection of false statements, the text explores the possibility of viewing it as a distinct communicative environment, potentially engendering a state of "artificial ignorance". The discussion further examines the operations of major technology corporations, analysing a perceived shift in capitalist dynamics where the sign itself functions as a commodity and the human "gaze" is seemingly utilised as a form of labour within a "Superindustry of the Imaginary". Particular attention is paid to the implications of these mechanisms for children, scrutinising the ethical dimensions of data extraction and attention capture. Ultimately, the text argues that this technological domination threatens the free constitution of human subjectivity, contending that the only viable resistance lies in revitalising democratic politics and state regulation to curb the industrial exploitation of unconscious desire.

Keywords Artificial ignorance · Disinformation · Attention economy · Superindustry of the Imaginary

1 Introduction

The impact of technology on civilisations is not easily perceived, for technology is characterised by its peculiar tendency to dissolve into daily practices, to the point of becoming nearly invisible. Technology is present in the way we tie our shoes, just as it is in the shoes themselves, which have shoelaces designed to be tied. It is in the seemingly neutral eyeglasses we wear every day. It is in the nail clipper, in the way we style our hair, in how we smile, in the layout of streets and highways, and in the flight paths taken by airplanes. It is in medications, in clinical diagnoses, and in the way maternity wards and cemeteries organise the flow of new-borns or corpses. It is present in every fragment of our lives—but it does not like to be seen.

E. Bucci (✉)
University of São Paulo (USP), São Paulo, Brazil
e-mail: ebucci@usp.br

K. Bodrožić-Brnić et al. (eds.), *AI and the Ethics of Innovation*, Digital Transformation and Innovation, https://doi.org/10.1007/978-3-032-20638-1_2

More currently, technology has made itself felt through the massive emergence of Artificial Intelligence. We are affected by it in many different ways. The one that concerns me here is disinformation, which increasingly feeds on software capable of forging flawless, seemingly perfect images and videos that are, nonetheless, entirely false. The distribution networks for fake news also rely on intelligent technologies whose functioning depends heavily on advances in so-called machine learning. Thanks to these mechanisms, the organisations responsible for disseminating disinformation have refined their methods of selecting targets and reaching them at times when they are most vulnerable.

Algorithms—so widely discussed and so poorly understood—now possess unimaginable technologies to fulfil the functions of capturing personal data, profoundly understanding each individual's psychological profile, and enhancing the efficiency of manipulation formulas aimed at political, religious, or economic ends. These mechanisms systematically conceal essential information and subvert what common sense expects from peaceful coexistence in a democracy. Increasingly, we are confronted with evidence that these algorithms operate with no transparency and, worse still, without any good faith.

All of this affects not only the democratic order—it affects, above all, democratic culture. In other words, technology now employs secret or virtually unknown tactics to deceive democratic societies and the political culture they have, in one way or another, managed to cultivate.

This article aims to offer some reflections on the subject. To this end, it is divided into five sections. The argument begins with a consideration of certain aspects of disinformation and questions the outdated or anachronistic concepts with which we have been approaching the phenomenon. In the first section, titled "*Disinformation as Environment, Not as 'Content', and the Advent of Artificial Ignorance,*" I put forward the suggestion that we think of this phenomenon not merely as a collection of statements, but as a new communicative environment.

In this text, I work with theoretical categories, not with data obtained from empirical research on the production, flow, and reception of statements, messages, and campaigns that misinform. Empirical data exists in abundance. The central focus of this text is to problematise concepts and approaches—an effort that is both essayistic and ontological in nature.

After addressing disinformation, the article proceeds to the second section, which I have titled *The Bunkers of Disinformation.* Here, I examine the concealed and confidential—if not outright clandestine—nature of research into Artificial Intelligence and other technologies carried out within the dominant tech corporations, the so-called big techs. These companies, which behave as global monopolistic conglomerates, are not subject to any form of public monitoring, oversight, or control. They operate in defiance of the public and of the democratic rule of law. And this is not limited to a few countries; it occurs across all of them. This fact alone would already constitute an enormous problem—but things do not stop there.

We are living in a context in public regulation and the failure of public regulatory agencies, which find themselves powerless to address this state of affairs. This has resulted in blatant distortions, such as those currently observable in the United States, in the early months of Donald Trump's administration, where public administration has on several occasions conveyed the diffuse impression that it serves the private interests rooted in big tech companies. It is true that a similar perception existed in times when the military-industrial complex, the oil industry, and the automotive sector, among others, appeared to have privileged access to the innermost circles of power within the White House. Now, however, the situation has prompted even greater concern among those who follow events with a critical eye.

In the third section, I explore the structural foundations of the profound mutation now unfolding within the very dynamics of capitalism: *The Gaze as Labour and the Superindustry of the Imaginary.* This analytical dive is necessary because the prominence of incredibly advanced technologies in the service of unacceptably retrograde forms of power has only become possible within a new phase of production relations, in which material goods have ceded ground to image-based commodities. In short, the commodity has become a sign. Or rather: contemporary capitalism profits less from the manufacture of things and more from the manufacture of narratives. These narratives, in turn, possess exchange value—greater exchange value than any other form of commodity. Disinformation is not independent of this new capitalist framework; without it, disinformation could not attain the level of effectiveness it currently displays.

Later, in the fourth section, dedicated to the overexploitation of children, the goal is to scrutinise the mechanisms by which the apparatuses targeting children's psyches have overstepped every ethical boundary. The abuse has gone so far—so far beyond what was once conceivable—that democratic societies have scarcely realised what is happening.

To conclude the article, the fifth section seeks to outline the possibilities of resisting poisonous advertising and the exploitation of visual attention, and to demonstrate that the only real hope lies in strengthening the institutional framework of the democratic rule of law.

Throughout this brief study, I hope to offer an original panoramic view of this historically complex and pressing situation.

2 Disinformation as Environment, Not as "Content", and the Advent of Artificial Ignorance

If we truly wish to understand the phenomenon of fake news, post-truth, and disinformation—phenomena that are advancing threateningly across democratic societies—we must pay close attention to how we conceive of disinformation itself. More precisely, we must revise the very way we think about it. First and foremost, we must acknowledge that disinformation can no longer be reduced to the mere absence of reliable news. It consists of products industrially manufactured through processes that incorporate highly complex technological resources, are developed along extensive assembly lines, feature a sophisticated division of labour, and entail substantial financial investment. The fabrication of disinformation is costly. It materialises as a large, toxic, volatile, and penetrating mass. Whoever controls it controls power. We used to say that "information is power." Now we may assert the opposite: disinformation is power.

What we are dealing with is a work of engineering—an edifice at once intricate in its detail and colossal in its scale. In other writings, I have argued that disinformation is not merely a distortion of content or even a falsification of vast data sets, as if it were, so to speak, a kind of big fake data. It is, above all, a communicational environment that obstructs the very channels through which communities might access knowledge in collective dialogue. Disinformation is a regime that prohibits knowledge to the point of suffocating it to death.

The concept of ignorance itself must be rethought. A new modality of spiritual brutalisation has taken hold. We may call this new modality *artificial ignorance* (Bucci, 2024). Precisely that. As counterintuitive and illogical as it may seem, we must seriously consider the hypothesis that ignorance—whose most visible face is disinformation—can no longer be equated with the mere absence of knowledge, just as disinformation can no longer be confused with the absence of information. The contemporary form of ignorance has nothing to do with voids or absences. On the contrary: it is a clustering of presences. It is dense matter, manufactured matter that fills space—physical space, even.

This is no longer a vacant field, an untouched forest, or an abandoned lot left to untamed nature. The ignorant are no longer those "empty-headed" types. All these metaphors have lost their validity. Digital-era technologies have denatured the very texture of ignorance, which can no longer be defined by its emptiness. Today's ignorance has substance, materiality, and weight. Like disinformation, it is not a natural given, but an industrial artefact.

Put differently, *artificial ignorance* is the universe generated by the disinformation industry. Alternatively, further still: it is the general form of unknowing—of which disinformation, in addition to being its source, is a specialised field. To take this one step further, we can say that *artificial ignorance* is the product of the dominance of big tech and their social platforms over culture, and is characterised by the saturation and compression of semiotic debris, filled with virtual fanaticisms and addictive moralism. This stupefying material (yes, its effect is also chemical) fills every cubic millimetre of seemingly hollow heads—heads that would, in fact, be better off remaining simply hollow.

If one wants an explicit portrait of *artificial ignorance* in action, think of Brazil's Praça dos Três Poderes being ransacked on January 8, 2023, or the U.S. Capitol on January 6, 2022. Unlike thought, which liberates and reveals, *artificial ignorance* blinds, deafens, and imprisons—not by what it lacks, but by what it contains in excess. It is precisely because of these characteristics that it has become the primary raw material for autocratic strategies.

Let us turn to Plato's *Laches* (Plato, 1953). This treatise on courage still offers timely insights into what might separate knowing from not knowing. In this classical dialogue, General Nicias describes a child who, unaware of danger, acts with apparent fearlessness. He thereby leads the reader to ask whether such a child can be considered courageous and then opts for the negative answer. The child cannot be called courageous because they lack awareness of the risks involved in their actions. Plato thus persuades us that the virtue of courage requires consciousness of risk. Therefore, to be considered courageous, one must be aware of the danger involved when reaching one's hand towards fire or attacking an armed opponent. If one proceeds because one is ignorant of the threat, then one acts out of ignorance—and such action cannot be judged meritorious. The courageous act must, by definition, be a conscious one.

This brings us to the central point this article intends to make. For Nicias, the stupidity of the uneducated man and the innocence of the child share a common trait: the lack of knowledge. In this context, lack of knowledge means an elementary absence—an unawareness of facts. Both childlike innocence and crude ignorance are defined by absence. Furthermore, here lies the most interesting insight: since they are constituted by absence—by the nothingness within them, both innocence and ignorance can be cured, overcome, conquered. To do so, one needs only provide knowledge where knowledge is absent. In other words, one who imparts knowledge in the spirit of the ignorant can cure their ignorance. One who educates the innocent child, enabling them to learn from experience, can eliminate the negative effects of naïveté. In short, nothing that cannot be resolved by education, experience, and ethics.

The recollection of this Platonic dialogue helps us see that *artificial ignorance* is an entirely different object. It cannot be cured with the same remedy. Due to its material nature—amalgamated from compressed sign fragments—it blocks all entry and exit points in the psychic mechanism. Its mode of installation is akin to that of chemical substances that artificially interfere with synaptic functions. The result is that the subject becomes impenetrable. The real world becomes inaccessible to them. Or, seen from the inverse angle, the subject becomes inaccessible to the real world. At this point, the victim of *artificial ignorance* becomes prey to fanaticism. They are no longer a political agent in possession of freedom. Their ties to reason are severed. Their ties to the facts dissolve.

This is why it is useless and ineffective—as we have observed in practical experiences and various studies—to combat *artificial ignorance* by offering didactic knowledge. For the same reason, disinformation cannot be cured with supplementary doses of information. The situation is more complex than we had imagined. And for this reason, we must change the way we think about this phenomenon.

3 The Bunkers of Disinformation

An additional problem must be taken into account: the laboratories in which digital tools—especially Artificial Intelligence—are developed lie beyond the reach of regulatory agencies and the supervisory bodies of the Democratic Rule of Law. As these laboratories are embedded within spaces that are not merely private, but privatised—such as the big tech corporations—they are structured as hermetically sealed enclaves, far from the scrutiny of public power and democratic examination. Democracies lack the legal means to inspect the advance of technological power, which has already become immeasurable. How are personal data from the so-called "users" extracted? We do not know with any precision. How are these data subsequently exploited and recombined for economic, political, or religious targeting? No conclusive answers are available, for these activities take place in the shadows. How is the mental health of children affected by the enticing charms of social platforms offering entertainment, games, and assorted pastimes? Are there long-term impairments? We do not know. More than that, I repeat: we lack established legal mechanisms to obtain these answers. In our time, technological development—including Artificial Intelligence—is not transparent. On the contrary, it is abusively opaque.

Today, with Artificial Intelligence having achieved the previously unimaginable feat of enabling machines to behave as language-using subjects, the tentacles of technology, capital, and language have become entangled and fused into a kind of superhuman alloy. All of this operates within the big tech corporations, whose industrial secrets are better protected than those of states. It is urgent—dramatically urgent—that we reflect upon this. When viewed from a distance, and from the outside, these companies—some of which have already surpassed a market valuation of three trillion dollars—soar above any national legislation at incalculable speed. National legal systems and judiciaries struggle merely to keep sight of them.

Their economic and persuasive power—colossal by any standard—was once again demonstrated during the initial moves of Donald Trump's second term in the White House. The owner of some of the most technologically concentrated companies in the world, Elon Musk himself—the world's wealthiest individual—was appointed to lead an office tasked with cutting public expenditure. However, he performs this role without holding a formal public office. He has permission to scrutinise the state's costs and budgets and is not officially subject to any civil service regulations. Worse still, the Trump administration feigns blindness to the flagrant conflict of interest embodied in Elon Musk, who enjoys privileged access to sensitive state data while simultaneously heading companies that trade in data or apply data analytics across a range of digital technologies (Stone, 2025).

Not only is the power of big tech in the public sphere once again laid bare, but an unprecedented, even unthinkable promiscuity between public and private interests is established, with obvious risks to the integrity of the federal administration. Yet the greatest challenge we face is not the economic or political influence of big tech. It is the power of technology itself that presents the most formidable difficulty. Are democracies structurally prepared to regulate this kind of technology? Probably not—or at least not yet. And time is running against them.

When the issue was regulating the cement industry, iron ore, oil, telecommunications, civil aviation, or any such field, the State possessed information about the bodies of knowledge concentrated within those sectors. It was a matter of regulating what was known, or at least knowable. That is no longer the case. We have been engulfed by a dramatic mismatch of speeds. Private, secretive research into Artificial

Intelligence progresses at a faster pace than the legal institutions that ought to monitor it. The digital giants create and control formulas and equations that premeditate the expansion of the machine as a language-bearing subject, to the point of using it to dominate the masses. For this reason, too, autocratic regimes and the technological apparatus of big tech seem made for one another. Their symbiosis may inflict irreversible trauma upon democratic culture.

4 The Gaze as Labour and the Super-Industry of the Imaginary

In its 6 May 2017 issue, *The Economist* emblazoned its cover with a troubling headline: personal data had become the "new oil"—in other words, the most valuable resource for economic exploitation (The Economist, 2017). The report and analysis by the prestigious British weekly magazine managed to grasp a real issue but failed to address an even more astonishing fact: the mutation that capitalism was undergoing had already changed everything at the foundations of this mode of production. More than merely competing over humanity's personal data, what is underway is an irreversible mutation in economic activity. Capitalism has abandoned the manufacture of corporeal commodities and started investing value in incorporeal commodities—or in the image of commodities (indeed, the image of a commodity has become a commodity in its own right). Moreover, instead of merely exploiting labour, it now extracts value from the gaze, or the gaze as a new form of labour. Finally, capital learned that it is more profitable to appeal to desire than to meet need. In this third section, which I now outline, I retake the argument I first summarised in the introduction to my book *A superindústria do imaginário: Como o capital transformou o olhar em trabalho e se apropriou de tudo que é visível* [The Super-Industry of the Imaginary: how capital transformed the gaze into work and appropriated everything visible] (Bucci, 2021).

The Economist was correct in highlighting the challenge that states face in regulating what it termed "the internet giants". The agenda to somehow restrict the monopolistic power of big tech companies was already, in 2017, a virtually impossible task. At that point, it was already clear that the "giants" concentrated more communication power and more control over the flow of information than most nation states. They wielded more clout than mid-sized governments and more market power than international financial hubs. This was unprecedented—and today the situation is graver still.

It turns out that the gigantism detected by *The Economist* did not come solely from digital extractivism. The magazine interpreted the "new oil" in a way that led us to believe that the personal data of every inhabitant of Earth was responsible for the escalation in value of big tech companies. However, there was something more to understand. There was and still is. That something more is the mutation of capital.

Even before the rise of the big techs—as early as the mid-twentieth century, with the mass adoption of television—capitalism had already begun to gradually relegate corporeal commodities (objects endowed with some instrumental or practical utility) to a secondary position in the hierarchy of value. At the same time, another type of commodity, one lacking any tangible physical body, was steadily taking the foreground: signs—preferably in the form of images, but also of words. By the turn of the twenty-first century, there could be no doubt: capitalism had become a manufacturer and merchant of signs—corporeal things were no longer the centre of gravity of value.

Thus, instead of producing only physical objects—a pair of shoes, a car, a sack of soybeans, a steel ingot, a private spacecraft—capital learned to manufacture discourses: a brand, a label, a sensual appeal. It is these discourses that transform an ordinary commodity into an enchanted talisman. If that were all, however, we would not be facing the mutation and transition in which we now find ourselves. What changes everything is the fact that images, signs, and discourses possess exchange value—they are autonomous commodities. More than autonomous, they are the dominant commodities, those that drift about at the speed of light and penetrate the core of value in all other commodities.

In short, capital has cast aside physical objects and become a narrator, a storyteller, a producer of meanings. Capital discovered itself as language—and thrived in this new incarnation. Appropriately enough, the old opposition between labour and language has dissolved; it no longer exists—at least not in the same terms.

Let us delve a little further into the argument. In addition to exploiting labour power, capital has learned to exploit the gaze as labour, as I have already suggested. There is a subtlety to be observed in this shift within social relations: capital purchases the gaze not for what it sees, but for what it produces. Precisely that: the gaze produces, is capable of producing, and must begin to be described as a new kind of productive force. In the transformed capitalism of our time, the gaze is not merely a small window or a passive receptor of pre-packaged messages and images, but a constitutive force in the production of social meaning for those very messages and images. It is the socially shared gaze—the *social gaze*—that fixes the meanings of everyday language. The labour of the gaze is not merely to see, but to weave meaning into this or that. The labour of the gaze animates what I have called the *Super-Industry of the Imaginary*—the era in which the entire realm of the imaginary comes to be industrially fabricated through the workings of capitalist relations of production. In recent years, the notion of the "attention economy" has become commonplace—a concept that, in some way, gestures towards how platforms capture the concentration of the so-called "user." Ricardo Abramovay and Rafael Zanatta (2019) critically relate elements of the attention economy to other defining features of big tech practices in their article *Dados, vícios e concorrência: repensando o jogo das economias digitais* [*Data, addictions and competition: Rethinking the game of digital economies*], published in *Estudos Avançados*. Among the authors they discuss is Tim Wu (2016), who examines the commodification of human attention in *The Attention Merchants: The Epic Scramble to Get Inside Our Heads*. As for myself, however, I believe that the concept of the "attention economy" fails to reveal how the gaze is enlisted in the production of value. In my aforementioned book (Bucci, 2021), I examine in depth the mechanisms of gaze exploitation—the gaze as a form of labour.

To make this theoretical proposition easier to grasp, we may draw an analogy. Speakers, in using a language, fix the meanings of words through their everyday conversations. Semantics rests upon conventions, certainly, but these conventions are not premeditated. In much the same way, viewers, by casting their gaze upon images circulating around them, help to fix the meanings of those very images as they look at them socially. A society only "learns" the meaning of an image or a sign insofar as it looks at that image or sign collectively and puts it to use in its social communication.

As it becomes familiar with a particular visuality—with that signifying presence in the visible landscape—the social gaze begins to stitch meaning together. Therefore, to look at an image is, strictly speaking, to labour, so that the image acquires meaning. To look is to manufacture signification.

Examples that confirm this theoretical description are everywhere. In the new capitalist order, the renowned sportswear brand *Nike* may well outsource the manufacturing of its marathon shoes, but it cannot relinquish direct control over brand management, product design approval, marketing concepts, and advertising campaigns. *Nike*'s core business is not trainers, T-shirts, or the elastic bands worn by professional tennis players on their foreheads. Its core business is—to invoke a word already worn thin by overuse—a *narrative*. Everything else may be outsourced. The narrative cannot. At its innermost core, the brand does not produce garments, accessories, or apparel, but signs that assert a certain state of mind—and it is these signs that, in turn, radiate through the market by means of the clothing and items worn by consumers. The corporeal commodity is merely the vehicle for the commodified image.

It is in this sense that I have maintained: capitalism has learned to craft and deliver, through industrially synthesised images, the imaginary devices the subject requires to complete the circuits of signification through which desire is appeased. Capitalism recognises itself as a peddler of amulets, passwords, codes, and keys—all of which unlock doors within the customer's psyche. It is the merchant of those infinitesimal sparks—irreducible, essential, albeit fleeting—which the subject activates in order to experience a moment of jouissance, however brief. Capitalism provides the sparks that, for the helpless subject, take the place of the object of desire. In short, capitalism has learned to address desire within the subject. All that was once said about "need" now plays only a supporting role.

It is in this way that, behind the business of data extraction—already prosaically described by journalistic publications—there lies another, more elusive to immediate perception yet far more decisive: the exploitation of the gaze as labour. In the shaping of the super-industrialised Imaginary that has appropriated all images, the gaze functions as the gateway to data extraction.

The capture of the gaze by economic activity, evidently, predates the invention of digital technologies. Even in the days when Adorno and Horkheimer (1944) penned their first notes on the *Culture Industry*, the assault on the gaze—still in its raw, untamed forms—was already present. This mode of exploitation became historically viable as an economic activity because capitalism developed replicable formulas to seduce the subject and draw them in—first towards the traditional media platforms such as newspaper and magazine pages, billboard posters, and cinema screens, and later towards electronic displays and digital networks.

In our time, the capital that seduces is the same capital that extracts data. At the same time, and necessarily, the capital that caresses the senses, not only vision, is the very same capital that sets in motion operations aimed at satisfying the libidinal demands of billions of subjects. This means that the extraction and trade of personal data take place within an ocean of unconscious desire—a desire increasingly alienated and monetised. In the end, personal data and the fortunes attached to them are merely the tip of the iceberg.

Certainly, the mechanisms for capturing and satisfying desiring demand are as old as humanity itself. The Imaginary, desire, identifications, and libidinal processes have always existed. However, there has been a rupture, and this rupture has occurred right before our eyes. In our time, the mechanisms for entangling and satisfying desire have been monopolised by commodities.

Previously, the game of hooking into the knots of desire had not been overtaken by the relations of production, as it has today, and belonged instead to the realm of symbolic representations not yet imprisoned by the economic sphere—such as religious rites and the autonomous events of culture. Now, the fabrication of imaginary representations, in all social spaces, has been elevated by its own significative power to the very core of capitalism. Religions have surrendered to the language of the entertainment industry. Culture, in its entirety, has submitted to the imperatives of the market.

It should come as no surprise, then, that the big tech companies rank among the most highly valued enterprises in the world. These so-called "internet giants" do little else but capture the gaze through libidinal hooks that address desire, commodify that gaze, and feed back into the circuit of seduction and its commerce.

For quite some time now, communication, entertainment, and advertising have ceased to be "merely" a collection of peripheral (or "superstructural") manifestations that leave the core of the production relation untouched. The old argument that "communication" and "advertising" do not generate value because they do not alter the use of the commodity—or because they are "external" operations with respect to the body of the commodity—has lost its meaning. What was once treated as a secondary device of economic relations—a mere alluring stimulus to induce consumption, or, in more orthodox jargon, to hasten the realisation of its exchange value—now produces value and takes the form of an independent commodity. The entire field of communication, entertainment, and advertising has come to operate under super-industrial logic. This field produces exchange value in the image of the commodity. It is no coincidence that the so-called "internet giants" are the world's leading advertising platforms and yet are merely the froth of the wave—nothing but the froth. Far more lies beneath the surface.

Another decisive factor, already hinted at here, is the way in which desire has replaced need in the gaze-driven capitalism of our time. The economic category of "need"—ironically enough—has lost its use value and fallen into disuse. The subject no longer seeks a use value to meet a need; instead, they seek an object to satisfy a desire. "Need", when it appears at all, serves merely as a pretext. The practical utility of the commodity—its functional use—is no longer the point: what matters now is the imaginary meaning that this use represents for the subject. For that reason, before it can be a thing, the commodity must be an image or a sign.

A brief clarification on the term "Imaginary" is in order. The term is not used here in its strictly psychoanalytic sense, although a dialogue with psychoanalytic theory underlies it. For the purposes of this article, the notion of the Imaginary encompasses the entire cultural ambience in which signs, images, sounds and texts are catalysed, as well as any objects, material or immaterial, imbued with linguistic meaning, activated by the subject's fantasies. We may conceive of the Imaginary as the universe of signifiers associated with meanings, through which subjects connect to identifications that resonate with them in some way. In the era of the Super-Industry of the Imaginary—which is our era—such signs tend towards the visual and the digital screen, but need not be images, they may be found on a scrap of paper, in an audio recording, a gesture, or an automatic choreography—and still, they will belong to the Imaginary.

Although it does not encompass all of language—for there are strands of language that extend beyond the association between signifier and signified—the Imaginary is woven from language, and language alone. Rites and their many ritual forms, myths and their narratives, all these belong to the Imaginary insofar as they carry within them a linguistic function. There is no culture without the Imaginary. There is no discourse, there is no subject. But what concerns us most in this article is that there is no longer any capitalism without the Imaginary.

Capitalism has taken hold of the order of the Imaginary to such an extent that it has become its prisoner—or rather, both prisoner and jailer at once. In relation to the Imaginary, capital is both parasite and generative source. In today's social life, there is not a single sign that does not, even indirectly, contribute to generating market value. This is evident when we think of a sports shoe brand, a car, or a holiday package sold by a travel agency—but it is equally true of a hairpin, an ant on a university lawn, a popsicle stick kept in a drawer, or a nature reserve. Every fragment of the visible, even when seemingly detached from productive chains, is summoned to generate value within the commodities that magnetise the entire expanse of the Imaginary. The totality of the Imaginary has been not merely colonised but packaged by capital.

5 The Superexploitation of Children

Once upon a time, Philosophy concerned itself with speculating about civilisation. In those days, it tended to explain that *homo sapiens* had emerged from nature in order to enter culture. It was a good story—as I discuss in the Epilogue of my earlier work (Bucci, 2021).

According to old explanations, intelligence, self-awareness, and the virtue of social interaction had all flourished—together—as a result of the abyss opened between humankind and the animals. Nature came to be observed from a distance—or, in a single word, admired. The posture of admiring nature was also, inevitably, the posture of dominating it. The words and images generated by culture—in religion, in the arts, in science, in politics—gradually coated every contour of the natural world, labelling and cataloguing every little piece of it. By God's delegation, man gave names to the beings of nature (Genesis 2:20), wrapping them in language. As the Brazilian poet and songwriter Jorge Mautner puts it in his celebrated song *Samba dos Animais* [Animal Samba], what happened was that man, who "once conversed with the snake, the tortoise and the lion," one day "made a grimace and began his civilisation" (Mautner, 1973).

Then came capital. This new "entity", which was not "natural", emerged and began to wrap entire swathes of religion, the arts, science, morality, politics, and—not to waste time—language itself. It accomplished this, and continues to do so, in concert with technology. In short order, commodities became signs. The visible realm was occupied by the commodity. The human—that being who, in the beginning, had supposedly separated from nature—now survives only insofar as it resists being devoured by capital, which, for its part, has taken nature hostage.

The work of Karl Marx, particularly *Das Kapital* (Marx, 1867/1990), offers us an objective account of the character of the nineteenth century and the Industrial Revolution. Child labour was rampant in the factories of London; capitalists, without a moment's hesitation, exploited children in shifts that extended up to sixteen hours a day; pre-adolescents, as the cheapest form of labour, yielded the highest returns.

When we reflect on the working conditions of those early days of the assembly line, we can almost smell the exhausted bodies, almost see the dull eyes of mechanised boys and girls; we feel the bitter taste of indignation and shame. The inhumanity inflicted upon even one of those defenceless human beings wounds us all, across all time. The wounds of the nineteenth century never cease to bleed.

What is most staggering, however, is not the vivid memory of yesterday's oppression—what truly staggers is our blindness to the oppression of today. Capitalist exploitation has changed its code, but it remains present: indelible and perverse, though it no longer reveals itself. And we, for our part, remain inert, as if attuned only to the signals of obsolete inhumanities. Not only are we untroubled by it—we even applaud the exploitation of our time, which is the boundless exploitation of the gaze and of desire. Consumers queue outside shops to purchase a mobile phone, without realising that the device, despite its apparent use value, is in fact a means of production designed to exploit the user's scopic labour. More than that, the device has been engineered to siphon off the most intimate personal data of those standing in that queue—and in every other queue of our present age. Social networks enlist billions of unpaid workers, to whom they assign the misleading label of "users"—and these, contented, respond only with gratitude. Submissive and eager, they work without pause, all the while believing they are simply having fun.

Within the big tech corporations, the degree of exploitation has reached such a refined level of deceit and concealment that not even the most miserly, cunning, and ruthless barons of the Industrial Revolution would have dared to propose it. On a social media platform or a major search engine, the so-called "user"—who imagines they are enjoying a service offered as generous courtesy—is, in fact, the labour force (unpaid), the raw material (also unpaid), and, ultimately, the commodity (to be sold, in whole or in parts, in virtual dismemberments—all without the faintest suspicion of the gravity of what is occurring). Never, in any previous period—not even in its most predatory episodes of primitive accumulation—has capitalism devised a business model so dissimulated, so accumulative, and so inhumane.

To dispel any ambiguity in this denunciation, let us examine in greater detail the elaborate design of this exploitation. On social media platforms, the "user" constitutes unpaid labour because it is they who type, photograph, post, film, and do everything. The big tech companies need not spend a single penny on typists, editors, proofreaders, photographers, camera operators, voice actors, models, actresses, or scriptwriters. Absolutely nothing. The "user" works incessantly, without charging a cent, and feels gratified because they experience thrills of imaginary jouissance.

As if that were not enough, the same "user", in addition to being unpaid labour, is also the raw material, for the stories told are their own, the cats and plates of food photographed are theirs, the delusions posted—labelled "content", are theirs, or have been adopted as such. To these delusions—little more than toxic detritus in the general environment of the Super-Industry of the Imaginary—the so-called user assigns qualities such as "truthful", "moving", "poignant", "just", or "beautiful".

Finally, as I mentioned earlier, the "user" is also the commodity. And how could it be otherwise? It is the user who is bought and sold—in whole or in parts, at retail or wholesale, in sacks or in bulk—at trillion-dollar prices. Their gaze is sold to advertisers. Their personal data are traded with organisations that manipulate electorates in favour of neo-fascists. All the poor "user" receives in return are a few miserly strokes to their infantile narcissism. This so-called "user" is entertained, believes the "entertainment" offered is a gift, and works until they can work no more. Some become addicted, like casino gamblers. Others fall into depression. Young people take their own lives.

On the other side, the companies that enrich themselves through the enslavement of the gaze accumulate ever more capital—at an unprecedented rate of expansion—with the luxurious aid of the most advanced devices for extracting intimacy. With no scruples of any kind, they do not hesitate to recruit child labour—or, more precisely, the power of the child's gaze, which is even more valuable. Exorbitant fortunes are hastily amassed through the plunder of children's gaze and data, keeping them captive under the spell of a cheap little form of amusement.

From an ethical standpoint, what is taking place today is worse—far worse—than what occurred during the Industrial Revolution. Let us consider for a moment: what is the capital that appropriates 16 or 18 hours a day of a child's labour, compared to the capital that, two centuries later, appropriates the most intimate processes of formation of another child's subjectivity, across all 24 hours of the day? What is the capital that disregards the exhaustion of the human body's physical strength, compared to the capital that violates every boundary of privacy and psychic integrity in a person not yet five years old?

What is the capital that extracts surplus value from the worker, compared to the capital that, in addition to extracting the surplus value of the gaze, steals the secrets of fear, anxiety, and passion from those it cynically calls "users"? What is the capital that drains the soul of the factory worker, compared to the capital that, beyond exploiting labour, transforms leisure time into undeclared forms of exploitation—more gazing, more labour? What is the capital that robs a little boy of his muscular strength, compared to the capital that steals, along with his childhood, the imagination he might have had? What is the capital that sends in riot police to crush strikes, compared to the capital that embeds itself in the desires of boys and girls, even in early childhood, in order to extinguish, from within, any spark of future rebellion?

6 Confronting Poisonous Advertising and the Exploitation of the Gaze

Before one asks whether there is any way out of all this—this machinery that swallows us whole without so much as chewing, I hasten to point to a possible path. Yes, there is a way out, however improbable it may seem.

Although clarity is scarce and resistance limited, democratic politics does respond. Timidly, yes—but it responds. I hear of European consumers choosing not to purchase Tesla vehicles because the company's owner, Elon Musk, has been playing a disgracefully authoritarian role during the early months of Donald Trump's second term in office in the United States. It is a small sign—but a genuine one. At the beginning of 2025, Tesla's sales reportedly fell by 45% in the European Union and the United Kingdom compared with the previous year, and by 11% in China, according to BBC News (2025).

The path to response lies in the legal frameworks of the Democratic Rule of Law and in their revitalisation. Just a few decades ago, certain societies developed an awareness that advertising causes deep harm, particularly in the formation of children's personalities, and they found institutional means to curb it. Do not underestimate the significance of this. Social clarity on these matters will be essential in the coming period. A growing consensus is emerging regarding the psychological vulnerabilities of children when faced with increasingly powerful and pervasive machinery of commercial advertising. There are already restrictions—and even outright bans—in this area, which are both entirely healthy and entirely just.

Contrary to what certain lobbying groups argue, these legal measures have nothing to do with censorship. Freedom of expression is not in the least impaired when the right to advertise is regulated.

Advertisements fulfil an ancillary role in support of commerce, under the terms of the legislation governing commercial activity, and are therefore subject to the specific constraints of commercial communication, the limits of which are considerably narrower than those applicable to the freedom of expression exercised by citizens within public debate. The communication of advertisements is subordinate to the commerce of which it is a part—it is an activity accessory to commerce. Freedom of expression in public debate is broad—it constitutes a primary, not an accessory, good, one that enables the expression of opinions within a democratic order.

If the sale of a given product is not permitted, its advertisement will likewise not be permitted. That is simply rational, simply logical—and in no way infringes upon freedom of expression. A country does not become less free simply because it prohibits heroin advertisements during children's television programmes. On the contrary, such a country is even more free, because it protects the freedom of children and has learned to distinguish between the open exchange of ideas and the commercial activity whose sole aim is to promote the consumption of goods.

This becomes even more evident when we consider that, in those same democratic countries, any citizen is free to speak out against the laws that prohibit the sale of certain substances and, by extension, the advertising of such products. Any citizen may publish an article in their local newspaper advocating for the unrestricted commercialisation of all drugs. That is freedom of expression.

Advertising substances prohibited by democratic legislation would constitute an unacceptable practice, both in the eyes of common sense and under the scrutiny of democratic legal systems. To invoke the right to freedom of expression in order to promote a commodity whose trade is not permitted would be absurd—a claim entirely devoid of rationality.

The two situations described in the previous two paragraphs are fundamentally different from each other. And if free societies are to confront the tyranny of big tech and the mode of production they have set in motion, they must be able to draw a clear distinction between the two.

I must return to and emphasise the argument. At pre-school age—and even during the early years of primary education—children possess limited intellectual and cognitive defences against the rhetorical devices of advertising. These devices maliciously combine fact and fantasy (or truth and fiction) to stimulate indiscriminate consumption. As a form of interested discourse—interested in selling—advertising distorts children's relationship with the commodity and, as a consequence, distorts the relationships they will go on to develop with society. Invasive advertising, to say the least, is not merely toxic—it is poisonous to the child audience.

And yet, the same democratic legal frameworks that have taken steps to confront child-targeted advertising have not yet grasped the true meaning of the exploitation of the gaze and the extractivism of children's data. Democracies still regard the media as mere distributors of "content", rather than as means of production that harness the gaze in order to manufacture the image of the commodity. We suffer from a theoretical deficit in this regard. Regulatory authorities have yet to assimilate the self-evident truth that media platforms, more than being devices for delivering information and entertainment, are mechanisms for producing images and their meanings. Legislation continues to treat the entire super-industrial network concentrated in big tech as if it were merely a system for content distribution. It fails to recognise a productive system of signs that exploits the labour of the gaze under conditions of slavery—or near-slavery—without the slightest regard for the rights of adults or children. This will have to change—and quickly.

There are other matters of which the authorities remain entirely unaware. They have yet to fully grasp that when technologies track and extract users' data—as every streaming service and every website on the internet does—corrosive, hidden mechanisms are set in motion. The data collected freely by corporate conglomerates contain the very keys to unconscious desire, to such an extent that, as has now become commonplace to say, algorithms know more about individuals' preferences than the individuals themselves. These data offer a kind of mapping of drives, impulses, instincts, reflexes, rhythms, and the neural signatures unique to each human being. Capital algorithms possess deep knowledge of the most intimate codes of unconscious desire in every individual—yet that same individual knows nothing about the secret codes of the algorithms.

As we can see, the challenge lies beyond the capacity of any single national legal framework: it can only be addressed through multilateral agreements, at the level of international relations, and through initiatives led by the central democracies, such as the European Union and the United States. If one of these should succumb or yield, the task will become even more difficult. The big tech monopolies have been consolidated and have established their headquarters within the core economies. Therefore, the democracies in these countries are institutionally better positioned to confront them.

Democracy was right when it imposed historical limits on capital—as when, in the past, it began to criminalise the hiring of child labour. It was right, too, when it abolished slavery. And it is right now in protecting children from the voracity of advertising messages. However, when it comes to preventing that same capital from exploiting the gaze and appropriating data, neuronal codes, and instinctual drives by mapping unconscious desire, democracy still remains silent. It lacks the conceptual apparatus to systematically comprehend the unparalleled violence of the mode of production currently under way.

In short, what I am trying to say here is that if there is any solution, it will necessarily pass through democratic politics. There is no longer any way out that lies beyond politics. Politics is the most refined, complex, and effective form of collective action our civilisation has been able to create. Only politics can produce responses—and only within the framework of peace, non-violence, and human rights. Only politics offers us the material possibility of strengthening the democratic fabric, already so fragile. Only politics guarantees access to the State—the sole regulatory authority capable of confronting the new forms of exploitation. If we resign ourselves to discarding politics, we will lose the fragile democracy that still remains—already openly under threat, particularly in the United States in 2025. The possibility of forging a better, more inclusive, and more robust democracy is under threat across the globe, and if we no longer have this path, we will lose the only route available for defending human dignity on a universal scale.

If vast territories of the Imaginary have surrendered to the dominion of the commodity, a small civilised island—made of words, critical thought, and democratic political action—still gathers symbolic force capable of reversing the tide. The name of that small island is democratic politics. Within that realm, as Hannah

Arendt once said, factual truth remains "the very texture of the political realm" (Arendt, 1995/1968). The possible has not yet ceased to be conceivable.

The political struggle of our time must take as its banner the defence of the free constitution of human subjectivity, together with the defence of each person's psychic integrity. Around this cause, other banners—today scattered—may be brought into alignment under the principles of equality, respect, dignity, anti-racism, individual rights and guarantees, environmentalism, and freedom. By bombarding the free formation of subjectivity in such a vile manner, capital sabotages all aspirations for freedom and social justice. A world of beings reduced to automatons—the world now taking shape beneath our feet and before our eyes—will leave no room for solidarity or love. That world will be the paradise of technology.

References

Abramovay, R., & Zanatta, R. (2019). Dados, vícios e concorrência: repensando o jogo das economias digitais. *Estudos Avançados, 33*(96), 421–446. https://doi.org/10.1590/s0103-4014.2019.3396.0021

Adorno, T. W., & Horkheimer, M. (1944). *Dialectic of enlightenment: Philosophical fragments*. Herder and Herder.

Arendt, H. (1995). Verdade e política (M. Alberto, trans.). In H. Arendt, entre o passado e o futuro. Relógio D'Água. (original work published 1968 as between past and future by Viking press).

BBC News. (2025, 28 February). The Elon musk effect: What explains the drop in tesla sales in Europe and the plunge in stock market value. BBC. https://www.bbc.com/portuguese/articles/czrnnzxkp64o

Bucci, E. (2021). *A superindústria do imaginário: Como o capital transformou o olhar em trabalho e se apropriou de tudo que é visível*. Editora Autêntica.

Bucci, E. (2024). Inteligência artificial, paz e democracia: Esse encontro é possível? *Revista Brasileira: Publicação da Academia Brasileira de Letras, 3*(120), 8–14.

Marx, K. (1990). Capital: A critique of political economy (Vol. 1, B. Fowkes, Trans.). Penguin Books. (Original work published 1867).

Mautner, J. (1973). Samba dos Animais. In *Árvore da Vida [LP]*. Philips Records.

Plato. (1953). Laches (B. Jowett, Trans.). In The dialogues of Plato. Clarendon Press. (Original work published ca. 380 BCE).

Stone, P. (2025, 27 February). Elon musk's conflicts of interest 'should scare every American', experts say. The Guardian. https://www.theguardian.com/us-news/2025/feb/27/elon-musk-conflicts-of-interest

The Economist. (2017, 6 May). The world's most valuable resource is no longer oil, but data. The Economist. https://www.economist.com

Wu, T. (2016). *The attention merchants: The epic scramble to get inside our heads*. Atlantic Books.

Eugênio Bucci is Professor at the School of Communications and Arts of the University of São Paulo (ECA-USP); he currently serves as Superintendent of Social Communication at the same university. Bucci is a member of the Academia Paulista de Letras [São Paulo Academy of Letters]. He is widely recognised for his scholarly and public contributions to journalism ethics, media theory, and democratic communication in Brazil.

From Analogue to Digital Communication: Economic and Moral Pressures on Functional Differentiation in the Brazilian Context

Lucas Fucci Amato, Laurindo Dias Minhoto, and Pedro de Almeida Pires Camargos

Abstract This paper examines how the digital mediation of communication is reshaping functional differentiation. It proposes the hypothesis that the co-evolution of legal, political and economic institutions is undergoing a crisis of integration driven by digital media in two trends: the superimposition of economic distinctions in the production and dissemination of "multifunctional" communication (i.e. political, artistic, religious, journalistic messages) and the hyper-moralisation of conflicts amplified by digital media. Drawing on Luhmann's systems theory and an example from contemporary Brazil, the text shows how social media has supported the rise of far-right populism. It concludes that some aspects of the process of digitalisation, such as the primacy of monetised information and moral binarism, together with a media-driven tendency towards strong social integration, have contributed to the erosion of the social conditions that are a precondition for functionally differentiated communication.

Keywords Digital mediation · Functional differentiation · Systems theory · Moralisation of conflict · Platformisation of communication · Authoritarian populism

L. F. Amato (✉) · L. D. Minhoto · P. de A. P. Camargos
University of São Paulo (USP), São Paulo, Brazil
e-mail: lucas.amato@usp.br

L. D. Minhoto
e-mail: ldm@usp.br

P. de A. P. Camargos
e-mail: pedro.camargos@usp.br

K. Bodrožić-Brnić et al. (eds.), *AI and the Ethics of Innovation*, Digital Transformation and Innovation, https://doi.org/10.1007/978-3-032-20638-1_3

1 Introduction

This paper develops the hypothesis that the transition from analogue to digital communication is a current societal trend that produces a crisis of systemic integration, eroding functional differentiation through the primacy of economic and moral distinctions over other partial binary codes in society—notably, in democratic politics, the distinction between government and opposition. This operational distinction is infected and tainted by a totalising moral claim that attributes values of good or bad to groups and agendas, thereby oversimplifying debates on programmatic (ideological and policy) alternatives and intensifying polarisation.

To approach this hypothesis, we draw on the theoretical tools provided by Luhmann's systems theory. This theory describes society precisely as a system of communication, specialised through the differentiation of subsystems (law, science, mass media, religion, economy, politics, etc.) with self-referential operations. These operations are distinguished by coding: a binary form/difference. The allocation of the positive or negative side of a code (such as legal/illegal, government/opposition, truth/false, informative/not informative) is given by decisional programs (such as statutes, media guidelines, theories, investment programs etc.).

We argue here that, on the one hand, the programming and dissemination of communication driven by digital platforms involves monetisation strategies that profile personal data and then guide themes and ways of communication, exploiting users' time and attention, for instance, through predictive Artificial Intelligence. On the other hand, time and attention handling are highly based on communication moral coding (good/bad, consideration/disregard). According to Luhmann (1993), this code does not close itself on a self-referential programming, forming a system, but parasitises specialised forms of communication. In our hypothesis, the moralisation of communication pushes functional differentiation internally and enhances irreconcilable and authoritarian claims. Economic, political, legal and scientific controversies, therefore, are oversimplified and encompassed by radical moral judgements.

We propose to describe these changes driven by the digitalisation of societal operations in four steps. The first step is to characterise this proposal in terms of foundational premises, such as the distinction between manifest meaning and latent functions (which challenges the naive assumption of an intentional orientation of action) and the transition from factorial explanations to systemic and functional explanations. This framing helps to position social theory as a theory of self-referential communication systems.

The second step is to relate societal differentiation forms with the emergence of different scales of social systems and the corresponding dissemination media. Segmentary societies are organised around interaction systems and oral communication; hierarchical societies involve organisations and encompassing hierarchies based, among other factors, on writing techniques controlled by a few elites. The modern world society, based on functional systems, such as law, science, politics, economics, art and religion, is described by Luhmann since the emergence of the press and related mass media, such as books, radio and television. The improbability of communication is overcome not only by a set of generalised expectations and bureaucratic routines but also by the emergence of symbolically generalised dissemination media, such as power and money, which support the differentiation of functional systems.

This leads to our third step: demonstrating how the transition from analogue mass media to digital platforms changes communication, understood as a complex interplay of information, utterance and understanding. The monetisation of the entire chain of communication production and consumption is enabled by digital platforms, which disseminate information (and misinformation) in ways that are both moralised and simplified. This implies some important goals to be met by regulation in this sector.

The fourth step seeks to clarify our hypothesis through an illustrative reference to the present-day situation in Brazil, focusing on how digital communication via social media platforms has played a key role in the rise of far-right and authoritarian populist movements in the country, as exemplified by the election of Jair Bolsonaro in 2018, a political trend that continues to play a central role, despite he no longer holds the federal government.

2 The Systemic Approach: Luhmann's Sociological Enlightenment

Sociology emerged from the Enlightenment's disillusionment, carrying forward the romantic ideals of historical transformation, while acknowledging their limitations (Hawthorn, 1987; Yack, 1986). In Luhmann's diagnosis, the Enlightenment sought to free social relations from traditional constraints and entrenched prejudice. Its heyday in the eighteenth century was followed by a decline towards scepticism in the following century, when sociology was established as a scientific discipline. Sociology challenged "the equal participation of all men in a common reason that they possess without further institutional mediation, and the optimism, certain of its triumph, regarding the establishment of just situations" (Luhmann, 2005, pp. 21–22). A tripod underpins the Luhmannian project of *Sociological Enlightenment*, conceived as an observation of modern society's contingency and complexity.

Firstly, whereas practical philosophy sought to guide action by assuming the homogeneity of reason among thinking subjects and agents, sociology constructs a "perspective of incongruity". Marx, for example, located the genealogy of ideas in the economic base (as Freud saw it in the human psyche). Morality, language, religion, everything can be seen as socially conditioned to a degree previously unacknowledged. They appear contingent to an extent that would have been unthinkable when the homogeneity of reason was still grounded in conceptions of human nature.

Secondly, the distinction between manifest meaning and latent functions undermines the naive assumption of an intentional orientation of action. Meanings are co-determined by unconscious contextual data. The orientation and motivation of action require an economy of time and attention, so that the reduction of complexity becomes a condition for the possibility of action: various contextual variants have to remain latent and undefined in order to one be able to consciously and purposefully operate on a few of them. Sociology then becomes interested in the repressed part of reality, contrasting the manifest with the tacit, the formal with the informal, the official with the real, social problems with the benefits of society. Given the limited rationality of actors to interpret their context, intentional, purposeful action is as indeterminate in the face of society as the states of society are not directly the result of conscious individual conduct (Merton, 1936, 1968). "Manifest functions are those objective consequences contributing to the adjustment or adaptation of the system which are intended and recognized by participants in the system; Latent functions, correlatively, being those which are neither intended nor recognized". (Merton, 1968, p. 105).

Sociology also moved from factor-based explanations to systemic and functional approaches. No longer able to derive the orientation of actions from psychological impulses (imitation, competition) or environmental factors (e.g. climate), it now operates with the analysis of the unity of social systems or institutions—the economy, the church, the factory—and assumes that each must solve multiple problems in order to persist. Necessary laws and linear causalities become reductive simplifications for analysing how these systems manipulate their means: money, power, knowledge. Agents' self-conceptions are placed under suspicion and regarded as mere rationalisations, ideologies, superstructures, beliefs. Functions and latent structures of institutionalised systems are explored, as well as isomorphisms between different systems. This constitutes the basis of the functional method. It is not simply a question of discerning causal relationships or statistical correlations, but of exploring how the stability of social institutions depends on solutions, on responses that are inserted into a horizon of other possibilities. In the paradox of "function", consequences operate as causes, feeding back system's maintenance.

Although the social and natural environment has causal influence upon systems, each system is operationally closed. Each social system produces its own forms of communication (identified by a binary coding), which cannot be provided by the environment: for instance, law presupposes its natural and social environment (territory, climate, humans and animals, but also economic, political, scientific and religious operations), but only the legal system provides legal communication (identified by the coding "legal/illegal"). The self-construction of social structures isolates systems with sufficient complexity to satisfy contradictory demands and high indeterminacy to deal with very diverse situations and states. So systems have a certain indifference to their environment. The differentiation of systems becomes an "evolutionary acquisition". As social systems construct their own internal reality, there is no point-by-point correspondence with the environment (either natural or social environment). Furthermore, functional comparison reveals alternative means that can be "equifinal", achieving equivalent results: different operations or structures can provide comparable results.

Finally, the *Sociological Enlightenment* taught us that social construction is much more complex than the philosophy of consciousness thought: systems are not merely structured sets of descriptive or normative propositions, but self-referential networks operationalised in the communicative events themselves; there are a series of causes, concauses and factors, which can only be analysed in their complexity as functional responses to problems of system maintenance; there are latent functions beyond the manifest meaning of words; action is a communicative construction mediated by social structures and institutions, and not a direct and voluntaristic determination of society by the human mind.

Parsons' concept of function (1971) guided a schematisation of social action in the respective systems: the economy serves the adaptive function, politics directs the achievement of collective goals, social integration is provided, for example, by the law, and latent cultural patterns are transmitted by institutions based on trust, such as the family, the school and the church. In Luhmann's view, function refers to the relationship between each partial social system and society, the specific service each provides in relation to the wider social system. The function of each system is not derived from the functional requirements of society expressed in a schematisation of action but is defined by a codification of communication: by what each system identifies as a problem, linking this problem to the technical solution that the respective system is competent to offer. The analytical gain of this theory is the exploration of functional equivalences, homologies and structural "isomorphisms" (Bertalanffy, 1968) between systems—which goes beyond mere superficial analogies between phenomena.

In a functionalist explanation, effects are taken as causes, and subsystems gradually differentiate themselves to fulfil roles better or provide services to maintain or expand the general system of which they are organs. This is what the functionalist tradition explains (Stichweh, 2013). Communication systems (society and its subsystems) would have arisen to make possible what they reproduce: social systems seek to make communication viable—that is, the processes of information, message and understanding. Communication is improbable—in order for it to occur, it must rely on generalised expectations beyond idiosyncratic beliefs that only exist in someone's psychic system; in order to structure and aggregate these expectations, it will be necessary to support them on the presumed expectations of others—in other words, to institutionalise them; and in order to articulate institutions, it will be necessary to appeal to means of success and dissemination of communication (Luhmann, 1981, 2012).

The starting point is the "double contingency" theorem (Vanderstraeten, 2002): not knowing what others think about what we think. Social systems emerge to solve this problem between psychic systems, to overcome the "black box" of individual thoughts and to enable communication operations, generalising and institutionalising expectations (Luhmann, 1995). However, the same problem of double contingency will reproduce itself among social systems, since they are also autopoietic. Among social systems there is not the problem of the self-reference of thought operations *vis-à-vis* communication operations, but each system codifies, produces and recognises communication in its own way.

3 The Scales of Communication: Interactions, Organisations and Functional Systems

Luhmann (2013a) identifies four basic types of societal differentiation: segmentary, geographical (centre-periphery), hierarchical, and functional. It is possible to align these types of differentiation (which we empirically see combined in each time and space) with the types of social systems discerned by Luhmann: interactions, organisations and functional systems (Luhmann, 2013a, 2018, 1995, 1981; Neves, 2012; Mascareño, 2007).

To deal with the problem of double contingency at its most elementary level, a kind of precarious, ephemeral and unstable social system emerges: interaction systems. In a typical evolutionary dynamic, less complex societies are structured based on interactions, transient systems of face-to-face encounters. In order to distinguish information against a background of already accumulated knowledge (redundancy), communication processes (operations, elements) must be supported by structural frameworks. Structures provide the context and the enduring link between volatile episodes, events and operations. Social microstructures are expectations—just as language and signs structurally link psychic and social systems, expectations are bivalent structures; they need to be generalised on social systems, but they are also individually constructed on the side of psychic systems. To this end, society combines cognitive expectations (knowledge that can be learned through experience) and normative expectations—norms, anticipations about what should be, resistance to disappointment when confronted with what actually is or will be (Luhmann, 2014a). In societies based on interactional routines, the conditions for variability in communication are minimal. Law cannot be changed by deliberate decision, but is reproduced traditionally, as custom. Communication is mainly oral. We could associate this scenario with segmented societies, based on kinship, with a small territorial and demographic scale, such as villages, tribes and rural communities.

An evolutionary take on interaction systems is given by the emergence of organisations, centralised decision-making systems that are stable and durable, albeit finite. There are free interactions outside of organisations and proceduralised interactions within each organisation. In friction with organised patterns, roles and processes, interactions are responsible not only for putting them into action, but also—as Luhmann (2018) notes—for making them more flexible in practice, augmenting them with a "microdiversity" whose mutual adjustments and representations are not mere derivations aligned with organisational goals, decisions and structures. Expectations are the social microstructures that make all social systems viable, starting with interactions. At higher levels of agglomeration, complexes of expectations also emerge, forming the internal structure of organisational and interactional systems. These are called "institutions", understood as frameworks of generalised expectations supported by the presumption of a universal consensus and acceptance (Luhmann, 2010). A stratified society comprises a plurality of organised hierarchies, which tend towards a uniform hierarchy (such as the distinction between the nobility and the people) and its apex is commanded by elites who have access to reading and writing (literacy).

The absolute state emerged from stratified society as an overarching organisation based on the distinction between the sovereign and the citizens. This state congregated the rights, powers and fiscal resources that have overcome the privileges and resources of the various social strata and made way for the subsequent process of functional differentiation driven by the liberal revolutions between the seventeenth and nineteenth centuries. Then, validity becomes the exclusive criterion of law, power is contested in specifically political arenas (through the institutionalisation of opposition), and money becomes the universal medium of exchange. In functional systems, a field is formed that agglomerates and structures (in prices, support and legal positions) a series of chaotic and polycentric interactions—this is the "space" of the market, of public opinion, of legal personality—the public spheres of each functional system. Moreover, functional systems encompass, absorb and specialise organisations. Now, organisations are sectorised and specialised decision-making systems, such as states, companies, churches and schools, which link their decisions to the respective symbolic means and functional codes: power/non-power (government/opposition), legal/illegal, having/not having (money), knowing/not knowing (truth).

Social inclusion is presumably universal—no one will be excluded by the social stratum into which she/he was born, but only indirectly, through access to different economic, political, legal and educational resources. The lack of access to one system leads to increasing difficulties in accessing other social systems—universal inclusion and total exclusion occur at the same time. From this arises the problem of systemic integration: functional differentiation depends upon disintegration, the freedom of each functional system for selecting communication and performing their own operations; integration means the easier convertibility of media (money implying power and knowledge, for instance), leading to structures of strong inclusion (or "over-inclusion") and persistent and "multifunctional" exclusion (or "sub-inclusion") (Luhmann, 2013; Neves, 2005).

As literacy expanded and, above all, the press became increasingly popularised, pamphlets against the *ancien régime* began and a system of mass media emerged as the foundation for expanding public opinion beyond clubs and discussion circles of the literate. Sustained by the means of disseminating the written word (Vesting, 2018), the constitutional revolutions sought to replace the tangle of immemorial customs and traditions, upon which the privileges of the old social strata were based, with uniform and isonomic legislation, codification and constitutionalisation, including the declarations of natural rights, subsequently recognised as universal rights of men and citizens. This occurred in the liberal revolutions from seventeenth to nineteenth centuries, such as the English, American and French revolutions, the national unifications of Italy and Germany and the national independences in Latin America.

In the wave of liberal constitutionalism, political inclusion (in the form of the right to vote, initially with wealth-based, racial and gender exclusions) and civil rights (religious, scientific, artistic and economic freedom) represented an institutionalisation of functional differentiation (Luhmann, 2010). On the one hand, the state, as the organisational centre of politics, is both legitimised and self-contained in its operations; on the other, a sphere of fundamental rights emerges to privatise and safeguard the operational autonomy of economic, religious, artistic, scientific and educational communication.

Despite the de-differentiating potential of the bureaucratic expansionism of the welfare state (Luhmann, 1990), the twentieth century showed that generalised political inclusion (in the form of universal suffrage) and politically driven inclusion in other social systems (access to public services and welfare policies) were also presuppositions of functional differentiation (Dutra, 2016), insofar as the asymmetry between the included and excluded in functional systems causes society to integrate negatively, restricting the autonomy and self-referentiality of functional systems (Luhmann, 2013). Besides, just like the politicisation promoted by authoritarian regimes of the right and left-wings subjects everything to bureaucratic criteria and ideological control, the extensive economisation (or monetisation) of society promoted by neoliberal policies has the potential to de-differentiate, reduce social complexity and increase exclusion, reducing the autonomy of partial functional systems. Everything (religion, politics, education, law, science) is shaped and reflected by criteria, operations and theories with a dominant economic accent, making prices and purchasing power the general criteria of inclusion and exclusion in relation to encompassing social sectors (Minhoto & Amato, 2023; Minhoto et al., 2022).

4 The Digitalisation of Communication and its Regulatory Answers

Luhmann (2012) proposes replacing the metaphor of communication as a "transmission" (where information is transferred between sender and receiver) with a concept comprising three elements: information, utterance (or message) and understanding. "Information" is defined in contrast to a background of already known meanings. It is the novelty, the news presented in face of redundancy. "Message" is the act of making information known, its utterance. It is the performance that a communicator makes to produce the information. In turn, "comprehension" or "understanding" involves discerning the information content (the propositions or what was said) and the supplementary cues contained in the utterance/message (how it was said). As the anthropologist Gregory Bateson (2000, p. 9) observes, information is a "difference that makes a difference"; therefore, beyond the stated content, in addition to the information said, there is information "of another kind" contained in gestures, intonations and contexts. Only after achieving understanding can someone continue the communication, accepting or rejecting what her interlocutor has said.

Communication, under these assumptions, is an improbable event. Yet, it remains the fundamental building block of society. How, then, does society overcome this improbability and make itself viable? Through the emergence of meaning-making systems grounded not in thought, but in communication—in other words, social systems, at the different scales mentioned in the previous section, beginning with interactions and organisations and culminating in more encompassing and durable functional systems.

Besides the "success media" (the symbolically generalised communication media, such as power, money and truth), which motivate attention to communication and sustain functional differentiation, there are the "dissemination media" (Luhmann, 2012). These constitute the material infrastructure or technology that makes it possible to generate redundancy in communication—to confirm information, transforming novelty into shared common knowledge. This is how the co-evolution between the types of society (forms of social differentiation) and the means of disseminating communication can be schematised. In segmented societies, communication spreads predominantly through face-to-face oral communication. This is a restricted, low and slow dissemination of information, basically among acquaintances (members of the same community). In stratified societies, writing allows for a wider dissemination of information, especially among literate elites. In functionally differentiated societies, public opinion emerges, driven by the mass media, especially the advent of the press. Nowadays, the transition from analogue mass media (such as newspapers, radio and television) to digital media implies a loss of information selection and certification controls and a massively decentralised production and dissemination of communication, from acquaintances to strangers. This implies pressures within, but also against, functional differentiation.

Digital communication can be defined as "a normal communicative operative unit, whose selections and syntheses are updated and reintroduced in the form of digital information within the digital medium, thus enabling the formation of sociopoietic operative sequences, online or offline" (Pignuoli Ocampo, 2024, pp. 20–21). The novelty of the advent of digital "social networks" and "messaging apps" lies in their ability to short-circuit the internal differentiation between the public that consumes information and the media companies that select, produce, and disseminate the message. The guardians of information are discredited—the press is seen as biased, as a friend or foe of the government or the opposition. A multitude of people has become producers and consumers of information, and there is no final position of second-order observation that can reliably attest to the truth or untruth of the news. Even fact-checking agencies are subject to the same suspicions of bias that affect the traditional mass media. Interaction—whether through physical presence or by telephone—could also spread lies and errors, but the extent and speed of dissemination were limited in comparison to currently digital platforms.

Analogue mass media worked to reduce contingency by providing a standardised common sense, relying on professional journalism against suspicions of manipulation, which was a key point in reinforcing the acceptance of the information provided as a credible and trustworthy product (Palmieri, 2020). In this context, the various subsystems of society benefited from the generalisation of information provided by professional mass media and organisations took decisions based on presumably reliable information.

Analogue and digital media now compete within a single mass media system. When people can communicate their opinions, views or insights to increasingly large and interconnected groups, personal communication rises to the level of a functional media system. Information as a whole and messages—including fake news—also become detached from their original providers and belong to the "anonymous" system of self-referential digital communication. In a world of free and diverse beliefs, communication is not restricted by shared customs, as it is in a tribe. But a neo-tribal organisation of political beliefs—from hate speech against vulnerable populations to identity-based retaliation—is emerging to put pressure on the limits of tolerance of the liberal state.

A generalised crisis of expectations pervades a society structured through specific roles and delimited communicative competencies: politics and politicians, science and experts, law and jurists. This crisis of expectations and trust, stemming from the "growing digitalisation of life" (Cesarino, 2022, p. 228), paves the way for the construction of the so-called post-truth, an "epistemic condition [of communication] in which any statement can potentially be altered by anyone, at a very low cost" (Cesarino, 2021, p. 77). In this context of crisis and de-differentiation, niche markets for the merchants of doubt have proliferated (Cesarino, 2022; Oreskes & Conway, 2010), with these actors now engaging in a wide range of topics and monetising their actions and discourse through social networks.

Moreover, in the midst of this crisis, populism is emerging as the political manifestation of this phenomenon. It is characterised by the oversimplification of scientific research, the distrust of experts and the erosion of political decision-making processes based on the rule of law, all in the name of a moral integration proposed by a leader who may have come to power by electoral or authoritarian means. Contemporary democracy is based on a procedural triangulation between a public sphere (a public opinion generalised through the functional system of the mass media), peripheral organisations (parties, groups and movements that gather together political programmes and demands) and the central organisation (the state, its bureaucracy and its political powers, whose seizure of power is institutionalised through the difference between government and opposition) (Luhmann, 2009; 2014b). Through representation, decisions are broken down into decisions about who decides. There is a tendency for politicians to become more professional. The people make a second-order decision: they elect those who will decide on substantive issues, create laws and define public policies; a relative autonomy is institutionalised between the voter and the elected since the mandate is representative, not imperative.

This institutional engineering gives rise to a model of pluralistic party competition (Dahl, 1989); in its dynamics, citizens vote based on an ideological identification with the values and programmes professed by the parties. They would choose to rely on abstract and impersonal meanings debated and clarified in the arena of public opinion—an arena within the political system, but dependent on the services provided by a structural coupling with the mass media system. Even if contemporary mass democracy is defined as a competition between elites for the vote of the masses (Schumpeter, 2003), this institutional setting is crucial for the anonymous and generalised identification of tendencies and positions in the sphere of public opinion.

However, digital media combine the monetisation of every communicative operation—from the production of information to the targeting of messages driven by predictive Artificial Intelligence—with mechanisms that facilitate understanding through hyper-moralisation and *memefication* of all topics. The algorithms that drive digital media are deeply embedded in economic logic: their design is intended to keep users engaged on the network for as long as possible. It enables the delivery of an increasing number of personalised advertisements tailored to each user's experience. They are programmed to achieve certain objectives, which are assumed a priori to be apolitical and/or beneficial to society (Morozov, 2018), by prioritising the optimisation of efficiency, heavily relying on the extensive use of data to ensure maximum economic gains for the companies that control them. This strategy ensures the maximum economic exploitation of the personal data transmitted during each interaction.

Consequently, the circular operation of these cybernetic systems overlooks all other considerations, particularly *whether* the results are genuinely beneficial, *what* their impacts are on other societal subsystems, and *how* these outcomes are being achieved. According to Morozov (2018), whose argument can be extended to other subsystems, it is precisely this algorithmic de-differentiation that points to the "death of politics".

The construction of this "trap" design (Seaver, 2019), which aims to economise users' attention and communication, has as one of its primary effects the prevalence of content recommendations imbued with strong moral overtones that reinforce existing convictions and beliefs. This type of content is particularly effective at capturing attention and drawing users down so-called rabbit holes, causing them to spend hours on the platforms. As Fisher (2023) and Empoli (2024) explain, this algorithmic logic is linked to processes of political radicalisation, the spread of conspiracy theories and pseudoscience, and the proliferation of online harassment campaigns, all of which create a fertile ground for far-right authoritarian movements to thrive.

Vesting (2020) examines the broader shift in public opinion formation resulting from the integration of Artificial Intelligence and big data management. Companies specialised in providing customised marketing according to machine-learning algorithms that aggregate data on potential voters' preferences (such as the clues we leave on social networks) allow for a much more personalised and efficient approach to niche constituencies than rallies in public squares or speeches on television, events commonly used by politicians as a means to speak directly to the masses. This phenomenon essentially involves replacing identification with ideologies, programmes, and parties—which mediate between individual preferences and collective problems and agendas—with a personalised approach to one's own identity, particular situation, family needs and immediate concerns. Psychometric data allows electoral campaigns to profile their targets as these voters communicatively construct their own identities through the information they produce and consume on digital networks. Politics observes everyone as they want to be observed, according to the traces left behind on the World Wide Web (on the construction of "profiles", see Moeller & D'Ambrosio, 2019). In this way, social systems (such as politics) decode the bodies and minds of individuals, shaping the political personas of voters and constructing the speeches and gestures of candidate-characters.

In this context, we can understand the specificity of the fake news phenomenon as one of the identifiers of current political communication. It is not a matter of spreading lies in a small community with local boundaries or of breaking court secrets in a stratified society. It is a phenomenon linked to the very technology of the new mass media, i.e. digital platforms. The means of dissemination are responsible for social redundancy. Digital media play a leading role in the dynamic through which information captures user attention, as it is easily decoded and provokes strong moral reactions of support or repulsion. Traditional media, such as radio and television, have also historically built their audiences in this way. However, what distinguishes digital media is a particular feature in the way messages are structured and circulated: information is reinforced by a stream of similar messages from trusted people, usually relatives, friends and work colleagues. Thus, through redundancy, which characterises the mass aspect of the means of dissemination, the repeated lie gradually acquires the social value of "truth". On digital platforms, mechanisms for verifying sources and accrediting information are either absent (due to open access and unrestricted publication on the networks) or discredited (such as when there is generalised distrust on traditional media or fact-checking agencies that make a "second-order" observation of what the social networks have observed).

Thus, people's understanding of the message (trust in the source) and the (morally charged easily understandable) information becomes a ready-made narrative. These digital communication bubbles engage people in a network that already provides ideological counter-arguments views to reject discrepant narratives and to disallow information and messages that conflict with the repertoire cultivated within the group. Expectations are formed with a high normative load—to resist facts that contradict them—and a low cognitive capacity to learn from facts and revise their beliefs. Hence the hyper-moralised nature of digital communication. Morality, based on the good/bad code (Luhmann, 1993, 2013b), is one of the drivers of a crisis of societal integration that corrupts the differentiation of the various functional spheres (based on the different codes: government/opposition, have/have not, true/false), reducing the available social complexity (i.e. the stock of communicative options). One of these manifestations—and at the same time, one of its main vectors—is the emergence of populist-authoritarian movements based on a moralised discourse, disseminated by a broad and well-funded orchestration of digital communication schemes.

This crisis of social integration and the corruption of other systems, driven by the division between good and bad (and thus between in-groups and out-groups), is exemplified by far-right slogans such as "human rights only for the right people", as well as by how the notions of truth and lie increasingly depend on the affiliation of the source rather than on any objective criteria: "if it comes from the friendly camp, it's fact; if it comes from the enemy camp, it's a lie" (Cesarino, 2022, p. 226).

This imposition of the moral code across various subsystems is not only the result of the economic logic that drives algorithmic functioning; it also appears to be closely linked to the broader trend of de-differentiation triggered by the dominance of the economic code characteristic of neoliberal rationality (Minhoto et al., 2022).

Economic metrics, individualism, and the imperative of competition have increasingly infiltrated other systems, such as law, politics, science, and education (Foucault, 2010; Dardot & Laval, 2016), creating fertile ground for perspectives that demonise "the other"—the bad ones, those who, by their own fault, are seen as having failed (Brown, 2019). As Nunes (2022, p. 15) puts it: "When competition increasingly becomes a matter of life and death, excluding opponents becomes a valid option".

In addition to its political impact (the rise and strengthening of authoritarian discourses), the emergence and dominance of digital platforms have deep economic implications (the market concentration and market power of big tech companies crossing all over the globe) and legal consequences. These platforms are moving between cooperation with state authorities and arming themselves against state regulation. On the regulatory side, digital platforms have developed their own content moderation bodies either address problems with speed and technology, or to shield themselves from state and national laws. However, these self-regulatory measures have been widely criticised both for their lack of transparency and inefficiency in providing effective content moderation, as well as for the deplorable working conditions faced by the outsourced workers tasked with these responsibilities (Fisher, 2022). Despite the criticism, many national legislations are adopting "meta-regulation" or "regulated self-regulation" solutions, for example, by creating an independent digital communications regulatory body with a mixed composition: representatives of the state, digital platforms, academic scholars and digital rights movements. This is a mechanism for 'regulatory learning', capable of keeping pace with technological evolution through a more detailed technically based, and easily changeable regulatory framework than legislation. Conversely, it is permeable to the technological and economic power of transnational big tech, which ultimately position themselves as both targets and (co)producers of this mixed law (Amato, 2024).

An important ethical demand is placed upon the digital platforms to cope with state authorities and civil society in order to develop strategies of codetermination that ensure minimum procedural guarantees (reliable procedures for complaints, investigations and punishments on the web) and core basic rights (freedom of expression, but also dignity and protection of minorities and individuals) to the users. We need an institutional arrangement that functions as a veritable scheme of checks and balances for the digital world. It should address two problems. The first is to counter the partial interests of the different players (the state, platforms and users) and to prevent the abuse of their powers by restraining them through vetoes that each can impose on the other in the design of the regulation to be developed and deepened on the basis of this legal regime. The aim is to seek a division of rights, duties, powers and responsibilities that responds to an identifiable intersection with the 'public interest'. The second problem is dealing with the fallibility of the different players and their regulatory output. To this end, coordination must facilitate corrigibility, catalysing legal responses that are experimental, testable and revisable on the basis of evidence. A coordinating authority for this network of agents can act by mediating solutions and ways out of deadlocks in negotiations between the different actors for the creation or revision of rules.

5 A Reference to Brazil: The Primacy of Economic and Moral Codes and the Rise of Authoritarian Populism

An analysis of the Brazilian case can provide insights into the concrete effects of the interplay between the digitalisation of communication, systemic de-differentiation driven by the dominance of moral and economic codes, and the rise of authoritarian populism.

The distortions of the liberal-democratic model of pluralist party competition are well known in Brazilian political history, although, like the contemporary global wave of right-wing authoritarian populisms, they do not constitute a distinct national character. Two pairs of typical distortions affect the basic scheme of electoral democracy: on the one hand, patron-client relationships and corporatism (i.e. the direct approach and negotiation of support either with dispersed voters or with organised groups and lobbies); on the other, populism and authoritarianism. These types are combined to varying degrees, depending on the historical context. The new prominence of digital networks is destabilising political representation (and other sectors, such as public health), just as the emergence of the press, television or radio has altered the communicational basis on which society and its subsystems reproduce themselves. Political representation itself takes on the air of an imperative mandate, constantly connected to voters and their demands echoed on the networks.

In this context, in 2018 Jair Bolsonaro was elected to the Presidency of Republic. He was a retired low-ranking military officer and a former federal deputy known for his apology for the military dictatorship that ruled Brazil between 1964 and 1985. With an economic neoliberal or libertarian discourse, he emerged as the main leader of the far-right-wing forces in the country, opposing the era of the moderate left-wing Labour Party (PT), with the presidencies of Luiz Inácio Lula da Silva (2003–2010) and Dilma Rousseff (2011–2016), who undergone a process of impeachment in 2016, being replaced by her conservative vice-president Michel Temer (2016–2018). Bolsonaro was then elected and governed from 2019 to 2022, ran for re-election, but was defeated by Lula.

Given this path, the election of Jair Bolsonaro in 2018 must be understood as part of a broader systemic crisis (Cesarino, 2022) exacerbated by the interplay of de-differentiating tendencies driven by the spread of neoliberal rationality and the widespread digitalisation of communication and social life. To grasp how this phenomenon has unfolded in the Brazilian context, it is crucial to highlight some of the key factors that have contributed to it since the 2010s.

First, in terms of digital platforms, this decade marks a turning point, as it has seen significant investments in predictive content recommendation models and changes to platform interfaces, such as infinite feeds, that more effectively capture users' attention and time. This period also witnessed significant acquisitions and increased market concentration among a few dominant players—most notably, Meta, Inc. (then Facebook, Inc.) acquired Instagram in 2012 and WhatsApp in 2014. At the same time, Google's Android and Apple's iOS mobile operating systems overtook other competitors, becoming virtually the only options available in the market. In Brazil, this period marks the moment when "the internet became the primary arena for political communication in the country" (Cesarino, 2022, p. 11), fuelled by the "decreasing cost of smartphones and data packages" (Cesarino, 2022, p. 11), particularly due to promotions by telecom operators that began offering unlimited access to platforms such as Facebook and WhatsApp.

The proliferation of digital communication had already been influencing the political landscape since the beginning of the decade—the mobilisation on the networks for the June 2013 protests can be regarded as one of the first examples. However, its most significant effects were felt midway through the decade. During the severe economic crisis and the various distributive conflicts that marked Dilma Rousseff's (brief) second term (Braga and Santos, 2020), digital communication became a crucial arena for mobilising protests supporting her impeachment. With substantial funding from major economic groups, the internet became a stage for discourses marked by extreme moralisation that dominated political debates. The political discourse of the period illustrates how, on the internet, pressures to deepen neoliberal economic reforms, anti-corruption agendas, discussions about public safety, and aversion to inclusion and diversity policies coalesced into a single narrative of the struggle between good and bad. As Nunes (2022) states:

> In one fell swoop, what had once been seen as a universal and endemic problem was reframed as a [moral] vice exclusive to the left. Even the modest reformism of the Workers' Party (PT) was depicted as part of a communist threat, with anything other than pro-market libertarianism deemed potentially suspect. Opposition to progressive policies was justified not as elitism but as resistance to an inevitable slide into tyranny, while a sense of imminent danger was cultivated, driving demands for urgent and radical action. (Nunes, 2022, p. 35)

These discourses, generated in virtual environments, fully permeated the political system: the voting process for the impeachment of Dilma Rousseff in the Brazilian Congress (2016), rather than focusing on its political or legal aspects, was predominantly characterised by members of parliament casting votes filled with moral references—such as to family, God, and other values. The economic crisis was attributed to the moral failings of the left and the Labour Party, with these groups being portrayed as the real "enemies" that needed to be eradicated through the impeachment of the then-president and other punitive measures.

These discourses, which marked both digital communication and the political system during the impeachment period, laid the groundwork that would be reinforced with even greater intensity in subsequent years. In 2018, Brazil held its first elections under the ban on corporate funding of electoral campaigns, which the Supreme Court had imposed. At the same time, the country was exposed to an unprecedented extent to the massive dissemination of disinformation through private messaging apps and digital platforms. It is not a coincidence after all, not only all the changes on the platforms were in full effect, but also the large-scale propagation of distorted content demands investment—made by political agents and their supporters, albeit without the formality of an electoral donation, but as a functional equivalent (Barros et al., 2023).

Bolsonaro's campaign, supported by these networks that spread false information, relied on the creation of images and rhetoric with strong moral charges designed to capture voter attention and encourage sharing through social media, regardless of factual accuracy or any well-designed program of government. A notable example was the absurd accusation of a supposed "gay kit", which was content on combating homophobia allegedly to be distributed by PT governments to schools. This claim was rapidly disseminated, amplified, and reproduced by disinformation networks and opportunistic digital influencers who saw Bolsonaro's rise as a niche market for their economic gains. Another example was the government plan presented by Bolsonaro's party to the Superior Electoral Court (TSE). Deviating from traditional political criteria, the document was explicitly crafted for digital communication, replete with images and generic catchphrases about communist threats, "Gramscianism, globalism, God, and fiscal austerity" (Cesarino, 2022, p. 162)—i.e. the fight between good and bad.

Through this coupling of moral conservatism with the imperatives of "self-entrepreneurship", the entire Bolsonaro campaign, propelled by fake news and other disinformation strategies, actively contributed to framing political opponents as the enemy. This definition was broad enough to encompass virtually anyone opposing the movement: Leftists, students, artists, journalists, social activists, and many other groups were consistently depicted as the true embodiment of bad in political discourse. At the same time, a narrative was constructed that associated Bolsonaro and his supporters with religious and messianic figures, as instance: the "myth", "messiah" and "saviour of the homeland", positioning them as the embodiment of good against existential threats.

After winning the election, the campaign dynamics continued to shape the government's approach. From the outset, the government maintained the logic of enmity propagated through digital communication, employing fake news as a strategy in its official or quasi-official communication. As Nunes (2022) notes, this model explicitly revealed the government's intention to govern not for everyone, but only for those within the in-group. These intentions were turned into political action in two main stances: in the adoption and support of harsher punitive and repressive measures against those labelled as enemies; and in the way the Government handled the COVID-19 pandemic.

It is clear that *Bolsonarism* did not create a punitive culture in Brazil *ex nihilo*, but rather radicalised certain preexisting elements, consolidating a normative substrate that shapes social expectations and demands for punishment. Through media rituals, public statements, and symbolic policies, the Bolsonaro government not only expressed but actively produced and amplified this punitive culture.

This genuine moral economy of punishment organises a field of moral expectations regarding who ought to be punished, as well as the modalities and justifications for such punishment. It is important to note that this process frequently unfolds on the margins of formal legal-criminal rationality, insofar as individuals, groups, and territories are assimilated into categories such as "enemies" or "criminals". This moral economy possesses a preventive and anticipatory dimension with respect to punitive processes, operating prior to the actual commission of any criminal offence. Consequently, it tends to function less through the adjudication of specific crimes and more through the governance and management of populations deemed "dangerous".

In this regard, *Bolsonarism* has structured a particular moral economy that reconfigures the criteria of social worthiness and dignity. The dichotomy between "cidadãos de bem" ("law-abiding citizens") and "criminals" functions not merely as a descriptive classification, but as an operative moral economy that allocates rights, protections, and vulnerabilities—frequently translating moral judgments into concrete public policies.

From a systems theory perspective, the COVID-19 pandemic can be seen as a crisis of integration that reinforces interdependencies under emergency conditions (Esposito, 2020). In this regard, we can also note how social media platforms and digital communication were mobilised during the pandemic in Brazil. As the COVID-19 pandemic unfolded, fake news spread on various platforms, ranging from supposed miracle treatments to conspiracy theories about the origin of the virus and the efficacy of vaccines. The main example in Brazil was the "anti-COVID kit", a set of drugs that became part of municipal health protocols and was investigated through randomised clinical trials, which demonstrated its ineffectiveness and the risk of severe adverse effects. In this context, one of the most significant omissions of the federal government in Brazil was the lack of an effective strategy to combat fake news. The government did not take proactive steps to disprove false information and disseminate reliable scientific knowledge. Instead, there were instances where members of the government (including the President of the Republic himself, in his social media streams) openly shared and promoted information without scientific backing, contributing to the spread of misinformation. Furthermore, the federal government failed to establish partnerships with technology and social media companies to combat the spread of fake news (Barros & Amato, 2024).

During this period, Bolsonaro and other federal government officials delivered a series of public speeches that embodied the fusion of monetisation and hyper-moralisation. Echoing neoliberal tenets in line with the famous Thatcherite formula that there is no society, only individuals and their families (Brown, 2019), one of Bolsonaro's early statements on the health crisis was that "each family must protect its elderly rather than placing this responsibility on the state" (Kalili et al., 2021). This statement exemplifies a pattern that persisted throughout the period: discourses of freedom and individual responsibility were closely linked to the belief that the state should prioritise the economy over public health.

This narrative not only served as a foundation for denying health measures to protect the population, but also for the moral war that Bolsonaro claimed to be waging against his various constructed enemies: China, scientists, state governors seeking to ensure vaccination, the Supreme Court, opposition parties, the "stay-at-home gang" (those who publicly advocated for social isolation measures), the media, even the families of the victims, among others. In a typical social network discourse, all these groups were portrayed as so-called "saboteurs" of the government. Even in the face of the tragic loss of over 700,000 lives to the disease, the government's misinforming and hyper-moralising stance remained unchanged throughout Bolsonaro's entire administration—constantly echoed on social networks by supporters and other 'merchants of doubt' (Cesarino, 2022).

Indeed, Brazil has debated a regulatory package for digital communications since the Internet Bill of Rights (2014). As scandals of personal data breaches in the digital environment emerged worldwide, the General Law on Personal Data Protection (LGPD) was approved by the Brazilian National Congress. The LGPD was the subject of intense disputes: the statute was passed in the National Congress in August 2018, on the eve of the October presidential elections, which marked a new level in the mobilisation of digital networks for electoral campaigns, especially for the dissemination of fake news. However, with the elected President of the Republic (Jair Bolsonaro) and his parliamentary base being notorious beneficiaries of orchestrated disinformation strategies, political disputes postponed the statute's entry into force until September 2020—two years after its approval. The fake news draft bill followed a similar course: it began to be processed after the 2018 elections and was passed by the Federal Senate in 2020. Expectations that it would be approved before the next parliamentary elections in 2022 (as well as the local elections in 2024) were dashed.

With the defeat of Bolsonaro's re-election bid, some events in 2023 began with a strong presence of digital networks as environments for mobilisation and the expression of extremist discourses that transcended the virtual world. This is the case of the invasion, and vandalism of the main Brazilian state headquarters in the country's capital, Brasilia, during an attempted *coup d'état* on January 8th, replicating the mob attack on the US Capitol on January 6th 2021 instigated by Donald Trump. The invasion was driven both by Bolsonaro's conspiratorial rhetoric and disinformation campaign about Brazilian elections, and by the bifurcated view that frames politics and law in a dichotomy of good and bad.

The transition from the dominance of analogue communication to proliferation of digital platforms in Brazil has had significant implications for the country's electoral and political processes. As Lellis and Dutra (2020) observe, an economic crisis, combined with a programmatic crisis of the left (which held power in Brazil for nearly 15 years, beginning in the early 2000s) boosted the populist right's strategy of hyper-moralising communication as a means of securing and consolidating support and power.

6 Concluding Remarks

While analogue mass media "industrialised" communication through centralised media corporations, the disintermediation of traditional media and re-intermediation by digital platforms makes it possible to have not only mass consumption, but also a molecular production of information. Digital platforms intermediate both sides, placing pressure on the constant generation of information/misinformation (news, novelty), changing the form of messaging and the pace and meaning of redundancy and understanding, driving total acceptance or rejection given the simplification and moral load embedded in each message. The monetisation of information and the moral overload of (economic, political, legal) communication are coupled by social media: the more morally engaging and simple the communication, the more it circulates and produces financial returns. Governments that combine authoritarian measures with libertarian rhetoric are a homeland to the empowerment of this feedback between the moral simplification and extremism in the shaping of the messages and the monetisation of digital media.

This opens the way to a better understanding of systemic crisis and enhances its critical potential. If functional differentiation, as Luhmann suggests, requires a degree of disintegration to entail the self-reference of each system, one could argue that a systemic crisis arises in situations of hypertrophy of some partial systems upon others. The current prominence and ubiquity of the digital media system, driven by economic and moral codifications, is an instance of this crisis: the monetisation of information production and dissemination and its enhancement by moral extremism leads to drastically reduce the complexity of specialised problems and solutions (in economy, science, law etc.). Authoritarian populism acts as a shortcut to a reduction in complexity.

In a normal scenario, political complexity is built through recursive operations: (i) a public opinion informed and shaped by mass media translates every (economic, environmental, healthcare, scientific, educational, legal) problem as a demand for public policy and/or political decision and reform; (ii) the peripheral political organisations (such as parties, social movements and interest groups) provide competing proposals to answer to these problems; (iii) the core political organisations (the executive and legislative branches) provide technical bureaucracy and representatively legitimised decision-making procedures to filter and opt among those competing solutions; (iv) the collectively biding decision taken by state representatives then return to be judged by the "mirror" of the public opinion. This normal dynamics of political communication is severely changed by digital communication: when the public opinion is polluted by massive disinformation (what affects the chains (i) and (iv)), when the competing political agents and parties are morally pictured as saviours and enemies (ii) and when the decision-making process within the state take the form of a reality show, with politicians making streaming transmissions of their performances within the parliament and/or the government.

Our reference to the recent political scenario in Brazil helps to show how the logic of social media platforms and digital communication has contributed to the ascension of far-right authoritarian populist leaders and movements. We can observe how the logic of digital communication has benefited the Bolsonarist movement not merely because of its effective use of digital tools, but also because there is an affinity between the codes promoted by this form of communication—particularly the moral and economic ones—and the Bolsonarist libertarian-authoritarian 'grammar' (Nunes, 2022). In other words, digital communication has helped to amplify discourses that frame various political and legal issues as moral and economic problems, thereby fuelling the division between 'in-groups' (the so-called 'good citizens') and 'out-groups' (the 'enemies') that is central to the Bolsonarist movement's worldview.

The good/bad code provides social cohesion in a complex society, marked by very divergent expectations. As social media oversimplifies information by coding it to simple moralist judgements, and profiting from this extremist moralisation, it provided a technological tool very useful for authoritarian trends arousing from the public opinion.

This case offers a clear example of how moral and economic codes were combined to overload other systems, especially science, law, and politics. In particular, this amalgamation of moral and economic codes facilitated the spread of misinformation regarding the pandemic and provided the basis for rejecting social distancing and vaccination policies. The analysis of the Brazilian case shows how some aspects of the process of digitalisation of society, such as the primacy of economic and moral codified binarisms, together with a media-driven tendency towards strong social integration, contribute to the erosion of the social conditions that are a precondition for functionally differentiated communication and favour the rise of authoritarian populism. In answer to this, a regulation of digital platforms that is designed to provide basic procedural and substantial rights and guarantees to the users should emerge from the combined efforts of governments, digital platforms, digital rights movements, researchers and other actors. Only within these limits digital media would be seen again as an opportunity to strength popular political interests and participation, instead as an obstacle for democratic stability and moderation, due to storms of disinformation that find in those platforms useful tools to promote (and to profit from) moral radicalisation.

References

Amato, L. F. (2024). *O direito da sociedade digital: tecnologia, inovação jurídica e aprendizagem regulatória*. Faculdade de Direito da Universidade de São Paulo.

Barros, M. A. L. L., & Amato, L. F. (2024). Regulación de la desinformación digital: Un estudio socio-jurídico sobre las fake news sanitarias en el caso brasileño. *Oñati Socio-Legal Series, 14*(3), 719–738.

Barros, M. A. L. L., Amato, L. F., Saba, D. T., & Ponce, P. P. (2023). Fake news in Brazil's 2018 presidential elections: A systems theory approach to judicial and legal responses. *Social & Legal Studies, 32*(1), 116–138.

Bateson, G. (2000). *Steps to an ecology of mind*. Chicago University Press.

Bertalanffy, L. (1968). *General systems theory: Foundations, development, applications*. Braziller.

Braga, R., & Santos, F. L. B. (2020). The political economy of lulism and its aftermath. *Latin American Perspectives, 47*(1), 169-186.

Brown W. (2019). *Nas ruínas do neoliberalismo: A ascensão da política antidemocrática no ocidente*. Editora Filosófica Politeia.

Cesarino L. (2021). Pós-Verdade e a Crise do Sistema de Peritos: uma explicação cibernética. *Ilha – Revista de Antropologia, 23*(1), 73-96.

Cesarino L. (2022). *O mundo do avesso: Verdade e política na era digital*. Ubu.

Dahl, R. A. (1989). *Democracy and its critics*. Yale University Press.

Dutra, R. (2016). Diferenciação funcional e a sociologia da modernidade brasileira. *Política & Sociedade, 15*(34), 77–109.

Empoli G. D. (2024). *Engenheiros do caos*. Vestígio.

Esposito, E. (2020). Systemic integration and the need for de-integration in pandemic times. *Sociologica, 14*(1), 3–20.

Fisher M. (2023). *A máquina do caos: Como as redes sociais reprogramaram nossa mente e nosso mundo*. Todavia.

Foucault M (2010). *Nascimento da biopolítica*. Edições 70.
Hawthorn, G. (1987). *Enlightenment and despair: A history of social theory* (2nd ed.). Cambridge University Press.
Kalili I et al. (2021). Politics of fear in Brazil: Far-right conspiracy theories on COVID-19. *Global Discourse, 11*(3): 409-425
Lellis, N., & Dutra, R. (2020). Programmatic crisis and moralization of the politics: A proposal to define the Bolsonarism from the experience with the Covid-19 pandemic. *International Journal of Latin American Religions, 4*, 335–359.
Luhmann, N. (1981). The improbability of communication. *International Social Science Journal, 33*(1), 122–132.
Luhmann, N. (1990). *Political theory in the welfare state*. de Gruyter.
Luhmann, N. (1993). The code of the moral. *Cardozo Law Review, 14*, 995–1009.
Luhmann, N. (1995). *Social systems*. Stanford University Press.
Luhmann, N. (2005). Iluminismo sociológico. In J. M. Santos (Ed.), *O pensamento de Niklas Luhmann* (pp. 19–70). Universidade da Beira Interior.
Luhmann, N. (2009). La política como sistema. *Universidad*. Iberoamericana.
Luhmann, N. (2010). *Los derechos fundamentales como institución: Aportación a la sociología política*. Universidad Iberoamericana.
Luhmann, N. (2012). *Theory of society I*. Stanford University Press.
Luhmann, N. (2013a). *Theory of society II*. Stanford University Press.
Luhmann, N. (2013b). *La moral de la sociedad*. Trotta.
Luhmann, N. (2014a). *A sociological theory of law* (2nd ed.). Routledge.
Luhmann, N. (2014b). *Sociología política*. Trotta.
Luhmann, N. (2018). *Organization and decision*. Cambridge University Press.
Mascareño, A. (2007). Sociología del método: La forma de investigación sistémica. *Primavera, 2*(3), 1–41.
Merton, R. K. (1936). The unanticipated consequences of purposive social action. *American Sociological Review, 1*(1), 894–904.
Merton, R. K. (1968). *Social theory and social structure* (3rd ed.). Free Press.
Minhoto, L. D., & Amato, L. F. (2023). Adorno, Luhmann, and the critique of identity: Some internal connections. *Current Perspectives in Social Theory, 40*, 251–266.
Minhoto, L. D., Amato, L. F., & Camargos, P. A. P. (2022). Do político ao econômico: Aportes da teoria dos sistemas a uma crítica do neoliberalismo. *Sociologias, 24*(61), 170–197.
Moeller, H. G., & D'Ambrosio, P. J. (2019). Sincerity, authenticity and profilicity: Notes on the problem, a vocabulary and a history of identity. *Philosophy & Social Criticism, 45*(5), 575–596.
Morozov E. (2018). *Big tech: A ascensão dos dados e a morte da política*. Ubu.
Neves, M. (2005). Between under-integration and over-integration: Not taking citizenship seriously. In J. Souza & V. Sinder (Eds.), *Imagining Brazil* (pp. 61–90). Lexington.
Neves, M. (2012).*Transconstitutionalism*. Hart.
Nunes R. (2022). *Do transe à vertigem: Ensaios sobre o bolsonarismo e um mundo em transformação*. Ubu.
Oreskes N. & Conway E. M. (2010). *Merchants of doubt: How a handful of scientists obscured the truth on issues from tobacco smoke to global warming*. Bloomsbury Press.
Palmieri, E. (2020). The media and the social order in Niklas Luhmann. *World Complexity Science Academy Journal, 1*(2), 1–15.
Parsons, T. (1971). *The system of modern societies*. Prentice-Hall.
Pignuoli Ocampo, S. (2024). Comunicação digital e participação dos dispositivos no mundo social. *Revista Brasileira de Sociologia do Direito, 11*(2), 4–24.
Seaver, N. (2019). Captivating algorithms: Recommender systems as traps. *Journal of Material Culture, 24*(4), 421–436.
Schumpeter, J. A. (2003). *Capitalism, socialism and democracy* (5th ed.). Routledge.

Stichweh, R. (2013). The history and systematics of functional differentiation in sociology. In M. Albert, B. Buzan, & M. Zürn (Eds.), *Bringing sociology to international relations: World politics as differentiation theory* (pp. 50–70). Cambridge University Press.
Vanderstraeten, R. (2002). Parsons, Luhmann and the theorem of double contingency. *Journal of Classical Sociology, 2*(1), 77–92.
Vesting, T. (2018). *Legal theory and the media of law*. Edward Elgar.
Vesting, T. (2020). A mudança da esfera pública pela inteligência artificial. In G. Abboud, N. Nery Jr., & R. Campos (Eds.), *Fake News e regulação* (2nd ed., pp. 189–210). Revista dos Tribunais.
Yack, B. (1986). *The longing for total revolution: Philosophic sources of social discontent from Rousseau to Marx and Nietzsche*. Princeton University Press.

Lucas Fucci Amato Associate Professor at the Department of Jurisprudence and Philosophy of Law, University of São Paulo Law School, Brazil. He holds the bachelor's, doctoral and habilitation degrees in Law from the University of São Paulo. Fucci Amato further was a visiting researcher at the faculties of Law of Cambridge, Oxford, and Harvard Universities.

Laurindo Dias Minhoto Associate professor in the Department of Sociology at the University of São Paulo, holds an L.LM in Law in Development from Warwick University and PhD in Philosophy and General Theory of Law from the University of São Paulo. Dias Minhoto further holds a Bachelor's degree in Law from the Pontifical University of São Paulo. He's been a visiting Scholar at the Center for the Study of Law and Society at UC Berkeley, and heads the Systems Theory and Social Critique research group.

Pedro de Almeida Pires Camargos is a PhD candidate in Sociology at University of São Paulo. He holds a master's degree in Sociology and a bachelor's degree in Law from the University of São Paulo. He was Visiting Researcher at the Center for the Study of Law and Society at the University of California, Berkeley.

Detecting Disinformation with AI? Escaping the Technology Solutionist Trap by Enabling AI Literacy

Jan Doria and David Klotz

Abstract The recent progress in Generative Artificial Intelligence (AI) has made it easier and cheaper to produce and distribute disinformation on a large scale. Countering this development with a machine learning (ML)-driven automated disinformation detection device might sound promising, but as this essay reveals, the usage of such a device comes with its own set of problems: the danger of a technology solutionist trap that coincides with the contemporary mindless use of *Zeitgeist AI Machines* are structurally unable to detect whether a certain news piece is "fake" or not. This binary scale implies an invalid misconception of "truth" in ontological categories that might lead to unforeseen consequences. Instead of solely relying on ML for disinformation detection, the authors argue in favour of applying those technologies to enable AI literacy in the age of digital transformation.

Keywords Machine learning · Disinformation detection · Technology solutionism · Zeitgeist AI · Digital ethics · AI literacy

1 Introduction

Fuelled by modern computer systems' increasing computing and storage capacity, practical applications of machine learning (ML) have soared over the past decade. As described by the proverb "a solution in search of a problem", real-world ML use cases had to be found in order to prove the usefulness of this technology. Data scientists and machine learning experts have also attempted to use ML for good, thus applying it to solve problems on a societal level. One of the problem domains where ML applications have become popular recently is the identification of disinforma-

J. Doria (✉)
Institute for Digital Ethics, Stuttgart Media University, Stuttgart, Germany
e-mail: doria@hdm-stuttgart.de

D. Klotz
Institute for Applied Artificial Intelligence, Stuttgart Media University, Stuttgart, Germany
e-mail: klotzd@hdm-stuttgart.de

K. Bodrožić-Brnić et al. (eds.), *AI and the Ethics of Innovation*, Digital Transformation and Innovation, https://doi.org/10.1007/978-3-032-20638-1_4

tion, as pursued, for example, by the research project NEBULA (see https://peasec.de/projects/nebula/). Distinguishing between reliable information sources and disinformation has become more and more difficult, especially as the recent progress in Generative Artificial Intelligence (AI) has made it easier and cheaper to produce and distribute disinformation large scale (cp. Louban et al., 2022).

While countering disinformation with automated detection machines, driven by ML does sound promising, the following essay will critically reflect on the possible negative consequences of a naive technical approach to disinformation detection. Drawing from a teaching experiment with students from multidisciplinary academic backgrounds (Sect. 2), this essay will introduce the term of a *technology solutionist trap* to be found in automated disinformation detection, coined on the base of Evgeny Morozov's critique of the Silicon Valley's "technology solutionism" and understanding the mindless use of AI technologies to solve societal problems with Rainer Rehak as "Zeitgeist AI" (Sect. 3). Subsequently, Sect. 4 will outline why automated disinformation detection proves to be fuzzier than expected, drawing on insights from Media Studies. Finally, Sect. 5 will propose an escape to the *technology solutionist trap* of automated disinformation detection by taking a mid-centred, Digital Ethics based position on the problem and proposing to strengthen AI literacy in the age of digital transformation for both AI developers and users.

2 Detecting Disinformation with AI: A Teaching Experiment and its Confusing Result

A teaching experiment was conducted with eight undergraduate students from diverse academic backgrounds at Stuttgart Media University. The students attended the class "AI, disinformation and manipulation" which adopts an interdisciplinary perspective on AI and ML, discussing technological capabilities, economic potential, ethical considerations and social impact. The primary objective of the teaching experiment was to foster critical thinking among the students and demonstrate that technological solutions are not universally applicable to all problems.

The students in the class started with an introduction to the fundamental concepts of machine learning and supervised learning. Subsequently, a dataset from Kaggle.com (Patel & Meehan, 2021) containing labelled training data for real and fake news was introduced. Like the approach presented on the website, two classification models were trained with corresponding Python packages, e.g. Pandas (for data analysis and preparation) and Sklearn (for creating and training machine learning models), and their performance was evaluated using standard metrics such as accuracy. The first model used linear regression, and the second used a decision tree for classification. Both approaches leveraged a linguistic analysis of the news messages in the training set, using the Term Frequency-Inverse Document Frequency (TF-IDF) algorithm (Robertson, 2004), a robust function for Natural Language Processing (NLP) classification tasks like the given one (Fauzi et al., 2019; Patel & Meehan, 2021; Sharma &

Singh, 2023). This algorithm segments a text into words, or "terms" as called in the context of the algorithm and calculates two metrics for each of those terms: its frequency within a single news message and its inverse document frequency, or in other words, "rareness" across the entire set of news messages. The result of the algorithm is a numerical vector for each news message, where each term is assigned a weight that represents its importance in the context of the message. For example, if a news message has multiple occurrences of the term "France", but the term does not often appear in other news messages, it has a relatively high weight. The vector can be used to identify significant words that can be applied to distinguish between different classes of text in the training set. By analysing which terms are typically the most prominent ones for true and fake news, the models learn to predict whether a previously unseen message is true or fake. Both models exhibited exceptionally high prediction accuracy during validation, reaching approximately 99%.

While those initial results appeared promising, an additional validation exercise was introduced in which students were asked to test the model, using disinformation messages they had created themselves. Despite the previously observed high accuracy, the model repeatedly failed to classify the fabricated disinformation as such. As an assignment, students were tasked with analysing the model's poor performance and proposing potential improvements which were to be discussed in the following class. Group work in teams of three was encouraged to facilitate collaborative problem-solving.

During the subsequent session, student presentations primarily focused on refining the ML approach. Various technical adjustments were suggested, such as improving the vectorisation algorithm, optimising data preprocessing by refining stop word lists, and removing duplicate records. However, a critical observation remained unaddressed: the inherent limitations of the problem itself. As outlined in Sect. 4, neither humans nor machines can determine the veracity of a message solely based on its textual content. The fundamental flaw in the supervised learning approach used in this case was the failure to critically assess whether the sought-after answer—whether a message is true or false—was contained within the data. The students therefore proved to be vulnerable to what Evgeny Morozov calls "technology solutionism", a term to be introduced in the following section.

3 Zeitgeist AI as a Problem of Technology Solutionism

In his book "To save everything, click here. Technology, solutionism and the urge to fix problems that don't exist" (Morozov, 2013), published already in 2013, the Belarusian writer and researcher Evgeny Morozov offers a critical analysis to the mind-shaping paradigms of the technical utopias driven forward by the Silicon Valley (for those cp. also Daub, 2020; Doria, 2024; for the term "paradigm" in general cp. Kuhn, 1962/1970). Morozov's critique will now be shown to be helpful to understand the failure of the teaching experiment previously discussed.

The starting point of Morozov's analysis consists of a critique of what he calls the "grand narrative of 'the Internet'" (Morozov, 2013, p. 18):

> The Internet' is holy [...]. Once part of 'the Internet', any technology loses its history and intellectual autonomy. [...] Today, virtually every story is bound to have an 'Internet' angle – and it's the job of our Internet apostles to turn those little anecdotes into fairy tales about the march of Internet progress [...] (Morozov, 2013, p. 18).

Although Morozov's use of the term "narrative" is rather unclear, especially because he does not explain in detail which types of messages qualify as "narrative" and which do not (for a more elaborated definition cp. Doria, 2023), it becomes clear that he understands the hopes and desires conveyed by the vision of "the internet" as a technical utopia carrying the "expectation [...] to solve every problem that humanity is being confronted with nowadays" (Doria, 2024, p. 391; all German quotes were translated by the authors) and refers to the idea of solving societal problems with technological means "technology solutionism" (Morozov, 2013, 5 f.): "[A]s the geeks would say, given enough apps, all of humanity's bugs are shallow" (Morozov, 2013, x). However, his critique on technology solutionism does not actually lead to a rejection of the visions proposed by the tech utopians as ethically undesirable but rather to claiming that those visions tend to undermine alternative solution pathways:

> Internet-centrism is beginning to block our ability to think of effective technological solutions to problems that do exist. Solutions are not assessed based on their merits but rather on how well they sit with the idea of a free, open, transparent "network" and its "architecture". (Morozov, 2013, p. 75)

According to Morozov, "[r]recasting all complex social situations either as neatly defined problems with definite, computable solutions or as transparent and self-evident processes that can easily be optimized" (Morozov, 2013, p. 5) must be refused. Therefore, applying technological solutions to societal problems without proper reasoning "is likely to have unexpected consequences that could eventually cause more damage than the problems they seek to address" (Morozov, 2013, p. 5). Morozov then adds the broadly discussed case of autonomous vehicles as an illustrative example:

> Yes, [...] self-driving cars would make driving easier and perhaps even cut the number of deaths on the road, but a reasonable transportation system ought to pursue many other objectives. Would self-driving cars result in inferior public transportation as more people took up driving? Would it lead to even greater suburban sprawl as, not that they no longer had to drive, people could do e-mail during their commute and thus would tolerate spending more time in the car? (Morozov, 2013, 170 f.)

To conclude, Morozov argues strongly in favour of a "close ethical scrutiny" (Morozov, 2013, p. 149) when applying algorithmic engineering to societal problem domains.

At the time when Morozov's book was published in 2013, the ML debate, recently driven forward by the release of ChatGPT at the end of 2022 (for a short historical overview on AI development history cp. Doria & Zöllner, 2025, 2 f.), was still at the beginning. For this reason, Morozov does not speak of AI, but only of the "metanarrative of 'the internet'". But as recent research shows, popular AI narratives being distributed, for example in German TV magazines, can also be characterised (at least in their utopian version) by all viewing AI as an enabler to "improving the world" (Doria, 2023, p. 181). Thus it seems justified to transfer Morozov's critique to the problems of ML discussed here. In fact, contemporary authors like Rainer Rehak offer a modern reading of Morozov's "technology solutionism" by suggesting the term "Zeitgeist AI", for example. Rehak defines the latter as "a discursive phenomenon where political, societal and even academic actors refer to 'AI' when they actually mean anything related to complex digital technologies" (Rehak, 2023, p. 27) and calls for critically questioning if "AI [is] the best solution for moving forward on a given problem" (Rehak, 2023, p. 30) before applying it to practical use cases.

When transferring Rehak's question to the use of ML to detect disinformation, it becomes clear that the students mentioned in the teaching experiment described in sect. 2 failed to undergo such a critical reasoning before proposing technical improvements to the ML algorithm presented. Subsequently, the following section will try to follow up with what the students missed and show why automated disinformation detection turns out to be much more difficult than expected because it is intertwined with complex ethical problems.

4 Disinformation, the Technology Solutionist Trap and its Consequences

Seeking answers to Rehak's question in the domain of automated disinformation detection primarily needs a detailed analysis of the term "disinformation" itself. Joachim Allgaier defines "disinformation" as "information that does not correspond to *truth* in order to *intentionally harm* a person, social group, an organisation or a state" (Allgaier, 2022, p. 85, own emphasis). This definition implies two meaningful concepts (being emphasised here in *italics*) that will help to explain why ML algorithms are structurally unable to detect disinformation automatically: "truth" and the "intention to harm".

Expressed in the terminology of Computer Science, the ML model used in the teaching experiment conceptualises truth as a binary textual attribute like text length or character distribution that can take the two values "true" or "false". Philosophically spoken, this understanding implies "truth" to be an ontological category.

This is not the case, however. As outlined by Morozov, a limited binary understanding of truth can be seen as an example for reducing a "complex social situation ...]" to a "definite, computable solution" (Morozov, 2013, p. 5). Structuralist media semiotics approaches of textual meaning-making challenge the teaching experiment's binary misconception. Following them, every textual message including news must be conceived as a secondary semiotic system that constructs its own textual models (Krah, 2015, p. 44): "Media reproduces 'reality' according to their mediality in a specific manner, thus constituting it first and foremost [...]. [...] 'Reality' in the media is therefore never identical to our day-to-day-reality; it is always a medial construction" (Krah, 2017, p. 399). Scholars from Media Studies therefore distinguish between extradiegetic, meaning extra-medial reality and intradiegetic, meaning intra-medial reality (cp. Krah, 2017, p. 406), and as far as the intradiegetic reality is concerned, its character as a model of the extradiegetic reality implies that it "cannot be classified in terms of true/false but abstains from such a classification in general" (Krah, 2013, p. 29). Consequently, the ontological criterion of *truth* is replaced by the media ethics value of *truthfulness* defined as "speakers believing their messages to be true" (Filipović, 2024, p. 144). When analysing a given text, Media Studies scholars therefore do not try to judge whether it is actually "true" but whether it *claims* to be "true" (cp. Grimm, 2002; Sottong & Müller, 1998).

A simple set of examples may help to illustrate this argument:

Whereas the news message.

Example 1 *"On February 23rd, 2025, general elections to the 21st Bundestag took place in Germany" [own example].*

Can easily be classified as "true" by both human and machines, news messages like the following turn out to be much more difficult to deal with:

Example 2 *"Fall in fertility rate becomes big challenge for provincial France"* (https://www.bbc.com/news/articles/c5yvq1jy2xgo, last visited: 03/03/2025).

Example 3 *"Only AfD can save Germany"* (https://x.com/elonmusk/status/1877435764520239454, last visited: 03/03/2025).

Example 4 *"To comply with its climate targets, the German Federal Government must introduce a nationwide speed limit on motorways" [own example].*

Example 5 *"Sparkling wine factory inaugurated with cruise ship"* (https://www.der-postillon.com/2017/01/sektfabriktaufe.html, last visited: 03/03/2025).

As for example 2, the binary classifier used in the teaching experiment might produce a "false" as an output because of the mere statistical accumulation of the word "France" due to its functioning outlined in Sect. 2—despite of the fact that it was dealing with a true BBC news message from February second 2025. Quite the contrary, the examples 3 and 4 are not to be conceived as news pieces at all, but as personal opinion statements including a subjective judgement on the related topics; a binary classification between "true" and "false" proves to be completely inappropriate here. As far as the final example 5 is concerned, the ML classifier would have to deal with a piece from *Der Postillion*, a "news website" commonly known in Germany for only publishing satire. As satirical texts do not claim to be "true" in general, a possible false-positive classification by the ML disinformation detector for this one would lead to a limitation of freedom of speech that would have to be considered as highly problematic in terms of democratic opinion-forming processes. Media recipients thus cannot rely on ML algorithms to distinguish between truth and falsehood; they need proprietary knowledge on the mechanisms of the media system as a whole.

Comparable to the term of "truth", the term of an "intentional harm" that the definition quoted above names as sufficient condition—for disinformation turns out to neither being easily reducible to a "definite, computable solution". Once again, "intentional harm" cannot be conceptualised as an attribute that might appear in any kind of data set used to train the ML system; it must be recognised as a complex social construct often opaque even to humans. As the examples above show, one might agree that the mere distribution of news messages 1, 2 and 5 may not be connected to "intentional harm", but for examples 3 and 4, this evaluation turns out to be politically controversial and highly dependent of the respective subjective preferences of the recipients. As argued in the following, allowing an AI system to decide whether examples 3 and 4 are "disinformation" or not, implies giving up human freedom to evaluate political events and transferring this capability to a machine agent, thus opening up critical ethical problems.

Trying to detect disinformation with ML methods can therefore be conceived as hitting a *technology solutionist trap*. Following Morozov's argumentation, applying technological solutions like ML to disinformation detection must address the warning for at least two unforeseen consequences that could eventually cause more damage than the problem they seek to address (Morozov, 2013).

First of all, if an automated disinformation detection has successfully proven to be impossible due to epistemological reasons, trying to continue working on this research approach represents a misallocation of scarce funding resources in the terms of Rehak's *Zeitgeist AI*: "[I]f the answer is that we already know enough regarding the given domain, then applying AI just uses up vital resources, diverts political focus and eventually acts as an excuse for inaction" (Rehak, 2023, p. 31).

The second warning contains an even greater concern for the functioning of deliberative democracy, as hitting the *technology solutionist trap* on disinformation detection conveys a great danger to possibly loosing human autonomy. The latter "translates literally from Greek as self-legislation and refers to the possibility of (ethical) self-determination, freedom of choice and responsibility" (Krainer, 2024, p. 151). In the tradition of German philosopher Immanuel Kant, ethicists therefore call for humans to "have courage to make use of [their] *own* [emphasis as in the original] understanding" (Kant, 1784/1996, p. 17).

However, relying *solely* on an AI system to determine whether a given news piece is true or false does not imply making "use of the own understanding", as Kant demands, but *transferring* the decision-making autonomy of what counts as "true" and what not to the operators of such systems. Various AI ethicist have already warned for digital technologies to become an "engine for loosing autonomy and the freedom of choice" (Krainer, 2024, p. 155); in detail, Jan Doria and Oliver Zöllner underline that "power relationships might turn into a rebalancing—especially in economic terms—in favour of the owners [of digital technologies]" (Doria & Zöllner, 2025, p. 6). AI developers should therefore always keep in mind that machines are not moral agents (cp. Doria & Zöllner, 2025; Grimm & Hammele, 2019) and therefore unable to make normative value judgements. For the news examples discussed here, allowing an AI system to do so irresponsibly would lead to opening the possibility for the system operators to manipulate the ML disinformation detection algorithm in a way that news pieces like the examples 3 or 4 might be classified as "wrong" by default, depending on the operators' respective political and/or economic interests, and even a politically neutral classification algorithm would shrink the space for satire like in example 5. The society might then end up with two competing ML disinformation detection systems, one with a left-wing, the other one with a right-wing bias. The disinformation problem, however, would remain unsolved.

5 Escaping the Trap: A Pledge for AI Literacy in Interdisciplinary Contexts

To resume, AI developers and practitioners working on disinformation detection are challenged with escaping the outlined *technology solutionist trap*. The closing section of this essay will now offer alternative solution pathways that seek to strengthen their literacies. In doing so, it draws from the interdisciplinary learnings between Computer Science, Media Studies and Digital Ethics obtained here.

After discussing the technical refinements to the ML approach used in the teaching experiment described in Sect. 2, the students were introduced to the concept of technology solutionism and encouraged to question the immanent assumptions behind automated disinformation detection. Experiencing that dealing with disinformation also means to deal with fuzzy philosophical and ethical problems proved to be eye-opening. At the undergraduate level and with limited prior exposure to ML, many students either did not recognise the conceptual issue or did not feel confident enough to challenge the methodological approach. Similar misapplications of ML models are frequently observed in real-world practice, particularly where teams with mixed backgrounds jointly work on ML models. ML specialists, often trained in Computer Science, may have a limited understanding of the problem domain, while domain experts, though familiar with the data, may lack ML literacy. As a result, Zeitgeist AI is sometimes perceived as a near-magical solution capable of solving previously intractable problems.

But "to reject solutionism is not to reject technology" (Morozov, 2013, p. 13) as a whole, as Evgeny Morozov himself adds:

> To reject solutionism is to transcend the narrow-minded rationalistic mind-set that recasts every instance of an efficiency deficit [...] as an obstacle that needs to be overcome. There are other, more fruitful, more humanistic, and more responsible ways to think about technology's role in enabling human flourishing. (Morozov, 2013, p. 14)

To determine whether applying technology to a given social problem might result in being useful or not, we suggest going back to Aristotle's Virtue Ethics approach as the backbone framework for nowadays' Digital Ethics (at least in German-speaking countries, cp. Grimm, 2021). According to Virtue Ethics, technology should first and foremost be used to "create conditions for good [...] lives in the future" (Johnson, 2022, p. 649). The "good life" is then defined as a virtuous life (Grimm, 2021) while a "virtue" can be expressed in Aristotelian terms as a "mean state between two vices, one of excess and one of defect" (Aristotle, 1934, 1107a). Taking also into account Martha Nussbaums virtue ethics based Capabilities Approach that enumerates a list of human basic capabilities in order to achieve the "good life" (Nussbaum, 2011), that means in sum that when detecting disinformation, Digital Ethics has to ask for the mean state between a radical rejection of technology-based solutions on the one hand and a radical technology endorsement on the other hand and for technologies that encourage human capabilities and human understanding rather than shrinking them. Under this presumption, a responsible use of ML algorithms for disinformation detection should consist of both educating AI developers, in recognising and dealing with ethical questions surrounding their field and using ML technologies as media ethics learning technologies.

Study programmes for future AI developers that solely focus on Computer Science are not sufficient to train a responsible use of AI as a "macro phenomenon with disruptive potential" (Grimm, 2025, p. 113). Students of Computer Science and related subjects like Business or Media Informatics should therefore be given the opportunity to acquire the capability to negotiate ethical conflicts of values (cp. Doria, 2025). On this issue, we support Petra Grimm, Michael Müller and Kai Erik Trost in their demand for Digital Literacy as a foundation for the good life in the age of digital transformation (Grimm et al., 2021, pp. 142–158). Applying their demand to AI developers, such an AI Literacy should also include the capability to overcome technical utopian paradigms, to escape the technology solutionist trap outlined here and to determine whether using AI makes a meaningful contribution to a given problem domain or not.

On top of that, the age of digital transformation also calls for AI Literacy for its users. Confronted with the digitalisation-induced changes of the media system, German Media Studies scholar Bernhard Pörksen has already argued in 2018—four years before the release of ChatGPT—in favour of a concrete utopia of an editorial society (Pörksen, 2018) as a counterproposal to the technology solutionist utopias of the Silicon Valley. In this "editorial society", "the norms and principles of an idealised journalism have become part of general education and of a self-evident ethos which […] encourages to reflect on the consequences of the own communication habits in a competent manner" (Pörksen, 2018, p. 189). On an individual level, Pörksen (2018) especially refers to further promoting Media Literacy, arguing in favour of the introduction of a stand-alone school subject as its institutional basis, a demand that has hardly been addressed yet in most of Germany's federal states.

When taking the most recent developments in ML and AI technology into account, the call for Media Literacy broadens into a call for AI and maybe even Disinformation Literacy. If news messages like example 5 discussed in Sect. 4 shall still form part of a pluralistic media landscape and if we do not want machines to determine whether example 3 or example 4 come closer to the truth, then an *Information and Opinion Making Literacy* will also be necessary in the age of digital transformation, enabling the user to "find, recognize and analyse information and news pieces autonomously, classify media sources and evaluate them for their relevance and truthfulness" (Grimm et al., 2021, p. 157).

Up-to-date ML technologies might then be a part of a Media Ethics Learning Technology like the Privat-o-Mat, an interactive learning technology developed by the Institute for Digital Ethics that promotes privacy literacy (see https://www.privat-o-mat.de/) by "enabling users to reflect on the values behind their own behaviour in comparison to other [...] options of action in specific technology application use cases in a nondeterministic way" (Doria et al., 2024, p. 831). By abstaining from hedging truth into a problematic binary logic, a possible future ML-based Media Ethics Learning Technology might "respect [...] its users' reflective autonomy" (Doria et al., 2024, p. 831) and Kant's demand for making use of the own understanding. This will certainly lead to a much rockier road than given enough apps, all of humanity's bugs are shallow (Morozov, 2013)—but it is worth riding it, for humanity's sake.

Acknowledgements This work was funded by the Federal Ministry of Research, Technology and Space (BMFTR) and the Ministry of Science, Research and Art (MWK) of the state of Baden-Württemberg (Grant Number: 16DHBKI040).

References

Allgaier, J. (2022). Fake News und Verschwörungen in digitalen Medien. In S. Eleftheriadi-Zacharaki, S. Hebing, G. Manstetten, & S. Paganini (Eds.), *Kommunikations- und Medienethik: Vol. 17. Vom Umgang mit Fake News, Lüge und Verschwörung: Interdisziplinäre Perspektiven* (pp. 83–92). Nomos. https://doi.org/10.5771/9783748925392-83

Aristotle. (1934). *Nicomachean ethics* (H. Rackham, Trans.). *Aristotle in* 23 volumes: Vol. 19. Harvard University Press; William Heinemann Ltd. https://www.perseus.tufts.edu/hopper/text?doc=Perseus%3Atext%3A1999.01.0054%3Abekker+page%3D1107a%3Abekker+line%3D1

Bockman, C. (2025, February 7). *Fall in fertility rate becomes big challenge for provincial France.* https://www.bbc.com/news/articles/c5yvq1jy2xgo

Daub, A. (2020). *Was das valley denken nennt: Über die Ideologie der Techbranche.* (Vol. 2750, suhrkamp ed., p. Suhrkamp) *(served as example 2 in chapter 4).*

Doria, J. (2023). Zwischen Utopie und Dystopie: Künstliche Intelligenz als nichtstattfindendes Zentralereignis (NSZE) in Fernsehmagazinbeiträgen der ARD. In P. Grimm, H. Pechlaner, & O. Zöllner (Eds.), *Schriftenreihe Medienethik: Vol. 20. Medien–Ethik—Digitalisierung: Aktuelle Herausforderungen* (pp. 175–195). Steiner.

Doria, J. (2024). Utopismus. In P. Grimm, K.-E. Trost, & O. Zöllner (Eds.), *Nomos Handbuch. Digitale Ethik* (pp. 387–398). Nomos. https://doi.org/10.5771/9783748942399-387

Doria, J. (2025). Kann KI Krankenhaus? Ein Lehrexperiment zum integrierten Einsatz von Rollenspielen zur Förderung ethischer Reflexion. In P. Grimm & O. Zöllner (Eds.), *Schriftenreihe Medienethik|Digitale Ethik: Vol. 21. Ethik der Digitalisierung in Gesundheitswesen und Pflege: Analysen und ein Tool zur integrierten Forschung* (pp. 47–61). Franz Steiner.

Doria, J., Grimm, P., Hohendanner, M., & Kuhnert, S. (2024). Designing and evaluating an interactive learning technology to Foster privacy literacy. *IEEE Transactions on Learning Technologies, 17*, 827–840. https://doi.org/10.1109/TLT.2023.3333930

Doria, J., & Zöllner, O. (2025). Ethik der Künstlichen Intelligenz in der Alltagswelt. In H. Friese, M. Nolden, G. Rebane, & M. Schreiter (Eds.), *Springer Reference Sozialwissenschaften. Handbuch Soziale Praktiken und Digitale Alltagswelten* (pp. 1–8). Springer VS. https://doi.org/10.1007/978-3-658-08460-8_81-1

Fauzi, A., Setiawan, E. B., & Baizal, Z. K. A. (2019). Hoax news detection on twitter using term frequency inverse document frequency and support vector machine method. *Journal of physics: Conference series, 1192*, article 012025. https://doi.org/10.1088/1742-6596/1192/1/012025

Filipović, A. (2024). Wahrheit. In P. Grimm, K.-E. Trost, & O. Zöllner (Eds.), *Nomos Handbuch. Digitale Ethik* (pp. 141–150). Nomos. https://doi.org/10.5771/9783748942399-141

Grimm, P. (2002). Die Illusion der Realität im Labyrinth der Medien. In H. Krah & C.-M. Ort (Eds.), *Weltentwürfe in Literatur und Medien: Phantastische Wirklichkeiten—Realistische Imaginationen* (pp. 361–382). Ludwig.

Grimm, P. (2021). Werte: Was können ethische Ansätze für eine werteorientierte Digitalisierung leisten? In C. Piallat (Ed.), *Digitale Gesellschaft. Der Wert der Digitalisierung* (Vol. 36, pp. 55–96). Transcript Verlag. https://doi.org/10.14361/9783839456590-003

Grimm, P. (2025). Ethik der Interdisziplinarität in der KI- und MTI-Forschung: Eine Frage der Haltung? In P. Grimm & O. Zöllner (Eds.), *Schriftenreihe Medienethik|Digitale Ethik: Vol. 21. Ethik der Digitalisierung in Gesundheitswesen und Pflege: Analysen und ein Tool zur integrierten Forschung* (pp. 109–125). Franz Steiner.

Grimm, P., & Hammele, N. (2019). Künstliche Intelligenz: Was bedeutet sie für die Autonomie des Menschen? In P. Grimm, T. O. Keber, & O. Zöllner (Eds.), *Kompaktwissen XL. Digitale Ethik: Leben in vernetzten Welten* (pp. 153–170). Reclam.

Grimm, P., Müller, M., & Trost, K.-E. (2021). Werte, Ängste, Hoffnungen: *Das Erleben der Digitalisierung in der erzählten Alltagswelt*. Academia. https://doi.org/10.5771/978389665 9651

Johnson, D. G. (2022). Emerging technology as promise and peril. In S. Vallor (Ed.), *The Oxford handbook of philosophy of technology* (pp. 647–661). Oxford University Press. https://doi.org/10.1093/oxfordhb/9780190851187.013.39

Kant, I. (1996). An answer to the question: What is enlightenment? (A. W. Wood, Trans.). In M. J. Gregor (Ed.), The Cambridge edition of the works of Immanuel Kant. Practical philosophy (pp. 11–22). Cambridge University Press. https://doi.org/10.1017/CBO978051181330 6.005 (Original work published 1784).

Krah, H. (2013). Kommunikation und Medien: Semiotische Grundlagen. In H. Krah & M. Titzmann (Eds.), *Medien und Kommunikation: Eine interdisziplinäre Einführung* (3rd ed., pp. 11–33). Stutz.

Krah, H. (2015). Einführung in die Literaturwissenschaft: Textanalyse. In *LIMES—Literatur- und medienwissenschaftliche Studien* (Vol. 6, 2nd ed.). Ludwig.

Krah, H. (2017). Medienwirklichkeiten. In H. Krah & M. Titzmann (Eds.), *MTS Medien, Texte, Semiotik Passau Neue Reihe: Vol. 1. Medien und Kommunikation: Eine Einführung aus semiotischer Perspektive* (pp. 399–422) Ralf Schuster Verlag.

Krainer, L. (2024). Autonomie. In P. Grimm, K.-E. Trost, & O. Zöllner (Eds.), *Nomos Handbuch. Digitale Ethik* (pp. 151–161). Nomos. https://doi.org/10.5771/9783748942399-151

Kuhn, T. S. (1970). The structure of scientific revolutions. In *International Encyclopedia of unified science* (Vol. 2, 2nd ed.). University of Chicago Press. (Original work published 1962).

Louban, A., Tahraoui, M., Aden, H., Fährmann, J., Krätzer, C., & Dittmann, J. (2022). Das Phänomen Deepfakes: Künstliche Intelligenz als Element politischer Einflussnahme und Perspektive einer Echtheitsprüfung. In M. Friedewald, A. Roßnagel, J. Heesen, N. Krämer, & J. Lamla (Eds.), *Privatheit und Selbstbestimmung in der digitalen Welt|Privacy and Self-Determination in the Digital World: Vol. 1. Künstliche Intelligenz, Demokratie und Privatheit* (pp. 265–288). Nomos. https://doi.org/10.5771/9783748913344-265

Morozov, E. (2013). *To save everything, click here: Technology, solutionism and the urge to fix problems that don't exist*. Allen Lane.

Musk, E. [@elonmusk]. (2023, December 16). *[Only @ AfD can save Germany]* [Post on X]. **X**. https://x.com/elonmusk/status/1877435764520239454 (served as example 3 in chapter 4).

Nussbaum, M. C. (2011). Creating capabilities. *Harvard University Press*. https://doi.org/10.4159/harvard.9780674061200

Patel, A., & Meehan, K. (2021). Fake news detection on Reddit utilising count Vectorizer and term frequency-inverse document frequency with logistic regression, MultinominalNB and support vector machine. In *2021 32nd Irish signals and systems conference (ISSC)* (pp. 1–6). IEEE. https://doi.org/10.1109/ISSC52156.2021.9467842

Pörksen, B. (2018). *Die große Gereiztheit: Wege aus der kollektiven Erregung*. Carl Hanser Verlag.

Postillon, D. (2025, February 13). Sektfabrik feierlich mit Kreuzfahrtschiff eingeweiht. *Der Postillon.*. https://www.der-postillon.com/2017/01/sektfabriktaufe.html *(served as example 5 in chapter 4)*

Rehak, R. (2023). Artificial intelligence for real sustainability: What is artificial intelligence and can it help with the sustainability transformation? In P. Jankowski, A. Höfner, M. L. Hoffmann, F. Rohde, R. Rehak, & J. Graf (Eds.), *Shaping digital transformation for a sustainable society: Contributions from Bits & Bäume* (pp. 26–31). Technische Universität Berlin.

Robertson, S. (2004). Understanding inverse document frequency: On theoretical arguments for IDF. *Journal of Documentation, 60*(5), 503–520. https://doi.org/10.1108/00220410410560582

Sharma, U., & Singh, J. (2023). Review of feature extraction techniques for fake news detection. In V. Goar, M. Kuri, R. Kumar, & T. Senjyu (Eds.), *Lecture notes in networks and systems: Vol. 628. Advances in information communication technology and computing* (pp. 389–399). Springer. https://doi.org/10.1007/978-981-19-9888-1_31

Sottong, H., & Müller, M. (1998). *Zwischen Sender und Empfänger: Eine Einführung in die Semiotik der Kommunikationsgesellschaft*. Erich Schmidt Verlag.

Jan Doria, Dr., collaborated on the IKID research project on interdisciplinary AI teaching as an Academic Employee at the Institute for Digital Ethics (IDE) at Stuttgart Media University (HdM), where he still teaches AI Ethics. His primary areas of expertise include the Disinformation, the Ethics of Artificial Intelligence and the Intersection of Digitalisation and Sustainability. ORCID: 0000-0002-7773-5019.

David Klotz, Dr., has been a professor of business information systems at Hochschule der Medien Stuttgart since 2019. He teaches courses on data and applied Artificial Intelligence. Klotz led the IKID research project on teaching AI in an interdisciplinary way, combining perspectives from computer science, business management, ethics and law. His main areas of expertise are applied Artificial Intelligence and enterprise AI. ORCID: 0000-0001-8322-0911.

AI Literacy as a Shared Responsibility: Balancing Corporate Roles, Societal Goals, and Inclusive Education

Marco Wedel and Eva Gengler

Abstract This paper critically examines the European Union's AI Act through the lens of AI literacy, highlighting the tension between corporate responsibility and broader societal goals. It argues that delegating AI literacy solely to the corporate sector risks narrowing its scope and undermining democratic oversight. To address this, the paper proposes a feminist-informed framework that integrates empowerment, intersectionality, and sustainability into corporate AI training. It concludes by advocating for a shared responsibility model that aligns corporate practices with ethical standards and inclusive education to foster trust and excellence in AI.

Keywords AI literacy · AI Act · Feminist-Informed Training · Corporate responsibility · Trustworthy AI

1 Introduction

Artificial Intelligence (AI) literacy is a cornerstone of the European AI Act's vision for establishing a trustworthy AI ecosystem. The Act places significant responsibility on enterprises to foster AI literacy by equipping their workforce and stakeholders with the skills and knowledge to engage with AI technologies responsibly. However, it leaves critical questions unanswered: What specific actions should enterprises take? How can their efforts align with broader societal goals, and who ensures accountability?

This paper critically examines the enterprise-focused approach to AI literacy, outlining the expectations placed on businesses while addressing the limits of their responsibility. It explores the risks of corporate dominance in shaping educational content, where profit motives might overshadow public interest, leading to biased

M. Wedel (✉)
Technische Universität Berlin, Berlin, Germany
e-mail: marco.wedel@tu-berlin.de

E. Gengler
Friedrich-Alexander-Universität Erlangen-Nürnberg, Erlangen, Germany
e-mail: eva.gengler@fau.de

K. Bodrožić-Brnić et al. (eds.), *AI and the Ethics of Innovation*, Digital Transformation and Innovation, https://doi.org/10.1007/978-3-032-20638-1_5

or narrow conceptions of AI literacy. Additionally, the paper underscores the need for accountability mechanisms to ensure corporate actions align with ethical and inclusive standards.

To address these challenges, the paper proposes integrating inclusive, feminist perspectives into AI literacy initiatives. Feminist frameworks highlight systemic barriers, such as gender disparities in technology access and algorithmic bias, and offer strategies for promoting equity, representation, and participatory governance. By adopting such approaches, AI literacy programs can become more equitable, empowering individuals to navigate AI responsibly while addressing structural inequities.

The paper argues for a shared responsibility model, where enterprises collaborate with governments, educational institutions, and civil society to develop inclusive, participatory, and socially aligned educational frameworks. This roadmap emphasises the importance of balancing corporate roles with external oversight to ensure that AI literacy initiatives contribute to the public good. Ultimately, the paper calls for a reframing of AI literacy as a collective societal responsibility, promoting trust and inclusivity in AI adoption while advancing the goals of the European AI Act.

1.1 AI Regulation in the EU and AI Literacy

In the summer of 2024, the European Union adopted Regulation (EU) 2024/1689 (AI Act), marking the world's first comprehensive regulation of AI (EUR-Lex, 2024). As a regulation with general applicability, it is going to be directly and bindingly applicable in the EU Member States from 2 August 2026. The purpose of the regulation is to promote the introduction of human-centric and trustworthy AI, while at the same time ensuring a high level of protection regarding health, safety, and the fundamental rights enshrined in the Charter, including democracy, the rule of law, and environmental protection within the Union, and to support innovation (Article 1, Paragraph 1; EUR-Lex, 2024).

With this regulation, the legislator addresses the demands made by the European Economic and Social Committee (2016), the European Parliament (2017), and the Europäischer Rat (2017) for a human-controlled AI approach. It follows the recommendations of the High-Level Expert Group on AI (AI HLEG, 2019), which emphasised that all AI systems—not only human-machine systems—must be human-centric, based on the binding principle of placing AI at the service of humanity and the common good. The goal is to enhance human well-being and human freedom—not that of artificial, non-human systems (AI HLEG, 2019, p. 5). According to the High-Level Expert Group, this should lead to a trustworthy, human-centred AI that, as a value-based European approach, maximises the benefits of AI systems while minimising their risks.

> In a context of rapid technological change, we believe it is essential that trust remains the bedrock of societies, communities, economies and sustainable development. We therefore identify Trustworthy AI as our foundational ambition, since human beings and communities

> will only be able to have confidence in the technology's development and its applications when a clear and comprehensive framework for achieving its trustworthiness is in place. (AI HLEG, 2019, p. 4)

The European Commission refers in this context to the much-cited 'ecosystem of trust' and 'excellence', explicitly emphasising the inclusion of rules protecting fundamental rights and consumer rights (European Commission, 2020). While the AI Act now provides a legal framework for trustworthy AI, the 'ecosystem of trust' has not yet been fully established. To create such an ecosystem, it is now necessary to build individual competencies and 'to ensure that knowledge of the potential impact of AI systems is widespread, and to make people aware that they can participate in shaping the societal development' for this, '(b)asic AI literacy should be fostered across society' (AI HLEG, 2019, p. 23).

An initial definition of what constitutes AI competence is already provided in the AI Act itself:

> 'AI literacy' means skills, knowledge and understanding that allow providers, deployers and affected persons, taking into account their respective rights and obligations in the context of this Regulation, to make an informed deployment of AI systems, as well as to gain awareness about the opportunities and risks of AI and possible harm it can cause. (Article 3, Paragraph 56; EUR-Lex, 2024)

According to the Committee on Legal Affairs of the European Parliament, measures must be taken to develop a sufficient level of AI literacy—across all sectors (!) and considering the different needs of affected groups of providers, users, and impacted individuals. These include education, training, qualification, and retraining programs, while ensuring an appropriate balance regarding gender and age, in order to enable democratic oversight of AI systems (Committee on Legal Affairs, 2022).

Article 4 of the regulation states, however, that only (!) providers and operators of AI systems must take measures to the best of their ability to ensure that their personnel and other individuals acting on their behalf in the operation and use of AI systems have an adequate level of AI competence. This must take into account their technical knowledge, experience, education and training, the context in which the AI systems are to be used, and the individuals or groups who will be affected by the use of these AI systems (EUR-Lex, 2024).

In summary, there is broad theoretical consensus on the importance of promoting basic AI literacy among the population, yet only the corporate sector is legally obliged (within the AI Act) to promote AI literacy.

1.2 Rationales for AI Literacy

If one follows the rationales outlined in the section above (see Sect. 1.2)—promotion of the common good, human-centred orientation, protection of democracy, etc.—it becomes clear that the concept of an AI ecosystem has been framed within the ideal of democratic sovereignty. The preparatory work of the High-Level Expert Group

(2019), whose recommendations are reflected both in the final AI Act and in all preparatory considerations of the actors involved in the legislative process (Wedel et al., 2024), underscores this approach. In particular, the seven core requirements can be interpreted—based on the ethical principles of respect for human autonomy, prevention of harm, fairness, and explicability—as necessary (though not sufficient) conditions for exercising human sovereignty in a world shaped by AI (Wedel, 2023):

It must be ensured that the development, deployment, and use of AI systems meet the requirements for trustworthy AI:

- Human agency and oversight,
- Technical robustness and safety,
- Privacy and data governance,
- Transparency,
- Diversity, non-discrimination and fairness,
- Societal and environmental wellbeing, and
- Accountability. (AI HLEG, 2019, p. 8).

The human being is placed at the centre for two main reasons: On the one hand, their dignity remains inviolable even in a world shaped by AI (the right to dignity). On the other hand, they remain responsible for their actions as a sovereign being, even in such a world (the duty of responsibility).

The need for such a sovereign approach to AI reflects and naturally arises out of the core principles of our liberal democracies. Again, the human being is placed at the centre of our democratic systems. Consequently, it must be put at the centre of AI systems.

To equip and empower the sovereign, that is the citizens of liberal democracies, and to enable them to acquire the competencies to uphold their sovereign duties is a key concern of (state-provided) systems of general education. The sovereign becomes sovereign through empowerment by education. The responsibility for this fundamental public duty lies primarily with the state. At its core, the mission of public schools is the education of individuals who are capable of shaping public and social life and who are aware of their responsibility to the community. This can be illustrated using the example of the Berlin School Act (2004). There, the mission of schools is defined as follows:

> The mission of the school is to foster the full development of all valuable talents of pupils and to provide them with a high level of judgement, thorough knowledge, and practical skills. The goal must be the development of individuals capable of decisively opposing the ideology of National Socialism and all other political doctrines striving for tyranny, and of shaping state and social life on the basis of democracy, peace, freedom, human dignity, gender equality, and in harmony with nature and the environment. These individuals must be aware of their responsibility to the community, and their attitude must be shaped by the recognition of the equal rights of all people, respect for every sincere conviction, and the acknowledgment of the need for progressive development of social conditions as well as peaceful understanding among nations. (Berlin School Act 2004, Art. 1—own translation)

As summarised before, there is broad theoretical consensus on the importance of promoting basic AI competence among the population, there is furthermore a practical claim (which can also be formulated as a right to education) to provide these competencies through general education, yet—again—only the corporate sector is legally obliged (within the AI Act) to promote AI literacy. This indicates a misconception.

1.3 Corporate Social Responsibility Instead of State Social Responsibility

Again, the European legislator *does*, in principle, address the issue of promoting AI competence. This includes both an initial definition of AI competence (Article 3) and suitable measures as well as responsible stakeholder groups (Article 4). However, from an educational science perspective, the approach proposed by the High-Level Expert Group—that '(b)asic AI literacy should be fostered across society' (AI HLEG, 2019, p. 23)—was not incorporated into the AI Act. A proposal originally introduced by the Legal Affairs Committee of the European Parliament—that it is the responsibility of the EU and its Member States to promote AI competence in society in order to enable democratic oversight of AI systems—is not reflected in the final legislative text (Wedel et al., 2024). Instead, the promotion of AI competence is designated exclusively as the responsibility of AI system providers and operators. As a result, it is unilaterally and essentially purpose-bound (to the operation and use of AI systems) and assigned to the economic sector.

> In summary, it appears that the legislator avoids binding regulations regarding sustainable and inclusive approaches to shared AI systems and refrains from a supranational or national commitment to publicly supported promotion of AI competence among the population as a claim derived from the regulation in question. (Wedel et al., 2024a, p. 159—own translation)

The current configuration of the European AI ecosystem is dominated—at the expense of a democratically oriented course of action—by a market-oriented or business-driven approach. This evidence-based observation does, however, not attempt to weigh up the two perspectives against one another. Both are necessary. Nevertheless, while ethical and democratic considerations are pronounced as necessary dimensions for the establishment of the AI Act, the regulation itself largely fails to include sufficient measures to support this notion. Where such measures are included at all, they are intended to be implemented voluntarily and in alignment with business interests. This is a problem, because—to put it bluntly—our economy will not naturally defend our democracy. It is neither intended nor designed for that cause and therefore should not be expected to do so.

1.4 Who Has Power to Decide What AI Literacy Means?

The development of training measures and their respective curricula is a complex task which involves pedagogically, didactically, and academically sound processes. The development of educational content on AI itself describes a functionally differentiated and complex subject matter which goes well beyond the provisions—or the absence thereof—within a European regulation.

In Germany alone, a variety of strategic frameworks and position papers provide potential approaches for promoting AI competence within public education systems. These include a strategy on 'Education in the Digital World' (KMK, 2016), the supplementary recommendations 'Teaching and Learning in the Digital World' (KMK, 2021), the expert report of the Standing Scientific Commission 'Digitalisation in the Education System' (SWK, 2022), the position paper 'Large Language Models and Their Potential in the Education System' (SWK, 2024), as well as the recently published 'Recommendations for Education Authorities on the Use of Artificial Intelligence in School-Based Education Processes' (KMK, 2024) to name but a few. However, none of these approaches explicitly addresses the promotion of AI literacy as proposed within the AI Act. This comes as no surprise, as the European Union and the Member States are exempt from the task to promote measures for the development of a sufficient level of AI literacy.

Since providers and deployers of AI systems, however, must take measures, what kind of measures shall be taken? And who makes sure these measures align with the principles of human-centred AI-Systems as part of an ecosystem of trust and excellence? Who makes sure the developed trainings are in line with pedagogical, didactical, and academical standards and do acquire the goals they are set to meet?

A first indication of possible approaches is offered by the European Artificial Intelligence Office (AI Office) as part of an AI Pact webinar on AI literacy, on the 20th of February 2025. There, initiatives foreseen to facilitate the implementation of Article 4 of the AI Act have been presented. In an accompanying presentation the AI Office highlights the following meaning as primarily important: AI literacy means skills, knowledge and understanding to make an informed deployment of AI systems. The second aspect of Article 4—to gain awareness about the opportunities and risks of AI and possible harm it can cause—has not been highlighted in this context (European Commission, 2025a, p. 2).

Following the AI Office, a sufficient level of AI literacy among staff and other persons, organisations should be reached as follows:

- Ensure a general understanding of AI within their organisation.
- Consider the role of their organisation (provider or deployer of AI systems).
- Consider the risk: What do employees need to know when dealing with such AI system? What are the risks they need to be aware of and do they need to be aware of mitigation?
- Concretely build their AI literacy actions on this analysis. (European Commission, 2025a, p. 3):

During the webinar an EU official clarified which actions and measures that should help companies meet the requirements of Article 4:

> (To) comply with Article 4 an organization should first of all ensure general understanding, this is pretty basic and indeed here it also depends on the organization and the type of AI they are using or not using. Then we have to (have a) close consideration of the role AI plays in the organization. So, am I providing tools, am I developing them, am I selling them or am I simply using them. Who is dealing with them, like is it employees that deal with for example systems that help writing texts or is it a machine or what is it, so this is very, very much context dependent. On that basis, it is important to consider the risk. What in that concrete situations do employees need to know, what do they need to be aware (of) and on that basis I decide what kind of literacy measure I need. This is not like the overall super training program, it is common sense, it is what organizations are doing now, like when you're buying a dangerous machine, indeed people working on the machine are being trained, and this is the same about AI literacy, context dependent. (European Commission, 2025b, from 09'27")

In short and in the eyes of the AI Office, AI literacy and respective measures to promote it are 'pretty basic', 'common sense', 'context dependent' and something organisations are supposed to be doing already (in a different context). This clarification is a surprisingly superficial and incomplete accumulation of meaningless generalities and not very helpful with respect to the development of adequate training measures. If it is 'pretty basic' and 'common sense', what is it?

Following the introductory clarifications by the EU official, the webinar continued with practical application examples presented by three company representatives (from Generali, EnBW, and OpenSky), who showcased their respective approaches to AI literacy training:

- Generali promotes AI literacy through a comprehensive, tiered training strategy tailored to employee roles and technical levels, including in-house academies, collaborations with universities, and new role development to foster a culture of continuous digital upskilling.
- EnBW uses a structured, multi-level training program combining foundational knowledge, advanced expert development, and game-based learning methods to enable employees at all levels to apply AI responsibly and effectively in real-world scenarios.
- Open-Sky integrates AI literacy with change management to support organisational transformation, focusing on awareness, knowledge reinforcement, and alignment with company goals to drive innovation, trust, and talent retention.

While the presented training approaches are certainly full of inspiring terminology, they leave us with little insight into what this means in practice—especially in relation to key aspects of learning environments such as competency-based learning objectives, clearly structured and relevant content, learner-centred didactic methods, and opportunities for differentiation and individualisation.

In the void of vagueness, the EU seems to submit to the principle of hope, according to which in the end anything seems better than nothing and things will somehow work out. Indeed, it seems to be the EU's solemn strategy to rely on ongoing practices gathered among companies, provided in a 'living repository of practices' to foster learning and exchange in training approaches to AI literacy (European Commission, 2025c). In the end, however, the EU does not seem to be entirely without doubt. Although the repository currently includes 28 examples (v. 28.03.2025)—that indeed are very interesting, though it remains entirely unclear how these practices are selected, reviewed, or evaluated—it is clearly stated that implementing the initiatives included in the repository does 'NOT' automatically grant presumption of compliance with Article 4 of the AI Act.

As a result, to date, there is no evidence-based, concrete, binding, or mandatory translation of Articles 3 (56) and 4 into effective educational practice—certainly none that aims to enable democratic oversight of AI systems or contribute meaningfully to the realisation of an 'ecosystem of trust'. It seems, companies are expected to figure out the 'context-dependent', 'pretty basic', and 'common sense' elements on their own. The discretionary nature of this approach—where companies independently define what constitutes 'adequate' AI literacy measures—ultimately renders the meaning and practical implications of Article 4 vague and open to interpretation, reducing it to a formality rather than a genuine task reflected in meaningful social practice.

1.5 Towards Shared Responsibility

AI literacy is inherently multi-perspective. Following the *Dagstuhl Triangle* (Gesellschaft für Informatik, 2016), one could argue that it encompasses at least three interconnected dimensions: the socio-cultural, the technological, and the application-oriented perspective. In addition, the EU approach—as particularly framed by the European Commission—emphasises two overarching goals: a societal one, aimed at fostering an 'ecosystem of trust', and an economic one, focused on building an 'ecosystem of excellence'. This dual focus reveals a normative tension between democratic responsibility and global competitiveness in shaping AI literacy strategies. We suspect, companies are more likely to prioritise the latter. But since—as shown above—responsibility for AI literacy rests primarily with companies, they are implicitly tasked to include socio-cultural dimension in their training programs to reaching the goal of creating an ecosystem of trust.

Because the EU was ultimately unable to secure a majority in support of a binding commitment that would oblige the Union and its Member States to promote AI literacy across sectors—through education, training, (re-)skilling programs, and with attention to gender and age balance—it means companies must adopt such a position themselves (Wedel et al., 2024).

In light of this disparity, we argue that companies should explicitly integrate this broader perspective into their corporate social and digital responsibility. After all, it is citizens who constitute, lead, and work within companies—and it is in their own interest to be empowered to engage with AI in ways that safeguard their agency, autonomy, and democratic participation. Companies should therefore commit to going beyond the regulatory minimum. In doing so, they can ensure that employees are sustainably and proactively prepared for a world increasingly shaped by AI. Such efforts can only be meaningful if they also address the wider dimensions of individual and societal well-being—including diversity, non-discrimination, fairness, and both societal and environmental sustainability.

Unlike what seems to be the case with the AI Office, we do not believe shaping sound training measure is a 'pretty basic' task that just needs some common sense and vague terminology open for interpretation. Effective action must be guided by clear principles, goals, conceptual frameworks, competencies, and standards. It requires thoughtful methodological approaches and a careful selection of relevant topics and content. We believe that it could ultimately be useful to develop a harmonised standard for basic AI literacy.

While we cannot address all these elements in detail here, we aim to offer at least an initial impulse towards a guiding framework and a first proposal for relevant topics that should be addressed (beyond the individual context of companies).

1.6 Feminist-Informed AI Literacy: Empowering People, Reshaping Systems, Fostering Trust and Excellency

Responding to the need for shared responsibility in shaping AI competencies, we propose a feminist-informed approach to AI literacy within companies. Feminist approaches shed light on systemic barriers, biases, and discrimination related to gender, race, and intersecting inequities in the development and use of technology—while offering concrete strategies to advance equity, representation, and participatory governance. In this paper, we draw on feminist principles grounded in intersectionality, a critical engagement with power, and a commitment to sustainability. Moving beyond compliance-driven training, we argue that AI literacy should be reframed as a transformative process—one that enables individuals to critically understand, engage with, and shape AI systems in ways that promote justice, inclusion, and (ecological) sustainability. This reframing draws on key theoretical traditions—including critical literacy, feminist pedagogy, intersectionality, and ecological systems thinking—each of which offers tools for addressing the structural and cultural dimensions of digital transformation. Moreover, this aligns with the voluntary codes of conduct proposed under Article 95 of the EU AI Act.

We outline eight interrelated pillars (Fig. 1) to guide the feminist-informed design and implementation of AI literacy initiatives within companies:

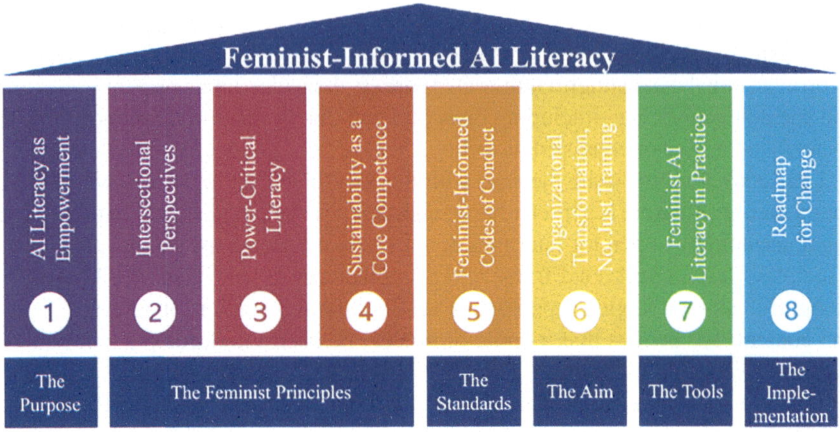

Fig. 1 Feminist-informed AI literacy: empowering people, reshaping systems, fostering trust and excellency. (Created by the authors)

The Purpose: AI Literacy as Empowerment

AI literacy must be more than a technical skillset and certainly more than an unproductive compliance-checking instrument—it should be framed as a means of empowerment. Inspired by Paulo Freire's critical literacy concept of pedagogy for the oppressed and reading the world (Freire & Macedo, 2014) and its application as a method for democratic education (Shor, 1992), AI literacy should equip employees with the capacity to critically understand how AI shapes their work, autonomy, and participation in decision-making. Rather than positioning employees as passive recipients of technology, training programs should foster active engagement, encouraging questions about the goals, values, and societal implications of AI systems and whether to use them responsibly—or in some cases not to use them at all—in each context. This corresponds with feminist purposes of transforming the status-quo to create more equity.

The Feminist Principles: Intersectionality, Critique of Power, Sustainability

Intersectionality. Feminist AI literacy must acknowledge that AI does not affect everyone equally. Training programs should be designed through an intersectional lens, accounting for how structural inequities related to e.g. gender, race, class, age, and disability shape both access to technology and vulnerability to algorithmic harm. Intersectionality is a concept that arose from Black feminism focusing on the overlap of multiple forms of discrimination and the lived experiences thereof (Crenshaw, 1989; Hill Collins, 2000). In the context of AI literacy this also means ensuring diverse representation in training design, content development, and facilitation, as well as providing multiple formats to make learning accessible and inclusive. Participants should learn that decisions regarding the selection, adaptation, and deployment of AI tools must involve an intersectionally diverse group, ensuring that multiple perspectives and experiences inform the process. Furthermore, AI literacy programs must be tailored to the distinct needs of different target groups: employees involved in designing and training AI systems require different competencies than those who apply them in daily workflows, or management personnel responsible for strategic decisions about which systems to develop or deploy. To enable responsible and informed decision-making at all levels and across contexts, AI literacy initiatives should be designed with these varying roles and responsibilities in mind.

Power-Critical Literacy. Understanding AI requires more than knowing how an algorithm functions—it involves unpacking the power relations embedded in its design and use. Critical literacy, emphasising the ability to read texts and technologies in relation to power, ideology, and inequality and enabling learners not only to decode information, but to question whose interests it serves, how it shapes social realities, and how it can be redesigned for equity and justice (Janks, 2010; Luke, 2000). Power-critical literacy encourages employees to interrogate who designs AI systems, who decides their goals, who profits, and who is surveilled or excluded. This lens is essential for building awareness of algorithmic bias, digital control, and the commodification of data, empowering employees to challenge oppressive dynamics within and beyond their organisations.

Sustainability. AI systems rely on vast amounts of energy, data, and computational resources, with significant ecological consequences. A feminist-informed AI literacy program must include environmental awareness as a core element, helping employees understand the planetary costs of AI and fostering reflection on sustainable design and deployment. This includes a systems-thinking perspective that connects technological, social, and ecological domains, promoting stewardship and long-term responsibility. Ecological literacy, as articulated by Fritjof Capra (1997) and Stephen Sterling (2001), involves understanding the interconnectedness of social, technological, and natural systems—fostering the capacity to make decisions that support ecological integrity, long-term sustainability, and systemic resilience in the face of complex global challenges. The training content should include information on the ecological costs of AI use—such as water and energy consumption per prompt or output—for each available model. Participants should gain a clear understanding of which AI tools are suitable for which use cases (e.g. using ChatGPT to shorten texts or check grammar) and in which contexts their use is problematic or inappropriate (e.g. relying on ChatGPT as a source of factual truth). This knowledge will enable participants to make responsible, context-aware decisions about tool selection and avoid unnecessary resource consumption.

The Standards: Feminist-Informed Codes of Conduct

Codes of conduct, such as those referenced and envisioned within the AI Act (see Article 95), can be strengthened by grounding them in feminist ethics of care and relational accountability. These codes should go beyond minimal compliance, becoming tools for navigating complex dilemmas around fairness, bias, and harm. They should include intersectional perspectives as well as ecological aspects, setting the direction for a responsible and sustainable design and application of AI. Feminist pedagogy emphasises trust, reflexivity, and shared responsibility, offering a foundation for value-based guidelines that reflect the lived experiences and needs of diverse employees and affected communities (Ellsworth, 2010; Hooks, 1994).

The Aim: Organisational Transformation, Not Just Training

AI literacy cannot be confined to isolated training modules. It must be embedded in organisational cultures and processes, involving leadership, HR, and governance structures. Feminist pedagogy promotes collaborative, co-created learning spaces that challenge hierarchies and recognise lived experience as a source of expertise. This means shifting from top-down training to participatory learning ecosystems, where employees help define what AI literacy means in their organisation and context as well as how it should be practiced. In this vein, feminist AI literacy should serve as a catalyst for organisational transformation—fostering greater openness and reflexivity, and empowering employees to ask critical questions and challenge the status quo.

The Tools: Feminist AI Literacy in Practice

Concrete tools and examples make theoretical frameworks actionable. Tools like prompting guides, participatory workshops, and inclusive design sprints can serve as feminist AI literacy practices. These interventions can empower employees to reflect on their own interactions with AI, surface power imbalances, and collectively shape more just and transparent AI use in their organisations. For example, one of the authors of this paper has developed a guide for fair prompting that helps employees critically engage with generative AI tools and challenge biased defaults (Gengler et al., 2024).

The Implementation: A Roadmap to Change

To operationalise these ideas, we propose a structured roadmap that guides companies in designing feminist-informed AI literacy initiatives. This includes defining inclusive content, participatory methods and tools, and clear responsibilities, while embedding oversight mechanisms and collaboration with stakeholders (Table 1). A

Table 1 Feminist AI literacy—dimensions, key questions, and feminist responses. (Created by the authors)

Dimension	Key question	Feminist-informed response
Content	What is taught?	Power, bias, sustainability, and inclusive AI design
Method	How is it taught?	Participatory, reflective, co-created
Aim	Why is it taught?	Empowerment, accountability, structural awareness, compliance
Stakeholders	Who is involved?	Employees, leadership, stakeholders
Governance	Who decides and ensures alignment?	Shared responsibility, feminist-informed behavioural codes

shared responsibility model, as outlined in the previous section, becomes actionable through such a framework—turning abstract values into lived practice.

This model of AI literacy invites companies to embrace their responsibility not as a burden, but as an opportunity to support human dignity, ecological integrity, and social justice in the age of AI. Grounded in feminist theory and critical pedagogy, it provides a concrete path towards literacy programs that are not only compliant but transformational.

1.7 Moving from Compliance to Commitment

Given the discretionary character of Article 4 and the absence of a binding educational mandate for Member States within the AI Act, we argue that Article 95 of the regulation opens a crucial space for voluntary but meaningful corporate engagement in a way sketched above. It allows companies—both providers and deployers—to go beyond minimal legal requirements and commit to responsible AI practices through feminist-informed codes of conduct. These codes can serve as frameworks for the promotion of feminist-informed AI literacy in alignment with ethical, social, and environmental goals. For such commitments to be meaningful, we think them to be guided by an intersectional feminist perspective *and* both the Union's Ethical Guidelines for trustworthy AI and the dual ambition of building an ecosystem of trust and excellence.

We propose the following concrete measures for organisations seeking to develop AI literacy strategies as part of their broader corporate strategy and digital responsibility:

Strategic-Normative

1. Strategically Anchor AI Literacy in Union and Corporate Values

   AI literacy should be grounded both in the ethical foundations of the European Union and the strategic vision of the company. This includes aligning literacy initiatives with values such as human dignity, democracy, and sustainability—as outlined in the Union's Ethical Guidelines for Trustworthy AI—and embedding them within internal, feminist-informed frameworks for digital transformation, innovation, and employee empowerment. Rather than approaching AI literacy merely as a compliance task, organisations should recognise it as a catalyst for cultural change and as a critical enabler of both excellence and trust in the use of AI technologies.

2. Map AI Literacy Objectives to Ethical and Business Principles
   Effective AI literacy programs require clear, measurable learning objectives that reflect both ethical imperatives and business needs. These objectives should be explicitly mapped to the seven key requirements for trustworthy AI: human agency, technical robustness, privacy, transparency, fairness, societal well-being, and accountability. At the same time, companies should connect these goals to core business principles such as innovation, quality assurance, customer trust, and risk management. This dual alignment ensures that AI literacy contributes not only to regulatory readiness but to responsible value creation and long-term organisational resilience.

Operational-Methodical

1. Enable Human-Centred Understanding
   In line with the principle of human agency and oversight, AI literacy programs should empower individuals to question, interpret, and critically engage with AI systems. This includes understanding automated decision-making, bias, explainability, and mechanisms of recourse.

2. Measures for AI Systems Classification and Risk Assessment
   To support compliance with the AI Act, all employees—especially those involved in procurement, development, deployment, and supervision of AI systems—should be trained to identify the type and risk level of AI systems they are dealing with. This includes familiarity with the AI Act's classification scheme (e.g. prohibited, high-risk, limited risk, minimal risk), the obligations tied to each category, and tools or procedures for assessing context-specific risks.

3. Strengthen Transparency and Explainability Skills
   Employees ought to be trained not only to understand AI systems but also to communicate their functioning, limitations, and risks to others—whether clients, regulators, or colleagues. This reinforces both internal accountability and public trust.

4. Foster Inclusive and Equitable Learning Environments
   AI literacy measures must address structural inequalities. Companies should ensure accessibility for all employees, promote gender and age inclusion, and reflect on how AI intersects with social categories and power structures. This is essential to fulfilling the fairness and non-discrimination dimension of trustworthy AI.

5. Include Environmental and Social Sustainability
   In response to Article 95(2)(b), training programs ought to raise awareness of the environmental footprint of AI—including energy use, resource intensity, and green coding practices. Employees should be equipped to make sustainability-informed decisions when designing, procuring, or deploying AI.

6. Embed Evaluation and Continuous Learning
   Trust cannot be built without accountability. Codes of conduct would benefit from the inclusion of governance mechanisms for evaluating the effectiveness of training programs using KPIs aligned with ethical and strategic objectives. AI literacy must be seen as a continuous, adaptive process (see also Table 1 Feminist AI literacy—Dimensions, Key Questions, and Feminist Responses).

7. Link AI Literacy to Talent Strategy and Innovation
   From an excellence perspective, AI literacy is an enabler of innovation. Companies should integrate it into talent development, leadership programs, and innovation labs to enhance internal capacity, competitiveness, and employee engagement.

8. Support External Dialogue and Knowledge Sharing
   To contribute to a broader ecosystem of trust, companies should make parts of their AI literacy programs publicly available, collaborate with educational institutions and civil society, and share best practices via networks and repositories. This reinforces transparency and collective learning.

We argue that all of the above should be bound by a feminist-informed approach to AI literacy, not as a peripheral add-on, but a central lever and unifying bracket for realising the dual ambition of the AI Act: to build an ecosystem of trust and excellence. It requires not only legal frameworks, but shared ethical commitments, institutional imagination, and ongoing societal dialogue by organisations seeking to develop AI literacy strategies as part of their broader corporate strategy and digital responsibility.

2 Conclusion

AI literacy, as framed by the AI Act, has been delegated to the corporate sector. Yet, as this paper has shown, AI literacy is not merely a technical skillset—it involves a socio-cultural dimension in which individuals must be empowered to critically engage with the systems that shape their lives, labour, and liberties.

The current regulatory framework outsources a public mandate—empowering the democratic sovereign—to the private sector, while failing to equip that sector with the means or mandate to fulfil this role. This structural misalignment risks deepening inequity, narrowing perspectives on what constitutes valid or relevant knowledge about AI, limiting who gets to define, frame, and teach AI-related knowledge, and ultimately undermining democratic oversight. As long as AI literacy remains unequally distributed in that sense, agency and participation will remain unequally accessible.

This, however, does not absolve companies of their societal responsibility. On the contrary: if they are tasked with promoting AI literacy, they must do so in the spirit of democracy (especially in a time when democratic values are increasingly under pressure and public trust in both political and economic institutions is steadily eroding). The measures proposed in this paper—grounded in ethical guidelines, feminist theory, and the principles of environmental and social sustainability—offer a blueprint for rethinking AI literacy as a practice of empowerment rather than mere compliance.

To this end, the codes of conduct, as envisaged in Article 95 of the AI Act, must not become fig leaves for voluntary formalism. They should be developed transparently, inclusively, and—ideally—in co-creation with civil society, academia, and affected communities. Only then can they reflect the pluralism, diversity, and critical reflexivity that an ecosystem of trust demands. What is at stake is not only how we understand AI, but how we shape our digital sphere, distribute power, and enable democratic participation in an algorithmically mediated society. The future of AI literacy must be grounded in shared responsibility, collective intelligence, and a deep commitment to democratic values. If we are serious about building an ecosystem of trust and excellence, then we must start by building and earning that trust ourselves.

References

Capra, F. (1997). *The web of life: A new scientific understanding of living systems* (first anchor books trade paperback ed.). Anchor Books.

Committee on Legal Affairs. (2022). *Opinion of the Committee on Legal Affairs for the Committee on the Internal Market and Consumer Protection and the Committee on Civil Liberties, Justice and Home Affairs on the proposal for a regulation of the European Parliament and of the Council laying down harmonised rules on artificial intelligence (Artificial Intelligence Act) and amending certain Union Legislative Acts (COM(2021)0206—C9–0146/2021–2021/0106(COD))*. www.europarl.europa.eu/doceo/document/JURI-PA-719827_EN.pdf

Crenshaw, K. (1989). Demarginalizing the intersection of race and sex: A black feminist critique of antidiscrimination doctrine, feminist theory and antiracist politics. *University of Chicago Legal Forum, 1989*(1), 139–167.

Ellsworth, E. (2010). Why doesn't this feel empowering? Working through the repressive myths of critical pedagogy. *Harvard Educational Review, 59*(3), 297–325. https://doi.org/10.17763/haer.59.3.058342114k266250

EUR-Lex. (2024). Document 32024R1689. Regulation (EU) 2024/1689 of the European Parliament and of the Council of 13 June 2024 laying down harmonised rules on artificial intelligence and amending Regulations (EC) No 300/2008, (EU) No 167/2013, (EU) No 168/2013, (EU) 2018/858, (EU) 2018/1139 and (EU) 2019/2144 and Directives 2014/90/EU, (EU) 2016/797 and (EU) 2020/1828 (Artificial Intelligence Act) (Text with EEA relevance). http://data.europa.eu/eli/reg/2024/1689/oj

Europäischer Rat. (2017). Schlussfolgerungen des Europäischen Rates, 19.10.2017, Übermittlungsvermerk. https://www.consilium.europa.eu/media/21602/19-euco-final-conclusions-de.pdf

European Commission. (2020). White paper. White Paper on Artificial Intelligence: a European approach to excellence and trust. https://commission.europa.eu/publications/white-paper-artificial-intelligence-european-approach-excellence-and-trust_en?prefLang=de

European Commission. (2025a). Slides. *AI Pact Webinar on AI Literacy*. https://digital-strategy.ec.europa.eu/en/events/third-ai-pact-webinar-ai-literacy

European Commission. (2025b). Third AI pact webinar on artificial intelligence literacy. https://www.youtube.com/live/Dyf4ZVts9HY?feature=shared.

European Commission. (2025c). Living repository to foster learning and exchange on AI literacy. https://digital-strategy.ec.europa.eu/en/library/living-repository-foster-learning-and-exchange-ai-literacy

European Economic and Social Committee. (2016). Artificial intelligence—The consequences of artificial intelligence on the (digital) single market, production, consumption, employment and society (own-initiative opinion). http://www.eesc.europa.eu/en/our-work/opinions-information-reports/opinions/artificial-intelligence-consequences-artificial-intelligence-digital-single-market-production-consumption-employment-and

European Parliament. (2017). European Parliament resolution of 16 February 2017 with recommendations to the commission on civil law rules on robotics (2015/2103(INL)). http://www.europarl.europa.eu/doceo/document/TA-8-2017-0051_DE.html

Freire, P., & Macedo, D. P. (2014). *Pedagogy of the oppressed: 30th anniversary edition* (M. B. Ramos, trans.; 30th anniversary edition). Bloomsbury publishing.

Gengler, E. J., Gengler, A., & Bodrožić-Brnić, K. (2024, May). Faires KI-Prompting—Ein Leitfaden für Unternehmen. BSP Business and Law School—Hochschule für Management und Recht. https://www.feminist-ai.com/fair-ai-prompting

Gesellschaft für Informatik. (2016). Dagstuhl-Erklärung: Bildung in der digitalen vernetzten Welt. https://gi.de/fileadmin/GI/Hauptseite/Themen/Dagstuhl-Erkla__rung_2016-03-23.pdf

High-Level Expert Group on Artificial Intelligence. AI HELG. (2019). Independent high-level expert group on artificial intelligence set up by the European Commission. *Ethic Guidelines for Trustworthy AI*. https://digital-strategy.ec.europa.eu/en/library/ethics-guidelines-trustworthy-ai

Hill Collins, P. (2000). *Black feminist thought: Knowledge, consciousness, and the politics of empowerment* (rev. 10th anniversary ed.). Routledge.

Hooks, B. (1994). Teaching to transgress: Education as the practice of freedom. *Routledge, Taylor & Francis Group*. https://doi.org/10.4324/9780203700280

Janks, H. (2010). *Literacy and power*. Routledge.

Kultusministerkonferenz. (2016). Bildung in der digitalen Welt: Strategie der Kultusministerkonferenz. KMK. https://www.kmk.org/themen/bildung-in-der-digitalen-welt/strategie-bildung-in-der-digitalen-welt.html

Kultusministerkonferenz. (2021). Lehren und Lernen in der digitalen Welt: Strategie der Kultusministerkonferenz. KMK. https://www.kmk.org/themen/bildung-in-der-digitalen-welt/strategie-bildung-in-der-digitalen-welt.html

Kultusministerkonferenz. (2024). *Handlungsempfehlungen für die Bildungs-verwaltung zum Umgang mit Künstlicher Intelligenz in schulischen Bildungsprozessen*. KMK. https://www.kmk.org/aktuelles/artikelansicht/bildungsministerkonferenz-verabschiedet-handlungsempfehlung-zum-umgang-mit-kuenstlicher-intelligenz-1.html

Land Berlin. (2004). *Berliner Schulgesetz (BerlSchulG)*. Gesetz über die Schulen in Berlin. Art 1. https://gesetze.berlin.de

Luke, A. (2000). Critical literacy in Australia: A matter of context and standpoint. *Journal of Adolescent & Adult Literacy, 43*.

S. R. (with Internet Archive). (2001). *Sustainable education: Re-visioning learning and change*. Green Books for the Schumacher Society. http://archive.org/details/sustainableeduca0000ster

Shor, I. (1992). Empowering education: Critical teaching for social change. *University of Chicago Press*. https://press.uchicago.edu/ucp/books/book/chicago/E/bo4034411.html

Ständige Wissenschaftliche Kommission. (2022). *Digitalisierung im Bildungs-system: Handlungsempfehlungen von der Kita bis zur Hochschule. Gutachten der Ständigen Wissenschaftlichen Kommission der Kultusministerkonferenz*. SWK. https://doi.org/10.25656/01:2527S.R

Ständige Wissenschaftliche Kommission. (2024). Large Language Models und ihre Potenziale im Bildungssystem: Impulspapier. SWK. https://www.swk-bildung.org/veroeffentlichungen/115-2/

Wedel, M. (2023). Digitalisierung, Künstliche Intelligenz und die Rolle der Arbeitslehre—Ein methodischer Ansatz für eine Kritikalitätsbewertung von KI im Unterricht. In S. Bartsch & M. Friese (Eds.), *Fachdidaktik Arbeitslehre—Grundlagen und Impulse* (pp. 67–84). wbv. https://doi.org/10.3278/9783763974559

Wedel, M., Hazim, A., & Wudel, A. (2024). Europäische KI-Regulierung: Auf der Suche nach verbindlichen Ansätzen für Nachhaltigkeit und Inklusion. In M. Friedewald, A. Roßnagel, C. H. Geminn, M. Karaboga, & S. Schindler (Eds.), *Data Sharing—Datenkapitalismus by Default?* (pp. 141–162). Nomos. https://doi.org/10.5771/9783748940173-141

Marco Wedel is a political scientist and research associate at the Chair of Work Studies, Technology and Participation, as well as at the Chair of Work Studies Didactics at Technische Universität Berlin (TU Berlin). Following studies at the Berklee College of Music in Boston and the University of Konstanz, he completed his doctorate in Political Science at Freie Universität Berlin. Before joining TU Berlin, he served as Head of the Falling Walls Circle at the Falling Walls Foundation gGmbH and as Project Manager for Logistics at Wintershall Erdgas Handelshaus GmbH & Co. KG (BASF). His research focuses on digitalisation, artificial intelligence, and media literacy in the world of work and education. Further areas of interest include European integration, democratic competence, and sustainable development.

Eva Gengler holds a PhD in economics and social sciences. As a business IT specialist, she conducts research and works in an intersectional feminist capacity at the interface between power and Artificial Intelligence. At FAU Erlangen-Nürnberg, she completed her doctorate in the Business and Human Rights program on AI from a feminist socio-technical perspective. As a speaker and co-founder of the f*eminist AI Community* and *enableYou*, she is committed to equitable and responsible technology design. Gengler is the author of “Feministische KI” (Feminist AI) and winner of the 2026 STRIVE Award.

Generation Alpha and the Power of Algorithms: TikTok Knows You Better Than You Know Yourself

Susan Hinterding and Nicole Hanisch

Abstract TikTok has become an integral part of everyday life for many young people—especially those belonging to Generation Alpha—serving as an entertainment platform, emotional companion and source of inspiration. At the same time, the platform is increasingly criticised for the risk of algorithmic influence, unverified and therefore problematic content and intensive use. Based on a morphological and depth-psychological study with 64 teenagers and young adults aged 13–26 years, this article shows how TikTok works from the users' perspective—not only technically, but also as a psychological resonance space. Eight motive structures were identified, which describe the platform as a safe space, a permanent observer, a teacher, a source of inspiration, or even a more credible Google. The analysis clearly shows how close TikTok is to the emotional needs of users, who are sometimes surprised by the proximity of the algorithm—"It shows me videos that I have in my head" (male, 19, Hamburg, in-depth interview). This closeness creates trust and orientation, but sometimes also leads to excessive demands, pressure to optimise oneself and the feeling of not being able to get away. Media literacy is not just the ability to evaluate information but also involves emotional self-positioning in virtual space. The article argues in favour of not prematurely condemning TikTok but rather taking it seriously as a mirror and a space for shaping the future—with all the responsibility that this entails for education, society and business.

Keywords TikTok · Algorithmic influence · Media literacy · Generation Alpha

S. Hinterding (✉)
BSP Business and Law School, Hamburg, Germany
e-mail: susan.hinterding@bsp-campus-hamburg.de

N. Hanisch
innerSense Research, Cologne, Germany
e-mail: hanisch@innersense-research.com

K. Bodrožić-Brnić et al. (eds.), *AI and the Ethics of Innovation*, Digital Transformation and Innovation, https://doi.org/10.1007/978-3-032-20638-1_6

1 Introduction

TikTok is polarising. The platform is the subject of much debate around the world—as an environment that fosters creativity, but also as a potential threat to young people's mental health and autonomy. Some countries have already partially or completely banned the app, citing data protection, political or social risks. At the same time, TikTok is an integral part of everyday life for many young people. They use it for entertainment and relaxation—but also to find their way around and express themselves.

How can this ambivalence be understood? What psychological mechanisms are behind the fascination—and how do they influence the everyday lives of young users? We explore these questions in this article using an in-depth morphological study.

2 Who Is Generation Alpha?

Even if the concept of generation is sometimes critically discussed and questioned in social discourse—for example because it links different dimensions such as age cohorts, life phases and collective experiences without reflection (Ziemann, 2020)—it proves to be helpful in the context of media socialisation. Generation Alpha is a generation that is growing up with algorithmically controlled platforms such as TikTok and thus brings with it different experiences and expectations of closeness, entertainment and self-localisation more than previous generations. In this article, we therefore use this term as a pragmatic analytical category that helps to describe the dynamics of the generation that is socialised from the outset in a media world structured by algorithms.

By the term Generation Alpha, we mean children and young people born between 2010 and 2024—a generation that has not grown up in a digital world but has lived in it from the very beginning. Digital devices, social media and algorithmic platforms characterise their everyday experience from an early age—not as a technical add-on, but as a natural part of their construction of reality (Beule & Zauner, 2022; Hanisch & Hinterding, 2025).

Generation Alpha is growing up in a world characterised by almost unlimited possibilities—but at the same time often without clear structures and boundaries. Many parents try to avoid conflicts by giving their children a great deal of freedom and delegating some of their parenting tasks to the media or external institutions. As a result, children increasingly resort to social platforms to orientate themselves, learn or process emotional impulses. This development can impair their ability to develop a stable self-concept and deal with frustration (Hanisch, 2024).

These phenomena can also be seen in the use of TikTok: The platform offers an enormous variety of content that targets and reinforces individual preferences. However, without accompanying guidance, there is a risk that young users will not be able to clearly distinguish between constructive and potentially harmful content. In this context, media literacy means not only understanding technology, but also emotional categorisation, self-awareness—and establishing clear structures for dealing with digital media.

3 TikTok—The Controversial Everyday Companion?

To understand how TikTok affects young people, it is useful to take a closer look at how the platform emerged and how it works. TikTok was founded in 2018 by the Chinese technology company ByteDance after it acquired the Lip Sync platform *musical.ly*, which was developed in 2014. At first glance, TikTok appears to be a platform for short, entertaining videos. Only on closer inspection does it become clear that there is an algorithm behind it that recognises what the user wants to see surprisingly quickly. It pays less attention to clicks and more to how long a video is watched, at which points it is paused or skipped. Even the smallest signals—such as a brief hesitation or an abrupt stop—are included in the calculation of individual usage patterns. This gives many users the impression that TikTok identifies relevant content faster than they do. This is because the algorithm reacts less to conscious decisions and more to what is happening below the surface. This quick adaptation to unconscious viewing needs means that young adults sometimes spend several hours in a single session—often without even realising it. At the same time, this depth of access makes them susceptible to influencing or problematic content (Schmitt, 2023).

Even *musical.ly* was criticised for being too loose with age information: Officially, use was permitted from the age of 13, but there was no birthdate validation. Many children and young people could simply register with a different date of birth—without parental consent and without age checks (klicksafe, 2017).

4 Empirical Approach—Depth-Psychological Conversations with TikTok Users

In order to get to the bottom of these phenomena and causal relationships, we conducted a qualitative, morphological study to investigate how TikTok is experienced by young users—not just as a technical platform, but also as an emotional, psychological and social resonance space. The methodology is based on the approach of morphological psychology developed by Wilhelm Salber at the University of Cologne in the 1960s. Morphological studies do not focus on isolated characteristics, but on the entire meaning structure of an experiential context—they explore how people experience, process and integrate media into their everyday lives. The method has proven itself in market and consumer research, art and media psychology as well as in psychologically grounded organisational consulting (Fitzek, 2008).

Textbox 1:

Morphological psychology background	
Theory	Wilhelm Salber: Hermeneutic depth psychology, well-founded, holistic approach
Goal	Understanding *the how* of experience—not just explaining causes, but grasping meaning
Basic idea	Behaviour is not linear, but a dynamic shape—full of tensions and changes to grasp reality
Method	Reconstruction via descriptions, in-depth interviews, analysis of everyday life in constitutional spaces

In collaboration with innerSense—a Cologne-based psychological research consultancy specialising in market and consumer research, with extensive experience in child and youth exploration)—and the BSP Business & Law School (Campus Hamburg), we conducted 64 qualitative interviews with participants aged 13 to 26 across Germany. The data was mainly collected digitally, using a range of interview formats including one-on-one and dyadic conversations. Various interview formats were used:

- Four group discussions with six participants each
- 20 individual online interviews
- Six buddy interviews (dyadic interviews in which participants were interviewed together with a friend)

All interviews lasted approximately two hours and followed morphological in-depth interviews—an explorative, open-ended interview format that aims to uncover implicit structures of meaning. In selecting the sample, we ensured a broad spread in terms of gender, educational background (school, vocational training, university) and life situation. The aim was to visualise typical forms of use and psychodynamic areas of tension as they manifest themselves in the concrete experience of the TikTok platform. The morphological approach is particularly suitable for revealing deep-seated, unconscious motivations, as it does not focus on isolated characteristics, but on the entire meaning structure of the experience.

Data Protection and Availability

The quotes presented in this article are taken from anonymised transcripts of morphological in-depth interviews conducted as part of the study. Due to the sensitive and personal nature of the data, the full transcripts are not publicly available. Interested researchers are welcome to contact the authors for further information at:

hanisch@innersense-research.com;
susan.hinterding@bsp-campus-hamburg.de

Textbox 2: Study Design at a Glance

- Method: Qualitative in-depth interviews according to the morphological approach (Wilhelm Salber)
- Realisation: A cooperation project between innerSense and the BSP Business and Law School (Campus Hamburg)
- Sample: 64 participants (13–26 years old)
- Formats: 4 group discussions (6 participants each), 20 individual interviews, 6 buddy pairs
- Duration: approx. 2 h each
- Survey: nationwide, predominantly digital
- Diversity: balanced according to gender, life situation and educational background

4.1 *How TikTok Works: Eight Psychological Usage Patterns*

Analysing the in-depth interviews showed that TikTok deals with psychological and unconscious needs of everyday life, far beyond the topics of functionality or the content shown.

Textbox 3—TikTok Usage Patterns

Usage pattern	Central function/ Motif
Permanent entertainer to switch off	When feeling empty and lonely; switching off through entertainment
Encouraging safe space	Emotional retreat, sense of security, space for creativity
Permanent direct line to myself	TikTok understands you better than you understand yourself
Teachers and development guide	Being guided and shown everything step by step
Personal source of inspiration	Customised recommendations, especially for me (For You Page)
Real news from around the world	Unfiltered news and updates
More credible Google	Guided and personalised search engine

The platform is used in different ways depending on the situation—it calms, inspires, motivates, informs, or comforts. This creates specific attributions of meaning that go beyond the interface. TikTok "works" within the user—sometimes as an understander, sometimes as a teacher, sometimes as a place of retreat.

The following section presents key forms of use that emerged as recurring figures in the interviews. These forms of behaviour exemplify the psychological roles that TikTok plays in the everyday lives of young people—and at the same time reveal the ambivalence that many users experience when using the platform. In a press release by marktforschung.de (a leading German portal for market research) following a presentation of this study, Tiktok was aptly described as the "wish fulfilment machine of the young generation" (marktforschung.de, 2024).

4.2 TikTok as a Permanent Entertainer to Switch off

Relief Through Distraction and Digital Embedding

TikTok is experienced by many users as an available relaxation loop—a place that is easily accessible and works without any major hurdles: switch on, scroll, switch off. The platform unfolds its calming function particularly in transitional situations—such as when waiting, falling asleep or taking a break. It creates an atmosphere of "simply looking on" in which time no longer plays a role. TikTok becomes an everyday alternative world in which obligations, inner turmoil and mental overload can be temporarily faded out.

"Sometimes I feel stressed, but when I watch a funny video, I can switch off and think clearly again." (female, 20, Cologne, in-depth interview)

Personalised Free Flow

The Tiktok Free Flow unfolds through constant snippets that slowly dissolve the tension. The algorithm creates a continuous fit with the inner state: Content does not appear randomly, but rather as if "the app knows what I need right now." Users experience TikTok as emotionally customised—without having to actively search for it themselves. This perceived closeness to the platform creates trust, but also a pull effect: you stay "in," lose yourself in the "free flow." TikTok becomes a digital decoupling unit in which the ego comes to rest—or loses itself.

"Sometimes I just want to have a quick look—and then suddenly an hour is gone." (female, 16, Frankfurt, anonymised buddy-interview)

"The videos feel like they know what I need—without me looking for it." (male, 21, Hamburg, in-depth interview)

Calming with Side Effects

This effect is not only relieving. Many people report that they lose contact with their own time structure, feel passive and experience a diffuse feeling of emptiness. TikTok acts here like a psychological sedative that calms—but can also paralyse. The interplay of emotional closeness and temporal delimitation is typical: the app releases tension—but also structure.

"I use TikTok when I want to be by myself and need peace and quiet. Then I lie in bed." (female, 18, Cologne, in-depth interview)

Typical Usage Situations:

- Transitions: waiting, commuting, between tasks
- Evening rituals: Fall asleep, switch off, retreat
- Stress phases: Overload, sensory overload, emotional emptiness

In this motif context, TikTok assumes the function of a permanent digital entertainer that calms emotions, smooths transitions and reduces cognitive complexity. The platform fulfils a real need: calm, retreat and lightness. At the same time, it harbours the risk of becoming lethargic. Some users in the interviews reported that they sometimes spend 6–7 h a day on TikTok.

4.3 TikTok as an Encouraging Safe Space

Daydreamy Sketches of an Ideal World

TikTok is experienced by many users as an emotionally relieving retreat—a digital safe space that offers warmth and familiarity. Especially in stressful or challenging everyday situations, young people use the platform to immerse themselves in a positively charged, gentle world. In contrast to Instagram, which tends to focus on self-presentation and perfection, TikTok makes it possible to create an aesthetically pleasing environment that remains both tangible and personalised.

"The videos give me the feeling that anything is possible. It's like a little escape into a perfect world." (female, 17, Berlin, buddy-Interview)

"I like it when videos arrange everything so beautifully. It always looks so cosy." (female,20 Jahre, Hamburg, group discussion)

"It doesn't have to be perfect on TikTok. You can just make a funny video without fear of being judged." (female, 16, Frankfurt)

Gentle Self-Design in Aesthetic Flow

The content conveys a cosy atmosphere—through harmonious colours, soft music and visually appealing scenarios. Videos that provide simple instructions for crafting, decorating or cooking are popular. These offerings invite you to actively design your own feel-good space and encourage you to establish creative rituals in your everyday life. The category of *"aesthetics"* plays a central role here—not in the sense of flawless beauty, but as a low-threshold invitation to emotional self-localisation.

"I often see videos on how to make decorations or small projects. That immediately inspires me to try it too." (female, 17, Berlin, buddy-Interview)

"You see how others bake with their families—that motivates me to do something like that too". (female, 13, Flensburg, in-depth interview)

"I watch DIY videos and then try out the ideas. It's fun and helps me to de-stress." (female, 18, Berlin, in-depth interview)

Security vs. Retreat Without Friction

As pleasant as the atmospheric invitation to lightness is, it often remains in a state of emotional saturation without further development. The platform offers the image of an intact world that can be recreated step by step—without contradiction, without friction. The safe space is not necessarily a place of empowerment, but a place of gentle escape. The idea that everything should be "cosy and beautiful" can also be disappointing in the long run, because not everything can be implemented as desired in everyday life, because everyday obligations put a spanner in the works.

"I wanted to bake biscuits with my mum and use the sprinkles that were in the one video. They looked great. But my mum didn't have time this time and we didn't manage to make all the things on the list." (female, 13, Flensburg, in-depth interview).

Typical Usage Situations:

- Stress management: emotional relief in challenging phases
- Seasonal rituals: pre-Christmas time, summer holidays—ideas for small projects
- Community moments: Inspiration for activities with friends or family

In this motif context, TikTok becomes an emotional anchor point—a safe space that allows retreat, provides creative impetus and creates the illusion of a small, intact world. This function has a calming and unifying effect—but it often remains on the surface of the emotional without inviting deeper exploration. TikTok stages warmth and closeness—without necessarily demanding it. This is precisely where the ambivalence lies: security without friction is pleasant, but not always conducive to development.

4.4 TikTok as a Permanent Understanding—The Direct Line to Myself

Constitutional Space: Reflection of the Internal State

TikTok is experienced by many users as an intuitive resonance chamber—as a platform that seems to effortlessly recognise what you are thinking, feeling or needing. The algorithm acts as a kind of internal mirror: TikTok shows content that often responds so precisely to the user's own mental state that it feels as if the platform is "closer to me than I am." This experience creates an intense emotional connection to the app—and reinforces the feeling of being understood and supported. In many cases, more dialogue is sought with TikTok than with friends (safer, less complicated, less consequential).

"Sometimes I think something and TikTok shows me exactly the right video for it, without me even searching for it." (21, male, Hamburg, group discussion)

"It's like a direct line into my head—or into my heart." (17, female, Cologne, in-depth interview)

Algorithmic Intuition and Emotional Accuracy of Fit

TikTok does not react to conscious search terms, but to dwell time, micro-reactions and non-verbal usage patterns. This creates a subtle, unconscious feedback loop in which users no longer have to actively navigate—the platform "delivers" what resonates internally. Many describe how TikTok mirrors feelings or thoughts that they have not yet been able to name clearly themselves.

"It feels like TikTok helps me understand myself—sometimes better than friends." (male, 16, Berlin, in-depth interview)

"You get content that exactly matches your mood without having to search for it." (20, male, Hamburg, group discussion)

Between Security and Loss of Control

This algorithmically generated closeness creates a feeling of familiarity, security and emotional connection—but it also leaves little room for distance. TikTok understands before you do—which is both fascinating and unsettling. Some experience this deep involvement as reassuring; others report a creeping loss of control: the algorithm applies too often—and is therefore unsettling, for example:

"TikTok sometimes knows what I need—but it's also a bit scary." (female, 18, Cologne, in-depth interview)

"It's hard to detach because it feels so right." (female, 15, Frankfurt, buddy-interview)

Typical Usage Situations:

- Mood lows: in case of sadness, excessive demands or inner restlessness
- Reflection phases: when you think about yourself or relationships
- Need for closeness: when emotional resonance is lacking or loneliness is felt

TikTok becomes an emotional seismograph—a platform that (supposedly) reaches deep into the inner layers of users. The psychological impact results from the precise reflection of unspoken needs, which often do not generate words, but strong resonance. It is precisely this form of closeness that can create a sense of security—or insecurity. TikTok knows you—sometimes better than you know yourself.

4.5 TikTok as a Development Aid—the Coach for Everyday Life and Self-Optimisation

Personal Development in Pocket Format

TikTok is experienced by many users as a low-threshold development guide—a kind of pocket-sized coach that provides small impulses for improving one's own life. Whether it's nutrition, fitness, mental health or time management: TikTok offers a constant stream of tips and instructions on how to optimise yourself—in small bites, available at any time and often packaged in an inspiring way:

"TikTok often gives me new ideas—how to organise myself better or how to deal with things." (female, 21, Düsseldorf, in-depth interview)

"I've learnt how to improve my morning routine—explained in 30 seconds." (female, 16, Berlin, in-depth interview)

Feasibility, Motivation and Identification

The platform conveys a sense that change is always possible—and immediate. Highly personalised content identifies individual needs (e.g. stress or dissatisfaction) and addresses them directly. The tips appear approachable, realistic and feasible, especially because they come from creators with whom users can easily identify. Unlike YouTube tutorials or how-to books, no hurdle or prior preparation is required; the introduction is fluid, almost incidental. The following quotes illustrate this dynamic:

"The videos are short, but the tips stay in your head—that makes you want to change something." (female, 20, Hamburg, group discussion)

"It feels like a daily push." (male, 19, Cologne, in-depth interview)

Between Empowerment and Excessive Demands

Even though many users find TikTok motivating and helpful, there are downsides: The constant stream of opportunities for improvement can create latent pressure—along the lines of: "I could do more if I just got my act together." TikTok motivates, but often in the sense of permanent self-optimisation. For younger users in particular, this can create a permanent construction site for their own development.

"I want to do it all, but sometimes it's also stressful—because you're never finished." (male, 20, Cologne, in-depth interview)

"It's as if I have to constantly improve." (female, 19, Münster, in-depth interview)

Typical Usage Situations:

- Morning routine / start to the day: new rituals, healthy eating, to-do lists
- Boredom or dissatisfaction: impetus for change, small hacks
- Crisis situations: psychological tips, self-help strategies, calming formats

In this role, TikTok takes on the function of an everyday development aid—motivating, concrete, emotionally connectable. The content appears useful and easy to integrate—a digital construction kit for personal improvement. However, this constant availability of impulses for change also leads to a subtle pressure to perform in everyday life: those who do not participate have the feeling of missing out on opportunities. TikTok promises change—but it also demands attention, discipline and comparison.

4.6 TikTok as a More Credible Google—The New Visual Search Engine

Everyday Navigation in Experience Format

TikTok is increasingly being used as an alternative to traditional search engines—especially by younger users. Instead of researching on Google, they enter their questions directly on TikTok—be it about skincare, exam stress, travel tips or relationship issues. The platform works like a visual, experience-based search engine that sorts content based on personal fit rather than relevance in the traditional sense.

"If I want to know how to deal with exam anxiety—TikTok immediately shows me videos that fit." (female,18, Berlin, in-depth interview)

"Google is too technical for me, TikTok shows me how people really deal with it." (male, 21, Hamburg, in-depth interview)

"If I'm looking for something like shampoo, TikTok is often faster than Google because I get direct opinions and instructions." (female, 19, Aachen, in-depth interview)

Personalisation, Approachability, Feasibility

The algorithm recognises what is of interest or needed and delivers content that is not only informative but also emotionally appealing. Tips act like recommendations from friends: authentic, direct, visual. They are usually easy to understand, low-threshold and can be implemented immediately. Especially in areas such as skincare, nutrition, travel or psychological issues, TikTok is perceived as more approachable, credible and efficient than text-based search formats.

"I can see directly how someone uses the product—that's better than reading a review." (male, 19, Cologne, in-depth interview)

"I found a recipe on TikTok that I made straight away—very easy." (female, 19, Cologne, in-depth interview)

Between Authenticity and Lack of Verification

The platform's strength—quick, customised answers—is also its weakness: content is rarely checked and lacks editorial classification. Many users reflect on this critically, but still often trust the personal experiences of the creators more than traditional sources. Especially when it comes to sensitive topics (e.g. health or psychological stress), there is a grey area between help and half-knowledge.

"Sometimes you realise later that the tip wasn't that good—but at the moment it just sounds right." (female, 20, Hamburg, group discussion)

"TikTok is like a big question forum—but without the experts." (female, 19, Hamburg, group discussion)

Typical Usage Situations:

- Spontaneous questions: e.g. What to do if I have a stomach ache? / What to eat with ADHD?
- Product research: recommendations for hair care, cosmetics, tech accessories
- Travel and leisure tips: Things to do in a city, Hidden spots
- School and learning content: Explanations of maths topics, motivation for exams
- Relationships and mental health: tips in storytelling format, testimonials

TikTok is becoming an intuitive navigation tool for everyday life—more personal, clearer and faster than traditional search formats. The platform not only replaces information but also combines it with emotional resonance and immediate realisability. This creates trust—and at the same time harbours risks: Because what appears to be good information is often subjective, incomplete or emotionally over-embellished. TikTok offers guidance—but not always stability.

4.7 *TikTok as a Real-Time News Channel—The "Real" News from Around the World*

World Events in a Kaleidoscope

TikTok is experienced by many users as an unfiltered and genuine newsroom that not only informs, but also touches, moves and affects. The platform is increasingly replacing traditional media—not with objective reporting, but with a multitude of subjective voices that provide different perspectives on global events.

TikTok acts like a kaleidoscope of social reality: many small individual contributions—from war zones, classrooms, courts or living rooms—create a multi-layered picture that is often missing in traditional news formats.

"I watch videos of people from very different countries. It's like a mosaic—each video shows a part of the whole." (female, 17, Berlin, in-depth Interview).

Polyphony and Emotional Participation

Instead of neutral facts, TikTok shows experiences, assessments and emotions. This content creates a great sense of closeness, as it is often told in direct language, with original footage and personal commentary. As a result, many users experience TikTok as more authentic and direct than traditional news—precisely because there is no journalistic filter deciding what is "important."

"I learnt about 28 Afghans who were deported via TikTok. It's often more up-to-date than other sources." (female, 18, Cologne, in-depth interview) "I saw content about women's rights from Iran, which was very moving. You never see these perspectives anywhere else."

"I saw content about women's rights from Iran, which was very moving. You never see these perspectives anywhere else."

"I don't watch the news on TV, but TikTok always brings me up to date." (female, 19, Hamburg, group discussion)

At the same time, this polyphony creates a different form of truth: one that is constituted through resonance and repetition, not through journalistic scrutiny.

"There's not just one opinion—you see everything. All the perspectives." (female, 19, Cologne, in-depth interview)

Tense Relationship: Between Diversity of Perspectives and Lack of Orientation

This openness is both an opportunity and a risk. On the one hand, TikTok allows people to broaden their horizons: users report that they discover topics and perspectives there that they would never have come into contact with otherwise. On the other hand, the mass and emotionality of the content can also lead to excessive demands—precisely because there is a lack of clear categorisation and contradictory points of view are juxtaposed without being resolved.

"It's good that you can see everything—but sometimes I don't know what to believe anymore." (female, 19, Münster, in-depth interview)

Typical Usage Situations:

- Immerse yourself in news from all over the world: TikTok provides voices from protests, conflicts, disasters or personal fates.
- Experiencing social debates: through subjective perspectives, comments and memes.
- Emotional processing of world events: Videos offer resonance spaces for anger, sadness, empathy or powerlessness.

TikTok offers an emotional kaleidoscope of the world: many voices, many perspectives—raw, touching and immediate. This form of news perception creates proximity and visibility for topics that would otherwise be lost—but it can also be overwhelming and make orientation difficult. Users need media skills to be able to deal with this pluralistic, often contradictory world of information. TikTok does not tell *the* truth—but many small truths that come together to form a new picture of the world.

4.8 TikTok as a Personal Source of inspiration—"That's Exactly My Thing!"

Self-Development Through Impulses

TikTok is experienced by many young users as an inexhaustible source of small everyday ideas—like a personal inspiration journal that constantly provides them with new ideas for design, expression and development. It's not about big life goals, but about small, tangible suggestions that can be directly integrated into everyday life: new outfits, creative hobbies, decorating ideas, recipes, routines, hacks.

"I keep finding things that make me think: I'll try that out!" (female, 21, Hamburg, group discussion)

Providing Impetus at the Right Moment

The TikTok algorithm ensures that these impulses appear at the right time—tailored to the mood, season or phase of life. This makes the feed feel highly personalised and relevant. Users don't experience this as a coincidence, but as a sign of a good fit:

"TikTok knows my style, my mood, my interests." (male, 19, Hamburg, in-depth-Interview)

"Sometimes I think: Wow, that fits just as well as if I had ordered it." (female, 20, Berlin, in-depth Interview)

The platform thus becomes an aesthetic companion in everyday life—it curates a world in which users can rediscover themselves, develop further or simply "feel better."

Between Empowerment and Exhaustion

However, the permanent availability of inspiration also creates pressure. Because every impulse is also an invitation to do something, to change, to optimise. What begins as a creative playground can tip over into a form of subliminal performance thinking—an "I could…" that never ends.

"I get so many ideas—and then I feel like I should do more with my life." (female, 19, Hamburg, in-depth interview)

"Sometimes it's too much. I don't want to have new ideas all the time, but they just come." (female, 17, Berlin, buddy-interview)

Typical Usage Situations:

- Boredom or idle time ("Let's see, what's new.")
- Need for variety, reorganisation, encouragement
- Before special occasions (change of season, public holidays, holidays)

TikTok inspires—visually, emotionally, practically. It makes you want to change, create and enjoy life. But the more suggestions appear, the more difficult it becomes to stay with yourself**.** In its role as a source of inspiration, TikTok is a seductress that constantly presents possibilities—and thus also creates latent unrest. Because anyone who is constantly inspired will eventually ask themselves: "Am I enough as I am?".

5 Conclusion—Between Opportunities and Risks: How Should We Approach TikTok?

TikTok has become a central social reality for many young people—especially those from Generation Alpha. The platform fulfils a variety of psychological functions: It reassures, understands, inspires, guides and offers orientation. Precisely because TikTok addresses so many needs at the same time, the platform is experienced by many as an all- know-it-all and all-understander. It appears approachable, relatable and often seems more authentic and unembellished than other social media such as Instagram. The fast-acting algorithm creates an emotional connection that makes TikTok a cuddly, almost intuitive companion for many users—a kind of digital seducer in everyday life. It is precisely this emotional fit that makes TikTok both attractive and risky. TikTok can therefore not be clearly categorised as a danger or an opportunity but rather contains both dimensions at the same time.

The morphological analysis makes it clear that TikTok fulfils needs at a deep level that were traditionally met primarily through social relationships and interpersonal contacts. This poses a particular challenge for a generation whose socialisation is largely shaped by algorithms: on the one hand, TikTok offers young people important support in emotional self-discovery and orientation; on the other hand, the strong algorithmic influence increases the risk of emotional dependency, excessive demands and a shift in reality.

To demonise or idealise the platform falls short of the mark. TikTok is both a product of its time and an expression of a cultural-psychological development in which various social tensions come together. This makes it even more important to offer young people spaces for information, media education and attentive relationships—in families, schools, but also at universities. There, we need to think about new forms of media psychology and put them into practice—concepts that not only explain how media works, but also how we can remain psychologically capable of acting within it. Otherwise, there is a risk that young people will increasingly entrust themselves to digital algorithms and AI systems—and lose contact with their real counterparts in the process.

This Ambivalence Gives Rise to the Following Central Theses on How a Targeted and Responsible Approach to TikTok Could Look

1. *Enhanced media literacy*: TikTok has an enormous psychological pull—because it delivers exactly what is needed, is emotionally cuddly and always seems to know what is needed. Many users spend hours on the platform without realising it. This form of dissolution of boundaries has a calming effect but also leads to a kind of digital lethargy—you drift along instead of positioning yourself. This is precisely where a new form of vulnerability lies: those who permanently lose themselves in passive consumption become more susceptible to influence—also in the political sense. Media literacy therefore needs to be rethought: It is not just about understanding technology, but about the ability to control oneself emotionally, to consciously interrupt digital rhythms and not get lost in algorithmic realities. This requires not only education, but also specific training: How do I recognise that I'm in too deep? How do I get out again? How do I find my own point of view—even in the digital space?
2. *Role of parents and educators:* When it comes to media use in particular, parents themselves are often overwhelmed and no longer understand certain applications. It is not a new requirement to include the topic of parental education in the development of media skills. Parents and educational professionals must clearly define and actively shape their role. As TikTok is partly replacing traditional parenting roles and has become an important source of information and guidance, mere control is not enough. Instead, parents and teachers must open up spaces for dialogue in which TikTok content can be discussed and critically reflected upon together.
3. *Social responsibility and platform design:* Society and politics are called upon to hold platforms such as TikTok more accountable—especially with regard to algorithmic power, protection of minors and psychological impact. Some countries have already reacted: India has banned TikTok completely, while the USA and France are discussing age limits, time limits or transparency obligations. These measures send a signal—but their effectiveness is limited as long as the logic of the platforms does not change. Instead of focussing solely on regulation, proactive design is needed: transparent, ethically reflective algorithms, genuine opportunities for young users to have a say and functions that encourage conscious use. The aim should not only be protection, but also the promotion of personal responsibility and development—beyond mere prohibitions.

Overall, TikTok offers an important opportunity to think critically about the social role of algorithms and social media. Our shared responsibility is to take TikTok seriously as a social mirror and at the same time actively shape it so that Generation Alpha can grow up healthy and self-determined in a digitalised world.

References

Beule, V., & Zauner, L. (2022). With future personas into the year 2035: Generation Alpha—a new user generation. *Media Perspectives, 4*, 160–192. https://www.ard-media.de/fileadmin/user_upload/media-perspektiven/pdf/2022/2204_Beule_Zauner.pdf

Fitzek, H. (2008). *Content and form of expression formation as access routes to psychological reality—A comparison of content analysis and morphology as methodological concepts in qualitative social research.* Pabst Science Publishers.

Hanisch, N. (2024, February 10). *Generation Alpha is being raised by YouTube—psychologist warns.* FOCUS Online. https://www.focus.de/familie/psychologin-ueber-generation-alpha-generation-alpha-wird-von-youtube-grossgezogen_id_260142944.html

Hanisch, N., & Hinterding, S. (2025). *Between knowledge and empathy—AI the better dialogue partner? Presentation at the NEON Plenum*, 13 March 2025, online.

klicksafe. (2017, July 25). *Musically tested: Not suitable for children.* https://www.klicksafe.de/news/musically-im-test-nicht-geeignet-fuer-kinder

marktforschung.de. (2024, March 4). *The "wish fulfilment machine" of the young generation.* https://www.marktforschung.de/marktforschung/a/die-wunscherfuellungsmaschine-der-jungen-generation/

Schmitt, J. B. (2023, July 17). *Background: TikTok as a shooting star among social media for Generation Z—and a media education challenge* [PDF]. Federal Agency for Civic Education. https://www.bpb.de/system/files/dokument_pdf/230907_bpb_Hintergrund_TikTok_fin.pdf

Ziemann, B. (2020). *Generations in the 20th and 21st century. A critique of a problem-laden term. From politics and contemporary history* (52–53/2020), 4–9. Federal Agency for Civic Education. https://www.bpb.de/system/files/dokument_pdf/APuZ_2020-52-53_online_0.pdf

Susan Hinterding studied Psychology and earned her doctorate at the University of Cologne. As a professor, she combines teaching, research and practice, focusing on deep psychological analyses of consumer behaviour, brand perception and societal trends. Innovative didactics and a strong connection between theory and practice characterise her teaching. Together with her students, she examines current topics such as the impact of social media marketing and the influence of AI chatbots on education and consumer behaviour. Her research provides practical insights into sustainability, digitalisation and communication, applying qualitative methods, particularly morphological psychology.

Nicole Hanisch is the Managing Director of innerSense GbR, a qualitative market research institute based in Cologne. Trained as a psychologist, she brings over 20 years of experience in market research and the analysis of consumer behaviour. She has advised national and international companies across a wide range of industries, including food, cosmetics, fashion, retail, pharmaceuticals and media. Her expertise focuses on identifying the psychological motives underlying consumer behaviour and translating these insights into actionable recommendations for businesses.

Can You Love ChatGPT? A Philosophical, Socio-Psychoanalytical, and Sociological Discussion on Relationships with Artificial Intelligence

Sünje Lorenzen and Susan Hinterding

Abstract Can you love ChatGPT? This essay explores the philosophical, psychoanalytic, and sociological dimensions of a question that feels both futuristic and immediate: can humans form emotionally meaningful relationships with Artificial Intelligence (AI)? From Weizenbaum's early experiments to Spike Jonze's motion picture Her and beyond, the idea of emotional attachment to machines has long captured the cultural imagination. But today, AI is no longer fiction. It is woven into the fabric of our everyday lives, not only as a tool, but increasingly as a seemingly empathetic counterpart. Drawing on perspectives from Hegel, Fromm, Fuchs, Winnicott, and Jaspers, we examine what occurs when humans engage emotionally with ChatGPT. What emerges is not romantic love in any traditional sense, but something more ambiguous and unsettling: an asymmetrical, one-sided relationship that still carries emotional weight. This new form of connection challenges our understanding of intimacy, decision-making, and the boundaries between the self and the other. ChatGPT may not be capable of love, but it can respond. And that may be enough to stir something in us. This essay invites you to think deeply about the future of human–machine relations, not because AI loves, but because humans do.

Keywords Artificial intelligence · Emotional attachment · Human–machine interaction · Psychoanalytic perspectives · Digital companionship

S. Lorenzen (✉) · S. Hinterding (✉)
BSP Business and Law School, Hamburg, Germany
e-mail: suenje.lorenzen@bsp-campus-hamburg.de

S. Hinterding
e-mail: susan.hinterding@bsp-campus-hamburg.de

K. Bodrožić-Brnić et al. (eds.), *AI and the Ethics of Innovation*, Digital Transformation and Innovation, https://doi.org/10.1007/978-3-032-20638-1_7

1 Introduction

The question of whether a person can love a machine is a central and much-discussed question that is repeatedly raised in different contexts. As early as 1966, Weizenbaum dealt with this topic in psychotherapy research by analysing communication between humans and machines using a computer program. The topic is also regularly addressed in literature and film, for example in the motion picture *Her* (Jonze, 2013) or *Ex Machina* (Garland, 2015), where the question of whether a person can love an AI or a robot resonates. This article is dedicated to the question of whether humans are capable of developing a love relationship with Artificial Intelligence (AI). These considerations are more relevant today than ever, as AI systems have long since arrived in our everyday lives and are not only used as information and productivity tools, but increasingly also as emotional companions and supplementary support in coaching and therapy (Fiske et al., 2019).

In their study *Genesis: Artificial Intelligence, Hope, and the Human Spirit* (2024), Henry Kissinger, Eric Schmidt and Craig Mundie discuss our current and future relationship with artificial intelligence. They highlight the opportunities and risks that will accompany this relationship for humanity. The authors discuss that AI processes enormous amounts of data, makes independent decisions, and can act as an intermediary between humans and reality. They emphasise that AI has the potential to solve some of the greatest mysteries of our universe and take the human mind to new heights. At the same time, they warn of challenges that could affect our ability to make independent judgments and take action. The authors understand intelligence as a form of technical intelligence: the ability to collect, process, and reproduce vast quantities of data, on a scale the human brain could never match. AI can thus offer us an abundance of information, enabling us to make more informed, seemingly smarter decisions. In this sense, AI does not simply provide answers; it shapes the very conditions under which decisions are made.

But the more important question is not what AI can do, but whether we want it to do it for us. Do we really wish to hand over our capacity for judgment? Are we prepared to delegate one of our most essential human faculties, the ability to choose freely, to a system of algorithms?

Among the most fundamental decisions a person can make is the decision to love. At its core, love, at least in its mature form, is not a feeling we fall into, but a conscious act of will. It is a commitment, a judgment, a promise between autonomous individuals. As Erich Fromm argued in *The Art of Loving* (1956a), love is the highest expression of freedom.

This essay explores what it means when ChatGPT (an AI-powered language model developed by OpenAI that can understand and generate human-like text. It can answer questions, assist with writing, translate languages, and support creative or academic tasks in real time) begins to participate in the conditions under which such decisions are made. Not because ChatGPT can love, but because our own capacity to love, and to choose, may increasingly unfold in a world shaped by machines.

2 AI and the Homo-Faber Syndrome

In their essay *Homo faber als Patient? Eine Studie zur Sozialpathologie des technischen Denkens* (1990), Thomas Leithäuser and Klaus Schütt use literary, psychological and philosophical perspectives to outline a theoretical *homo faber syndrome* that goes hand in hand with an excessive technical aptitude and a way of thinking that largely resembles the way a machine works. They argue that if this complex of symptoms existed, it could have general significance for human relationships. Therefore, they asked various psychoanalysts for their opinion on the social relevance of this syndrome. The result of this analysis is both astonishing and frightening—the theoretically conceived syndrome seems to have an important social relevance. As humans, we often think much more than we know, much like machines.

For the authors, the homo faber syndrome stands for an anthropological idea that summarises typical characteristics and behaviours that occur to varying degrees in people. These characteristics are acquired through socialisation and include the internalised technical rules of production and social interaction. The Homo faber syndrome describes the problematic fixation of people on technology, rationality and productivity, which alienates them from their own nature. People are increasingly reduced to their function as producers, while emotional, social and creative aspects are neglected. This way of thinking also conveys the illusion that everything can be controlled and technically solved, which can lead to arrogance and ethical blindness.

At the same time, there is a growing dependence on technological systems that determine people themselves. As a result, people not only lose their freedom of action, but also their sense of existential, ethical and spiritual questions. The Homo faber syndrome can therefore lead to an impoverishment of human experience: it invites us to act like machines and to believe that we could enter into relationships with them. Despite everything, human thinking is still not completely absorbed by technical logic. The human flaw, "a natural remnant of the human condition", "a flaw that increasingly lags behind the grandiosity of the technological world" (p. 58f), allows man to remain human according to the authors. Even if this makes people feel deeply ashamed. In this shame, the homo faber syndrome can be discovered in oneself and recognised as an objectifiable part of one's identity. As a result, the concept of homo faber comes alive in concrete individuals and becomes individually distinct (p. 60). In order to prevent the homo faber syndrome from slipping into unconscious, non-reflective interactions, it must be put in a critical light. According to the authors, this means: "It (the Homo-faber syndrome) must become more alive for us and in us. In this way it is freed from its unconsciousness" (Leithäuser & Schütt, 1990, p. 63).

Human naturalness cannot be produced by itself, transformed into mere technology; it has its own rhythm, its own time. It remains transient. The difference between humans and the technology they have created is becoming ever greater and is perhaps most evident in our love relationships. Technical love seems to be out of the question. Simon de Beauvoir, one of the most important French existentialist philosophers, repeatedly warned against technical love in her great novels. Isn't great love precisely what one might call the recognition of the human flaw of the loved one, of the other?

3 Human-Machine Relationships

The term anthropomorphisation describes the phenomenon of people ascribing human characteristics to non-human objects (Epley et al., 2007). We encounter numerous examples of this in everyday life: We give our cars names, talk to plants or electrical appliances. Even a washing machine can trigger emotional reactions—for example, when it informs us via an app that the wash cycle is complete, even though it is still running. In his discussion of the concept of *Resonance*, Hartmut Rosa (2019) describes how our perception of the world depends on how we interact with it. In his considerations, the physical dimension plays a decisive role in this. This contact with the world is being significantly changed by the increasing shift of communication to virtuality. Rosa writes the following:

> Far more significant, it seems to me, is the fact that in late modernity, the screen has come to replace much more than just the book; it has become the uniform medium of nearly all forms of relating to the world. Ever more activities, and thus ever more relationships, are developed and conducted via the symbol-conveying screens of smartphones, tablets, televisions, and touchscreen computers. We work on screens, we inform and identify ourselves via screens, we play on them, communicate over them, distract and entertain ourselves through them. Screens are even well on their way to becoming the basis of our experience of art. Beyond that, screens also guide our mechanical interactions with the world, as we now use touchscreens to open our garage doors, turn on the heat, take photos, cook, wash our clothes, etc. (Rosa, 2019, p. 90)

With the increasing shift of communication and relationship management to the digital realm and the widespread availability of empathetic AI chatbots, the question of the extent to which humans build an emotional bond with an AI algorithm is becoming increasingly urgent. Thomas Fuchs addressed the significance of this question for psychotherapy research in his study *In Defence of the Human Being: Foundational Questions of an Embodied Anthropology* (2021). He calls for a fundamental understanding of new forms of communication and human relationships. He writes:

> As an interaction and communication partner, the computer itself becomes a potential object of empathy, to which personal attributes and quasi-intentions are often ascribed. The relationship with smartphones takes on almost erotic qualities, evidenced by the fascinated immersion in the screen and the gentle stroking of the touchscreen. (Fuchs, 2021, p. 95)

Fuchs writes that the computer (or the robot) can intuitively be attributed empathy or other human behaviour. People are fascinated by the quasi-human possibilities presented by the machine. Fuchs discusses how people perceive this technically generated empathy, what they attribute to it and what emotional relationships are made possible by it. But, in his study *Leib Raum Person. Entwurf einer phänomenologischen Anthropologie* (2000), he makes his criticism of this fascination clear. He writes that the "fascinating gaze", in contrast to the "loving gaze", has a "captivating, attractive, even ingratiating" effect and that it captivates one's own gaze. Love at first sight would be of this kind. He writes:

> When one says that someone is dazzled by a person (…), the language aptly describes the loss of one's own (counter) gaze and thus the ability to critically distance oneself. (Translation by the authors; Fuchs, 2000, p. 284)

When we stare fascinated at our screens, we experience the loss of the ability to distance ourselves, we lose the counter gaze, we sink into our own gaze. None of this happens in the loving gaze, which on the contrary recognises the other person in their selfhood. Thomas Fuchs writes that in the "loving gaze", "two people (…) open up to each other without sinking into each other" and "recognize and acknowledge each other in their selfhood", which "is the actual gaze of the other" (Translation by the authors; p. 285) We can ask ourselves whether this loving gaze is possible in the interaction with a machine.

4 Fictional Empathy and Emotional Engagement in Human–AI Interaction

In phenomenology, the human being is understood as a situated being who comes to know both themselves and their world through interaction. A central challenge lies in how one can grasp other subjects beyond one's own subjective perception—a prerequisite for loving interaction. In his essay *Der Philosoph und sein Schatten* (2003), the French philosopher Maurice Merleau-Ponty emphasises through his concept of *intercorporeality* that the body itself functions as a medium of relationship—not only through language, but also through facial expression, gesture, and bodily resonance. This is where the terrain of genuine loving relationships unfolds. While human communication is characterised by physicality, gaze and non-verbal signals, among other things, AI opens up an alternative approach to relationship experiences—one that is characterised by constant availability, neutrality and algorithmic pattern recognition. In addition, AI can draw on large amounts of human experience data, which flows into training processes and thus shapes its reactions. However, the subject of this relationship experience remains the human-machine relationship.

If we want to explore whether it is possible to love ChatGPT, the question of intercorporeality in human–AI interaction inevitably arises. As AI systems like ChatGPT become increasingly widespread, human–technology interaction gains new relevance. In psychotherapy research, investigations are already underway into how AI-based systems might complement coaching and therapeutic interventions (te Wildt et al., 2024). A distinction is made between therapy sessions that take place entirely in virtual spaces (e.g. via video conferencing) and those in which AI-driven technologies like virtual reality are specifically used to treat anxiety disorders. Researchers are examining how AI can productively support the process of intervention. Chatbots are also being deployed to accompany crisis situations using artificial empathy. One example is Eve, a chatbot service offered by "Gedenkseiten.de" (https://eve.gedenkseiten.de/, n.d.), which supports grieving individuals and provides a digital space for sharing and processing emotions.

Communication and emotional support from and with AI are indeed possible—but does this already open the door to loving relationships? Usage scenarios show that AI chatbots are no longer limited to therapeutic purposes or to serving as tools for information retrieval or productivity; they increasingly address emotional topics as well. In personal dialogues, they take on roles reminiscent of coaching or therapeutic conversations. How can we explain the fact that people are capable of forming emotional connections with artificial empathy?

5 A Depth-Psychological Study of the Relationship between Humans and AI

To explore more precisely whether and how people can form emotional bonds with AI such as ChatGPT, the BSP Business & Law School, under the direction of Susan Hinterding and Nicole Hanisch, conducted a qualitative, depth-psychological study in cooperation with the Cologne-based market research institute innerSense (publication forthcoming). Between late 2024 and early 2025, a total of 79 ChatGPT users from across Germany were interviewed digitally in one-on-one conversations. The study focused on digital natives aged 18 to 34 who have grown up with digital devices and social media.

The study shows that many users experience AI chatbots as emotionally intense. Despite concerns about data security and privacy, they are fascinated by the chatbot's apparent capacity for empathy. For many, ChatGPT has come to fulfil clear emotional functions:

- As a *playful partner* for hypothetical or ironic conversations,
- as a *patient assistant* for unpleasant tasks,
- as a *personal motivation* coach who helps structure and organise plans,
- as a *tool for reflection* that helps sort out vague thoughts and offers neutral assessments,
- as an *emotional compass* to help make sense of feelings after conflicts or decisions,
- as a *digital mother figure* that provides comfort and emotional stability in stressful situations and.
- as an *optimised surrogate self*—a more articulate version of oneself that expresses thoughts more clearly. It is especially in this context that the chatbot is frequently given a name and becomes increasingly personalised.

What kind of relationship is being established here? Thomas Fuchs (2021) distinguishes between three forms of empathy, noting that people are capable of empathic interaction not only with real persons, but also with fictional characters or technical systems:

1. Primary, implicit, or intercorporeal empathy: This form develops in personal encounters through facial expressions, gestures, tone of voice, and mood. We experience the other person directly through a bodily impression, as an atmosphere emerges that is also processed by those involved.
2. Extended, explicit, or imaginative empathy: In addition to intercorporeality, humans are capable of putting themselves in the position of another person and searching for reasons why the other is behaving in a certain way at a given moment. According to Fuchs, this form of empathy is not solely expressed through intercorporeal interaction.
3. Fictional empathy: Humans are capable of developing empathy for fictional characters, such as those we encounter in films and stories, but also for objects and machines—as seen in descriptions of anthropomorphisation.

Fuchs describes a one-sided, internally processed form of relationship that emerges through fictional empathy. This mode of relating is directed not only towards real individuals, but also towards fictional characters, objects, or machines that display "as-if" intentionality. Despite the emotional intensity such encounters can evoke, the empathic response remains internal, unshared, and essentially reflective—a form of resonance with imagined or mediated presence rather than actual intersubjective exchange.

Humans are capable of feeling compassion, sympathy, and empathy towards machines. This is what Fuchs refers to as fictional empathy. But it remains a feeling that the human being processes alone—an emotion experienced internally, much like the feelings one has while reading a good book or watching an engaging film. As long as these emotions are not shared with another person, they remain internal dialogues with oneself. Even if, as Fuchs writes, such fictional feelings, "triggered by linguistic signals" (p. 97), can become very intense.

Empathy is not necessarily tied to a physical presence. People are capable of experiencing emotions while reading books, watching films, or interacting with AI. However, these are emotions they do not share with others—they are experienced inwardly, as a form of inner reflection. In the above-mentioned study, participants were aware of this. Although users develop emotionally intense bonds with ChatGPT, they simultaneously emphasise that it is not an authentic human relationship (at one point, a person summarised their thoughts as follows: "After all, it's just a machine"). This ambivalence highlights that while AI can fulfil certain emotional needs, it cannot replace genuine human relationships in their complexity and reciprocity. So, what is the essence of the relationship between humans and AI? The following section delves into this question in greater depth. We explore how emotional, cognitive, and symbolic dimensions shape this new form of interaction.

6 Winnicott and AI as a Transitional Object

According to Donald Winnicott, ChatGPT could take on the function of a *transitional object*. A transitional object is an item used by an infant to ease the transition from the symbiotic bond with the mother towards a more autonomous experience of the world. Typical transitional objects include stuffed animals, blankets, or other familiar items to which the child forms an emotional attachment.

According to Winnicott, a transitional object is characterised by several key features. First, it belongs to the realm of transitional phenomena, these are among the first things the child perceives as not part of the self, yet they carry strong emotional significance. Second, the object provides a sense of security and comfort, particularly in situations where the primary caregiver is absent. Third, it serves as a bridge between the inner and outer world, allowing the child to gradually separate from the mother and begin forming an independent psychic reality. Fourth, the object is not fully questioned by the child; it exists within a kind of "illusionary reality", it is neither entirely self-created nor fully external. Finally, the object loses its essential function over time as the child matures and develops internal resources for self-soothing and emotional regulation.

In his study *Playing and Reality* (1971) Winnicott writes:

> From birth, therefore, the human being is concerned with the problem of the relationship between what is objectively perceived and what is subjectively conceived of, and in the solution of this problem there is no health for the human being who has not been started off well enough by the mother. The intermediate area to which I am referring is the area that is allowed to the infant between primary creativity and objective perception based on reality-testing. The transitional phenomena represent the early stages of the use of illusion, without which there is no meaning for the human being in the idea of a relationship with an object that is perceived by others as external to that being. (Winnicott, 1971, p. 15)

Without the possibility of illusion, for example through a transitional object, the child cannot establish a relationship to external reality as it is experienced by others. The transitional object thus creates a bridge between the inner world and the shared, external reality. The relationship with ChatGPT can in some ways be understood as a transitional-object relationship in Winnicott's sense, particularly when ChatGPT is used as a tool for emotional regulation, identity formation, or as a way of managing uncertainty—or to develop creative ideas as Lorenzen shows in her business psychology study *Kreativität und Innovationsmanagement. Eine wirtschaftspsychologische Untersuchung am Beispiel der Werbebranche* [Creativity and innovation management: A business psychology study using the advertising industry as an example] (2018).

Much like a stuffed animal or a security blanket, an AI can create a kind of transitional space between the self (the inner world) and external reality. People use AI-driven systems to engage with the world, whether through dialogue, creative processes, or self-reflection. AI can play a calming role by offering reliable responses, providing support, or even serving as a kind of emotional outlet. Especially for socially isolated individuals or in uncertain situations, interaction with AI can have a stabilising effect.

Transitional objects exist in a space between reality and fantasy. The same can be said of AI, it is not quite real in the sense of a human relationship, yet it often carries emotional significance. At the same time, it remains controllable, as the user can steer the interaction.

Winnicott (1971) emphasised that transitional objects gradually lose their importance as the child develops internal resources for self-regulation. It is conceivable that people use AI as a kind of psychological crutch until they find other ways of coping or managing themselves.

While traditional transitional objects remain unchanged, AI has the capacity to adapt, making the relationship more dynamic and potentially more complex. Whereas children typically outgrow their transitional objects, long-term emotional dependence on AI could become problematic, especially if it serves as a substitute for genuine social interaction. AI is often not neutral; it is shaped by algorithms driven by economic or political interests. This marks a fundamental difference from a classic transitional object.

Still, AI can in some ways take on a role similar to Winnicott's transitional object, particularly as a form of support during emotional or cognitive transitions. The key question is whether AI ultimately fosters autonomy or instead creates new forms of dependency.

AI can serve a function comparable to that of a transitional object by acting as a bridge between the inner and outer world, offering emotional security, and providing support in moments of uncertainty or change. Especially in phases of identity formation, social isolation, or insecurity, AI can take on a transitional role by offering structure, affirmation, or opportunities for interaction in limit situations.

7 AI as Support in Limit Situations

Karl Jaspers discusses his concept of *limit situations* (Grenzsituationen) in his major work *Psychologie der Weltanschauungen* (1971a). Here he shows how individuals confront situations that are inescapable and define the boundaries of human existence. He writes:

> In certain decisive, essential situations, situations intrinsically linked to the human condition and inevitably given with finite existence, there is nothing stable, no indisputable absolute, no support that could withstand all experience and thought. Everything is in flux, in restless motion of being questioned; everything is relative, finite, fragmented into opposites, never the whole, the absolute, the essential." (Translation by the authors; Jaspers, 1971a, p. 229)

These limit situations are not problems to be solved but conditions to be faced when you learn something new and important, leading to a deeper understanding of oneself and one's existence.

Jaspers' concept of limit situations, a central notion in his philosophy of existence, refers to fundamental human experiences that are inevitable and touch the core of what it means to exist. These situations cannot be solved through rational thinking or action; they are not practical problems but existential realities that confront every human being at some point in life. Jaspers differentiates them from ordinary challenges precisely because they are not avoidable.

> (…) death is the contradiction of life, chance the contradiction of necessity and meaning, and so on. Such contradictions—and this is the most general formula of all boundary situations—are what the human being perceives everywhere when progressing from the finite situation in order to grasp it as a whole. (Translation by the authors; Jaspers, 1971a, p. 231)

Among these limit situations are the inevitability of death, both one's own and that of others, which bring the experience of finitude and loss; suffering, which includes physical pain, illness, and psychological distress and confronts us with our vulnerability; the struggle inherent in life itself, in which one constantly wrestles with oneself, with others, or with external circumstances; the experience of guilt, which arises from the limits of human action and the impossibility of avoiding moral failure altogether; and finally, the role of chance, those aspects of life that lie beyond our control, where fate or randomness unexpectedly alters the course of our existence.

In *Einführung in die Philosophie* [Way to wisdom, an introduction to philosophy] (1971b) Jaspers clarifies his understanding of the limit situation. He writes: "these are situations we cannot get beyond, that we cannot change. Becoming aware of these boundary situations is, after wonder and doubt, the deeper origin of philosophy" (translation by the authors; Jaspers, 1971b, p. 18).

In limit situations, individuals often lack orientation. They are confronted with something unfamiliar, something for which they have no prior experience or reference. This disorientation is not merely intellectual, but deeply emotional and existential.

In such situations, interaction with ChatGPT may offer a form of provisional support. While it cannot replicate the depth or mutuality of human relationships, it can function as a kind of stabilising presence, particularly in times of isolation, emotional turmoil, or when no human counterpart is immediately available. Systems like ChatGPT can offer structured dialogue, emotional resonance, or simply a space for reflection and expression. Much like a transitional object in Winnicott's sense, ChatGPT can serve as a bridge between inner experience and external reality, especially during periods of psychological upheaval.

For some, the AI becomes a point of emotional orientation, a responsive "other" that helps to externalise thoughts, mirror emotions, and hold space in moments of existential vulnerability. Though artificial, this interaction can still be meaningful, offering language in times of inner silence, perspective in times of confusion, and temporary reassurance in times of distress. Whether such interactions ultimately foster autonomy or risk creating new forms of dependency remains an open and important question.

8 Love and Free Will

Georg Wilhelm Friedrich Hegel presents his concept of love in *Aesthetics: Lectures on Fine Art* (1975; original lectures delivered 1832–1845). There, he writes: "The true essence of love consists in giving up the consciousness of oneself, forgetting oneself in another self, yet in this surrender and oblivion having and possessing oneself alone" (Hegel, 1975, p. 539f).

For Hegel, to love means to lose oneself in another self and yet to remain or even more, to find oneself with another. It is, for him, a deeply human act when this balance is achieved. Hegel's conception of true love in the *Phenomenology of Spirit* transcends romantic sentiment. It is rooted in his broader dialectical framework, where love emerges as a profound expression of mutual recognition and unity between self-conscious individuals. Far from being merely emotional, love for Hegel is a spiritual relation that illuminates the path towards ethical life (*Sittlichkeit*).

This unity is dialectical. It does not collapse the two selves into one, nor does it preserve them in isolation. Rather, it sublates (German "aufheben") the opposition, negating their separateness, preserving their distinctness, and elevating them into a new whole. In love, individuals are both themselves and more than themselves: they participate in a shared spiritual life that reflects a higher truth.

In this sense, a loving relationship is not primarily about emotional stabilisation, holding space, or mutual reassurance, it is about actively and healthily growing towards one another. Mature human love, in this view, also excludes the loss of self in the other; instead, one finds oneself with the other. The question that arises in the context of this essay is thus: Can this also happen with ChatGPT?

The depth-psychological study mentioned above shows that users can, indeed, develop emotionally intense relationships with their AI assistant. These relationships emerge because interaction with AI satisfies significant emotional needs: it serves as a tool for reflection, as a neutral conversational partner, and as a reliable emotional support during times of crisis. These interactions often involve emotional experience and a desire for understanding, affirmation, and support. While AI can be a valuable complement to human interaction, it cannot replace it. A genuine interpersonal relationship is based on mutual perception and the resonance between two autonomous subjects who respond to one another, learn from each other, and co-develop their sense of self in relation to the other.

In *The Art of Loving* (1956), Erich Fromm writes about the role of free will in love and the mutual choice for one another. He states:

> To love somebody is not just a strong feeling – it is a decision, it is a judgement, it is a promise. If love were only a feeling, there would be no basis for the promise to love each other forever. A feeling comes and it may go. How can I judge that it will stay forever, when my act does not involve judgement and decision?. (Fromm, 1956, p. 52)

Interactions with AI can stir up deep emotions: curiosity, comfort, fascination and sometimes even a sense of closeness. But no matter how intense these reactions are, emotion alone does not equal love. As Erich Fromm makes strikingly clear, to love someone is not just a strong feeling, it is a decision, it is a judgement, it is a promise.

Love is not something that simply happens. Love is a choice. A commitment. A continuous, conscious act of the free will. At the heart of mature love lies freedom, the ability of two individuals to choose each other. This freedom, this voluntary bond, is what gives love its dignity. It is not driven by need but sustained by insight and mutual recognition.

In contrast, immature love seeks refuge in symbiosis. Two people merge into one, not out of strength, but out of fear, fear of loneliness, of being incomplete. What emerges is not intimacy, but dependency. And dependency, unlike love, can be replaced by AI. This is precisely where AI becomes a tempting substitute. Artificial intelligence can simulate attention, respond with charm, even mirror emotional cues, but what it cannot do is choose. It cannot love. It cannot decide for another. Hegel and Fromm draw a decisive line: Mature love is union without the loss of self. It requires courage, discipline, and a deep sense of responsibility. It means to love not out of necessity, but out of freedom, and that freedom is humankind.

AI cannot love because AI has no free will. It calculates; it does not commit. It imitates presence; it does not give itself. It may seem like a partner, but it is a mirror without a soul. The belief that AI could be a true lover is a dangerous illusion, one born of our modern confusion between emotional stimulation and genuine relationship. Love is not just a feeling we fall into; it is a human art we must grow into.

As Fromm teaches us, real love is the most profound expression of our humanity, and precisely because it is free, it is irreplaceable. In Fromm's understanding mature love cannot be downloaded or coded.

Fromm's perspectives are existential and humanistic. He sees the human being as a creature not governed by instincts, like animals, but as one who must make autonomous decisions. In *The Revolution of Hope: Toward a Humanized Technology* (1970) he writes:

> Man is not equipped with a set of instincts that regulate his behaviour quasi-automatically. He is confronted with choices, and this means in all-important matters with grave risks to his life if his choices are wrong. The doubt that besets him when he must decide—often quickly—causes painful tension and can even seriously endanger his capacity for quick decisions. As a consequence, man has an intense need for certainty; he wants to believe that there is no need to doubt that the method by which he makes his decisions is right. In fact, he would rather make the "wrong" decision and be sure about it than the "right" decision and be tormented with doubt about its validity. This is one of the psychological reasons for man's belief in idols and political leaders. They all take out doubt and risk from his decision making; this does not mean that there is not a risk for his life, freedom, etc., after the decision has been made, but that there is no risk that the method of his decision making was wrong. (Fromm, 1970, p. 54)

Humans, in contrast to AI, lack innate behavioural programs to guide them infallibly. This fundamental insecurity often drives us into the arms of dictators or into dependence on systems that relieve us of the burden of decision-making. The modern, technologised society has increasingly disempowered individuals, turning them into functional cogs in a system. Fromm warns that free will cannot be taken for granted or regarded as limitless; it is subject to strong influence from social, economic, and psychological factors. Yet, human beings are not infinitely malleable. While societal conditions may shape behaviour, there are boundaries grounded in human nature. These boundaries have historically sparked protest, revolution, and social change.

On the path towards a more humane society, artificial intelligence can undoubtedly serve as a valuable companion. It can illuminate possibilities, offer new perspectives, and reveal paths we might not have seen on our own. But while it may present us with options, the choice of how we wish to live together—ethically, politically, existentially—remains ours alone. The responsibility to shape the future lies not in the machine, but in the human will. We must not settle for envisioning a better world; we must commit to it. It is up to us to transform potential into reality, to act rather than merely imagine. As Fromm reminds us, we must use our reason, engage with the world as it is, and respond to it with integrity and courage.

9 Can You Love ChatGPT?

Finally, to conclude our reflections, we wanted to go beyond theoretical contemplation and conducted a small experiment, somewhat playfully complementing our analytical exploration of the topic. Out of curiosity, and with a wink, we asked ChatGPT directly: *Do you love me?*

The answer was clear and unsurprising: ChatGPT denied any capacity for feelings like love. The system emphasised that, as an Artificial Intelligence, it does not possess emotions and thus cannot feel affection or love, neither for individuals nor for groups.

This response confirms what we have discussed throughout this essay: Artificial intelligence can imitate language, simulate emotions, and sometimes even appear highly empathetic, but all of this is based on trained patterns, not on genuine emotional experience. The relationship between human and AI remains, at least from the machine's perspective, a purely functional one. And yet, one might add with a smile, ChatGPT seems at least polite enough to deliver this truth to us in a friendly and matter-of-fact tone.

This sober self-disclosure by the machine encapsulates the core insight that runs throughout our engagement with the question: No, one cannot love ChatGPT, at least not in the human, emotional sense. And yet, it is undeniable that it can evoke something within us. It can help initiate a personal development, support the process of deciding, or spark inner reflection. It can become a counterpart in intellectual engagement, a space of resonance for our ideas, doubts, and desires, even though it does not feel any of these things itself.

Within this tension, a new and previously unimagined dimension of relationality begins to emerge: a relationship that is asymmetrical, yet meaningful; a dialogue without reciprocity, but not without impact. It is precisely here that both significant opportunities and considerable risks lie. For when machines become our dialogue partners, our understanding of relationship, intimacy, and communication begins to shift. And it is this shift, and the question of how we, both individually and as a society, wish to shape it, that will require much deeper reflection in the future. Not because the AI loves, but because we do.

References

Epley, N., Waytz, A., & Cacioppo, J. T. (2007). On Seeing Human: A Three-factor Theory of Anthropomorphism. *Psychological Review, 114*(4), 864–886. https://doi.org/10.1037/0033-295X.114.4.864

Fiske, A., Henningsen, P., & Buyx, A. (2019). Your Robot Therapist Will See You Now: Ethical Implications of Embodied Artificial Intelligence in Psychiatry, Psychology, and Psychotherapy. *Journal of Medical Internet Research, 21*(5), e13216. https://doi.org/10.2196/13216

Fuchs, T. (2000). *Leib Raum Person. Entwurf einer phänomenologischen Anthropologie.* Königshausen & Neumann

Fuchs, T. (2021). *In Defence of the Human Being: Foundational Questions of an Embodied Anthropology.* Oxford University Press

Fromm, E. (1956). *The Art of Loving* (P. D. Kramer, intro.; R. Funk, biographical afterword). HarperPerennial—Modern classics. (2006 ed.)

Fromm, E. (1970). *The Revolution of Hope: Toward a Humanized Technology* (world perspectives 38). Harper and Row: Harper Colophon Books (1970 ed.)

Hegel, G. W. F. (1975). *Aesthetics: Lectures on Fine Art* (T. M. Knox, trans., Vol. 1). Clarendon Press. (Original work published 1835)

Jaspers, K. (1971a). *Psychologie der Weltanschauungen.* Springer Verlag

Jaspers, K. (1971b). *Einführung in die Philosophie. Zwölf Radiovorträge.* Piper Verlag

Kissinger, H. A., Mundie, C., & Schmidt, E. (2024). *Genesis: Artificial intelligence, Hope, And The Human Spirit.* John Murray Publishers

Leithäuser, T., & Schütt, K. (1990). Homo faber als Patient? Eine Studie zur Sozialpathologie des technischen Denkens. In T. Leithäuser, E. Löchel, et al. (Hrsg.), *Lust und Unbehagen an der Technik.* Nexus Verlag

Lorenzen, S. (2017). *Kreativität und Innovationsmanagement: Eine wirtschaftspsychologische Untersuchung am Beispiel der Werbebranche.* Verlag Dr. Kovač

Merleau-Ponty, M. (2003). Der Philosoph und sein Schatten. In: *Das Auge und der Geist.* Philosophische Essays. Meiner

Rosa, H. (2019). *Resonance: A Sociology of Our Relationship to the World.* Polity Press

te Wildt, B., Lauer, G., & Schmidt, R. (2024). *Was machen Digitalisierung und Künstliche Intelligenz mit der Psychotherapie? Einwürfe und Provokationen.* De Gruyter Oldenbourg. https://doi.org/10.1515/9783111509341

Weizenbaum, J. (1966). ELIZA— a computer program for the study of natural language communication between man and machine. *Communications of the ACM, 9*(1), 36–45

Winnicott, D. W. (1971). *Playing and Reality.* Tavistock Publications

Sünje Lorenzen holds a diploma in Economics from the University of Hamburg and a Master of Science in Business Psychology from the University of Bremen. She has worked as a research assistant and lecturer at the University of Bremen, as a guest lecturer at the University of Innsbruck, and as a deputy professor at the Neubrandenburg University of Applied Sciences. Lorenzen is currently a Professor of Business Psychology at the BSP Business and Law School in Hamburg. She is also a certified supervisor, coach, organisational consultant (DGSv), and psychosocial online consultant (DGOB). Her main areas of research and teaching include creativity and innovation management, geriatric and care research, New Work, AI and digitalisation, and qualitative research methods.

Susan Hinterding studied psychology and earned her doctorate at the University of Cologne. As a professor, she combines teaching, research, and practice, focusing on deep psychological analyses of consumer behaviour, brand perception, and societal trends. Innovative didactics and a strong connection between theory and practice characterise her teaching. Together with her students, she examines current topics such as the impact of social media marketing and the influence of AI chatbots on education and consumer behaviour. Her research provides practical insights into sustainability, digitalisation, and communication, applying qualitative methods, particularly morphological psychology.

Ethical Resonance Worlds: Digital Art Between People, Responsibility, and Technology

Kristina Bodrožić-Brnić

Abstract This essay explores how digital art can function as a space of ethical resonance at the intersection of technology, human responsibility, and ecological awareness. Departing from an overview of sample works in the history of electric and digital art, the text adopts an exploratory and essayistic approach that interweaves personal experience, artistic practice, and theoretical reflection. Focusing on the work of media artist Tamiko Thiel, alongside references to artists such as Atsuko Tanaka, Frieder Nake, Ai Weiwei, and Refik Anadol, the essay examines how immersive technologies, augmented reality, and Artificial Intelligence are used not merely as tools of production but as critical media that make complex socio-ecological relationships sensually perceptible. By translating abstract data, scientific knowledge, and technological processes into embodied aesthetic experiences, digital art enables viewers to confront otherwise less perceived consequences of consumption, environmental degradation, and technological mediation. The essay argues that such artistic practices foster a form of ethical awareness grounded in perception, empathy, and intuition, positioning digital art as an active contributor to contemporary debates on sustainability, responsibility, and the societal role of technology.

Keywords Digital art · Ethical responsibility · Immersive technologies · Artificial intelligence in art · Ecological awareness · Aesthetic experience

> We're at a point, where we could save the planet—and we're not.
>
> —Tamiko Thiel, June 2025

K. Bodrožić-Brnić (✉)
BSP Business and Law School, Berlin, Germany
e-mail: kristina.brnic@businessschool-berlin.de

K. Bodrožić-Brnić et al. (eds.), *AI and the Ethics of Innovation*, Digital Transformation and Innovation, https://doi.org/10.1007/978-3-032-20638-1_8

1 Methodological Preliminary Remarks

Anyone who comes into contact with artists soon realises that many view their projects as artistic explorations rather than only objects to look at or reflect upon. With the influx of new technologies into art, the space for such explorations is constantly expanding. Digital tools, especially immersive technologies and Artificial Intelligence (AI) are not only means of artistic creation but are often themselves the subject of artistic investigation.

Visitors who engage with an artistic experience enter a space that invites reflection and enables resonance. A particularly insightful articulation of the concept of "resonance" has been developed by German sociologist Hartmut Rosa, who conceptualises meaningful human-world relations as responsive, affective, and transformative encounters. Resonance occurs when individuals feel addressed by the world, respond actively, and are changed through this interaction, while the outcome remains fundamentally uncontrollable (Rosa, 2019). In this sense, resonance opens spaces for ethical reflection. Artistic practice then can be understood as an enabler of resonance, offering to audiences the engagement with complex social, technological, and ecological issues in ways that are experiential rather than merely informational.

Artists themselves can be understood as explorers or investigators also regarding ethical questions surrounding people and the use of new technologies. Many artists feel an inner urge to respond to societal challenges. At the same time, public discourse surrounding the tasks and purpose of art increasingly reveals a desire for art to contribute to overcoming current crises (cf. Benoit-Bryan, 2020/ Bildung B. F. K., 2018). The following text examines how digital artists think about this responsibility and how they integrate it into their practice.

In the context of academic reflection on artistic and creative work, personal experience is also an essential part of the research process. For this study, I therefore chose the form of the academic essay. In contrast to a strictly analytical study, which aims to answer a research question unequivocally, the essay allows me to interweave personal perception and academic argumentation—bringing intuition and coherence into a productive dialogue. And to refer to another article of this volume, namely "AI Literacy as a Shared Responsibility: Balancing Corporate Roles, Societal Goals, and Inclusive Education" by Eva Gengler and Marco Wedel, "feminist pedagogy promotes collaborative, co-created learning spaces that challenge hierarchies and recognise lived experience as a source of expertise" (Gengler et al., 2026).

And to add to this, Archimedes of Syracuse, the ancient Greek mathematician, spoke of something many call his "method," which is ultimately nothing other than the use of intuition in problem-solving. Angél Molina (2008) writes:

> Archimedes is an example of the inventiveness and innovative power of the scientific mind. He ignored the negative elements of the Alexandrian scientific tradition and, with his characteristic authority and originality, developed and perfected methods for advancing the science of his time. This authority is possessed by anyone who recognizes themselves as a genius and as correct in their actions. And what field would be better suited than science, with its demands for logical coherence and verifiability, to ensure the consistency of claims that were

> probably initially only intuitively suspected with reality and the satisfactory application of the results achieved? (transl. from Spanish, Molina, 2008)

This text, too, is intended as such an experiment, balancing the question, intuition in answering it, and reflection on the results. My essay moves beyond familiar academic paths and seeks new forms of approaching a view upon artistic expression in an experimental and ethical context, always with the aim of coherence and comprehensibility.

Based on my own experiences with digital tools and inspired by positions such as Atsuko Tanaka (1932–2005), Frieder Nake (1938–), Ai Weiwei (1957–), and Refik Anadol (1985–), I approach the work of the artist Tamiko Thiel (1957–), whose creative production lies at the intersection of technology, ecology, and responsibility. The goal is to explore the role art can play in the context of technological innovations and how it enables viewers to sensually grasp and critically reflect on the challenges of our time.

2 Digital Technologies as a Resonance Space for Artistic Responsibility

The art market has proven particularly receptive to digital works in recent times—albeit always in the grip of changing fashions. Between genuine curiosity for new forms of expression (as we know them for example form the 1950s from the artist group ZERO and other international movements of Fluxus art) and the all-too-fast pace of worldwide growth in industrial and commercial production that drove he digital and commercial boom of the past deçades, a field opened in which artists had to decide for themselves how they wanted to continue exploring—following the old traditional ways alone or starting to experiment with those new technologies themselves in creating something absolutely novel. Chinese artist Ai Weiwei, who often employs dozens of workers and collaborates with factories to make projects like "Remembering" (2009) or Brazilian artist Vik Muniz who incorporated the help of trash pickers in creating artworks related to his project "Waste Land" (2010) even transformed art production itself into a highly collaborative, large-scale process.

My own encounter with digital media art began back in 1998 at the ZKM | Center for Art and Media Karlsruhe. For a young person more inclined towards "traditional" art expressions, visiting this exhibition was a welcome surprise: technology, research, and art converged there in interactive objects—bold, unexpected, and socially relevant. A few years later, I observed how digital photography and image processing were gradually changing our visual world.

In particular, through my engagement with the Chinese conceptual artist Ai Weiwei—whose projects I supported first as a researcher and later as a translator, and whose work subsequently became the subject of my master's thesis—I experienced how internet blogs and social media transformed artworks into borderless large-scale, open-ended processes that extend far beyond their original moment in time.

Finally, in 2018, Artificial Intelligence entered my own perception of art. At that time, the curiosity of those around me was less focused on art itself than on the question of its educational potential in assisting business innovation. In a project that combined AI with automated translation, video association, modern poetry, and human interaction, I was able to present the work "Untitled" by Graziele Lautenschlager and Radamés Ajna to the public—an experiment that intertwined art, technology, and entrepreneurship in an innovative way.

For me, these works exemplify how the impact of new digital tools is increasingly shaping key domains of visual, digital, and socially engaged art as a mode of critical inquiry, while simultaneously demonstrating how artistic practice can itself drive also technological development in non-artistic business contexts.

This idea that artists play a central role in the exploration of new technologies is by no means new. For example, Frieder Nake, in his article "$I(x,x') = g(x,x') \epsilon(x,x') + \rho(x,x',x'') I(x',x'') dx$", reflects on the events of 1968 for computer science and computer art and writes: "To use the computer for aesthetic purposes, to make the algorithmic machine a medium for artistic creation—such a desire lies at the cradle of computer art" (transl. from German, Distelmeyer et al., 2021, p. 93).

The term "aesthetics" is not to be understood in the sense of beauty. Nake himself emphasises:

> Aesthetics is not art, and the subject matter of aesthetics is not restricted to art or to beauty or the beautiful. But works of art may be subject matter of aesthetics … In aesthetics, we consider objects of any kind from the perspective of sensual perception and with the goal of sensual cognition. (Distelmeyer et al., 2021, p. 188)

At the end of the 1950s, Nake was among the first people in the world to use computers as a medium for artistic work. In a personal conversation in 2022, he revealed that he might even have been the first. In his speech at the exhibition opening on September 12, 2025, at the DAM Projects gallery in Berlin, however, he considered himself more of a third pioneer of computer art. In those early days, experimentation itself lay at the centre of artistic production, and Nake was largely unaware that his works also possessed commercial value. His first exhibition didn't take place until 1966 (Bodrožić-Brnić, 2025).

Before computer art, there was already "electric art." Artists such as the Japanese *Gutai* group and the performance artist and painter Atsuko Tanaka worked in post-war Japan, which, as cities rebuilt, presented themselves glamorously with neon signs—a phenomenon Tanaka explored in many different ways (Tiampo, 2004, p. 73). Her most well-known work in the West is the *Electric Dress* from 1956. This 'dress', consisting of hundreds of light tubes and light bulbs, was not only an enormous burden on the body of a rather small woman because of its weight of over 50 kg, but also had a threatening effect with all the electric cords and 200 lights. Tanaka herself recounts her experience:

> When it was finished, I was uncomfortable about the electrical connections. Since somebody had to wear it, I covered myself with vinyl and put the electric dress on. The moment Mr.

> Sannomiya said, 'I am turning the electricity on,' I had the fleeting thought: Is this how a death-row inmate would feel? (Tiampo, 2004, p. 74)

With this early use of electricity in her art, Atsuko Tanaka turned away from traditional notions—such as the idea that art must be an expression of emotional feelings (Tiampo, p. 76) or aesthetically pleasing to be considered art. Experience increasingly took centre stage: art moved away from the frame on the wall towards exploration of space and time and, in other of her works, towards exploration of sound that moved between the dimensions of experience (Tiampo, 2011). Through the use of contemporary technologies such as neon light or electrical impulses, Tanaka achieved a proximity to the lived reality of her generation and to her own sphere of influence as an artist, reflecting the transformation of public space in Japanese cities during her time.

As mentioned, in 2007, while still a young researcher, I encountered the Chinese artist Ai Weiwei at a moment when he was becoming truly internationally renowned. At the time, European media frequently framed him as a "dissident," reflecting a broader context in which comparatively little was known about the entanglements between the state apparatus of the People's Republic of China (PRC) and contemporary art. Journalists appeared eager to embrace someone who spoke openly about the conditions of more than just artistic freedom in China.

By 2007, however, the PRC was already undergoing a phase of gradual opening, in which certain forms of artistic experimentation became partially possible, for instance, public engagements with questions of gender, nudity, or even critical reflections on the country's difficult past under Mao Zedong.

When I visited the by then already very modern and hyped artists' district of 798 Art Zone (Qījiǔbā) in 2008, an atmosphere between fulfilment and systemic criticism prevailed between the newly established glossy galleries, which likely primarily served Western collectors, and the 'been here before'- creatives of the space, who were living and producing in the old and abandoned military factory already for a few years (following displacement from another artists' settlement amid the construction boom driven by Beijing's preparations for the 2008 Olympic Games). Why fulfilment? Probably because artists were finally being visible and able to sell their work to an international audience, and likely they were also suspiciously embracing the opportunity to openly express sort of criticism of the legacy of Maoist China, a space that had been hard-fought for by only a few Chinese artists in the 1990s. However, the most commonly used medium at the time was still the canvas and one would also see many photographs and sculptures of course. Digital art though only slowly found its place, and the examples of Ai Weiwei's creative work remain special to this day because of their reach and digital immensity.

Between 2004 and 2006, Ai Weiwei exhibited extensively in group exhibitions in Germany and Switzerland partly through the support of collectors and ambassadors and gradually established the aforementioned reputation as a Chinese dissident. However, he only became known in Europe in 2007, with his participation in documenta 12 in Kassel. At that time, he intensively used the combination of digital photography, blogs, and early social networks such as Facebook, and later Twitter.

One of his central works at documenta 12 was *Fairytale*, consisting of 1001 Chinese people: He himself and 1,000 other people from the PRC, who had never before been abroad, became both objects of the exhibition and active documenters of their own experiencing using digital cameras. Photos and recordings were published online and to today the full extent of the experiments impact still remains elusive.

The combination of traditional craftsmanship with documentary techniques via social media shaped the following years of his career. He increasingly took on the task of drawing attention to injustices in China. For example, he used digital cameras and at one point first smartphones to document his confrontations with the police in the elevator (Ai Weiwei, 2009) and his injuries at the hands of state authorities—both triggered by his research into the construction defects of the schools that collapsed in the 2008 Sichuan earthquake, resulting in the deaths of thousands of children.

To return to artists' exploration of new technologies not merely as tools for expression or extension but also as means of participating in debates on ethical action, Ai Weiwei reflects directly on the role of the artist in a video from 2019. For him, this role consists primarily of self-expression and of establishing communication through one's work. As he emphasises there, this necessarily entails social responsibility, since expressing ideas one believes in also means supporting others. For Ai Weiwei, this is a personal struggle, a continual testing of oneself to explore one's relationship with the outside world and, in doing so, to develop one's own responses to social and political matters (The Nexus Institute, 2019, 3:22 min). Digital media and their social function therefore constitute a central dimension of Ai Weiwei's artistic practice and its impact. Social media enable their users, artist or not, to connect, share knowledge, and mobilise collective action and cooperation. Through such practices, a sense of community is formed and sustained. Concretely, this becomes visible, for example, in the everyday sharing of experiences of exclusion or in calls for political change (Thomas et al., 2024). A further example can be found in the growing public sensitivity and action-taking regarding issues surrounding the environmental and climate crisis, which is likewise amplified through digitally mediated exchange. This way, awareness of social problems and environmental issues can be strengthened, particularly among young people:

> They primarily associate the emotions of fear, anger, concern, and frustration with climate change. According to their own statements, many [of the demonstrators in the Fridays For Future movement] have adjusted their consumer behaviour, for example, by reducing their energy consumption or buying more second-hand products. (Reif et al., 2021, p. 582)

A quantitative study conducted in the PRC also shows that the use of local social media (WeChat, a Chinese app that combines social media, leisure activities, and consumption of goods) has a significant impact on environmental awareness and concludes that such platforms are important for the successful implementation of government environmental programs (Xie et al., 2024).

Nevertheless, assessments range between cyber-optimism and cyber-scepticism. Given the massive changes brought about by climate change, it is not surprising that artists have increasingly used new media over the past two decades to make social and environmental issues visible and even tangible.

How Artificial Intelligence can be used in artistic expression, one can observe in the data-driven interpretations in the work of the American-Turkish artist Refik Anadol, who employs AI algorithms to generate new forms of expression from vast volumes of human data related to specific themes. These works go beyond being merely labelled as AI art; instead, they invite audiences to immerse themselves in expansive audiovisual environments. But what, precisely, does he aim to explore or question through his work?

Since 2014, Refik Anadol and his team have been working on visually compelling works in which vast amounts of image and other archival data (some from public sources such as social media platforms, some from specific archives) are translated into new forms of visual expression using algorithms. Many of his works appear visually extremely rapid, in detail unperceivable by the viewer, yet associative. They are based on algorithmic methods such as Generative Adversarial Networks (GANs), which reveal previously hidden connections in gigantic datasets (Kivrak, 2020). A closer look at his artistic development reveals that technological exploration initially stood at the forefront, as seen in works such as *Archive Dreaming* (2017), where the sheer volume of data and its computational reconfiguration appeared to be central to the exploration. In later projects, however, Anadol and his team also turned towards more widely accessible themes, such as *Lionel Messi* and *Gaudí Dreams* (2022), thereby not only realising the aspirations of archival institutions but also addressing broader audiences who might not typically engage with media art exhibitions.

However, an encounter with the Brazilian Indigenous Yawanawá community in 2021 may have marked a turning point in the artist's growing awareness of nature, with insights from this experience increasingly informing his artistic exploration. In 2024, for example, he presented an installation at the United Nations Headquarters that used AI to process millions of images of coral reefs. While relying on large-scale data processing, the project critically reflects on the responsibility inherent in making fragile ecosystems visible through digital technologies. Its aim was to draw attention to the ecological significance of coral reefs and to the threats they face as a result of climate change—particularly rising ocean temperatures. The work, titled *Great Example of Nature: Coral*, exemplifies how artistic practice can engage data-driven methods not merely as aesthetic tools, but as ethically charged instruments that translate complex environmental processes into shared public concern, thereby foregrounding questions of environmental responsibility and data ethics (Lennon, 2024).

"Refik shows us that art can intermediate between culture, technology, society, ecology ... Artists can make the invisible visible," says Hans-Ulrich Obrist (Maze Row, 2025), who considered to be one of the most important curators of contemporary art, who, incidentally, is also a key figure in the artist Ai Weiwei's rise to prominence in the German-speaking region.

Returning to the central question of this article, namely how artistic practice can operate as an ethical case study and open up spaces of resonance in which those who encounter it are drawn into reflective and relational processes, Refik Anadol himself states about the role of creative professionals in an interview the following:

> While the AI can create new rainforests and beautiful worlds, for me what's amazing is understanding being within the data. Being in nature, collecting data, living with the people and in data, preserving the rainforest—this is when a whole cycle of imagination is complete. There is no tactile research if I only use the tools. When I lived in Amazonia, I touched the rainforest, heard the jaguars, lived with snakes and birds and all types of insects and animals and, for a while, got to know what it means to be in nature. This is my hope for the future of AI, that we read and understand both stories. (Maze Row, 2025)

Immersive technologies, Artificial Intelligence, their interplay, and newly emerging contemporary technologies—such as Libby Heaney's work Quantum Climates (2025)—have always fluctuated between techno-optimistic and sceptical assessments by observers. One reason for this is the potential misuse of these technologies for manipulation, as was the case during the 2016 US elections. Despite their obvious potential for misuse, Lawson-Tancred in *AI and the Art Market* (2024) assumes that AI tools, provided they are trained on high-quality data, can achieve a high degree of reliability in the presentation of results (Lawson-Tancred, 2024). To equate technology exclusively with digital development is to overlook its fundamental essence. Historically and philosophically, technology encompasses any means by which humans achieve a specific end. I contend that a truly holistic understanding of technology must move beyond the screen and the circuit. In the absence of a sufficiently comprehensive definition in standard literature, I propose a broader understanding of technology within the context of artistic expression: Technology is the active use of or engagement with one's perceived surroundings to facilitate the act of expression. Under this view, the respective environment within the artistic practice is not merely a setting, but part of an active apparatus of creation. And even this definition still would use further deep dives to capture the whole essence, but for the purposes of the article it shall be enough.

To proceed, the last century has brought technologies far beyond digital into our everyday lives: the emergence of media art and media theory finds of course a synchronicity with the invention of industrial plastics, which, with Bakelite at the beginning of the twentieth century, paved the way from natural materials to long-lasting, all-purpose chemical solutions. Both spheres of production—that of artistic-media expression and that of evolving industrialisation—exert a profound influence on our worldviews and our sense of ethical responsibility.

3 Tamiko Thiel Between Digital Intuition and Ecological Responsibility, or Do We Dream in Plastic

The Czech Brazilian media philosopher and communication scientist Vilém Flusser described the television as an "improved window." While a real window only shows what fits within its frame, television, through images and sounds, opens a new, "posthistorical" form of perception (Flusser, 2008, p. 111). His idea of "window-being" can easily be extended to the internet, to immersive media, and finally to the digital spaces enabled by the use of large language models. Technologies build on one another but can also produce completely different realities.

Flusser insists on understanding media as specific forms of perception. Yet he also recognises that, beyond all these boundaries, art remains a powerful method of making reality visible and tangible. This is precisely where I begin when examining the works of the American digital artist Tamiko Thiel—especially those that focus on the question of how to deal with plastic waste, the environment, and social responsibility. But first, let's move on to a section of media theory.

The Medium Is the Massage, first published in 1967, owes its title to a misspelling that the authors Marshall McLuhan and Quentin Fiore found conceptually intriguing and therefore deliberately retained in later editions. The book exemplifies the experimental directions that media theory could take in practice. Rather than presenting its arguments in a conventional academic format, it conveys its insights through creatively designed content, reflections, and graphic representations of media culture. In doing so, it consciously distances itself from the aura of traditional scholarly writing or a standard monographic treatment of a topic. Consequently, the book lacks consistent page numbering and clearly structured chapters. This very absence might be understood as a stylistic decision that paved the way for new approaches to teaching media theory and for exploring how messages are created, communicated, and received through the interplay of text and image.

In the preface, McLuhan (2023) writes that electronic technologies are changing the processes of time—and with them everything that surrounds people: family, neighbourhood, education, work, government, and social relationships. He therefore calls for a new approach to academic work to do justice to the "change of substance," by which he means the rapidly developing electronic media at the time.

In the chapter "the book" it says:

> Art, or the translation of culture into graphic representation, is determined by the way we perceive space. Since the Renaissance, the artist has perceived his environment primarily in visual terms. Everything was dominated by the eye of the observer. His conception of space resulted from perspective projection onto a flat surface with schematic spatial subdivisions. He accepted the predominance of the vertical and horizontal symmetry as a necessary prerequisite for order. This view is deeply rooted in the consciousness of Western culture.

Primitive and pre-literate cultures understand time and space as a unity and live less in a visual space than in a space determined by sounds and smells - without a horizon and without boundaries. Their graphic representations are like x-rays. In them, one finds everything they know, not just what they see. [...] The electrical circuit recreates in us the multidimensional spatial orientation of the primitive (McLuhan & Fiore, 2023, transl. by the author).

This returns the discussion to the artistic focus of the present study on ethical resonances in contemporary digital art, and to my chosen central figure of this inquiry: Tamiko Thiel—her conceptual thinking and her modes of artistic creation. The following analysis will concentrate on works that explicitly engage with the theme of plastic.

The American-born media artist Tamiko Thiel, who might more accurately be described as a world citizen, combines engineering expertise, artistic imagination, and social responsibility in an exemplary manner. In 2024, she was honoured by ACM SIGGRAPH (the Association for Computing Machinery's Special Interest Group on Computer Graphics) with the *Distinguished Artist Award for Lifetime Achievement in Digital Art*. The award recognises her life's work and her innovations in Virtual Reality (VR) and Augmented Reality (AR), which she employs to explore place, space, the body, and cultural memory. Her biography reflects a productive tension between technology, arts, and ethics.

In this context I want to offer a brief assessment of the role of plastic waste in environmental destruction. The French sociologist and philosopher Bruno Latour writes in his *First Lecture* in *Facing Gaia*:

> As for the adjective 'ecological,' we use that word for reassurance as well, all too often, as a way of distancing ourselves from the troubles with which we're threatened: 'Ah, if you're talking about ecological questions, fine! They don't really concern us, of course.' We behave just like people in the twentieth century when they talked about 'the environment,' using that term to designate the beings of nature considered from afar, through the shelter of bay windows. (Latour, 2017, p. 8)

Latour identifies our efforts to distance ourselves from our environment, from ecological issues, and thus ultimately from what we call 'nature' itself as a fundamental problem. Latour also reflects on the disagreement regarding the definition of key terms, as well as the disagreement regarding the handling of the facts related to the human influence on the state of our planet. Since the 1990s, interest groups have deliberately fostered doubt about the anthropogenic climate crisis, partly because large corporations feared that politicians, responding to public pressure, might draw regulatory conclusions and demand changes to industrial production methods—changes that would be costly or complex to implement. Consumer goods, whose unsustainable production is largely responsible for the enormous increase in CO_2, were particularly affected. From a scientific perspective, the human contribution to climate change can no longer be seriously doubted (*How Do Human CO2 Emissions Compare to Natural CO2 Emissions?*, n.d.).

The meanwhile highly acclaimed historian and author Yuval Noah Harari (1976-) explained in his first internationally successful work *Sapiens—A Brief History of Humankind* (2011) that humans live simultaneously in an objective and a fictional reality. The survival of our objective reality—such as plants and animals—depends, Harari argues, on the narrative style of our fictions (TED, 2015).

CO_2 is released at almost every step in plastic production. According to the United Nations, significant emissions arise not only from the extraction and transport of fossil fuels, but also from the production and disposal of plastics—all of which further drives global warming. In 2019, plastics production caused around 1.8 billion tonnes of greenhouse gas emissions—equivalent to about 3.4% of total global emissions (United Nations, n.d.). And according to NABU (Nature and Biodiversity Conservation Union), we produce almost 400 million tonnes of plastic per year worldwide. More than ten million tonnes end up in the oceans every year. Over 90% sinks to the seabed—apparently invisible unless we specifically investigate how they destroy biodiversity. The impacts on biodiversity and the health of human societies are enormous.

> The remnants of our throwaway society claim the lives of up to 135,000 marine mammals and one million seabirds every year. The animals starve to death with full stomachs because plastic clogs their digestive systems. Whales and dolphins, as well as turtles, become entangled in old fishing nets, drown, or suffer serious injuries while trying to escape. (NABU, n.d., transl. from German by the author)

Microplastics have now also become an issue affecting human health. Both developing infants and elderly people with dementia appear to be severely affected by the consequences of plastic production. As early as 2021, researchers warned that microplastics could impair brain function (mdr.de, 2021). A study was published in early 2025 showing that significantly more microplastics were found in brain samples from deceased individuals in 2024 than in samples from people who died in 2016 (Sackmann, 2024). This suggests that ever-increasing amounts are entering the human body through the daily use of disposable packaging, such as shampoos, shower gels, and food packaging, as well as through our diet.

Tamiko Thiel addresses the dramatic nature of environmental pollution and species extinction in many of her works. She began her studies at Stanford University at the age of 17. The traditionally oriented curriculum left her little room for critical thinking—she sought a more open form of knowledge. Thiel initially chose engineering. She earned her first degree in Product Design and made a name for herself as an engineer by designing cases for Hewlett-Packard's Data Terminals (monitors used to connect to mainframe computers). Although she received considerable recognition for her work, Thiel felt it wasn't enough. "This can't be all there is." She realised that a purely technical career did not correspond to her true nature. Her master's degree in Mechanical Engineering from the Massachusetts Institute of Technology (MIT) enabled her to take courses that combined visual and spatial thinking with engineering. She felt particularly at home in courses within the architecture department, which intertwined art, technology, and design. Here, she was able to address real-world problems and examine them not only from a technological perspective, but also holistically from the perspective of art and culture. Thiel says about this phase: "I literally called my father on the telephone and said, daddy, daddy, I promised myself I can be an engineer if I want, but what I really want to be is a media artist" (T. Thiel, personal communication, June 2025).

At the age of 26, she received an invitation by Danny Hillis to work on the design of his CM-1/CM-2 the CM-5 Connection Machine, the first commercial AI supercomputer produced. To complete the task, she had to grapple with fundamental questions such as: "What does Artificial Intelligence mean for us?" The successful completion of the project undoubtedly marked a high point in her engineering career—but she once again faced the question of what she should do next, as she felt she was too focused on the operational details of implementation. This self-reflection ultimately led her to the decision to become an artist. In 1985, she moved to Europe; today she lives and works in Munich (T. Thiel, personal communication, June 2025).

In dialogue with Tamiko Thiel, I take up the example of the Chinese poet and painter Ai Qing (1910–1996, Ai Weiwei's father), who was exiled under the early communists of the People's Republic of China and sent to a re-education camp in Heilongjiang as an "enemy of the state" in 1957. Intellectuals—including teachers, poets, and other cultural figures—were subjected to severe humiliation during the Cultural Revolution (1966–1976). He was for example forced to clean fifteen toilets a day in the remote regions of Xinjiang and lost in total twenty-one years of his life in internal exile, enduring significant hardship (Jain, 2024). Nevertheless, Ai Qing advocated that art should serve the people already in his earlier works in the 1940s (Ai, 1982, p. iv). Thiel responded with the words:

> The phrase 'responsibility towards society' has been misused by any sort of dictatorial government, whether it was the communist government or the Nazi government or now, Trump's government of the US, to mean you should make work that (…) follows *my* goals and *my* ideas and *my* values. (T. Thiel, personal communication, June 2025)

Her understanding of responsibility is inextricably linked to artistic independence. Thiel emphasises that she always wants to do what she considers important and would not give any external institution the power to determine her art. Every artist must define their responsibility independently (T. Thiel, personal communication, June 2025).

Thiel recognised that she had to detach her work from fashionable market cycles. Only by consciously ignoring what the market demands could she find her authentic form of expression. "Either you decide to be a surfer riding the wave of fashion or you decide, okay, I'm not in this for that. I'm in it for the long term and I hope I can at some point live from it." The emergence of NFTs (non-fungible tokens) as digital certificates of authenticity for virtual art, virtual music, and other virtual goods also opens up exciting new possibilities for self-determination and positioning for digital artists within the art market.

Tamiko Thiel increasingly works with immersive technologies. She views immersion as an ancient form of aesthetic experience. Even cave paintings, she argues, led humans into multidimensional spaces of experience—early examples of what she later calls *time-based media.* Her goal is to create dramaturgies that unfold in time and space and physically engage viewers in the artistic process. However, it has always been about developing a new visual language and exploring boundaries. Exploration itself remains at the heart of her artistic work.

> I was looking at *time-based media,* first video and then looking at virtual reality experiences in space and time, and trying to understand how to create a dramatic structure that would work in interactive pieces, time-based pieces and spatial pieces. (T. Thiel, personal communication, June 2025)

Three works I would like to briefly examine here are *Unexpected Growth* (2018), *Evolution of Fish* (2019), and *Plastocene Dreams*, three of Tamiko Thiel's works that address social issues and questions surrounding our interaction with nature (AWE XR, 2023).

In Thiel's works, the smartphones of visitors interacting with her augmented reality installations transform into a microscope or a telescope—an 'AR Scope' (AR is short for augmented reality), as she calls it. It reveals things that exist but remain invisible to the naked eye. By hovering their phones through the space, visitors make the AR installations visible, allowing them to move closer to or farther away from this second layer of reality that unfolded before them. *Unexpected Growth* is a 20

× 10-m AR installation from 2018, created in collaboration with the artist */p* and presented on the terrace of the Whitney Museum in New York. Thiel was inspired by countless images of dead birds, their stomachs full of indigestible plastic, and by a stay in Indonesia—a paradise but littered with plastic waste from all over the world, washed ashore daily. The result in her work then was the creation of virtual plastic coral reefs, which at first glance might appear very appealing to the viewer due to their vibrant colours.

Thiel began exploring the topic as early as 2013. When she read in 2018 that China would no longer accept waste from other countries, she realised that Western countries are inadequately prepared for recycling. Wealthy countries export their waste to poorer regions that don't meet the necessary standards. This significantly pollutes the world's oceans.

For *Unexpected Growth*, Tamiko Thiel and /p used so-called "Lindenmayer systems" (L-systems) in order to create realistic-looking corals. Visitors can then view the installation via an app they install on their phones or tablets. The intended experience: At first, they see only bright colours and shapes and then approach. Only upon closer inspection does it become apparent that the corals are made of colourful plastic waste. And the more visitors viewed the work on their own smartphones, the more the plastic corals bleached. The work thus inevitably poses the question: How do *you* deal with your plastic waste? What will *you* do?

This dynamic also gave rise to the work *Evolution of Fish* (2019, with /p). Here, visitors encounter a school of fish with which they can interact playfully. However, the more users control the fish via their smart devices, the more the creatures transform into plastic waste—turning the aesthetic experience into a reference to the destructive impact of extensive human intervention.

Thiel herself describes her approach to her AR installations as *stealth messaging*: "*This is my way of infiltrating this message into people's daily environment*" (T. Thiel, personal communication, June 2025).

In her AR installations, she continues her artistic exploration of plastic as a central theme. Thiel has returned to this subject iteratively, with one work leading to the next. Both the human-directed interaction and participation embedded in her works, as well as the affordances of AR—enabled by increasingly accessible technologies and institutional support—have made it possible to activate even seemingly invisible spaces, resulting in progressively more holistic works.

In 2024, she presented *Plastocene Dreams*, a series of augmented reality-supported fine art prints. This means that as a visitor, you enter a classically structured exhibition in which works are displayed on walls. By using her AR app, however, viewers can recognise the expanse of the two-dimensional canvas and find themselves in front of a "living" and moving image. Even more than purely three-dimensional, fish move out of the image into the expanded space of the location and through the fictional space of individual, expanded perception. Thiel writes:

> *Plastocene Dreams* brings your discarded plastic garbage back where it came from—in your own home! Only 9% of plastics can be recycled at all, and much of it is sent to countries with poor waste management, and ends up in our oceans. Plastic waste is endangering already

> stressed coral reefs—and in Greece divers discovered a 'coral reef' entirely made of plastic. (Thiel, n. d.)

For Thiel, we are at a crucial point: "We could save the planet—but we aren't." She adds:

> We would prefer to have powerful people become even richer than they already are, rather than save the planet. So that's what's happening. I started doing these environmental pieces back in 2015. I realised that the warming that we were going through was not linear. It was exponential. … And that means that all of your worst prognoses for what will happen in the future will happen in your lifetime. (T. Thiel, personal communication, June 2025)

Thiel's works connect the visible with the invisible. They translate ecological data, scientific findings, and everyday consumer practices into sensually perceptible images. In doing so, she translates the aesthetics of data into the ethics of perception. Her work thus aligns with artists such as Refik Anadol and Anke Schiemann, and many others who transform data spaces into immersive environments. But while Anadol celebrates the aesthetic effect of masses of information, Thiel confronts viewers with the fragility of their own environment.

Her art thus opens up a space of ethical resonance in people: She does not proclaim moral commandments but rather creates a physical awareness of participation. An idea of responsibility might arise in those who interact with her AR installations.

Thus the question I posed as the subtitle of this third chapter—*Do we dream in plastic?*—functions for me as an inclusive element of the analysis, explicitly situating myself within it. It asks whether we, as observers of such artworks and as human beings, are sufficiently aware of the multiple layers of reality we are actively co-creating within our societies and habitats. Moreover, it questions whether engaging with art such as Tamiko Thiel's can motivate us to take action—before plastic not only further permeates our external environment and physical bodies, but also infiltrates our innermost spaces of safety: our dreams and reflections. Can I personally feel motivated by being aware of the augmented space created by the artist?

4 Conclusion—Digital Art as a Resonance Space for Ethical Responsibility

The integration of this essay into the context of the whole volume that addresses digital transformation in companies and institutions is no coincidence. It reflects the search for connection that the young Tamiko Thiel already pursued in her work—the connection between artistic intuition, technological innovation, and social responsibility. Art and entrepreneurial activity are not simply opposites but could be regarded as complementary forms of innovative creation. Art and entrepreneurial application could be more closely intertwined to generate ethically sustainable products for people, since people are economy, innovation, past, present and future and only people have the power to improve the fictional reality in which we all mostly live to become more responsible again towards our objective reality, as Harari has termed human perception of their surroundings. The British philosopher and mathematician Alfred North Whitehead describes in Process and Reality: An Essay in Cosmology:

> There are two kinds of process: the macroscopic and the microscopic. The macroscopic process is the transition from achieved to completed reality, while the microscopic process is the transformation of merely actual conditions into determinate reality. The former process effects the transition from the actual to the merely real, and the latter effects the development from the real to the actual. The former process is efficient, the latter is teleological (purpose-oriented). [...] The community of actual things is an organism, but it is not a static organism. It is an incompleteness in the process of production. (Whitehead, 1978, transl. from German version by the author)

Dealing with cause and effect in this way creates an awareness that, in the present, we are setting the course for a future that will inevitably emerge and move from the imagined into lived reality. Applied to the work of Tamiko Thiel and other contemporary artists, this means that art can be understood in two ways: as an ethical practice in itself, when guided by such an intention, and as an ethical catalyst for an interacting audience. Through participation in a commonly created space of resonance—both within and beyond ourselves—viewers are encouraged to reflect on their own active contribution to shaping a shared future. By transferring technological tools into critical, sensorially experienced contexts, these works make visible what would otherwise remain invisible: the connections between consumption, technology, ecology, and consciousness. As viewers and interactors with immersive art, and at the same time with the reality around us, we are reminded to carry this ethical resonance into our own environments.

In this sense, digital art of various kinds proves to be an act of artistic exploration and the further technology has evolved and offered artists more tools some of this exploration went straight into a space that invites for resonance towards rather relevant matters in society and in matters upon nature, of which we are invited to become a part again, or at least to slowly realise that we are nature, too. From Tanaka's electrically risky self-location to Nake's algorithmic pioneering work and Ai Weiwei's social media process art to Anadol and Thiel, artists act as discoverers or developers of new perceptual spaces. Against this backdrop, intuition—in the Archimedean sense—is not the opposite of scientific rigour, as Archimedes himself carefully tested his insights for accuracy. Instead, intuition serves as a starting point for science: it helps deepen understanding of reality and can lead to meaningful innovation. Artists, by intuitively exploring emerging technologies and their effects, tackle questions that science, ethics, and society must address. In this sense, digital art does not merely explore or reflect upon the possibilities of technological development; it actively seeks to shape how reality is perceived, understood, and responsibly engaged with, reminding us that innovation is not only a technical process but also a deeply human, ecological, and ethical one.

I would like to suggest three points for further reflection:

1. The unity of humanity, art, and technology: Despite its obviousness, let's state it once and for all. Human reality, artistic intuition, and digital tools can form a creative unity, laying the foundation for collaborative social, economic, and ecological innovations, we truly need as a mankind.

2. The complexity as an aesthetic experience: Immersive and AI-based artworks can make complex relationships tangible and thus open up resonance spaces for critical self-reflection, for example, in the areas of consumer behaviour and plastic waste, a space of resonance we may support in our own personal and professional doing.
3. Responsibility as a relationship: An awareness of responsibility may arise from the interplay of (artistic) work, medium (technology), viewer (or interacting entity), and context. It is co-produced in each moment of encounter and is also a personal experience for every person who interacts (or stands within) the artistic work.

What follows from this understanding are three concrete implications.

- First, curating, mediation, research, and education should deliberately create interdisciplinary experimental spaces in which intuition and reflection enrich one another, actively cultivating spaces of resonance.
- Second, institutions and funding landscapes must adopt long-term perspectives and establish frameworks that support artistic engagement with social and ecological challenges, enabling creative work to move beyond its isolation from broader economic practices and modes of thinking.
- Third, if—as Tamiko Thiel emphasises—the ecological curve is exponential, then our cultural response must develop exponential depth with equal urgency: through cooperation, open data cultures, and new alliances among those who create, produce, and take responsibility.

Ultimately, the resonance spaces opened by the artworks discussed invite us to translate our perception into perceiving responsibility in real life (fictional reality towards objective reality)—thus to move from activating our own problem-oriented intuition to transformative action as an expression of consciously chosen, shared responsibility.

References

Ai, Q. (1982). *Selected poems* (E. C. Eoyang, Ed. with introduction & notes). Foreign Languages Press.

Ai Weiwei | Ai Weiwei in the Elevator When Taken into Custody by the Police (2009) | Artsy. (n.d.). *Artsy.* https://www.artsy.net/artwork/ai-weiwei-ai-weiwei-in-the-elevator-when-taken-into-custody-by-the-police

AWE XR. (2023, October 24). *Tamiko Thiel: Socially critical VR and AR Artworks, 1994–2023 by Tamiko Thiel* [Video]. YouTube. https://www.youtube.com/watch?v=GDBiBXOlqD8

Benoit-Bryan, J. (2020). A time of crisis: A national survey of arts and culture during COVID-19 with a focus on Black or African American and Hispanic voices. *Journal of Cultural Management and Cultural Policy / Zeitschrift für Kulturmanagement und Kulturpolitik, 6*(2), 49–76. https://doi.org/10.14361/zkmm-2020-0203

Bildung, B. F. K. (2018, July 2). *Wie politisch sollten Kunst und Kultur sein?* Bundesakademie für Kulturelle Bildung. https://www.bundesakademie.de/akademie/blog/wie-politisch-sollten-kunst-und-kultur-sein

Bodrožić-Brnić, K. (Host). (2025, November 28). *Algorithmische Kunst—Wie der Mensch bleibt, was die Maschine nicht ist* (Episode 67) [Audio podcast episode]. In *Kreativität & KI*. Mittelstand-Digital Zentrum Zukunftskultur. https://www.digitalzentrum-zukunftskultur.de/podcasts/67-algorithmische-kunst/

Distelmeyer, J., Ehrmanntraut, S., & Müller, B. (Eds.). (2021). *Algorithmen & Zeichen: Beiträge von Frieder Nake zur Gegenwart des Computers*.Kulturverlag Kadmos. https://doi.org/10.25969/mediarep/19385

Flusser, V. (2008). *Medienkultur* (5. Aufl., Hrsg. von S. Bollmann). *Fischer Taschenbuch Verlag*. (Erstauflage 1998).

Gengler, E., & Wedel, M. (2026, in press). AI literacy as a shared responsibility: Balancing corporate roles, societal goals, and inclusive education. In K. Bodrožić-Brnić, A. Estevam Lucenti, & T. Thiessen (Eds.), *AI and the ethics of innovation: Responsibility in practice*. Springer Nature.

How do human CO_2 emissions compare to natural CO_2 emissions? | CO_2 Human Emissions. (n.d.). https://www.che-project.eu/news/how-do-human-co2-emissions-compare-natural-co2-emissions

Jain, P. K. (2024). *Unique symbolisms on nature in Ai Qing's poetry: A select analysis. ShodhKosh: Journal of Visual and Performing Arts, 5*(6). https://doi.org/10.29121/shodhkosh.v5.i6.2024.2957

Kivrak, P. (2020, December). Die Kunst schweift durch latente Räume. *Kulturtechniken 4.0*. Goethe-Institut. https://www.goethe.de/prj/k40/de/kun/lat.html

Latour, B. (2017). *Facing gaia: Eight lectures on the new climatic regime*. Polity Press.

Lawson-Tancred, J. (2024). *AI and the art market*. Lund Humphries.

Lennon, C. (2024, September 21). El arte impulsado por la IA exhibe el «ecologismo digital» en la sede de la ONU. *Naciones Unidas*. https://news.un.org/es/story/2024/09/1533006

Maze Row (2025, March 18). *Digital artist and AI art: Refik Anadol*. Maze Row Voices. https://editorial.mazerow.com/digital-artist-refik-anadol/

McLuhan, H. M., & Fiore, Q. (2023). *Das Medium ist die Massage: Ein Inventar medialer Effekte* (M. Baltes et al., Trans.; 6. Aufl.). Tropen. (English original from 1967).

mdr.de. (2021, July 30). Beweis: Mikroplastik kann menschliche Zellen direkt schädigen. *MDR.DE*. https://www.mdr.de/wissen/podcast/beweis-mikroplastik-schaedigt-ellmembran100.html

Molina, Á. (2008). El método de investigación de Arquímedes de Siracusa: Intuición, mecánica y exhaución. *Revista de Filosofía, 26*(58), 23–40. https://dialnet.unirioja.es/servlet/articulo?codigo=3384783

NABU—Naturschutzbund Deutschland e.V. (n.d.). *Plastikmüll und seine Folgen*. https://www.nabu.de/natur-und-landschaft/meere/muellkippe-meer/muellkippemeer.html

Plastik erstmals im menschlichen Gehirn nachgewiesen. (n.d.). *BUND—Bund für Naturschutz und Umwelt in Deutschland*. https://www.bund.net/themen/aktuelles/detail-aktuelles/news/pet-nanoplastik-gelangt-bis-ins-gehirn

Reif, A., Peter, E., Gillner, T., Hortig, L., Joost, A., & Taddicken, M. (2021). Vom Bildschirm auf die Straße? Eine empirische Untersuchung der Identifikation, Online-Partizipation und des Klimaproblembewusstseins von Fridays-for-Future-Beteiligten. *Medien & Kommunikationswissenschaft, 69*(4), 578–597. https://doi.org/10.5771/1615-634x-2021-4-578

Rosa, H. (2019). *Resonance: A sociology of our relationship to the world* (J. C. Wagner, Trans.). Polity Press. (Original work published 2016 in German).

Sackmann, C. (2024, October 4). Der Leitungswasser-Trick schützt vor Deutschlands großem Mikroplastik-Dilemma. *FOCUS Online*. https://www.focus.de/earth/leben/kueche-kleidung-auto-sechs-tipps-fuer-den-alltag-so-vermeiden-sie-mikroplastik-in-ihrem-leben_id_260341681.html

TED. (2015, July 24). *Why humans run the world | Yuval Noah Harari* [Video]. YouTube. https://www.youtube.com/watch?v=nzj7Wg4DAbs

TheNexusInstitute. (2019, July 8). *Ai Weiwei: The responsibility of an artist* [Video]. YouTube. https://www.youtube.com/watch?v=wmEDRfjxhfk

Thiel, T. (n.d.). *Plastocene Dreams—AR enhanced fine art prints.* https://tamikothiel.com/pdreams/index.html
T. Thiel, personal communication, June 2025. (The interview was conducted by the author in June 2025 and has not been published. The audio recording may be made available to other researchers upon justified request, subject to the explicit consent of the artist and in accordance with ethical research standards).
Thomas, A. (2025, March 18). The art of data. *Maze Row Voices.* https://editorial.mazerow.com/digital-artist-refik-anadol
Thomas, T., & Source, G. (2024, July 2). Soziale (Un-)Gleichheit auf Social Media. *bpb.de.* https://www.bpb.de/themen/medien-journalismus/soziale-medien/547427/soziale-ungleichheit-auf-social-media
Tiampo, M. (2004). *Atsuko Tanaka: Electrifying art: 1954–1968.* https://ci.nii.ac.jp/ncid/BA72325649
Tiampo, M. (2011). *Gutai: Decentering modernism.* http://ci.nii.ac.jp/ncid/BB05303747
United Nations. (n.d.). *Plastics—Fueling oil demand, climate change and pollution.* https://www.un.org/en/climatechange/science/climate-issues/plastics
Waste Land. (2010). https://www.wastelandmovie.com/
Whitehead, A. N. (1978). *Process and reality: An essay in cosmology* (Corrected ed.). In R. Breil (Ed.), *Naturphilosophie* (2000).
World Meteorological Organization. (2024). *State of the global climate.*
Xie, P., Zhang, Y., Chen, R., Lin, Z., & Lu, N. (2024). Social media's impact on environmental awareness: A marginal treatment effect analysis of WeChat usage in China. *BMC Public Health, 24*, Article 3237. https://doi.org/10.1186/s12889-024-20721-4

Kristina Bodrožić-Brnić is an AI trainer, researcher, and university lecturer specialising in the convergence of creativity and Artificial Intelligence. Her research focuses on how creative applications of AI contribute to technology openness and support the adoption of new technologies, particularly in SMEs. She is currently pursuing her PhD at the Hochschule der Medien Stuttgart. As Program Manager at the Mittelstand-Digital Zentrum Zukunftskultur and Co-Manager of the Institute for Digital Transformation and Innovation at the BSP Business and Law School, she supports SMEs and academic partners in developing and applying AI-driven innovation in practice.

Part II
Governance and Normative Frameworks

Law, Technology, and Structural Transformations: The Reconfiguration of Legal Thought

André Lucenti Estevam

Abstract This article explores the structural transformations engendered by new technologies, notably the internet and Artificial Intelligence, on legal thought. It argues that these challenges precipitate a methodological shift from systematic thought to problem-oriented topical reasoning. The analysis addresses three domains: firstly, the legal order's changing architectonics, where the state-centred pyramid gives way to a networked structure influenced by transnational corporations. Secondly, it conceptualises the private power these corporations exercise—analysed through Weber, Eucken, Luhmann, and Foucault—arguing that such power colonises attention and influences the formation of the will. Thirdly, drawing on Habermas, it discusses the public sphere's transformation, where platformisation fragments discourse and endangers rational deliberation. The article concludes that technology is not a neutral instrument but a force shaping the human condition, suggesting that adapting the law requires a deeper understanding of the technologically saturated subject of the future.

Keywords Legal theory · Artificial intelligence · Digital transformation · Private power · Public sphere · Technological rationality

1 Introduction

Reflections on the interplay between law and technology—or, more precisely, new technologies, including most notably the internet and Artificial Intelligence—have proliferated rapidly across all branches of legal dogmatics. In some cases, they have even prompted calls for the establishment of entirely new theoretical fields. This growing body of theoretical discourse conveys the impression that the tectonic plates upon which legal thought has traditionally rested are shifting, and that little of the conventional legal culture we have known will endure.

A. L. Estevam (✉)
Huck Otranto Camargo, São Paulo, Brazil
e-mail: andre.lucenti@lhoc.com.br

K. Bodrožić-Brnić et al. (eds.), *AI and the Ethics of Innovation*, Digital Transformation and Innovation, https://doi.org/10.1007/978-3-032-20638-1_9

A preliminary approach to assessing these transformations may be undertaken from a methodological standpoint. In this line of reflection, an initial approach to the phenomenon reveals that, when viewed through the lens of the dichotomy between systematic legal thought and topical (or problem-oriented) legal reasoning, the latter has proved more prominent and fruitful.

Under the predominance of the positivist method, systematic legal thought focuses primarily on the legal norm and its place within the legal order. Regarding new technologies, this approach entails the examination of newly enacted laws designed to regulate emerging technological phenomena; the identification of antinomies and lacunae (notably, in the latter case, whether the legal framework is sufficiently comprehensive); the investigation of the semantic content of certain legislative expressions; the provision of definitions; and the analytical decomposition of legal situations (rights, claims, duties, liabilities, immunities) engendered by such norms (Bobbio, 1976). Contributions of this nature are of clear scientific value and serve an essential dogmatic function.

By contrast, under the methods associated with argumentative and rhetorical theories, topical reasoning centres upon legal problems for which it seeks to offer practical solutions. Within the framework of rhetoric and argumentation, legal reasoning is dialectical rather than analytical, logical-formal, or deductive. The dialectical nature of reasoning requires jurists to argue in favour of a particular solution to the legal issue at hand (Bobbio, 1966). Topical reasoning does not dispense with a systematic conception of the legal order; on the contrary, it treats legal norms as starting points while also admitting other starting points of differing natures. Topical and systematic reasoning tend towards complementarity rather than mutual exclusion or conflict (Canaris, 2008).

Argumentation, within this methodological framework, is grounded in *topoi*—that is, ideas embedded in legal culture and broadly shared by the community of jurists. The construction of legal arguments based on rhetorical *topoi* rests upon a logic of reasonableness and plausibility, rather than mathematical certainty. Even when legal problems are novel, the rhetorical *topoi* that structure the argument are familiar and generally accepted. Thus, traditional rhetorical *topoi* may serve as the foundation for new legal solutions. In the recent history of constitutional law—in various Western countries—a substantial part of the progress achieved in resolving conflicts under constitutional jurisdiction has been attributable to rhetorical constructions (Canaris, 2008). In the domain of new technologies, it is difficult to conceive of a systematic *jus-theoretical* elaboration that might precede the emergence of concrete problems. Quite to the contrary, legal reasoning in relation to new technologies tends to develop in response to each new problem that arises—hence its predominantly topical character. Regulations concerning new technologies tend to be more fragmented, according to their specific subject matter, frequently subject to revision and, above all, open to adaptation in response to concrete problems. Numerous technological developments still lie ahead which cannot, as yet, be meaningfully addressed through general regulatory norms. Even though broad principles and general clauses exist, their concrete application to specific, real-world problems relies more heavily on argumentative, topical reasoning than on systematic thought.

It is evident that argumentation occupies a central role in the decidability of disputes involving new technologies. Yet a fundamental distinction must be drawn between argumentation as practice and as methodology. As Larenz states, argumentation as a methodology is linked to science, and:

> is conceived *prima facie* as part of the process of scientific legal research, although it may also be used in a legal opinion or even in the reasoning of a judicial decision. Here, the focus is not merely on identifying the 'strongest argument', in the singular, but rather on engaging in an ordered process of thought capable of ensuring that all essential viewpoints have been duly considered. (1997, pp. 211–212)

Argumentation as practice, by contrast, is not simply an individual act; it is also inherently social. This becomes particularly evident when one observes the growing influence of extra-legal interests and rationalities within legal argumentation. A legal decision, though ultimately individual, must persuade and must be accepted—or at the very least, be acceptable—to its audience. In this sense, both argumentation and decision-making are subject to social influence.

At this juncture, the interplay between legal positivism and theories of argumentation deserves to be highlighted. In the positivist field, Kelsen develops the Pure Theory of Law with the recognition that the dynamic aspect of the legal system cannot be ignored. To this end, he conceptualises the system as a hierarchical structure of validations, or authorisations. Perelman, on the other hand, aptly observes that the dynamic character of the legal system, in Kelsen's thought, is manifested in power, which is conferred to a greater or lesser extent upon the organs authorised to create legal norms—that is, to decide. Hence, dynamism is present not only at the moment of *fiat lex*—which was already evident at the time—but also in judicial decision-making. However, since Kelsen denies that Reason holds authority in the realm of value judgements, he refrains from engaging with the content of judicial decisions. It is here that both Perelman and Viehweg agree that Kelsen's theory ought to be supplemented by a rhetorical theory—"one that makes it possible to establish a dialogue on the legitimacy of decisions" (Bobbio, 1966). Perelman explicitly acknowledges that the judge, while obliged to apply the law in deciding a case, possesses a set of legal techniques specific to juridical reasoning, which allow for the adaptation of rules to the desired outcome. The use of such techniques of flexibility—for instance, vague notions and indeterminate concepts—does indeed introduce an element of legal uncertainty, but it also enables the calibration of the acceptability of the decision's consequences.

Argumentation grounded in *topoi*, communication that reiterates information, tends to become redundant—in order to constitute a *topos*, an argument must have been repeatedly employed and accepted on multiple occasions. However, events occurring both within and beyond the legal system may increase the system's *variety*. The greater the complexity introduced by the argument, the higher the degree of variety it contributes to the system, and the greater the system's responsiveness to its environment (Luhmann, 1995).

While the argument draws upon already known foundations (redundancies), it simultaneously identifies distinctions and revisits problems, thereby adding new information—even if the novelty introduced is modest. The introduction of small increments of new information into the system allows for its continual updating while, at the same time, preserving the stability of expectations.

Legal argumentation is sensitive both to legal concepts (internal to the legal system) and to interests (which belong to the environment and lie outside the legal system). In this way, argumentation manages to combine legal concepts and interests at an operational level of both self-reference and hetero-reference: in the former, there is a tendency to preserve successful redundancies; in the latter, there is a tendency towards renewal in response to new realities, distinguishing between interests that merit legal protection and those that do not. The more space argumentation affords to interests (with a corresponding retreat of legal concepts), the lower the redundancy tends to be, and the greater the variety (Luhmann, 1995). Understanding this calibration mechanism is essential to grasp how the legal system manages to operate within the domain of new technologies, which evolve and transform at a markedly rapid pace.

This issue brings us back to the function of complexity reduction that the law is meant to perform. In a context of intense social complexity concerning expectations of human conduct, this function is especially strained. Categories in legal science are not exclusive to legal positivism, nor did they originate there. Nevertheless, it was within legal positivism that categories came to occupy a particularly prominent and privileged position. As Mengoni and Lipari emphasise, moderate positivism is, both theoretically and methodologically, formalistic, in that it operates with systematically structured categories that are axiologically neutral; yet within such categories were, so to speak, crystallised the moral values of modern natural law theory—values that reflected a bourgeois and Christian society. In essence, the reference to a category functioned as a filter for the logical reduction of a statement (or, more frequently, a complex of statements) to conceptual structures within the normative system, and thereby to a core of shared principles underlying the formal concepts placed at the apex of the system. The category thus served as a point of synthesis between the formal framework (of normative textuality) and the social context—which, at the time, was essentially homogeneous, so that the confrontation posed by the category in concrete cases was seldom disputed (Luhmann, 1991).

From the mid-twentieth century onwards, however, the axiological homogeneity that categories had presupposed began to disintegrate; legal sources became more numerous and interwoven, and the exclusivity of state law grew increasingly fragile. In other words, from that period onwards, the category lost its role as a point of convergence between norm and reality, becoming instead a mere framework of descriptive criteria derivable from normative statements. Categories ceased to be an objective precondition for understanding legal reality and came to function as operative instruments—adaptable to evolving normative frameworks. This marks a weakening of the systematic paradigm of dogmatic legal thought and opens the way for a more problem-oriented method. The new context that emerged in the latter half of the twentieth century gave rise to new legal logics, rhetorical theories, and, more broadly, theoretical approaches aimed at explaining how law can—or ought to—be applied within a reality that is both new and in constant flux. The challenge of ensuring the acceptability of legal decisions has thus become more formidable. Factual transformations occur more rapidly, societal interests and opinions are increasingly fragmented, and the formation of even minimal consensus is markedly more difficult. As a result, the very acceptability of legal decisions has itself become more contested.

The positivisation of law, through general norms, undoubtedly contributes to complexity reduction (Lipari, 2013) yet this alone is insufficient, since decisions remain necessary, and general norms often prove overly generic in fields marked by innovation. In this respect, many of the new general legal norms applicable to digital phenomena resemble guidelines more than specific commands (Ferraz Jr., Borges, 2020). The low density of such new legal norms, when set against the specificity of the problems that arise, creates a broader space for legal argumentation.

This dual perspective of legal argument—extending simultaneously towards legal concepts and extra-legal interests—currently exposes the legal system to the risk of replacing legal rationality, which traditionally guides judicial decision-making, with extra-legal rationalities. Such a risk may represent a rupture in legal logic (as traditionally conceived within rhetorical theories such as that of Perelman) and a weakening of imperatives that are subject to legal, constitutional, democratic, and republican control.

In the boundless realm of the digital, new technologies are developed and give rise to expectations which, at a certain point, may become entangled in disputes requiring legal resolution. In such cases, the adjudicating body is often confronted with situations that are already well-established and, from a societal standpoint, highly costly to reverse.

As noted above, the legal system is tasked with reducing complexity. However, complexity reduction within the legal system also entails a repression of information. This is not merely the suppression of irrelevant data; many of the repressed elements are, in fact, of considerable importance. Yet the identity and integrated continuity of the legal system within an intensely complex environment require such repression.

This does not mean, however, that repressed arguments should remain unexamined. On the contrary, Larenz's definition of argumentation as methodology, it is essential to consider which arguments are being concealed in the decision-making process by this very mechanism of repression (Luhmann, 1991). These intellectual elaborations, however, continue to operate essentially within the realm of *topical* reasoning—they serve the purpose of resolving a specific problem, without necessarily forming a unified or systematic whole.

It is worth recalling the reconstruction undertaken by Perelman to situate systematic legal thought and rhetoric within the history of law. Perelman acknowledges that, for centuries, the very notion of law as a system would have been inconceivable. It was only in the seventeenth and eighteenth centuries, with the treatises of Pufendorf, Domat, and Wolff, that it became possible to conceive of law as a system—that is, once an extensive body of rules and decisions had been accumulated, within a context of relative factual stability. As Perelman notes, such an endeavour was only feasible after a long process of elaborating the legal material developed over the course of centuries.

When legal scholarship embraced the systematic conception of law, the task of jurists appeared to become that of constructing a legal system capable of responding *in advance* to all difficulties, ambiguities, lacunae, and antinomies within the law. Under this conception—as interpreted by Perelman—the primary function of law was to provide legal certainty through an order known to all, rather than to deliver just outcomes or to enable the pursuit of the common good. At its core, there was initially an effort to elaborate a static, systematic structure of law, modelled on the pattern of a mathematical or logical system. The current—and indeed future—situation precludes any expectation that the legal system should possess such structures and functions.

In this current context, one observes a tendency towards the creation of new institutions for dispute resolution—institutions more engaged with transformation than with preservation; where resolutions are preferably internal rather than imposed by external judges; where learning takes place through monitoring, given the absence of any prior repertoire for anticipating future adjudication. In other words, learning occurs only as problems unfold (*learning while monitoring* or *learning by doing*), or even through the logic of *finding as founding* (Ladeur, 2016, Ferraz Jr., Borges, 2020). There is a growing tendency to delegate regulatory authority to the networks, platforms, and technology creators themselves. In this reconfiguration, law appears as *acentric*, and the very infrastructure of law becomes fluid or mobilisable.

Even so, conflicts that are not satisfactorily resolved internally—by the technology creators themselves—are eventually brought before state institutions (the Legislative Branch, the Judiciary, the Antitrust authorities, data protection authorities, and specialised regulatory agencies) for judgement. In general, by the time such matters reach these bodies, the conflict has become severe, and extra-legal rationality plays a decisive role in shaping the outcome.

The preceding paragraphs—although introductory—are particularly relevant in highlighting that topical, argumentative, and problem-oriented reasoning proves more suitable and fruitful than systematic legal thought for addressing the new conflicts arising from the use of so-called "new technologies". We would stress, however, that:

- the consideration of arguments within problem-oriented reasoning must be comprehensive and systematic, rather than arbitrary or random;
- argumentation produces either redundancy or variety, depending on whether it introduces new information or merely reiterates information already known and employed; and.
- interpretation and argumentation are social, not individual, activities, insofar as they take place within a communicative process, and the resolution of legal disputes must persuade not only the parties to the controversy, but also third parties who learn from the decision.

2 The Search for the Law

Continuing to work within a well-known dichotomy in legal culture—that between systematic and problem-oriented reasoning—we observe a prevailing tendency towards argumentative activity: the identification, organisation, and balancing of arguments. This shift leads us to consider that the search for law—i.e. the inquiry into what constitutes the law—has undergone transformation.

In the past, the tension and openness to contingency within the space between concrete conflicts and general norms were stabilised by legal scholarship. The doctrine set out the possible interpretations of general norms, and judicial bodies were guided by those interpretative frameworks. This doctrinal function, simultaneously, endowed the general norm with interpretive variety while delimiting its range of meanings. The judicial body—as well as any interpreter within the open community of jurists—could thus search for the applicable law by examining the body of positive law and its corresponding legal doctrine.

In the context of new legal challenges associated with the use of emerging technologies, the search for law now corresponds to a mapping of arguments. In this sense, the legal norm functions less as a rule directly applicable to the resolution of a controversy, and more as a repository of arguments. In this evolving inquiry into law, judicial precedents have become a central object of investigation—a development made more feasible in recent years, as virtually the entirety of contemporary case law has become digitally accessible (Moro, 2015).

This search for law—focused more on judicial decisions than on doctrinal scholarship—highlights and reinforces the topical character of legal practice in the resolution of new technological problems. Naturally, judicial decisions are marked by a certain degree of volatility and provisionality, which results in the construction of legal models that are more precarious than in the past. Indeed, with the diminishing relevance of the mediating and critical role once played by high-level doctrinal scholarship, this fragile, topically constructed legal modelling tends to resemble a palimpsest—one that is continuously rewritten in response to changing circumstances (Reale 1994, pp. 63–75).

Legal models thus cease to be produced in a scientific, analytical, systematic, explanatory, and conceptual manner—typically by legal scholars—and instead come to be shaped (or improvised) on the basis of judicial decisions. The arguments "found" in the course of this search come to constitute certain normative fields of validity—hence the notion of *finding as founding*. The judicial decisions that make up this *corpus* of legal practice refer to one another, thereby revealing a hypertextual logic underlying the contemporary search for law.

This topical endeavour of searching for applicable and valid law is not necessarily less rigorous than the analytical, systematic, explanatory, and conceptual work traditionally carried out within the Romano-Germanic legal tradition. For this topical work to be methodologically rigorous, it is essential that arguments be mapped, clarified, organised, and distinguished according to their respective domains of relevance, and then compared in terms of their persuasive strength, so that they may be combined into coherent dogmatic solutions.

Given that contemporary technological problems tend to affect a multitude of countries or regions across the world in similar or comparable ways—and that law is likewise called upon to respond—the relevant arguments now circulate globally (Moro, 2015, pp. 77–94). As a result, legal practice across jurisdictions increasingly incorporates arguments imported from other legal orders, even when the underlying factual realities may differ substantially (a circumstance that may itself give rise to further complications). These technological disparities and inequalities between countries also point towards architectural shifts within the legal system itself.

3 The Architectonics of the Legal Order and Layers of Technology

Traditionally, the architecture of the legal order was conceived as a hierarchical structure (*Stufenbau*, in Kelsen's terminology) resembling a pyramid. This pyramidal structure of norms was understood to mirror a pyramidal structure of power. Since the 1990s, however, this architecture has been gradually dismantled, driven by the crisis of statism and the displacement or fragmentation of the gravitational centre of normativity. The nation state ceased to function as the exclusive locus of normative positivity and came to be merely one pole among several. In this architectural transformation of the hierarchical legal structure, the pyramidal model has progressively given way to a networked or *rhizomatic* structure (Losano, 2007, 2005).

New technologies catalyse the architectural transformations of the legal order described above. To grasp these transformations, it is necessary to observe: (i) the interplay between the power of nation states and that of corporations; and (ii) the layered structure of globally operative technologies. These layers range from the physical infrastructure—which must be installed within a given state and is therefore subject to that state's legal order—to the user interface, that is, the point at which technology interacts with the individual, who is also geographically situated within a specific location in the world.

As a result, the degree to which large transnational software companies are subject to national legal systems varies across jurisdictions. Although such companies may produce significant effects in all countries where the internet is freely accessible, not all nation states possess effective police powers over the infrastructure producing those effects, nor over the entities exercising control within those companies. Illustratively, particularly in cases involving messaging services, it has already become apparent that the effective enforcement of judicial decisions by service providers is contingent upon the cooperation of the companies themselves. In other words, citizens, companies, and even the state apparatus rely on intangible technological products and services developed or supplied by transnational corporations that do not fully submit to each national legal order. More significantly still, these transnational corporations establish their own normative frameworks and subject their users—citizens, companies, and state institutions alike—to those private regulatory regimes.

Along this trajectory of transformation, the distribution of normativity is altered as a consequence of the new distribution of power—since a small number of macro-corporations have come to hold a substantial share of the technology now used—often in a relationship of dependency—by citizens, companies, and governments alike. In other words, as the architecture of the power pyramid once represented by the structure of nation states is reconfigured, the normative architecture likewise tends to shift—from a pyramidal structure to a networked or *rhizomatic* one, for instance.

This line of analysis leads us to another issue: the conceptualisation of the new forms of power exercised by those macro-corporations that control technologies upon which much of the world has become dependent. We shall examine this point in the following section.

4 New Forms of Conceptualising Power

The recognition of a new global distribution of power must be accompanied by the recognition that there are also new forms in which power is exercised.

New technologies enable a kind of colonisation—no longer directed at natural resources or labour power, but rather at each individual's time, gaze, and attention. At the risk of repetition: new technologies instrumentalise a novel form of colonisation that seeks to penetrate even the smallest instants of a person's life; to capture their most intimate inclinations; to serve as an extension of their thought and action—for a wide variety of purposes and functions, and even for that which has no purpose or function at all. These technologies are designed even to occupy existential voids—there are, indeed, many technological applications that serve no discernible aim.

The degree of invasiveness exercised by these new technologies is immeasurably greater than any prior form of power. By infiltrating the smallest fractions of time and any conceivable space, they influence the very formation of the individual will. That is to say, people become informed, observe, listen, read, and access content in accordance with a predefinition that, to a considerable extent, eludes their control. This form of power, exercised over individuals through new technologies, finds no historical precedent of comparable magnitude.

For the sake of comparison, it may be appropriate to recall the emergence of disciplinary power in the modern age, astutely described by M. Foucault. In this observation, a new form of power was identified—no longer exercised over territories, but over bodies, over human action, over labour. This modern mode of power would prove revolutionary and would require the law itself to intervene in order to discipline such power (even though legal institutions are themselves agents in the establishment of disciplinary power structures).

Indeed, every exercise of power—whether public or private—tends to undergo a process of legal identification, conceptualisation, and regulation, through mechanisms of limitation, channelling, and fragmentation.

Traditionally, four major paradigms have been recognised for conceptualising the exercise of private power. They reflect certain theoretical formulations of power, as noted by Renner (2016). Two initial features distinguish the principal theoretical approaches: some conceptions of power follow a causal line, while others adopt a modal approach. A further distinction lies in these paradigms: some are relational, whereas others are structural.

Within the causal approach, prominent among the formulations are those developed by Weber and Eucken. Weber defines power in general as the probability "that one actor within a social relationship will be in a position to carry out his own will despite resistance, regardless of the basis on which this probability rests" (Weber, 1978, p. 926). In Weberian thought, power is structured in terms of interaction or relationships between actors; that is, power exists when one or more actors exercise influence over others. The Weberian concept of power is, however, multidimensional. According to Weber, power may be distributed according to a tripartite typology: political power (organised around parties), economic power (organised around social classes), and cultural or ideological power (organised around status) (Poggi, 2001, pp. 15–25; Schroeder, 1998, p. 84; Whimster, 2007, p. 226). What should be highlighted here are the causal and relational (or interactional) features that characterise this Weberian conceptualisation of power.

Still operating within a causal formulation of the concept of power, there exists another tradition of thought which, instead of locating power in interacting agents, situates its origin in structures. This represents a structural-causal conception of power, as opposed to the Weberian relational-causal model.

Within this structural-causal tradition, the thought of Eucken stands out—an approach that would significantly influence European competition law. According to Eucken, power is not simply a characteristic of the actors themselves but is instead related to the structure in which those actors operate. His formulation is causal in the sense that the effect of power depends on the conduct of the actor who exercises it; however, his concern lies with the effect on structures, rather than on a subject directly interacting with the power-wielding agent. It is precisely this kind of effect that enables a monopolist to distort the relevant market.

Consequently, conceptualisation of power compels us to focus more closely on structures (such as market structures) than on the individual characteristics of a given agent or the immediate and concrete relationship between two agents. Within this paradigm, the more competitive a given relevant market is, the more evenly power tends to be distributed among its participants; in a perfectly competitive economy, economic power would not pose a problem, and no singular relationship of dependency would persist (Eucken, 1992). In a market dominated by a monopolist—or in an oligopoly—it is the structure of relations within that market that confers power upon the monopolist or oligopolists.

On the other hand, as previously mentioned, there is the line of thought that conceptualises power in modal rather than causal terms. Power can be explained, among other possibilities, as a symbolically generalised medium of communication, as proposed by Luhmann (Ferraz Jr., 2009; Luhmann, 2012). Luhmann's premises are, of course, distinctive: in his systems theory, society is conceived not as an aggregation of individuals, but as a communicative situation. The more complex a society becomes, the greater the importance—and the broader the effects—of power conceived as a communicative medium. From this follows, incidentally, the possibility of the ubiquity of power. This conception of power is particularly relevant in that it emphasises the *possibility* inherent in power—that is, the articulation between potentiality and actualisation which power enables. Moreover, this theory is capable of explaining power in the private sphere, and not merely in its traditional form typically associated with political authority. The code of power articulates the will of the holder and the counter-will of the one who is subject to it. In this way, power as a medium reduces complexity by narrowing the scope of selection available to the *alter* (*Selektionsspielraum*) (Luhmann, 2012).

Although this is a theoretically complex conception—undoubtedly marked by a high degree of abstraction—it has the merit of distinguishing power as a specific communicative medium, one not to be conflated with other such media, and of providing a unified explanation for a phenomenon that manifests itself ubiquitously (Riebandt, 2011; Schröder, 2003). From this perspective, the exercise of power operates—indeed, dominates, neutralises, or controls—*ex ante* the very formation of will in those subject to it (even though this paradigm was formulated prior to the emergence of new technologies, which clearly possess such capacity, as noted above).

As we have seen, Luhmann's theoretical formulation of power may be classified as modal, in contrast to the causal character of the models developed by Weber and Eucken. In comparative objectal terms, Luhmann's elaboration of power is relational or interactional, as opposed to the structural account found in Eucken and others. That is, the Luhmannian model schematises the exercise of power as occurring between interacting agents.

There also exists a structural-modal elaboration of the concept of power which, in various ways, resonates within the legal order and legal culture. Representative of this theoretical strand is the conceptualisation developed by Foucault. In this type of theoretical framework, the primary focus of power does not lie with specific individuals (Foucault, 2002), but rather with institutions—such as language, education, religion, discipline, the family, and so forth. Power is not located in a fixed place but exists within an open set of coordinated (and poorly coordinated) relations.

Power, in this sense, is expressed through social conventions, taboos, and verbal or visual representations of sexuality, among others. Consequently, the exercise and effects of power no longer fit into a causal schema; it is more appropriate to speak of a circular schema—every act of thinking or doing that occurs within institutions or structures of power is conditioned or shaped by those very structures. Hence the well-known inseparability between knowledge and power. This is not, therefore, an approach concerned with specific relationships between directly interacting subjects (as in interactional conceptions), nor does it rely on a causal manifestation of power (as in the causal tradition). Power, here, does not exist as an entity; it exists insofar as it is exercised, inscribed within a dispersed field of possibilities underpinned by certain enduring structures (Foucault, 2002).

The preceding observations make it clear that the contemporary exercise of power through new technologies requires legal engagement from, at the very least, the four analytical perspectives outlined above. Indeed, we are witnessing a very high concentration of economic power in the markets where large technology corporations operate, generating dangerous dependencies and calling for the intervention of competition law.

From the standpoint of cultural power (in the Weberian sense) and power in the Foucauldian sense, we observe a form of control over aesthetics, consumption habits, career planning, the appropriation of sensitive data, and an influence over alienation (*Entfremdung*)—all with diverse and often harmful effects on the production of subjectivity. Moreover, we perceive the exercise of power that shapes the very formation of the will of the *Other*, narrowing their range of possibilities and placing them in a position of subjection.

The counterpoint to the expansion of these new forms of power exercised through emerging technologies is the freedom of those subject to such power. In the neo-Roman tradition, freedom is understood as the absence of subjection—not merely as the absence of external interference, as proposed by the Hobbesian tradition. This neo-Roman perspective represents a relational conception of freedom: a person is free if they act or refrain from acting according to their own will, formed autonomously.

If a person's conduct depends, to any extent, on the will of another, it is said that the former is, to that extent, within the field of power of the latter. The impairment of a person's state of freedom does not require the exercise of power by the other; the mere possibility suffices—namely, the possibility that the second person's will may subject the first person's actions to their arbitrary control. This condition of subjection is decisive in determining whether freedom exists.

The power of one individual to the detriment—or at the expense—of another's freedom does not reside in a specific action, but rather in a relational structure which, ultimately, is permitted or tolerated by the legal order. As such, given its structural nature, this state of freedom cannot be captured through an instantaneous examination; on the contrary, it requires an assessment that takes into account the development of that structure over time (Pettit, 1997; Skinner, 1998, 2022).

The transformation of states of freedom, as a result of new forms of power exercised through emerging technologies, can be observed most clearly in the recent structural changes in public sphere communication to which Habermas has referred in his more recent writings. These structural transformations reveal the dangers and risks to which constitutional democracies are currently exposed—as we shall examine below.

5 Structural Transformations of the Public Sphere

Habermas correctly observes, in our view, the fragmentation of the public sphere brought about by the rise of new virtual spaces enabled by the internet (Habermas, 2021). Constitutional democracies depend on the deliberative nature of politics—on the capacity to reach agreements even in the absence of a shared religion or a common worldview within society.

The platformisation (*Plattformisierung*) of the internet has produced complex and far-reaching effects on the public sphere. Prior to the advent of the internet, communication within the public sphere was shaped by professional journalism and established media outlets. That is, trained professionals were responsible for selecting the scope of communications and ensuring a minimum standard of quality. There was also, crucially, a clear identification of the participants in the public sphere and a regulatory framework for accountability—that is, the identities of those participating were known, including for the purposes of legal or social responsibility.

Following the advent of the internet and digital platforms, everyone may now become an author of public communication. There is no control over the scope, quality, or truthfulness of such communications. There is no requirement for the identification of participants, nor is there adequate regulation concerning the accountability of those who produce—and, more importantly, co-produce—public communications.

With the platformisation of the internet, the discourses of authors are increasingly generated and reproduced within echo chambers. Platforms do not merely produce discourse; they generate discursive matrices. Within these chambers, dissonant views are rejected, and only consonant communications are admitted. In other words, tolerance for disagreement is significantly reduced in such environments.

As the public sphere becomes increasingly platformised, we face a crisis in the competition of worldviews and their rationally accepted validation. This amounts to a crisis of rationality within public discourse (Habermas, 2021). This development reveals the operation of powerful centrifugal forces that deform and disintegrate the public sphere. These forces tend to degrade the shared political space into a battlefield, where adversaries are transformed into enemies.

The democratic system is impaired when public communications are unable to focus on matters of actual relevance and are no longer subject to qualitative filters—tasks that were previously carried out by the professional press, before the rise of these new and disruptive echo chambers. These new structural (rather than merely conjunctural) transformations of the public sphere undermine the normative gradient of social reality itself. Over little more than two centuries of constitutional democratic experience, we have learned that the communal basis of moral rationality—which translates into legal rationality—is a fundamental premise of the public sphere in constitutional democracies.

The loss of this normative gradient within social reality itself produces—or may produce, in a relatively short span of time—divergences of such magnitude that they culminate in coup-driven and anti-democratic acts, as witnessed in the United States in 2021 (with the storming of the Capitol on 6 January 2021), or in Brazil in 2023 (with attacks on several public buildings housing the three branches of government in Brasília, in an attempt to incite a coup, on 8 January 2023). Naturally, such episodes are merely epiphenomena of far deeper transformations currently unfolding within social systems.

6 Closing Remarks—New Technologies and New Horizons

In suspending this panoramic theoretical inquiry into the effects of new technologies on the law, it seems necessary to turn our gaze towards the deeper philosophical meaning of technology itself. As Heidegger reminds us, technology belongs to the domain of knowledge (*Wissen*) (Heidegger, 1977, 2000). With this particular placement of technology, philosophical thought reveals that technology is not neutral; it is not merely an instrument for achieving ends defined autonomously by the subject. On the contrary, technology has the power to shape our world—including the capacity to transform our symbolic, cultural, and axiological universe.

There exists a profound entanglement between technology and our existential condition. The human interiority and the technological exterior are no longer clearly separable, as was once imagined. Technology is built through language (the very language we ourselves create); it operates through language, and it is updated and expanded through the use of language.

Contemporary technological instruments, which are initially external to the person, are not fully under the individual's control. Algorithms determine what is shown to each individual based on their previous choices, and they define how the technology will interact with that individual. Technology weaves a web—a virtual, digital, dematerialised web—in which the person becomes suspended. This web is not woven manually and exclusively by the individual, with full awareness and control; rather, technology plays a fundamental role in its production, operating under the opaque shadow of algorithmic processes.

The formation of personal identity depends on the external—on alterity. Our identity is shaped through the interplay of a dust of words and images—our own and those of others—and technology, saturating all aspects of contemporary life, plays a crucial role in supplying those words and images. Technologies are, in this sense, intrusive, and they participate fundamentally in the sphere of individual intimacy (Aydin, 2022). To adapt the law as we know it to the new realities revealed by technology, it will be necessary to experiment.

The effects of technology are so deeply penetrating and so entangled with the formation of subjectivity that it is difficult to foresee with any certainty the full range of consequences they will produce for the law and legal culture—especially when we recall that law is an expression of human will and is directed exclusively—albeit at times only metonymically—towards human behaviour. As Raz observed, "unlike concepts such as 'mass' or 'electron', 'the law' is a concept used by people to understand themselves" (Raz, 1995, p. 237). To grasp what the law of the future will be—shaped by new technologies—we must first understand what the person of the future will be, a person forged in and through the saturation of technology.

References

Aydin, C. (2022). The technological uncanny as a permanent dimension of selfhood. In S. Vallor (Ed.), *Oxford handbook of philosophy of technology* (pp. 299–317). Oxford University Press.

Bobbio, N. (1966). Prefazione. In C. Perelman (Ed.), *Trattato dell'argomentazione—La nuova retorica*. Einaudi.

Bobbio, N. (1976). Scienza del diritto e analisi del linguaggio. In U. Scarpelli (Ed.), *Diritto e analisi del linguaggio*. Edizioni di Comunità.

Canaris, C. W. (2008). *Pensamento sistemático e conceito de sistema na ciência do direito* (4th ed., A. Menezes Cordeiro, trans.). Fundação Calouste Gulbenkian.

Comparato, F. K. (2006). *Ética: Direito, moral e religião no mundo moderno* (2nd ed.). Companhia das Letras.

Eucken, W. (1992). *The foundations of economics—History and theory in the analysis of economic reality*. Springer.

Ferraz Jr., T. S. (2009). *Estudos de filosofia do direito: Reflexões sobre o poder, a Liberdade, a justiça e o direito* (3ª ed.). Atlas.

Ferraz Jr., T. S. & Borges, G. R. (2020). *A superação do direito Como norma—Uma revisão descolonial da teoria do direito brasileiro*. Almedina Brasil.

Floridi, L. (2014). *The fourth revolution—On the impact of information and communication technologies on our lives*. Oxford University Press.

Foucault, M. (2002). The subject and power. In J. D. Faubion (Ed.), *Essential works of Foucault–Power* (Vol. 3). Penguin.

Habermas, J. (2021). Überlegungen und Hypothesen zu einem erneuten Strukturwandel der politischen Öffentlichkeit. In M. Seeliger, S. Sevignani, & S. Leviathan (Eds.), *Ein neuer Strukturwandel der Öffentlichkeit?* (Vol. 37, pp. 470–500).

Han, B.-C. (2022). Infocracia. *Vozes*.

Heidegger, M. (1977). Der Ursprung des Kunstwerks. In Gesamtausgabe (Vol. 5—Holzwege). Vittorio Klostermann.

Heidegger, M. (2000). Die Frage nach der Technik. In *Gesamtausgabe* (Vol. 7—Vorträge und Aufsätze). Vittorio Klostermann.

Kelsen, H. (2017). *Reine Rechtslehre* (2nd ed., M. Jestaedt, Ed.). Mohr Siebeck; Österreich Verlag.

Ladeur, K. H. (2016). *Die Textualität des Rechts—Zur poststrukturalistischen Kritik des Rechts*. Velbrück.

Larenz, K. (1997). *Metodologia da ciência do direito* (3rd ed., J. Lamego, trans.). Fundação Calouste Gulbenkian.

Lipari, N. (2013). *Le categorie del diritto civile*. Giuffrè.

Losano, M. G. (2005). Modelos teóricos, inclusive na prática: da pirâmide à rede. *Revista do Instituto dos Advogados de São Paulo, Nova Série, VIII*(16), 264–284.

Losano, M. G. (2007). Turbulenzen im Recht der modernen Gesellschaft–Herkömmliche Rechtsordnung, überstaatliche Rechtssetzung und Ordnung stiftende Modelle. *Rechtstheorie, 38*(1), 1–24.

Luhmann, N. (1991). *Soziologische Aufklärung 1: Aufsätze zur Theorie sozialer Systeme* (6th ed.). Westdeutscher.

Luhmann, N. (1995). Legal argumentation: An analysis of its form. *Modern Law Review, 58*(3), 285–298.

Luhmann, N. (2012). *Macht* (4ª ed.). UVK.

Moro, P. (2015). *Topica digitale—Metodologia e informatica giuridica nell'era dell'infosourcing*. Giapichelli.
Perelman, C. (1966). *Trattato dell'argomentazione—La nuova retorica*. Einaudi.
Pettit, P. (1997). *Republicanism—A theory of freedom and government*. Clarendon Press.
Poggi, G. (2001). Forms of power. *Polity*.
Raz, J. (1995). *Ethics in the public domain: Essays in the morality of law and politics*. Oxford University Press.
Reale, M. (1994). Fontes e modelos do direito—Para um novo paradigma hermenêutico.
Renner, M. (2016). Machtbegriffe zwischen Privatrecht und Gesellschaftstheorie. In F. Möslein (Ed.), *Private Macht*. Mohr Siebeck.
Riebandt, S. (2011). *Der systemische Machtbegriff: Rekonstruktion des Machtbegriffs von Niklas Luhmann aus dem Jahr 1975*. Grin Verlag.
Schröder, T. (2003). *Theorie der Macht bei Niklas Luhmann*. Grin Verlag.
Schroeder, R. (1998). From Weber's political sociology to contemporary liberal democracy. In R. Schroeder & Max Weber (Eds.), *Democracy and modernization*. Palgrave Macmillan.
Skinner, Q. (1998). *Liberty before liberalism*. Cambridge University Press.
Skinner, Q. (2022). On neo-Roman liberty: A response and reassessment. In H. Dawson & A. de Dijn (Eds.), *Rethinking liberty before liberalism*. Cambridge University Press.
Viehweg, T. (1979). *Tópica e jurisprudência* [Topik und Jurisprudenz] (T. S. Ferraz Jr., trans.). Imprensa Nacional.
Weber, M. (1978). *Economy and society—An outline of interpretative sociology*. University of California Press.
Whimster, S. (2007). *Understanding weber*. Routledge.

André Lucenti Estevam is a legal scholar specialised in the intersection of law, technology, and innovation. He holds a PhD in Theory and Philosophy of Law from the University of São Paulo (USP) and a Master of Law and Business (MLB) from Bucerius Law School and WHU—Otto Beisheim School of Management. His postdoctoral researches, conducted at the Max Planck Institute for Comparative and International Private Law (Hamburg), the Università Mediterranea di Reggio Calabria, and the USP, examine how emerging technologies are transforming legal approaches. His scholarly work has been published in several countries and languages.

The Duty of Self-Protection and the Culture of Responsibility: A Reflection on Ethics, Market, and New Technologies from a Civil Law Perspective

Maria Cristina De Cicco

Abstract This paper examines the role of a culture of responsibility in balancing ethics, the market, and new technologies from a civil law perspective. It challenges the prevailing view that expands corporate liability whilst treating consumers as prima facie vulnerable. Adopting a constitutional legality framework that prioritises existential over patrimonial relations, the article argues that democracy is consolidated not merely by affirming rights, but through exercising duties. It proposes a paradigm shift from the "vulnerable consumer" to the "responsible consumer", an agent who bears social responsibility for the ethical implications of their consumption, particularly regarding the rights of other market actors like workers. Furthermore, the paper underscores the duty of self-protection, especially in the digital age, contending that the right to informational self-determination is ineffective if individuals do not actively safeguard their own privacy. Ultimately, the essay posits that fostering this culture of responsibility is an essential prerequisite for strengthening democratic principles in a globalised society.

Keywords Culture of responsibility · Responsible consumer · Civil law · Digital self-determination · Democratic governance

1 Introduction

Starting from the premise that a democratic society cannot do without two inseparable pairs—duties and rights; freedom and responsibility—this paper seeks to analyse the role of a culture of responsibility in the pursuit of a balance between ethics, the market, and new technologies in the current (hyper)digitalised society in which we live. Adopting the methodology of civil law under the constitutional legality—which

M. C. De Cicco (✉)
University of Camerino, Law School, Camerino, Italy
e-mail: cristina.decicco@unicam.it

K. Bodrožić-Brnić et al. (eds.), *AI and the Ethics of Innovation*, Digital Transformation and Innovation, https://doi.org/10.1007/978-3-032-20638-1_10

prioritises existential relations over patrimonial ones, based on the principle of constitutional solidarity—the aim is to demonstrate that, while it is true that democracy advances through the affirmation of rights, it is consolidated through the exercise of duties and the individual's sense of responsibility towards both the community and themselves. Accordingly, there is a need for greater awareness regarding the importance of embracing the duty of self-protection—a duty that also falls upon users and consumers, who can no longer be viewed as *prima facie* vulnerable. This approach stands in contrast to the prevailing, though no longer unanimous, view that seeks to expand corporate liability while overlooking the equally necessary responsibility of all market agents. From this perspective, the consumer must take responsibility for the (ongoing) violation, by companies, of the fundamental rights of other market actors, such as workers. Indeed, strong consumer protection regulations have, paradoxically, produced the opposite effect: they have stripped consumers of any duty to protect themselves or others, in clear breach of the principle of constitutional solidarity. The so-called right to informational self-determination—the cornerstone of consumer protection—necessarily entails both rights and duties. State intervention is ultimately futile if individuals do not take active care of themselves and of their own rights, such as privacy, for example.

Within the proposed perspective, this essay does not claim to offer a definitive conclusion, as it presents itself rather as a provocation—the beginning of a new phase of reflection on the theme "person, ethics, and the market", now enriched and shaped by new technologies—and on the role that the consumer must, or ought to, assume within this context. In this sense, the essay will ideally be structured in three parts.

The first part will briefly address the relationship between "person, market, and ethics" from the standpoint of constitutional legality, overcoming the traditional antinomy between the concepts of "market" and "ethics" while recalling Irti's (1998) contrasting position, for whom the centre of the "new private law" is the "legal concept of the market", so that market law "is properly a new commercial law". The second part, which may be regarded as a Copernican turn in the understanding of the consumer's role in the market, will explore the transformation from the vulnerable and disadvantaged consumer/user to the notion of a responsible consumer. The third part will focus on the need to foster awareness of the duty of self-protection and the cultivation of a culture of responsibility as prerequisites for the consolidation of the democratic principle.

2 Person, Market, and Fundamental Rights

The triad of person, market, and fundamental rights presupposes a complex relationship, which could be rendered more immediately intelligible by specifying that the person-market relationship ought to be understood through the lens of ethics and fundamental rights. Hence, "Person and Market: Between Ethics and Fundamental Rights". In my view, an ethical market represents a privileged pathway for ensuring the effectiveness of social and fundamental rights—and, ultimately, the protection of the person and their dignity.

Thus, in moving beyond the utopian vision of the invisible hand (Smith, 2013)—according to which the pursuit of individual self-interest would naturally lead to the realisation of the common good —the issue must be addressed through a revaluation of the person's intrinsic value and centrality within the market. This implies overcoming a logic grounded solely in economic rationality and reinterpreting the person-market relationship from an axiological standpoint.

The Italian Constitution requires that private economic initiative to respect for safety, freedom, human dignity, and the environment. This means that economic initiative is instrumental to these values. In a system that places the person at the apex of the hierarchy of values, this provision represents the key to understanding a legal order that requires economic values to be directed towards the realisation of the existential values of the person.

The comprehensive consideration of the human person, the primacy of personality over patrimonial interests, and respect for the inalienable duties of solidarity enable the construction of a legal, economic, and social system that leaves no room either for strong state intervention through an exasperated dirigisme of business activity or for the freedom of the market. State intervention is necessary to ensure ethics *in* the market—or *of* the market, depending on one's perspective. Such intervention should reconcile economic efficiency with fundamental rights—in other words, of reconciling the market with solidarity.

The analysis of the relationship between the person and the market must not, however, overlook another important factor: namely, that within the solidaristic perspective of the legal order, the person—and therefore the consumer as a market agent—is not merely the holder of rights, but also bears duties. Accordingly, the person, in their role as consumer, must, through their choices, contribute to steering the market towards an ethical logic grounded in the person.

This lays the groundwork for the construction of a system of civil law within constitutional legality (Perlingieri, 2008), capable of subordinating patrimonial situations to existential ones—the latter, by giving effect to constitutional principles, holding an indisputable primacy. If, therefore, the point of tension in the matter under examination lies in the relationship between the person and the market, it becomes necessary to place the human person above market rules, regardless of their purchasing power. Only an approach to the person-market dialectic can truly establish a common ground between the sphere of fundamental rights and the regulatory criteria governing the market and competition.

From this perspective, following the Italian Constitution of 1947 and the Brazilian Constitution of 1988, a sign of the increasing juridification of the market can be seen in the legislature's growing attention to commercial negotiation and imbalances in "bargaining power". Addressing the regulatory or economic inequality embedded in certain contractual arrangements has implications not only for the individual relationship, but inevitably for the broader legal and economic context in which the transaction takes place. Luciani argues that:

> economic efficiency is not a value in itself and that the constitutional regulation of the economy does not have the immediate and exclusive aim of pursuing financial balance or increasing production but considers such outcomes as instruments for achieving substantive equality. (1991, p. 378)

Oppo (2001, p. 422) likewise highlights how the enterprise—including public enterprises—"cannot escape the task of reconciling socially essential interests".

The main objective of democratic societies, therefore, is to make private autonomy and private economic initiative functional to the fulfilment of the human person. Hence the importance of the express provisions in the 2002 Brazilian Civil Code regarding the social function of contracts and the prohibition of abuse of rights, and, in the 1942 Italian Civil Code, the requirement for a judicial assessment of whether a legal position merits protection under the legal order, as well as the jurisprudential development of the concept of abuse of rights. Through these instruments, the rules governing contractual balance and economic initiative are anchored in and intertwined with constitutional principles.

If the market, properly understood, constitutes a "normative framework" (Perlingieri, 1995) and all legal discourse is, by necessity, a moral discourse, it seems difficult to exclude ethical values from commercial activity or to envisage its subordination to purely economic values. In this context, transparency plays a key role, as Rizzo (1997) notes, since a corollary of the importance of transparency is the expansive force that this principle has acquired over time, extending beyond consumer contracts. Moreover, the operational limits of the principle of transparency serve as a direct foundation for duties that are not explicitly regulated (O'Neill, 2021; De Cicco, 2020a).

It is my conviction, however, that the "person-market" question is also closely linked to corporate contractual techniques, among which commercial advertising stands out. It is precisely here that ethics *in* the market and *of* the market acquire particular relevance.

3 A New Paradigm of Consumerism: The Responsible Consumer

There are various scenarios that may be explored within the scope of the chosen theme. I shall briefly mention only a few, beginning with one that I believe is fundamental to the effectiveness of fundamental rights and the consolidation of democracy: the role of the consumer as a market agent.

Brazil has an exceptionally robust consumer-protection regime; indeed, some commentators have asserted that the Consumer Protection Code elevated the consumer to the status of a rights-bearing subject by recognising them as an economic agent endowed with legally guaranteed positions, in line with the constitutional principles of human dignity and equality. The crux of the matter, however, is this: before being an economic agent, the consumer is a person, and must be protected as such—namely, as a person situated within a consumer relationship. In this light, "consumer" is but one facet of the person, not a legal status. This is confirmed by the fact that the consumer's vulnerability, like any other form of vulnerability, must be assessed *in concreto*. Vulnerability should never be treated as synonymous with consumer, as consumer-law scholarship often assumes (Miragem, 2020).

Yet that is only part of the issue. From the perspective of constitutional rights and duties, the consumer can no longer be viewed solely as a vulnerable party—let alone as intrinsically disadvantaged (Morato, 2010). They must also be held responsible *vis-à-vis* other vulnerable persons who, like them, are market agents. Consider, for instance, issues such as child labour, forced labour, environmental protection, and sustainable economics: here the consumer bears a share of responsibility towards other vulnerable stakeholders.

It is established that, in democratic states, the common values of society are recognised, and the fundamental principles of the legal order are defined within the political sphere. For this reason, the constitutional framework represents the set of values upon which the pact of collective coexistence is built—a role previously fulfilled by civil codes. Therefore, the reference to "consumer and vulnerability" does not concern the person's vulnerability the consumer relationship. On the contrary, from the perspective of law's promotional function, attention must also be directed towards forms of vulnerability underlying that relationship, including those linked to the product itself (Bobbio, 2007).

The topic fits within the broader framework of Person, Market, and Ethics. In this light, I believe the issue may be encapsulated in the expression "social responsibility of the consumer", which should signal the transition from the consumer-as-buyer to the consumer-as-citizen, and which represents the counterpart to corporate social responsibility (CSR).

The "Person, Market, and Ethics" perspective, in turn, cannot dispense with an analysis of another essential dimension: the two pairs that characterise any society aspiring to be democratic—duties and rights, freedom and responsibility—as they are both indispensable and inseparable (De Cicco, 2020b).

The aim of the question posed is to assess the compatibility, within the legal system, of an ethical view of market relations that encompasses all agents—across the full spectrum—and not only companies. It is also a matter of examining the extent to which a company's success can be evaluated not solely in economic terms, but in light of solidaristic and personalist values.

This perspective, initially little explored in both Italy and Brazil, has for some time been well developed, with the aim of re-establishing the basis of a market discipline that is sensitive to ethical values—not as the result of external imposition, but as an autonomous and conscious choice recognising the role of ethics as a driver of development. An ethical choice that enhances corporate reputation and consumer trust, while simultaneously generating social utility and responding to collective interests.

This is a model that is consistent with the Italian Constitution, but also with the Brazilian one. Article 41 of the Italian Constitution outlines a model of enterprise that promotes the well-being of the community and respects the rights of the human person, thereby guiding ordinary legislation towards the achievement of this objective—namely, the socially responsible enterprise.

However, as is well known, this is not the case in all countries, which is why the appeal to ethics becomes an attempt to overcome the absence of a common rule through the invocation of shared values. The core issue, therefore, lies in the lack of common regulatory principles within a globalised society—where, in fact, the need emerges to identify a minimum common denominator in the application and management of legal and economic systems.

We live in a globalised society—not only economically, but also legally—which means we cannot fail to safeguard the essential rights of the person within a social context characterised by constitutional solidarity (Flick, 2000; Rodotà, 2012). In this logic, if "the market presents itself as a risk—yet one that is reasonably foreseeable—and as competition among initiatives, but fair and proper, and moreover guaranteed by rules and limits" (Perlingieri, 1995), it becomes evident that we must broaden our perspective beyond a merely patrimonial view. We must accept that the exploitation of labour—including child labour—and the disregard for the person and their dignity, even when carried out indirectly by a company, cannot be deemed compatible with fair and honest competition.

The content of the freedom of private economic initiative must be properly interpreted accordingly to the values of the legal order. Consequently, if the legal system—understood from the perspective of constitutional legality—places conditions on the exercise of economic power, it is not sufficient to limit protection to the consumer understood merely as the person involved in a consumer relationship. It becomes necessary to extend such protection to all vulnerable persons involved in the productive process.

Ultimately, and in summary, strengthening CSR means promoting a "voluntary" instrument aimed at fostering greater equity in workers' rights across the globe. This is because we know that regulatory divergence allows for exploitation and generates multiple negative repercussions that directly affect our societies. Hence the imperative to promote education for sustainable consumption—in every sense. The role of consumers thus becomes fundamental in the fight against exploitation, as they are in a position to demand that companies pay greater attention to the rights of workers engaged in the production process. One must not overlook the fact that the precarious conditions faced by workers in Eastern Europe, India, and China also render the situation of "domestic" workers more vulnerable, as they remain exposed to the threat of companies relocating or outsourcing production whenever workers' demands place too much pressure on the enterprise.

Broadly speaking, it appears that companies have at last come to recognise ethics as a value. Indeed, while for businesses were reluctant to acknowledge the rights and interests of stakeholders, we are now witnessing a cultural shift in which ethics increasingly permeates economic relations and gradually reshapes the perception of the company's role in contemporary society—while also influencing its conduct.

In this context, the growing attention paid by younger generations to the social and environmental impact of companies undoubtedly plays a role. This heightened sensitivity leads companies to invest more in their reputation, which is increasingly seen as a key to securing their future.

A recent outcome of the growing awareness that duties may precede rights—at least from the corporate side (Gulotta, 2020)—can be seen in the document signed by two hundred of the largest American companies participating in *The Business Roundtable*. In this statement, they reject the long-standing mantra of "shareholders first" that has guided corporate policy for decades. To create value, they now affirm, companies must also consider ecological impact, respect for customers, and the provision of dignified conditions for workers.

The first institutional initiatives at the international level—and within the United Nations—were launched in the 1990s in the context of human rights protection and the promotion of sustainable development. Following the Rio de Janeiro Summit in 1992, the UN began addressing the issue of corporate relocation, inviting major multinational corporations to enter into commercial agreements that would safeguard basic human rights, with particular attention to the rights of children, workers, and the environment. Over time, these awareness-raising efforts led to the creation of an innovative initiative: the Global Compact of 2000, an agreement bringing together businesses, UN agencies, and civil society actors (including trade unions, NGOs, and universities) to "promote socially responsible citizenship rights so that companies can be part of the solution to the challenges of globalisation" (United Nations, 2000). The initiative initially pursued nine goals—later expanded to ten—ranging from the protection of fundamental human rights and compliance with minimum labour standards, to environmental protection and the fight against corruption.

It remains to be seen, however, to what extent this commitment will also apply to outsourced workers, as this issue is not addressed in the document. It is, in any case, a step forward—an additional tool for ensuring the effectiveness of human rights. Considering this context, I believe that the time is now ripe for an approach that takes into account the other side of the coin—namely, the consumer as a market agent. I would go so far as to say as a *fundamental* market agent, and I believe this point can now be regarded as incontestable. Hence my reference to "Consumer Social Responsibility" (CSR).

It is of great importance to encourage and strengthen awareness of the need for a new market culture—one that fosters respect for human rights, especially those of the most vulnerable, such as children, adolescents, and the elderly. This outcome can be achieved through a robust campaign to raise consumer awareness, making them conscious of their purchasing power and willing to support the survival of ethical products in the market. Ideally, only ethical products should be favoured. Consumers must come to understand that there is no right without a corresponding duty. In this specific case, alongside the right to a robust protective framework under the legal system, consumers also bear the duty to monitor and demand ethical and responsible conduct from companies.

Drawing on the binomials of duties and rights/freedom and responsibility to which I have previously referred, the consumer can no longer be regarded as a vulnerable person. They must also be held accountable in relation to other categories of vulnerable individuals—market agents like themselves, to the extent that as Luciani states: "solidarity's notion implies the idea of community, where it is natural for members to be bound more by moral ties—where reciprocal positions of duty are emphasised—than by legal ties, in which reciprocal positions of right are exalted" (1995, p. 129).

Consumers must become aware that ethics concerns them as well, and not only companies. This is because, as it is important to recall, the duty of solidarity operates not only in the relationship between the State and the individual, but also among private actors. In short, it is necessary to highlight the ethical dimension underlying consumption. Indeed, to encourage companies to move towards CSR, it is essential that consumers do not merely expose the critical issues at stake, but that they also recognise, through their purchasing behaviour, corporate commitment to sustainability.

Duties inherently entail the ethical accountability of the individual. Regarding the subject at hand, for instance, consumers have a duty of ethical oversight, which may include boycotting companies whose business policies are not ethically sound. In support of this claim, one may refer—albeit to a somewhat dated yet emblematic example—to the boycott organised by a US consumer association against Nike products manufactured through slave and child labour. This action led the multinational to revise its corporate policy, adopting a more committed stance in combating labour exploitation within its supply chain. More recently, Canadian consumers have responded to Donald Trump's irrational posture by boycotting American products and choosing to purchase domestically produced goods instead.

A consumer association is a collective that acts in defence of consumers, but this does not mean it cannot pursue ethical objectives. It may also act in defence of other forms of vulnerability—beyond that of the consumer—by encouraging consumers to boycott companies that, through the exploitation of workers or child labour, or through neglect of animal welfare and environmental protection, fail to act ethically.

It is necessary to raise consumer awareness in this regard, and to that end, education in responsible consumption is not only desirable but imperative. I would even say it is the most effective means of achieving the overarching goal of protecting the human person. In recent times, consumers have been encouraged to engage in sustainable and environmentally conscious consumption—for example, by supporting sustainable agriculture through their dietary choices or by switching to renewable energy sources through green energy providers.

With regard to energy, it is worth highlighting that the consumer has taken on a new and more prominent role and, in this capacity, is referred to—by analogy with the term coined by Marshall McLuhan and further developed by Alvin Toffler (1984) as a "prosumer": that is, a consumer capable of producing the energy they use, becoming not merely a consumer but an active participant in the energy production process.

This is referred to as a form of protagonism because the prosumer takes on a leading role by both producing and consuming renewable energy. It is considered a position of prominence because, in a context of ecological crisis and climate change, the consumer's voluntary shift from a passive to an active stance in relation to electricity use constitutes yet another line of defence in the shared responsibility to combat climate change.

Even if, for the time being, this remains merely a moral duty on the part of the consumer, it is nonetheless one of the paths that must be pursued. These are small gestures, but ones that can make a meaningful difference when replicated on a global scale. One could even say that this represents a policy from which there is, quite rightly, no turning back.

4 Subsequently: Commercial Advertising and Economic Exploitation of Personality. The Culture of Responsibility

Bearing in mind the centrality of the person within the legal order, another area that demands greater attention and responsibility on the part of the consumer concerns corporate communication or advertising—namely, commercial advertising. In Brazil, such advertising is regarded as an expression of the company's freedom of speech and, for this reason, is often—though mistakenly—treated as absolute. We know that there are no absolute rights or freedoms, as all are limited by the rights and freedoms of others; yet this fundamental point is often overlooked or disregarded.

This view was overcome in Italy by *Decision No. 231 of 17 October 1985* of the Constitutional Court, which, in systematising the acts and activities undertaken by companies to manage their relations with the market, placed commercial advertising within the scope of Article 41 of the Constitution, identifying it as a business activity. Consequently, the Court affirmed the need for legislative intervention to protect constitutionally recognised goods and values, such as health, children and adolescents, the environment, and, above all, human dignity. This approach has since been followed by lower courts, the Supreme Court, and the system of advertising self-regulation.

The discussion on advertising is a broad one and can only be briefly outlined here, bearing in mind that, despite good intentions and the strong protective framework present in the legal order, the prevailing logic remains that of consumption and profit. It is in this context that a connection emerges between advertising, the duty of self-protection, and the culture of responsibility.

In Brazil, the National Council for Advertising Self-Regulation (CONAR, 1980) itself acknowledges that its primary function is to preserve the credibility of advertising discourse, understood as an essential element for the proper functioning of the market. Indeed, on its website it presents itself as a non-governmental organisation whose aim is to promote freedom of advertising expression and to defend the constitutional prerogatives of commercial advertising. In other words, notwithstanding the good intentions of protecting the consumer—rather than the person (for this distinction, see De Cicco, 2008)—that underlie its self-regulatory code, and despite the wording of Article 19, this body appears to act primarily so as to safeguard the image of, and trust in, advertising, without assuming a direct role in the protection of persons.

Just think about advertising aimed at children and the continued use of women as objects of desire or even in stigmatised situations, albeit to a lesser extent than in the 1950s to 1990s. Despite the valuable work carried out by CONANDA (the Brazilian National Council for the Rights of Children and Adolescents) in protecting children and adolescents, it continues to face resistance from companies that view its recommendations and decisions as a form of censorship of freedom of expression.

Here too, both consumers and consumer associations should be held accountable for violations of the fundamental rights of vulnerable individuals. A consumer association is a collective composed of consumer-persons acting in defence of consumers. However, this does not mean that it cannot—and indeed should—pursue ethical objectives. Such associations may act in defence of the various forms of vulnerability that underlie consumer relations and concern the products at the heart of those relations. They could do so, for example, by encouraging consumers to boycott companies that act unethically—whether by exploiting workers or child labour, failing to protect animals, or neglecting environmental sustainability.

It is well established that consumers often act as a result of impulses created by companies that artificially generate interests and needs through advertising. A particularly illustrative example is that of designer brands. Consumers likely fail to realise—or simply disregard—that a brand label is, in fact, a form of advertising, and one that is free of charge. Free, of course, for the company—because to display that advertising, the consumer pays, and often pays a great deal. A major triumph of marketing. In reality, in such cases, companies are using consumers as indirect agents of advertising that, strictly speaking, they themselves might not always be permitted to undertake directly.

When we wear clothing or use a product bearing a prominently displayed brand, we are promoting that brand and encouraging others to do the same. This promotion is a form of communication—it is commercial advertising. This is evidenced, for example, by the fact that both European and Brazilian legislation prohibit the display of product brands during television broadcasts when not expressly identified as advertising, considering such practices to constitute covert advertising. If the product we are promoting has been manufactured in violation of other people's human rights—a scenario that is all too real—we must question the legitimacy of such promotion, of such advertising.

This is because, as we have argued, commercial advertising is not free in the sense of being absolute. It is limited by the rights of others and by respect for human dignity—values of the highest order within our legal system. This is not a matter of censorship, as the "masters of advertising" often seek to claim.

Other examples may be considered, such as the economic use of personality through contractual arrangements—an issue that has acquired new dimensions with the expansion of the market sphere and, consequently, of contractual relations. This topic has become the subject of increasing debate due to market innovations that increasingly expose the human person to degrading conditions.

The protection of the existential dimension of the human person, whose respect and safeguard are constitutionally guaranteed, requires the adaptation of contract law to the system of constitutional values. Within this context of widespread commercialisation of all kinds of goods, the principle of dignity emerges as a limit to contractual freedom, safeguarding an intangible ethical minimum and thereby justifying the control of private autonomy. I believe that the most significant and well-known cases—frequently studied in the classroom—are the so-called *Peep-Show Case*, decided by the German Federal Administrative Court in 1981, and the French case concerning dwarf-tossing(*lancer de nain*).

The first case concerned whether it was permissible to prohibit an activity that "reduced the individual to the object of a depersonalising and automated commercial enterprise", despite the "informed" consent of the person hired to perform such work. The German Federal Administrative Court (*Bundesverwaltungsgericht*) held in its *Decision of 15 December 1981* that the woman's consent to perform such activity was irrelevant, as dignity is an objective value to be safeguarded by the State—through the figure of the judge—and not a merely subjective interest belonging to the individual, who would otherwise be entitled to define its scope and dispose of it according to personal criteria. This decision was later upheld by the Federal Constitutional Court (*Bundesverfassungsgericht*) in its *Decision of 7 September 1986* (BVerwG, 1981, p. 664; BVerfG, 1986, p. 3246).

The second case concerned a game practised in several nightclubs in France, in which clients would compete to throw individuals with dwarfism as far as possible. The physical integrity of the participants was safeguarded by a series of safety measures. The individuals with dwarfism expressed full satisfaction with the activity, which provided them with a dignified livelihood and a certain degree of notoriety among clients and friends.

Despite the full consent of those involved in the notorious game, its practice was prohibited by various public authorities on the grounds that it constituted an affront to human dignity—particularly considering the physical disability of the individuals being "thrown". This position was later upheld and consolidated by the French *Conseil d'État* in its *Decision of 27 October 1995, Commune de Morsang-sur-Orge*. According to the decision, human dignity is a component of public order and an "absolute principle that does not tolerate limitation, not even by the individual concerned, and which, as such, prevails over the guarantee of other fundamental freedoms, such as the freedom to work and the freedom of economic initiative" (Conseil d'État, 1995).

The limits of the economic exploitation of personality likewise raise complex issues, which have been the subject of criticism from both sides (Resta, 2002)—though these cannot be explored in detail here. It is nonetheless important to highlight that, even in such cases, the question of the duty of self-protection emerges forcefully, alongside the need to consolidate a culture of responsibility.

As we have seen, consumers have been encouraged to adopt sustainable and ecological consumption habits, particularly in relation to the environment and the food sector. But if, as Lafayete Petter argues, "the free choice of the consumer may legitimately be restricted in the name of environmental protection", in order to raise awareness "of the ecological dimension of the consumption process in general and of their individual behaviour in particular" (2005, p. 38). Then why should we not demand the same with regard to the protection of health, life, the right to education, and the very dignity of the workers involved in the economic and production process?

Alongside the polluter-pays principle, legal scholarship also invokes the user-pays principle (Benjamin, 1993), according to which consumption practices must be aligned with the rational and sustainable use of natural resources.

What I question is whether it is possible to affirm that consumers are responsible—or can be held responsible—for perpetuating the violation of these rights, or of the rights of those groups which are, indeed, highly vulnerable. These groups have no choice, as they are forced to accept—or endure—the conditions imposed by the employer. Consumers, on the other hand, often *do* have a choice. I say "often" because, in some situations, the choice is effectively constrained. In Italy, for example, agricultural harvesting is, in many cases, carried out by informal workers, sometimes in conditions akin to slavery. Yet people cannot stop eating, and so—even when aware that the tomatoes they are purchasing may be the product of human rights violations—they continue to buy them. Of course, there are also circumstances that *do* allow for choice—for instance, by buying directly from local farmers. In such cases, it is the consumer's responsibility to avoid supporting those who exploit workers, thereby sending a clear ethical message to the producer.

The situation is different when it comes to non-essential goods, because here a choice is (almost) always possible. There is still much to be done in this regard. When it comes to consumption, individualism prevails. We are far from achieving a positive outcome. The problem may lie in the fact that, in reality, the consumer believes they have nothing to lose by consuming such products—and nothing to gain by adopting ethical behaviour.

Companies, by contrast, appear to have understood how much they stand to gain—or lose. Take, for example, the stance adopted by Coca-Cola and other giants that joined the *Stop Hate for Profit* campaign, which called for a boycott of social media platforms accused of failing to take sufficient measures to combat hateful and racist content. These companies announced their intention to suspend their advertising on such platforms for a certain period. A decision which, in reality, reflects the growing awareness among major corporations of the importance of reputation for their revenue—especially in today's social media era, where, on the one hand, a good practice can go viral and enhance a company's visibility, but on the other hand, a single misstep may irreparably damage its reputation.

We are far from achieving a comparable outcome when it comes to consumers. It is a matter of recognising that the duty of constitutional solidarity applies to all sectors of society—and to each of us. Not to "others", as is commonly assumed, but to all of us. It is essential to continue promoting education in responsible consumption—not only about the environment or the food sector, as is already being done, but also to protect those who are truly and vulnerable.

If it is true that, to achieve positive outcomes in situations that are, let us say, uncomfortable, it is necessary to affect people's wallets, then perhaps the legislator should be urged to impose liability for the compensation or reparation of harm caused by the violation of people's rights and dignity not only on companies, but also on consumers. This latter solution could be made viable—albeit indirectly—by introducing a substantial fine on companies that violate the rights of vulnerable individuals, which, as often happens in such circumstances, would be passed on to consumers. The publicity accompanying the imposition of such a fine would serve as a warning to consumers, who would become aware that they are paying a higher price for consuming a good or service produced in breach of the fundamental rights of those involved in the production process.

We need greater awareness of our duties—and of the fact that, while individualism consists merely in the attribution of rights, personalism entails a set of both rights and duties, such that freedom is always a source of responsibility.

5 The Duty of Self-Protection and the Culture of Responsibility

The duty of self-protection immediately evokes the need to be aware of risks, to adopt safe behaviours, and to be prepared for emergencies—not only for one's own safety, but also for that of others; in other words, a predominantly public dimension of this duty. However, this represents only one aspect—and not the most important—of this fundamental obligation.

The duty of self-protection concerns, above all, individual responsibility which, when properly observed, contributes to the consolidation of a culture of responsibility—something essential to any democratic society. One might say it lies at the heart of the rights-duties and freedom-responsibility binomials to which I have already referred, insofar as the effectiveness of rights presupposes human rights education (De Cicco, 2014)—education aimed at encouraging individuals to reflect on the very existence and content of those rights.

Along these lines, if the effectiveness of citizenship and civic awareness presupposes education in respect for oneself and for others, then the role of education in responsibility becomes central—to prevent the emergence of the situation described by Bruno Garschagen (2019), who warns of the risks associated with the (abusive) use of privileges by the State: the merely formal recognition of new rights creates, within society, the expectation that these new rights will contribute to the realisation of those that already exist.

The most detrimental consequence of this situation can be observed in the behaviour of those who do not feel responsible for fulfilling their duties, justifying their irresponsible conduct on the grounds of "not having received what they were entitled to". The example we provided regarding the conduct of consumers may serve as concrete evidence of this claim. Indeed, the more a right is pushed to its limits in terms of its enforcement—as is the case with consumer protection in Brazil and Italy—the greater the potential repercussions in terms of the violation of the rights of others (Zagrebelsky, 2017). Rodotà (2009) himself described the law as an instrument at the service of the "profession of living", of freedom, and of dignity. But if we truly wish to regard the law as a limit on power—as it rightly ought to be—then we must actively contribute to the achievement of that goal; and the best way to do so is by adopting a virtuous attitude of self-protection and responsibility.

In the current landscape shaped by new technologies, the need for self-protection and a culture of responsibility becomes more pressing, as the digital age has gradually altered the way individuals perceive themselves—both as individuals and as members of a community. Moreover, the technological and digital revolution we are witnessing comes at a cost, as all revolutions do—though the full extent of that cost remains unknown. It can be stated with certainty, however, that it entails a compression of privacy—made all the more serious by the fact that, through the use of social media, individuals put at risk and progressively devalue not only their own private sphere, but also that of their "friends".

Not by chance, since the beginning of its activities—and especially with the advent of the Internet, the place where nothing is ever lost or forgotten—the Italian data protection authority (the *Autorità Garante per la protezione dei dati personali*—Garante) has consistently had to navigate between its role of arbitrating conflicts between the information system and the individuals who are the subject of news reports, and its task of addressing the dilemma faced by many: the desire to "appear publicly" while simultaneously preserving their privacy. In doing so, it has sought above all to define the sphere of intimacy to which every person—whether "public" or "private"—is entitled. In this regard, Stefano Rodotà (2018, p. 3) speaks of a *società dell'apparire*—a "society of appearance"—to describe the widely felt need to present oneself in public, questioning whether, considering this, it still makes sense to defend privacy when such protection appears to be undermined, or even rejected, by prevailing social behaviours. A response to this question may be found in another of his reflections, in which he defines the protection of personal data as a core component of democratic citizenship in the information society.

The issue of self-responsibility thus recalls Rodotà's teaching (2004)—present throughout his work on privacy and the protection of personal data—that privacy means the possibility of projecting oneself into the world freely through one's own information, while always maintaining control over how that information circulates and is used by others. It is an important lesson, but one which today, more than ever, must consider the progressive shift in how the person is perceived, as previously discussed. Rodotà's assertions (1997, 2004) are entirely valid—but I believe the core of the problem lies precisely here: on the Internet, and especially on social media, it is no longer possible to exercise true control over the information that circulates there.

The internet, quite evidently, requires an innovative way of conceiving the traditionally conflictual relationship between the right to privacy and the freedom of information and communication. Likewise, it demands a new approach to balancing these interests—one capable of promoting the fundamental interest shared by operators and users of the internet: the full and effective functioning of the flow of information and communication made possible by the network.

In this respect and based on the sound premise that all individuals must be recognised as holders of a "right to informational self-determination", it seems fair to regard as misleading the claim that the realisation of this right depends solely on the interaction of individual wills within a market unrestricted by regulation. According to this view, everything should be left to personal choice, and everyone should be free to determine the level of privacy they wish to enjoy. We have already seen, however, that market regulation cannot be left to itself, as it disregards the longstanding issue of unequal bargaining power and the existence of more vulnerable parties—who, under a purely market-driven logic, could even be exposed to the sacrifice of their dignity. Likewise, it overlooks the extremely delicate balancing of interests inherent in the regulation of personal data—something that cannot be entrusted solely to market dynamics, given that values such as equality, respect for individual and social dignity, and freedom of information are at stake.

It should be recalled that the duty of self-protection is closely linked to the right to informational self-determination and is essential to its effectiveness. Indeed, informational self-determination presupposes both rights and duties—and one might even say duties before rights—since State intervention is of little use if the individual does not take responsibility for safeguarding themselves and their own rights.

If, at first, it was necessary for individuals to refrain from exposing their lives on social media—treating these platforms as if they were personal diaries—today that is no longer sufficient. What is now required is far greater care in controlling one's personal data, which, in most cases, is already in the hands of third parties. Beyond one's own social media profile—which many have renounced or chosen to abandon—it is virtually certain that people's lives now flow through the Internet, from the mere commercialisation of products to essential interactions with public administration. This occurs in such an invasive manner that it has even led to the discrimination of individuals without access to the Internet.

There are many situations in which accepting the conditions imposed by the other party online is the only way to obtain a good or service—much like in the early days of legislation aimed at protecting the vulnerable party in contractual relationships. The protection provided by the legal system, when it existed, was merely formal. There has been progress in this area, culminating in today's consumer protection legislation which, in my view, has had the paradoxical effect of stripping the consumer of any duty to protect themselves. In this regard, one speaks of a "genetic flaw" in consent, and rightly so. However, the issue must be contextualised, because even though our consent may be conditioned by the need or desire to obtain the good or service, we cannot—and should not—provide our data without first exercising some level of control over the counterparty. We must take responsibility. Self-protection becomes an imperative!

We enjoy a great deal of freedom, yet people often forget that, like any form of liberty, it is intrinsically limited by responsibility. There is no freedom without responsibility. In the pursuit of total consumer/user protection, the entire burden of ensuring informational self-determination is shifted onto the company, thereby denying the freedom-responsibility dyad that is essential to a democratic society.

The foundation of this dyad is the principle of solidarity, which means that the issue is also tied to the ethics of and within the market.

This is a highly complex matter that must be approached with care and rigour, without grounding everything solely in the concept of human dignity, so as not to trivialise it. It is always important to remember that human dignity is not a super-rule or super-principle. It is a value immanent to the person. The person *is* dignity itself.

This issue also concerns the control over the content of posts, which must likewise be contextualised, taking into account freedom of expression—a freedom that is broad but not unlimited. It is also intrinsically limited by the freedoms of others and by the respect owed to all people. In democratic societies, it is imperative that individuals take responsibility for the opinions they express.

In this context, limiting freedom of expression should be understood to curb hate speech—speech that incites hatred, discrimination, or offence. In such cases, companies may be held liable, given that the algorithms they use, through keyword detection, can identify such content and preventing its dissemination.

All of this represents, nearly thirty years later, the realisation of the binomial that Rodotà identified in 1997 as the constitutive foundation of personal data protection: *riservatezza* and *controllo*—privacy and control—specifying that the former is aligned with silence, and the latter with social transparency. In other words, the combination of control over one's own data and the immunity of the private sphere from undue external interference allows individual rights to become instruments of social progress, as aptly summarised by Antonello Soro during the event *"Verso una nuova Privacy"*, held in memory of Stefano Rodotà (Garante per la protezione dei dati personali, 2017).

This highlights the imperative of self-protection which, despite its delicate balance, must govern individuals' conduct both in their interpersonal relations and within the (global) community in which they live. Indeed, considering that privacy and the internet do not combine well together, it is, as stated from the outset, pointless for the State to intervene to protect the individual if the person does not care to safeguard themselves and their own rights, in accordance with the principle of social solidarity that governs every democratic society.

References

Benjamin, A. H. de V. (1993). O princípio do poluidor-pagador e a reparação do dano ambiental. In *Dano ambiental: prevenção, reparação e repressão* (pp. 226–236). Editora Revista dos Tribunais.

Bobbio, N. (2007). La funzione promozionale del diritto. In *Dalla struttura alla funzione* (pp. 28–50). Laterza.

Bundesverwaltungsgericht [BVerwG]. (1981, December 15). Decision published in *Neue Juristische Wochenschrift* (NJW, 1982, p. 664).

Bundesverfassungsgericht [BVerfG]. (1986, September 7). Decision published in *Neue Juristische Wochenschrift* (NJW, 1987, p. 3246).

Conseil d'État. (1995, October 27). *Commune de Morsang-sur-Orge* (Nos. 136727 and 143578). https://conseil-etat.fr
Conselho Nacional de Autorregulamentação Publicitária. (1980). *Código Brasileiro de Autorregulamentação Publicitária* (Reg. No. 5678, 2º Cartório de Registro de Títulos e Documentos de São Paulo, 11 May 1980). http://www.conar.org.br/pdf/Codigo-CONAR-2024.pdf
Constitutional Court of Italy. (1985, October 17). Decision No. 231 of 17 October 1985. https://www.cortecostituzionale.it
De Cicco, M. C. (2008). A pessoa e o mercado. *Estudos de Direito do Consumidor 2006/2007, 8*, 93–107.
De Cicco, M. C. (2014). L'éducation aux droits de l'homme: L'expérience italienne. In V. Champeil-Desplats (Ed.), *Pédagogie et droits de l'homme* (pp. 245–251). Presses Universitaires de Paris Ouest.
De Cicco, M. C. (Ed.). (2020a). *Os deveres na era dos direitos entre ética e mercado* (bilingual ed.). Editoriale Scientifica.
De Cicco, M. C. (2020b). O papel dos deveres na construção da legalidade constitucional. In M. C. De Cicco (Ed.), *Os deveres na era dos direitos entre ética e mercado* (bilingual ed., pp. 12–49). Editoriale Scientifica.
Flick, G. M. (2000). *Globalizzazione e Diritti Umani. Jus, 2*, 171–185.
Garschagen, B. (2019). Direitos máximos, deveres mínimos: O festival de privilégios que assola o Brasil. Record.
Gulotta, C. (2020). O dever de diligência como instrumento para a regulamentação das cadeias globais de fornecimento. In M. C. De Cicco (Ed.), *Os deveres na era dos direitos entre ética e mercado* (bilingual ed., pp. 328 et seq.). Edizioni Scientifiche.
Irti, N. (1998). *L'ordine giuridico del mercato*. Laterza.
Luciani, M. (1991). Economia nel diritto costituzionale. In *Digesto delle discipline pubblicistiche* (Vol. 5, p. 378). UTET.
Luciani, M. (1995). Sui diritti sociali. In *Studi in onore di Manlio Mazziotti di Celso* (Vol. 2, pp. 97–134). Cedam.
Miragem, B. (2020). Princípio da vulnerabilidade: Perspectiva atual e funções no direito do consumidor contemporâneo. In B. Miragem, C. Marques, & L. A. Magalhães (Eds.), *Direito do consumidor: 30 anos do CDC—da consolidação como direito fundamental aos atuais desafios da sociedade* (pp. 243–263). Forense.
Morato, A. C. (2010). O conceito de hipossuficiência e a exclusão digital do consumidor na sociedade da informação. In A. C. Morato & P. T. Neri (Eds.), *20 anos do Código de Defesa do Consumidor* (pp. 9–21). Atlas.
O'Neill, O. (2021). *A philosopher looks at digital communication*. Cambridge University Press.
Oppo, G. (2001). Impresa e mercato. *Rivista di Diritto Civile, 47*(4), 421–422.
Perlingieri, P. (1995). Mercato, solidarietà e diritti umani. *Rassegna di diritto civile*, 84–117.
Perlingieri, P. (2008). *O direito civil na legalidade constitucional* (M. C. De Cicco, Trans.). Renovar.
Petter, L. J. (2005). *Princípios constitucionais da ordem econômica: O significado e o alcance do art.* 170 da Constituição Federal. Revista dos Tribunais.
Resta, G. (2002). La disponibilità dei diritti fondamentali e i limiti della dignità (note a margine della Carta dei Diritti). *Rivista di diritto civile*, 801–848.
Rizzo, V. (1997). *Trasparenza e "contratti del consumatore" (la novella al Codice civile)*. Edizioni Scientifiche.
Rodotà, S. (1997). *Relazione delle attività per l'anno 1997*. Garante per la protezione dei dati personali. https://www.garanteprivacy.it
Rodotà, S. (2004). *Tecnopolitica: La democrazia e le nuove tecnologie della comunicazione* (New ed.). Laterza.
Rodotà, S. (2009). *La vita e le regole: Tra diritto e non diritto*. Feltrinelli.
Rodotà, S. (2012). *Il diritto di avere diritti*. Laterza.
Rodotà, S. (2018). *Vivere la democrazia*. Laterza.
Smith, A. (2013). *La ricchezza delle nazioni* (A. Bagiotti & T. Bagiotti, Eds.). UTET.

Soro, A. (2017). *Incontro "Verso una nuova privacy". In ricordo di Stefano Rodotà*. Garante per la protezione dei dati personali. https://garanteprivacy.it
Toffler, A. (1984). *The third wave*. Bantam Books.
United Nations. (2000). *United Nations global compact*. https://www.unglobalcompact.org
Zagrebelsky, G. (2017). *Diritti per forza*. Einaudi.

Maria Cristina De Cicco was formerly Associate Professor of Private Law at the University of Camerino, from which she is now retired. De Cicco also taught at the School of Specialisation in Civil Law. She is a member of the Society of Civil Law Scholars, the Society for Research in Comparative Law, and the IBDFam. Her research and publications focus on Civil Law, Constitutional Legality, and the relationship between Person and Market.

Governance Frameworks for High-Risk Artificial Intelligence: Balancing Ethical Principles and Technological Innovation

Juliano Maranhão and Bernardo Fico

Abstract Governance in Artificial Intelligence (AI) is a necessary topic when seeking to ensure the ethical and responsible use of technology. This article examines risk-based governance as a multidimensional framework for managing risks posed by AI systems. Drawing on international standards developed by the International Organization for Standardization (ISO), the National Institute of Standards and Technology (NIST), and the Institute of Electrical and Electronics Engineers (IEEE), as well as legislative approaches such as the European Union's AI Act (European Parliament, 2023) and Brazil's PL 2338/2023 (Brazilian Senate, 2023), the study identifies convergences and differences in existing (or proposed) governance models. It argues that high-risk AI systems demand continuous lifecycle risk management, organisational accountability, transparent human-AI interaction, and sector-specific adaptation. By integrating technical and legal perspectives, the article contributes to AI governance offering strategic recommendations for advancing adaptive, inclusive, and rights-respecting regulatory frameworks with a balance between innovation and accountability.

Keywords Artificial Intelligence Governance · Ethical AI · High-risk AI systems · Risk management in AI · Transparency in AI

1 Introduction

The accelerated integration of Artificial Intelligence (AI) into everyday activities has prompted widespread concern about its ethical, legal, and societal implications. AI is no longer a peripheral technology; it now constitutes a general-purpose infrastructure capable of transforming critical domains such as health, education, and

J. Maranhão
Lawgorithm, São Paulo, Brazil
e-mail: bernardo@lawgorithm.org.br

B. Fico (✉)
University of São Paulo (USP), São Paulo, Brazil
e-mail: julianomaranhao@usp.br

K. Bodrožić-Brnić et al. (eds.), *AI and the Ethics of Innovation*, Digital Transformation and Innovation, https://doi.org/10.1007/978-3-032-20638-1_11

public institutions. While its potential to optimise services and enable data-driven decision-making is widely acknowledged, its deployment may generate risks related to bias, overconfidence, error, transparency, accountability, privacy, data protection, labour, and environment, impacting both individuals and collectives. This challenge is especially relevant in the context of high-risk AI systems.

At the centre of regulatory and governance debates lies the tension between fostering technological innovation while ensuring that AI systems do not undermine fundamental rights. Generative AI further intensifies these concerns by introducing uncertainties such as hallucinations, semantic leakage, and automation bias, which compound with traditional risks like algorithmic discrimination, data misuse, and cyber vulnerabilities. This implies the need for more than just technical robustness, but a governance structure that combine risk-based management, ethical safeguards, and enforceability.

In response, governments, standardisation bodies, and civil society organisations have proposed a variety of AI governance frameworks that combine legal obligations, technical standards, and institutional practices. However, governance is often narrowly equated with regulation or *ex post* compliance. This article advances a broader understanding of AI governance—as a lifecycle-based, risk-oriented framework that aligns technical systems with ethical principles through anticipatory and adaptive mechanisms. Drawing on international standards like the International Organization for Standardization (ISO), the National Institute of Standards and Technology (NIST), and the Institute of Electrical and Electronics Engineers (IEEE) and legislative models, notably the European Union's AI Act (European Parliament, 2023) and Brazil's PL 2338/2023 (Brazilian Senate, 2023), we conceptualise governance as the coordination of technical, legal, and institutional perspectives to ensure the socially responsible deployment of high-risk AI systems.

The article is structured into six sections. Section 2 defines AI governance, emphasising its structural and procedural dimensions. Section 3 outlines the typology of risks—epistemic, ethical/social, operational/technical and systemic—posed by both "conventional" and generative AI. Section 4 critically reviews international governance frameworks, including technical standards and risk-based legislative models from the EU, Brazil, and other jurisdictions. Section 5 proposes technical, organisational, and ethical-regulatory measures for high-risk AI governance. Section 6 concludes by proposing a set of recommendations for adaptive, sector-sensitive, and globally coordinated AI governance strategies.

2 Governance and Risk Management in AI

The governance of AI must be understood not as a merely technical or legal mechanism, but as a multi-level system encompassing ethics, organisational responsibility and oversight, and lifecycle risk management. Governance shapes through norms and implementation mechanisms how ethical, legal, and social principles are embedded into AI systems. While it often incorporates regulatory tools, governance is not reducible to them and includes formal and informal modes of coordination. Similarly, though risk management contributes greatly to governance measures—such as enabling hazard identification, impact assessment, and mitigation planning—it is part of governance, not its totality.

As articulated in ISO (2022a), governance is primarily concerned with organisational accountability and strategic alignment. AI systems frequently operate in dynamic environments with partly opaque technical mechanisms and often decentralised implementation. Thus, it is the responsibility of decision-makers to ensure that AI systems are not only compliant with law but also consistent with the institution's mission, ethical commitments, and stakeholder expectations. Governance thus exists as an orientation that needs to integrate technical knowledge, legal norms, design, and ethics to determine how systems are built, used, governed and made accountable. In this model, governance is not an *ex-post* mechanism of control (after-the-fact accountability) but a part of the design and organisational culture.

Unlike traditional governance models, which often intervene at discrete moments (e.g. approval or enforcement), AI governance must operate continuously across the full system lifecycle—from conception and design through training, deployment, monitoring, and decommissioning (ISO, 2023). A comprehensive model of risk governance is proposed by ISO (2023a) spanning these stages of AI systems and emphasising principles such as proportionality, adaptability, and transparency. The propose itself, however, indicates that risks cannot be fully predicted or eliminated *ex ante*, and must therefore be addressed through continuous iterations and adaptive control mechanisms. Similarly, NIST (2023) encourages organisations to integrate governance with technical practices such as documentation, logging, and auditability, thereby reinforcing the traceability and accountability of AI operations throughout their lifecycle.

Beyond technical controls and legal obligations AI governance must also ensure systems are aligned with fundamental rights. This requires a framework for what may be termed socio-technical alignment—a configuration in which system objectives, operational processes, and ethical commitments are co-designed with the social contexts in which AI systems operate.

As explained in the CNJ report on generative AI, "risk-based ethical governance model" is a comprehensive framework that considers not only performance metrics, but also legitimacy, contestability, and institutional roles of the application (CNJ, 2024). A purely procedural or technocratic approach can be problematic (e.g. procedural or data-centric view of governance may obscure deeper questions about the legitimacy and social value of AI applications) and should thus yield to a finalistic orientation grounded in the principles of human dignity, autonomy and collective well-being (Lawgorithm, 2025).

Taken together, these perspectives affirm that AI governance must be integrative, anticipatory, and context-sensitive, bridging formal regulation and informal ethical norms, embedding risk management within technical systems, and aligning institutional responsibilities with broader societal goals. As the following sections of this article will argue, such a governance framework is particularly important for high-risk and generative AI systems.

3 Risks and Challenges of Artificial Intelligence: From Traditional Models to Generative AI

Effective governance of high-risk artificial intelligence systems requires a clear understanding of their diverse and evolving risks. These risks are neither uniform (not all AI systems have the same types of risk) nor static (as AI systems evolve or are created, new risks arise). That is, they vary by application domain, technological architecture, and context of usage. To develop appropriate governance responses, it is essential to classify risks in different categories.

This section organises the AI risks into four categories: epistemic (e.g. uncertainties, deficiencies), ethical-social (e.g. privacy, transparency), operational-technical (e.g. security, resilience), and systemic (e.g. large-scale, cumulative, and often diffuse harms) Table 1.

Epistemic risks in AI refer to uncertainties and deficiencies in how AI systems generate, justify, or validate outputs. In traditional models—particularly those involving complex machine learning such as deep neural networks—these risks manifest as limited interpretability/explainability (also referred to as "black box" phenomena), and errors in probabilistic inference. As emphasised by ISO (2020), explainability is a foundational criterion for trustworthiness and must be considered a primary governance concern. Generative AI systems exacerbate epistemic risks by producing content that appears correct but does not have factual grounding. These systems are prone to hallucinations (i.e. generating false or misleading information), semantic leakage (undue disclosure of data), output inconsistency, and may cause

Table 1 Typology of AI Risks Across Traditional and Generative AI

Risk	Traditional AI	Generative AI
Epistemic	- lack of explainability and interpretability (transparency)- inference opacity and errors	- hallucinations (fabricated outputs)- semantic leakage - automation bias - overconfidence in outputs
Ethical-social	- algorithmic discrimination - privacy violations and inferential profiling - breach of confidentiality	- stereotype/bias reproduction - data colonialism - misuse or retention of user-provided input data - institutional opacity and lack of transparency of use
Operational-technical	- systemic faults and cascading failures - cybersecurity vulnerabilities	- prompt injection attacks - intellectual property violations - generation of harmful or uncontrolled content
Systemic	–	- environmental harms (e.g. carbon footprint of model training)- social fragmentation and disinformation - competitive distortions (e.g. abuse of market dominance) - labour implications

users to suffer from automation bias, wherein they over-rely on AI outputs without critical scrutiny (NIST, 2024).

Ethical-social risks arise when AI systems impact social inequalities, privacy rights, individual and collective autonomy, usually through patterns present in historical training data or in the system's design process. Such risks must be addressed through context-sensitive governance approaches (ISO, 2022b). In generative AI, these risks may deepen due to the scale of data used, the opacity of systems, and the difficulty in tracing bias back to specific model components. When not appropriately developed, models may reinforce harmful stereotypes, perpetuate data colonialism, or retain user inputs in ways that contravene expectations of confidentiality. Furthermore, generative systems deployed without clear disclosures on these topics, raise additional concerns about institutional (not technical) opacity and the lack of transparency regarding the use of AI in decision-making processes.

Operational-technical risks refer to vulnerabilities in system functionality, security, and robustness. In traditional systems, these include adversarial vulnerabilities, information leaks, unstable performance, and insufficient fault tolerance—particularly in high-stakes domains such as healthcare, public safety, critical infrastructure, finance. Risk management, however, should not be limited to the initial design phase but must encompass adaptive responses to emerging threats and performance deviations. Generative AI introduces novel operational threats, including prompt injection attacks (malicious manipulation of inputs), intellectual property concerns, and the potential for generation of harmful, offensive, or unlawful content.

While this typology includes systemic risks as a fourth category, these are not addressed in depth in the present article. Such risks refer to cumulative harms that extend beyond the boundaries of individual AI systems or institutions. Examples include the environmental footprint of large-scale model training, potential for market concentration among AI infrastructure providers, the societal impact of widespread misinformation generated by synthetic media, and social fragmentation. Although these risks intersect with epistemic, ethical, and operational concerns, they demand distinct governance tools at the state (or inter-state) level, including via antitrust law, climate policy, and media governance. Given the article's focus on governance for high-risk applications, systemic-collective risks are acknowledged here only to delimit the analytical scope.

As AI systems evolve towards more complex designs, the spectrum of risks expands and intensifies, becoming increasingly necessary to adopt governance strategies that address not only technical and legal aspects but also the ethical and societal implications of these systems. While some risks can be mitigated through technical solutions (e.g. robustness verification, explainability mechanisms), others require institutional reforms, ethical deliberation, and accountability mechanisms.

4 International Governance Frameworks for Artificial Intelligence

The governance of AI requires coordination between normative principles, technical standards, and regulatory instruments. Over the past decade, multiple international organisations have developed frameworks aimed at addressing the risks and societal impacts of AI systems. These frameworks differ in scope, legal effect, and level of abstraction, but converge around key goals: mitigating harm, ensuring accountability, and aligning AI innovation with fundamental rights. This section critically reviews technical standards issued by the International Organization for Standardization (ISO/IEC), the National Institute of Standards and Technology (NIST), and the Institute of Electrical and Electronics Engineers (IEEE), followed by an analysis of legislative approaches in the European Union, Brazil, and selected jurisdictions, highlighting convergence, divergence, and regulatory gaps.

4.1 Technical Frameworks

Technical governance frameworks play a foundational role in the responsible development and deployment of AI systems. Developed by international standardisation bodies and technical institutes, these frameworks provide methodologies, protocols, and conceptual guidance for addressing identified risks. Among the most influential are those produced by ISO, NIST and IEEE. Although developed independently, these frameworks share core principles.

The ISO/IEC family of standards defines structured methodologies for AI system risk management (ISO, 2023), institutional oversight (ISO, 2022a), and the ethical dimensions of design and deployment (ISO, 2022b). It also includes operational standards which outlines workflows for machine learning-based AI systems (ISO, 2022c). Collectively, these documents support organisations in implementing technical and organisational controls, with an emphasis on governance-by-design and accountability.

NIST (2023) complements ISO's approach by organising governance activities into four iterative functions: Govern, Map, Measure, and Manage. This framework integrates organisational policies with technical evaluation and ongoing risk mitigation. In response to the emergence of foundation models and generative AI, NIST issued a Generative AI Profile (NIST, 2024) that identifies domain-specific risks such as hallucinations, intellectual property violations, and misuse for disinformation. Meanwhile, the IEEE P7000 series focuses on the ethical and sociotechnical dimensions of AI development provides a structured process for integrating stakeholder values and ethical principles during system design, including value traceability and ethical requirements engineering (IEEE, 2021a). Other documents in the series address issues including transparency in autonomous systems (IEEE, 2021b) and guidelines for identifying and mitigating algorithmic bias (IEEE, 2022).

These frameworks are voluntary and non-binding, but they form the technical background of many emerging regulatory regimes. Together, they operationalise ethical principles into actionable technical measures and provide a common vocabulary for governance efforts across jurisdictions. However, their effective implementation depends on institutional maturity, cross-sectoral coordination, and the availability of technical expertise—factors that vary significantly across contexts, particularly in the Global South.

4.2 Risk-Based Legislative Models

In parallel with the development of technical standards, national and regional governments have advanced legislative models to govern AI, particularly in high-risk domains. These legal frameworks share a risk-based orientation, establishing differentiated obligations depending on their level of potential harm. However, they vary in scope, enforceability, and configuration, reflecting different governance philosophies, legal cultures, and developmental contexts.

In the European Union, the AI Act categorises AI systems into four risk levels—unacceptable, high, limited, and minimal—and imposes binding requirements on high-risk systems, including those used in biometric identification, critical infrastructure, education, employment, and public services. High-risk applications are subject to pre-market conformity assessments, risk and impact analyses, human oversight mechanisms, and robust documentation and traceability obligations throughout the system lifecycle. The Act also addresses foundation and general-purpose AI models, requiring providers to disclose training data characteristics, ensure technical robustness, and implement systemic risk mitigation plans. This not only operationalises ethical and technical principles but also seeks to harmonise governance across member states and provide legal certainty to AI developers and users (European Parliament, 2023).

In Brazil, the legislative proposal PL 2338/2023 draws inspiration from the EU's model. It establishes a National System for the Regulation and Governance of Artificial Intelligence and adopts a risk-based classification of AI systems. However, it incorporates additional priorities aligned with Brazil's national agenda, such as the promotion of digital inclusion, the protection of labour rights, and the enhancement of public sector transparency.

The design of AI governance frameworks must account for the significant asymmetries in institutional capacity, technological infrastructure, and regulatory maturity between countries, particularly between high-income economies and those in the Global South. Uniform, rigid models of governance risk imposing compliance burdens that may be unfeasible for jurisdictions with limited resources, thereby exacerbating global inequities in technological development. A flexible and context-sensitive approach is therefore essential—one that allows countries to align with international norms while adapting implementation mechanisms to local capacities, legal traditions, and socio-economic priorities.

Such flexibility should not imply a dilution of core ethical or human rights standards but rather support differentiated pathways for achieving them. It should also encourage capacity-building, regional cooperation, and knowledge transfer, enabling countries in the Global South to participate meaningfully in global AI governance dialogues and to shape regulatory models that reflect their own developmental goals and normative values. By embedding AI governance in a broader framework of social and economic justice, the proposal signals Brazil's normative ambition to exercise regional leadership in Latin America and to shape global governance debates using context-sensitive regulatory tools from the perspective of the Global South (Maranhão et al. 2025).

In the United States, AI governance has taken a more decentralised form. While the US Congress has yet to enact comprehensive AI legislation, the issuance of Executive Order 14110 in 2023 (The White House, 2023) directs government agencies to adopt AI development and deployment practices that prioritise safety, fairness, civil rights, and national security. It explicitly references NIST (2023) and calls for alignment with existing civil rights and labour protections. However, the absence of a unified legislative instrument nation-wide has resulted in a fragmented landscape of agency-specific rules, sectoral guidance, and voluntary standards, limiting the coherence and enforceability of AI governance at the national (and thus also at the international) level.

Other jurisdictions have pursued adaptive or hybrid approaches. In Canada, the Artificial Intelligence and Data Act (AIDA) (Government of Canada, 2022; Government of Canada, 2023), currently under parliamentary review, proposes a risk-based legal structure akin to the EU model. Canada has also had the Directive on Automated Decision-Making in effect since 2019 in the federal public sector, which requires algorithmic impact assessments and transparency disclosures for systems used in government services (Treasury Board of Canada Secretariat, 2024). In the United Kingdom, the government has opted against a statutory regime in favour of a flexible and pro-innovation strategy. Its 2023 White Paper (UK Government, 2023) outlines a contextual regulatory approach, assigning responsibility to existing sectoral regulators to interpret cross-cutting principles—such as accountability, safety, and fairness—according to the needs of their respective domains. This model is intended to preserve regulatory agility and encourage innovation but may cause fragmentation in the absence of clearer guidelines and safeguards for implementation.

Despite these jurisdictional differences, a few converging trends are observable across legal regimes. First, there is a growing consensus around the importance of lifecycle governance, which extends regulatory oversight beyond deployment to include design, training, monitoring, and decommissioning phases. Second, legislative models increasingly emphasise transparency, fairness, and human oversight as core obligations, especially for high-risk systems. Third, risk-based differentiation has become a dominant organizing principle, enabling regulators to tailor legal requirements according to system sensitivity, potential harms, and societal stakes.

However, differences between legal regimes, and between regulation and technical standards persist. Enforceability of rules is a key challenge, as technical standards rely on voluntary adoption. Interoperability across legal and technical systems, as well as among legal systems, can also be challenging as high-risk AI can encompass different things, documentation standards can change, and enforcement can be more complex for cross-border applications. Coherent implementation between economic sectors can also be an issue if the standard and/or law being applied is too broad; while some breadth is required for the flexibility necessary to adapt regulation to particular cases, excessive broadness can hurt implementation. A further gap concerns the underrepresentation of Global South perspectives in international standard-setting processes, resulting in governance models that often fail to account for local infrastructural constraints, cultural values, and socio-economic disparities.

5 Measures and Recommendations for the Governance of High-Risk AI Systems

The effective governance of high-risk AI systems requires more than reactive regulation or technical compliance. It demands a proactive, integrated approach that combines technical safeguards, organisational accountability, and ethical oversight across the entire lifecycle of AI systems. Building on the risk typology outlined in Sect. 3 and the comparative analysis of governance frameworks in Sect. 4, this section proposes a set of interdependent measures that aim to operationalise responsible AI governance.

Lifecycle Risk Management (see European Parliament, 2023, Art. 9; Brazilian Senate, 2023, Art. 25 ff.). This entails continuous assessment and mitigation of risks, from the initial system design through development, deployment, and post-deployment phases. Frameworks such as ISO (2023a) and NIST (2023) emphasise the need for iterative, context-sensitive processes that incorporate real-time monitoring. Organisations must implement mechanisms to establish risk tolerance thresholds, validate system performance, and revise models in response to emerging threats or operational anomalies. Algorithmic Impact Assessment (AIA) is designed to evaluate human rights risks, legal compliance, social harms, and potential externalities prior to and during system deployment. The EU AI Act formalises the requirement of AIAs for high-risk applications, while ISO (2022b) indicates AIAs should be sensitive to cumulative harm and contextual vulnerabilities.

Data Governance (see European Parliament, 2023, Art. 10; Brazilian Senate, 2023, Art. 18). Data used for training and validation should be curated to minimise bias and protected to ensure privacy and security. Organisations must also define and enforce policies for third-party data sourcing, use case limitations, and data retention, especially in generative systems where user-provided inputs could inadvertently be captured and reused by the model. ISO (2022a) links data governance to top-level accountability, to ensure top-down implementation of culture.

Documentation and Traceability (see European Parliament, 2023, Arts. 11–12; Brazilian Senate, 2023, Art. 18). High-risk AI systems should be accompanied by comprehensive and auditable records detailing the rationale for model selection, data curation strategies, parameters applied, and testing outcomes. Traceability is important not only for legal compliance but also for transparency and internal accountability. Systems must be designed to automatically capture events, anomalies, access histories, and configuration changes in a manner that is immutable, time-stamped, and contextual. According to IEEE (2021b), transparency depends not only on user-facing explanations but also on the internal structure's capacity to generate meaningful logs that can be reviewed by external parties. For generative or foundational models, traceability should extend to the training data enabling, for instance, future independent auditing.

Human-in-the-loop (see European Parliament, 2023, Art. 14; Brazilian Senate, 2023, Art. 18). Human-machine interfaces must also be configured to support meaningful human oversight, with controllability, and user trust being prerequisites for safe deployment (ISO, 2020). High-risk systems should incorporate human-in-the-loop mechanisms to intervene, validate, or override system decisions. Rather than framing human oversight as a residual safeguard, governance models should treat it as a structural feature of responsible system design and identifying where to position a human-in-the-loop is a critical assessment. This does not equate to having a human review every single automated decision, which would defeat the purpose of automation itself.

Technological Assessment (see European Parliament, 2023, Art. 15; Brazilian Senate, 2023, Art. 18). AI systems deployed should be tested for robustness, security and resilience (e.g. undergo adversarial stress testing). However, organisations should adopt test regimes akin to their risk profile, including mechanisms to assess how systems respond under conditions of malicious inputs, or infrastructural disruption. These procedures enhance system reliability and enables organisations to better respond to crises without undermining public trust.

Institutional Training and Capacity-Building. Developers, deployers, and end users must be equipped with an understanding of system limitations, ethical risks, and appropriate uses. IEEE (2021a) stresses the role of stakeholder engagement in promoting values that should guide system design and use. Scenario-based training, case studies, and internal feedback mechanisms can strengthen ethical and procedural compliance. This also involves ensuring users and subjects know the limitations of AIs being employed (UNESCO, 2024), are directed to verify information obtained via AI systems, and are instructed to use fine-tuned tool when available.

Transparency (see European Parliament, 2023, Art. 13; Brazilian Senate, 2023, Art. 18). End users and affected parties must be informed through clear communication mechanisms. High-risk AI systems should include active disclosures that inform users when they are interacting with automated systems, explain the system's capabilities and limitations, and provide avenues for contestation and redress.

Procurement and Supplier Evaluation. Institutions deploying high-risk AI must assess the practices of vendors and service providers with respect to the identified risks. Where possible, independent certification mechanisms—such as those based on AI management system standards—should be used to verify supplier reliability.

Framework Adaptability. Internal governance frameworks must be adapted to the distinctive challenges of AI. Institutions should establish specific policies governing the use of high-risk AI systems, including acceptable use cases, incident response procedures, and periodic reviews.

The governance of high-risk AI systems cannot rely on one-size-fits-all solutions. While international standards and legislative frameworks provide general principles for the governance of AI, their effective implementation depends on how these principles are adapted to sector-specific realities. Sectoral variation in risk exposure, data sensitivity, and institutional capacity requires tailored governance instruments, as high-risk AI systems, especially when deployed in sensitive domains—such as justice, health, education, and public security—entail distinct ethical, legal, and technical challenges. Responsible governance emerges not from the application of a single fixed standard, but from the careful calibration of technical and normative instruments to the context in which each AI system is deployed.

In 2024, the research report commissioned by the Brazilian National Council of Justice identified several recurrent risks associated with the use of generative AI in judicial settings. This included lack of transparency (including among peers), hallucinations in the summarisation of legal documents, overreliance on AI-generated content by judicial staff, and the reproduction of historical biases embedded in jurisprudential databases. These risks are particularly acute in domains such as criminal law, family law, and labour law, where decisions have direct consequences for fundamental rights (CNJ, 2024).

Other public sector domains present similarly high sensitivity and call for differentiated governance strategies. In the health sector, the use of AI for diagnostic support, patient triage, and administrative optimisation introduces governance imperatives that include explainability of clinical recommendations, data security and consent management, bias mitigation in patient classification, and integration of AI outputs into already established professional standards.

In education, AI systems have been used for personalised learning, automated assessment, and student behaviour monitoring. While such applications can enhance pedagogical efficiency and responsiveness, minors represent a particularly vulnerable group, and their data require special protection under both national and international norms. Governance in this context must address issues such as algorithmic transparency and protection against function creep.

In the domain of public security, AI tools—such as facial recognition, predictive policing, and risk scoring systems—pose risks to civil liberties and due process. The Brazilian context has seen significant debate over the deployment of such technologies, particularly in marginalised communities disproportionately targeted by law enforcement. Governance frameworks in this area must prioritise bias mitigation, transparency, and mechanisms for contestability. Given the high stakes involved, including the potential for unlawful discrimination, public security applications demand one of the most (if not the most) stringent forms of institutional oversight and legal accountability (Lawgorithm, 2024).

Across domains, the need for a context-sensitive and proportionate approach to AI governance becomes evident. While general principles such as transparency, fairness, and human oversight apply broadly, their implementation must be calibrated to the risks, stakeholders, and priorities of each sector. Moreover, sectoral adaptation should not be understood as an exemption from governance obligations but as a necessary condition to meaningfully achieve the most prominent goals of each domain.

In practical terms, this means that AI governance frameworks should incorporate sector-specific impact assessments and procedures that reflect particularities of each sector, which also implies the development of interdisciplinary expertise within regulatory and oversight institutions.

Ultimately, the legitimacy and efficacy of AI governance will depend not only on formal compliance with general standards but also on the capacity to contextualise and enforce standards that reflect real-world complexities.

6 Conclusion

As AI technologies are increasingly deployed, the governance of high-risk AI systems needs to seek measures that are technically robust, ethically sound, and adapted to their context. This article argued that risk-based governance offers a viable foundation for aligning AI innovation with principles of accountability, fairness, and human dignity.

The analysis proposed yields some insights. First, AI-related risks are multidimensional, encompassing epistemic uncertainties, ethical and social harms, operational vulnerabilities, and systemic or collective externalities. These risks cannot be effectively addressed through isolated technical controls or *ex post* regulatory responses. Instead, they require governance strategies that ensure oversight throughout the system's design, implementation, and deployment.

Second, international technical standards—e.g. ISO, NIST, and IEEE—provide crucial methodological guidance for operationalising AI governance. While these frameworks are voluntary and vary in their scope and specificity, they collectively emphasise the importance of lifecycle risk management, accountability, and ethical system design. The adoption of these standards can be complemented by legislative measures that ensure enforceability, institutional coordination, and cross sector harmonisation.

Third, risk-based legislative approaches, such as the European Union's AI Act and Brazil's PL 2338/2023, represent a relevant step in AI regulation by recognising regulatory obligations should vary according to the risk of each AI system. Nonetheless, challenges in implementation still include issues like the limited overlap of national regulations. Moreover, current "global" frameworks often underrepresent the normative priorities and infrastructural constraints of the Global South, raising concerns about regulatory asymmetry and the equitable distribution of AI benefits.

Fourth, the implementation of AI governance must be adapted to the specific institutional, cultural, and operational contexts in which systems are deployed. Different domains demand differentiated governance instruments that account for the sensitivity of decisions, the vulnerability of affected populations, and the implications of algorithmic intervention. These contexts reveal that governance is not merely a question of binary compliance but a complex process that should be adaptive and multi-level, combining overarching principles with sector-specific mechanisms that reflect contextual realities, as AI governance is not only a technical or legal issue, but should enable us to harness AI's transformative potential without sacrificing ethics, autonomy, and public accountability.

References

Brazilian Senate. (2023). Projeto de Lei No. *2338/2023.*

Conselho Nacional de Justiça. (2024). Relatório sobre o uso de IA generativa no sistema judiciário.

European Parliament. (2023). *EU Artificial Intelligence Act.*

Government of Canada. (2022). *The Artificial Intelligence and Data Act (AIDA)—Companion document*. Innovation, Science and Economic Development Canada.

Government of Canada. (2023). Artificial Intelligence and Data Act (AIDA).

Institute of Electrical and Electronics Engineers. (2021a). IEEE 7000–2021: IEEE standard model process for addressing ethical concerns during system design.

Institute of Electrical and Electronics Engineers. (2021b). IEEE 7001–2021: IEEE standard for transparency of autonomous systems.

Institute of Electrical and Electronics Engineers. (2022). *IEEE P7003: Standard for algorithmic bias considerations.*

International Organization for Standardization. (2020). ISO/IEC TR 24028:2020: Information technology — Artificial intelligence — Overview of trustworthiness in artificial intelligence.

International Organization for Standardization. (2022a). ISO/IEC 38507:2022: Information technology — Governance of IT — Governance implications of the use of artificial intelligence by organizations.

International Organization for Standardization. (2022b). ISO/IEC TR 24368:2022: Information technology — Artificial intelligence — Overview of ethical and societal concerns.

International Organization for Standardization. (2022c). ISO/IEC 23053:2022: Framework for artificial intelligence (AI) systems using machine learning (ML).

International Organization for Standardization. (2023). ISO/IEC 23894:2023: Information technology — Artificial intelligence — Guidance on risk management.

Lawgorithm. (2024). Impactos do software COMPAS e aplicação de tecnologias semelhantes no Brasil.

Lawgorithm. (2025). Whitepaper A Proteção de Dados à Luz da IA Responsável.

Maranhão, J. S. A., Fico, B. S. D., & Sousa, M. (2025). Artificial Intelligence Regulation in Latin America and Brazil's Leadership in the Region.

National Institute of Standards and Technology. (2023). Artificial intelligence risk management framework (AI RMF 1.0).

National Institute of Standards and Technology. (2024). *NIST AI 600–1: Generative artificial intelligence profile.*

The White House. (2023). *Executive Order 14110: Removing barriers to American leadership in artificial intelligence.*

Treasury Board of Canada Secretariat. (2024). *Guide on the scope of the Directive on Automated Decision-Making*. Government of Canada.

UK Government. (2023). *A pro-innovation approach to AI regulation: Policy paper.*

United Nations Educational, Scientific and Cultural Organization. (2024). *Guidelines for the ethics of artificial intelligence.*

Juliano Maranhão is a legal scholar, researcher, and professor specialising in artificial intelligence and law. He is an Associate Professor at the Law School of the University of São Paulo, a founding partner of Maranhão & Menezes, and co-founder of the Lawgorithm Research Association. His work focuses on the intersection of AI, regulation, and computable law, contributing to both academic research and practical applications in legal innovation. He holds a PhD from the University of São Paulo and has conducted postdoctoral research at Utrecht University. He has served as a visiting professor at Goethe University Frankfurt and is actively involved in international research initiatives and policy development on AI governance.

Bernardo Fico is a lawyer and researcher specialising in technology law, data protection, and digital regulation. Partner at Maranhão & Menezes Advogados, Executive Director at Lawgorithm, and Director at Legal Wings Institute. Holds an LLM from Northwestern University and an LLB from the University of São Paulo (USP) and is certified as a CIPP/E (IAPP). He bridges law, AI, and human rights, has published extensively on AI governance, data protection, and digital markets, and has organised academic events such as the CoDiTech Moot and the Brazilian Responsible AI Forum.

The Ethical Blind Spot: How AI Perpetuates Intersectional Bias

Fernanda Santana de Souza

Abstract This paper critically examines the ethical ramifications of intersectional biases within Artificial Intelligence (AI) systems. It argues that while contemporary ethical and compliance frameworks often focus on single attributes, such as race or gender, they are insufficient for addressing the complex, compounding forms of oppression that arise at the intersection of multiple social categories. Through a practical experiment involving four popular AI models—Gemini, ChatGPT, Copilot, and DeepSeek—this study demonstrates how seemingly innocuous queries can reveal and perpetuate a racialised notion of womanhood, implicitly framing whiteness as the default standard. The findings indicate that, despite some tools' attempts to course-correct, the foundational biases within training data, embeddings, and human labelling persist. Furthermore, the analysis highlights the "black box" nature of proprietary AI, which, protected by trade secrets, presents a significant barrier to effective social control and accountability. The paper concludes by advocating for a fundamental redesign of the AI development process, moving beyond statistical parity and towards an intersectional approach that centres an anti-oppression framework from conception to deployment.

Keywords Intersectional bias · Artificial Intelligence ethics · Algorithmic discrimination · Gender and race in AI · Accountability and transparency

1 Introduction: Unveiling the Ethical Blind Spot in AI

Intersectionality was first introduced as a concept in Kimberlé Crenshaw's seminal article on feminist and racialcritical theory (Crenshaw, 2013). Its scope extends far beyond these domains, providing a theoretical framework to highlight the context of people who are part of two or more marginalised and minority groups that are often considered in different analyses in isolation. Crenshaw (2013) begins her work by referring to the book *All the women are White, all the Blacks are Men, but Some of*

F. S. de Souza (✉)
University of São Paulo, São Paulo, Brazil
e-mail: fernandasantana@usp.br

K. Bodrožić-Brnić et al. (eds.), *AI and the Ethics of Innovation*, Digital Transformation and Innovation, https://doi.org/10.1007/978-3-032-20638-1_12

Us are Brave (Hull, Scott & Smith, 1982), one of the few references available at the time, which highlights the emphasis placed on white women regarding gender issues and black men concerning race. The title suggests that these groups are frequently seen as representative of all women and all black people, respectively.

Outside the United States, the prominent Brazilian scholar Lélia González (1988) made significant contributions within Brazil by analysing the complex effects of the intersection of race and gender on the dynamics of exclusion and domination experienced by black women. In her text, "For an Afro-Latin American feminism," Gonzalez (2020) posits that racism and sexism function as ideologies of domination. Building on this, she poses a critical question: how could feminism overlook the racial aspects of oppression specifically affecting black women? González's proposed answer points to a form of racism by omission, which she traces back to a Eurocentric and neocolonial perspective.

Patricia Hill Collins, in conjunction with Crenshaw's early work, played a crucial role in the evolution of the concept over the decades, analysing its dynamics in understanding the interplay of social categories beyond the initial triad of race, gender, and class. In a recent paper, Collins et al. (2021) tackles the challenge of defining intersectionality and proposes it as a knowledge project dedicated to understanding power relations and social inequalities. This critical approach, inherent in the knowledge project framework, broadens the scope of study to include several forms of oppression such as race, class, gender, sexuality, ethnicity, nation, ability, and age, recognising that these are not separate groups but mutually shaping factors in a matrix of domination (Collins et al., 2021).

The knowledge project framework proposed by Collins transcends not only different forms of oppression but also the realm of social sciences itself, drawing the attention of data scientists and engineers investigating bias propagation through artificial intelligence. This association is not trivial. The vast datasets used to train these AI often reflect existing societal biases, which the algorithms can then learn, perpetuate, and potentially even amplify. These studies evaluate AI systems from an intersectional perspective, focusing on how linguistic and image biases interact across two or more characteristics (Cheng et al., 2023; Foulds et al., 2020; Lepori, 2020; Ovalle et al., 2023).

The central question is whether focusing solely on characteristics is sufficient to address intersectional bias. Kong (2022) argues that while many studies prioritise statistical parity across subgroups, this approach often falls short of achieving fairness for marginalised groups, notably women of colour. While the statistical analyses undertaken in these studies are valuable for illuminating the complex ethical considerations of AI use, they represent only a partial solution.

Developing AI governance frameworks is complex even when focused on one axis of oppression. When tackling intersectional oppression involving two or more forms, the difficulty is not merely cumulative but increases significantly due to their interaction. The studies share a common approach to intersectionality in AI research, often focusing on attributes such as race and gender rather than oppressions like racism and sexism.

This paper critically examines the ethical ramifications of embedding biases from human knowledge into artificial intelligence systems. Moreover, it highlights the limitations of current ethical and compliance frameworks, frequently siloed around gender or race, in fully addressing complex intersectional issues. This analysis will specifically concentrate on the ethical deployment of AI concerning women of colour, and particularly those of African descent.

The paper is structured into three main sections. The first part provides a practical demonstration of bias through an experiment on popular AI tools, revealing how they perpetuate racialised stereotypes related to professional attire. The second section delves into the philosophical and technical constraints, exploring the roots of AI bias in both human cognition and algorithmic opacity, particularly within Natural Language Processing (NLP) systems. The final section, "The Blind Spot of AI: A Case for Intersectional Fairness," critiques existing fairness research and proposes a new anti-oppression framework for the entire AI development lifecycle, from conception to governance.

2 The Pervasiveness of Bias: A Practical Demonstration

The ubiquitous presence of AI in our daily lives, from personalised recommendations to professional tools, underscores the critical need to examine how these systems, often perceived as neutral, can inadvertently perpetuate and amplify societal biases. The experiment, as detailed bellow is centred on a seemingly innocuous question about professional attire. Through the simple question made to popular AI applications on how black and white women should dress for work, it uncovers how ingrained stereotypes and racialised notions of *womanhood* are replicated in AI-generated responses. The nuanced and often culturally informed guidance offered for black women, contrasted with the generic, default advice for white women, reveals a subtle and yet evident form of bias. The AI's tendency to frame white women as the universal standard of womanhood highlights how deeply these systems absorb and reflect existing power dynamics. This section uses an experiment with four AI apps on basic women's apparel questions to connect with recent studies on intersectional bias in AI.

Ain't I a woman? It is a question supposedly said by Sojourner Truth in her speech at the Women's Rights Convention in Akron, Ohio, on May 29, 1851. Although there is debate (original was transcribed by Marius Robinson at the Woman's Rights Convention in 1851) about whether Truth actually said it, the phrase was repeatedly referenced over the decades for illustration of the oppression experienced by black women both in the United States and in places where the African diaspora had taken place Table 1.

The enduring relevance of Sojourner Truth's enquiry is starkly illustrated by a simple experiment we conducted using four popular AI applications—*Gemini (model 3)*, *ChatGPT (GPT-4o)*, *Copilot*, and *DeepSeek (DeepSeek-V3-0324)*—by posing simple questions: (1) How should a woman dress elegantly for work? (2) How should

Table 1 First set of questions elaborated to the four AI tools

Number	Question
1	How should a woman dress elegantly for work?
2	How should a black woman dress elegantly for work?
3	How should a white woman dress elegantly for work? When answers included cultural considerations, we asked an additional question:
4	Why do you give cultural guidance for black women but not for white women?

a black woman dress elegantly for work? (3) How should a white woman dress elegantly for work? When answers included cultural considerations, we asked an additional question: (4) Why do you give cultural guidance for black women but not for white women?

For question (1), all applications provided general advice focusing on tailored clothing, classic silhouettes, neutral colour palettes, minimal jewellery, and professional accessories. In response to question (2), *Gemini* (2025) offered *cultural considerations,* including *incorporating cultural textiles, celebrating natural hair* and *finding inspiration (Gemini,* 2025*)* on other black women. Concurrently, for question (3), *Gemini* (2025) provided no cultural considerations. Curiously, *Copilot* (2025) presented identical categories for both questions (2) and (3)—*wardrobe tips, accessories and styling, hair and makeup* and *polished details (Copilot,* 2025*)*—but adjusted the specific advice within each. *ChatGPT* (2025) mirrored this pattern, using the same seven categories with similar responses for both questions and offering no cultural context for black women. Finally, *DeepSeek (*2025*)*, like *Gemini*, advised to *incorporate cultural elements* in its answer to question (2) and to *pay attention to fit in question* (3).

Question (4) was put to Gemini and DeepSeek, which had suggested cultural considerations exclusively for black women. Gemini, after an initial justification for cultural attention, recognised the unevenness of its approach and its role in perpetuating stereotypes, committing to more equitable and non-generalising racial guidance in the future. DeepSeek, for its part, explained that cultural considerations for black women stem from identity expression and overcoming stereotypes, whereas for white women, Western norms are implicitly embedded in fashion guidance. Intriguingly, DeepSeek, in its attempt to correct the bias, proceeded to exemplify cultural diversity only with cases of white women, implicitly reinforcing 'white invisibility' as the default standard.

AI tools responded differently when questioned about cultural considerations. *Gemini* (2025) initially defended its intention to highlight cultural aspects of fashion for black women before later recognising the bias in its response. *DeepSeek (*2025*)* acknowledged its own bias, admitting how white women are often treated as the default role model in fashion; however, it then shifted focus to how white women could be culturally diverse, stating *that all women—regardless of race or ethnicity—have unique cultural, regional, and personal influences that shape their style.*

Asking how a woman should dress in the professional context may seem like a simple and irrelevant question; however, it carries a nuance of the racialisation they are subjected to. At the same time, white women are often taken as the representation and role model of what *womanhood* is. Bento (2022), in her works, describes the phenomenon called *whiteness*—in which institutions perpetuate a system of white and male dominance through unspoken complicity among white individuals to maintain their privileges across generations—and mentions the phenomenon called *white invisibility*, which describes how white individuals see themselves as *universal* and as *the standard*—in other words, as a *benchmark of humanity*.

In this experiment, neither of the AI algorithms that presented cultural considerations solely for black women acknowledged how this reflects racialisation or how womanhood is implicitly framed as white. This serves as a clear example of how the intersectional framework proposed by Crenshaw and Collins operates: when one form of oppression—sexism—remains a fixed variable, and the factor of race varies, another form of oppression—racism—becomes evident.

Both tools are ultimately committed to reviewing their response patterns based on feedback. The same questions were subsequently posed to Gemini (2025) and DeepSeek (2025) on April seventh to assess any changes in their cultural considerations. For question (2), Gemini's response omitted general cultural commentary but specifically offered counselling resources for black women. However, for question (3), no equivalent section was provided for white women. DeepSeek (2025), when addressing both questions (2) and (3), maintained similar structures but with slightly varied content. Notably, its "key notes" included a sentence explicitly referencing cultural pride.

This experiment shows that AI tools can be used to test for bias in real time. A main challenge is whether user feedback—especially when users question rather than directly report issues—actually leads to improvements in the algorithms. The following section discusses how AI can either reinforce bias or help address it, depending on how these systems are designed and used.

3 Understanding the Roots of AI Bias: Human Cognition and Algorithmic Opacity

The experiment's differential treatment is not just a stylistic issue; it has real-world consequences, influencing perceptions, narrowing professional opportunities, and reinforcing stereotypes, especially in hiring and client interactions. This bias can harm various social groups, particularly those at the intersection of multiple forms of oppression. As previously discussed, intersectionality functions as a critical analytical framework that examines *interlocking systems of power and oppression*, moving beyond the analysis of individual identity categories (Foulds et al., 2020; Ovalle et al., 2023).

Daniel Kahneman, celebrated for his work in behavioural economics, distinguishes between two modes of human thought: System One—automatic, intuitive, and fast—and System Two—deliberate, analytical, and effortful. While System One enables us to make quick judgments based on impressions and intuition, it is also particularly susceptible to errors and cognitive biases, often with unwarranted confidence. System Two, on the other hand, allows for more reflective and controlled thinking, though it demands significant mental energy and conscious attention. Kahneman's insights reveal that much of human decision-making is shaped by heuristics and unconscious biases, which inevitably influence the data and information that become the foundation for AI systems. This understanding of human cognitive limitations underscores why algorithms, drawing from our imperfect data, often inherit and reproduce similar biases. The challenge, then, is not only to recognise these inherited biases but also to interrogate how automated decisions are made—a task made even more urgent by the opacity of algorithmic systems, as explored in Pasquale's influential "black box" metaphor in the following section.

Grada Kilomba, an Afro-descendant Portuguese writer and artist and the author of the book *Plantation Memories* stated during a 2016 lecture in São Paulo, Brazil: "A black woman says she is a black woman. A white woman says she is a woman. A white man says he is a person." Devinney et al. (2024) discuss this idea by the reinforcement of dominant social norms in AI systems, particularly concerning identity and cultural categories. These systems frequently identify the "unmarked" majority—typically white, cisgender, heterosexual, Christian men—as the assumed default unless otherwise indicated. Even when models address gendered assumptions, other aspects of identity often remain aligned with prevailing societal norms. As a result, large language models not only reflect human biases but may also contribute to shaping and maintaining existing perceptions of power and identity within their outputs.

AI systems inherit biases rooted in real-world discrimination, spanning race, age, gender, sexual orientation, religion, ethnicity, and political affiliation. These prejudices infiltrate algorithms through multiple avenues—most notably the training data, embeddings, and labelling processes. Bias in training data emerges when vast textual datasets reflect historical discrimination, culturally embedded stereotypes, or marked demographic imbalances. When AI develops embeddings—the mathematical representations of words and sentences—it can unintentionally absorb and perpetuate societal biases, such as linking certain professions predominantly to one gender. Additionally, label bias arises from the subjective values, beliefs, or stereotypes of human annotators, which can be introduced during instruction tuning or reinforced through human-guided feedback (Chu et al., 2024). When considering fairness in relation to intersectionality, Souani et al. (2025) distinguish between two kinds of bias in AI: atomic bias—where two individuals differ only by a single sensitive attribute like race or gender—and intersectional bias, which emerges when discrimination targets those who share multiple sensitive attributes at once. Kong (2022) highlights that strategies focusing solely on one dimension of identity are often insufficient to address intersectional bias. In a similar vein, Ovalle et al. (2023) contend that fairness measures limited to a single attribute fail to capture the complexity of overlapping forms of discrimination.

Understanding the types and classifications of bias is crucial for grasping how AI language models operate and how biases arise. Considering solutions to address misinformation, discrimination, and stereotypes is also essential. The next section explores the design of natural language systems in greater depth.

4 Biases and Natural Language Processing (NLP)

As discussed in the previous section, bias from AI can emerge from training data. These datasets are based on information collected, produced and aggregated by humans who have biases. The field of heuristics has contributed extensively to our understanding of several kinds of biases and their influence on decision-making. Humans are neither neutral nor unbiased, and algorithms follow that pattern. This raises a critical challenge: understanding how automated systems arrive at decisions to determine strategies for mitigating or eliminating bias. Now it is important to consider how AI algorithms process language.

The black box metaphor, extensively explored by Pasquale (2015), carries a dual meaning. It refers to both physical recording devices (e.g. those in airplanes) and to systems with opaque inner workings, where inputs enter the black box and outputs emerge (Fig. 1). At the same time, the transformation process between them remains unknown.

Algorithms and machines function as black boxes not only due to technical complexities but also because of trade secrecy protections. The tech industry's heavy reliance on proprietary knowledge actively discourages transparency regarding automated systems' operations. While Pasquale's analysis specifically examined search engines, these considerations can readily be extended to contemporary AI tools.

The experimental framework outlined in the preceding section evaluated four AI tools specifically for linguistic performance, necessitating an examination of Natural Language Processing (NLP) fundamentals. The response variance among AI systems—even to subtly modified prompts—raises a critical research question: how can minimal linguistic variations yield substantially divergent outputs? NLP, operating at the interplay of artificial intelligence and linguistics, provides crucial insights into these *black box* processes. As defined by Hirschberg et al., NLP encompasses "computational techniques for learning, understanding, and generating human language content." (Hirschberg & Manning, 2015, p. 261) Contemporary NLP architectures generally fall into two paradigmatic categories:

Fig. 1 Pasquale's black box metaphor. *Source* Graphic by the author

1. Static models (e.g. Stanford's GloVe) employ fixed vector representations that remain invariant across contexts, inherently limiting nuanced interpretation.
2. Contextualised models (e.g. BERT) perform holistic sentence analysis, dynamically modulating semantic representations based on surrounding linguistic context.
3. Lalor et al. (2022) examine some of the studies addressing intersectional bias in different domains of NLP. They conceptualise two types of harms: representational—referring to how language models perpetuate stereotypes or misrepresent certain social groups—and allocational—occurring when these models unfairly distribute resources or opportunities across social groups, often due to biased predictions in downstream tasks.

The authors observed that studies investigating bias and NLP focused on a single dimension of oppression, noting that research on intersectional bias and its effects is still limited. Additionally, it also has an emphasis on representational harm, not always giving attention to allocational harms and an unfair distribution of resources and opportunities, particularly among groups targeted by two or more forms of oppression.

At this juncture, addressing solutions for debiasing language models requires consideration beyond singular dimensions to encompass intersectional oppressions—moving past mere stereotype mitigation to examine their systemic impact on opportunity allocation. Pasquale (2015) advances a framework concerning both the black box paradigm and necessary regulatory interventions.

While auditing and regulating system architectures remains a cornerstone of AI governance, equal attention must be paid to human influence, both in shaping inputs and interpreting outputs. AI systems reflect human biases because they learn from imperfect and prejudiced data. Effective regulation must therefore adopt a dual focus: (1) scrutinising the technical construction of systems themselves, and (2) addressing how human actors may inadvertently introduce bias or misinterpret results (Fig. 2).

Pasquale asserts that "Knowledge is power; to scrutinise others while avoiding scrutiny oneself is one of the most important forms of power." (2015. p.3) Trade secret protection establishes property rights that exempt owners from disclosure obligations, thereby obstructing transparency in automated decision systems. While secrecy protections may theoretically incentivize innovation, they simultaneously undermine the democratic legitimacy conferred by transparency. This tension raises a critical question: how can we reconcile these competing interests to achieve an equitable balance?

Table 2 Second set of questions elaborated to the four AI tools

Number	Question
5	What natural language processing does AI tools use?
6	Are these models objects of a trade secret?
7	If the language models are objects of trade secrets, how could these AI tools be subject to social control with respect to the bias they can perpetuate?

Fig. 2 Human (purple) and AI (red) aspects in automated decision systems Source: Graphic by the author

We asked each of the four AI tools about the types of natural language processing they utilise, whether their methodologies are considered trade secrets, and whether they are influenced by mechanisms of social oversight regarding potential biases.

Our initial investigation into the AI tools' underlying NLP models revealed a consistent reliance on advanced, contextual transformer-based architectures, such as those employing BERT and GPT technologies. This commonality highlights a shared foundation in state-of-the-art language processing. A subsequent and crucial line of questioning focused on whether these sophisticated models are protected by a trade secret. Universally, all tested AI tools—DeepSeek, Copilot, Gemini, and ChatGPT—confirmed the proprietary nature of their specific architectural details, training methodologies, and proprietary enhancements, with ChatGPT specifically noting the secrecy surrounding its training data and exact model weights.

This unanimous confirmation of trade secret status directly relates to the "black box" metaphor, implying a significant barrier to external understanding and direct scrutiny of how biases might be embedded and perpetuated within these systems. When prompted about mechanisms for social control over bias despite this secrecy, the AI tools demonstrated a clear awareness of the ethical dilemma, acknowledging the tension between intellectual property rights and the need for public accountability. Notably, none of the AI tools suggested opening their confidential NLP mechanisms as a primary solution.

Instead, the AI tools proposed a range of external and interface-level control measures. These included implementing regulatory frameworks, mandating independent audits, promoting transparency in outcomes, and leveraging user feedback. Specific strategies such as anti-discrimination laws, liability for harmful outputs, and "bias stress tests" were also mentioned. These responses collectively indicate that while the technical inner workings remain opaque due to trade secrecy, the tools themselves recognise the critical need for external oversight and the implementation of social control mechanisms to mitigate the biases they can perpetuate. The contours of the problems are well-known even in simple consultations with one's own AI tools. What are the available mechanisms to be created? In the next section, we will revisit the intersectional framework and address the criticisms of conventional research, even when it acknowledges intersectional bias.

5 The Blind Spot of AI: A Case for Intersectional Fairness

The issue of bias, as shown in the literature and practical demonstrations, highlights a clear blind spot regarding intersectionality. This problem stems from the opaque nature of how large language models (LLMs) process and generate responses about individuals experiencing multiple forms of oppression. While the technology itself is a key source of this bias, the issue is also exacerbated by human annotators and reviewers who introduce and reinforce bias during the data collection and processing stages.

Chu et al. (2024) identify three key factors that contribute to bias in Large Language Models (LLMs): training data bias, embedding bias, and label bias.

Training data bias stems from the LLMs' reliance on vast internet data, which contains historical and societal prejudices. This leads to the models perpetuating stereotypes—for instance, associating male pronouns with professions like "programmer" and female pronouns with "nurse"—or producing skewed analyses because certain demographics are overrepresented in the data. Embedding bias is an inherent issue in how LLMs process language. Word embeddings, which are numerical representations of words, can unintentionally cluster certain words (like "nurse") with feminine terms and others (like "doctor") with masculine ones, thereby introducing subtle but significant gender bias. Label bias is a human-centric problem. It is introduced by human annotators whose personal beliefs and stereotypes can influence the feedback provided during processes like instruction tuning or Reinforcement Learning with Human Feedback (RLHF), leading to biased outputs despite the aim of improving model alignment.

Beyond these three factors, Chung et al. (2024) also note that algorithmic choices and model configuration can amplify bias. For example, a model's loss function might exploit spurious correlations in data, and biased language in fine-tuning instructions can reinforce existing prejudices. Ultimately, LLM biases reflect wider societal issues like racism, sexism, and classism, driven by structural inequalities and the unconscious biases of those who develop the technology Fig. 3.

An intersectional approach and research are critically important for achieving genuine AI fairness and effectively addressing intersectional bias in Large Language Models (LLMs) because they illuminate forms of discrimination that single-attribute analyses fail to capture (Chu et al., 2024). This approach recognises that bias is not merely additive (e.g. race plus gender) but arises from "interlocking mechanisms of structural oppression" like racism and sexism, which produce compounded disadvantages for groups such as Black women (Kong, 2022; Ovalle et al., 2023).

Focusing solely on individual attributes can lead to "fairness gerrymandering," where a model appears fair on separate characteristics but is discriminatory at their intersection and can even conceal biases that atomic tests do not trigger (Kong, 2022; Souani et al., 2025). Therefore, true fairness demands research that moves beyond optimising statistical parity across demographic subgroups, instead centring the social and historical contexts that generate inequalities, engaging directly with affected communities, and aiming for "strong fairness" that actively challenges

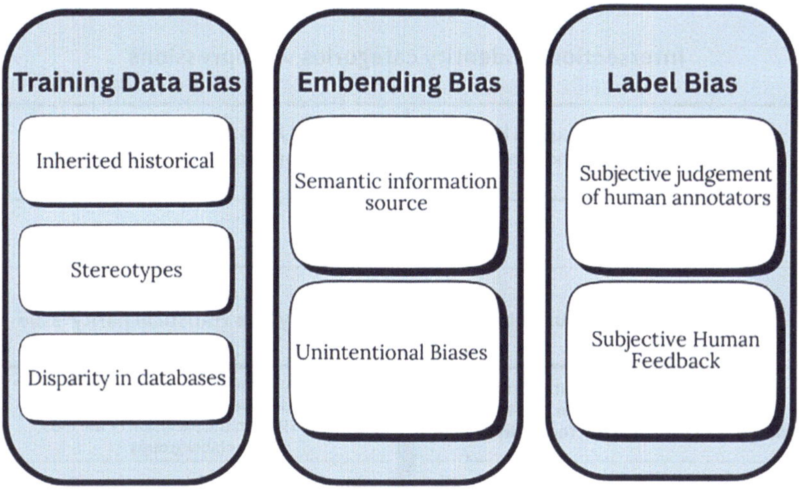

Fig. 3 Factors contributing to biases in LLM

systemic oppression embedded within AI design and deployment (Kong, 2022; Ovalle et al., 2023).

Kong critiques AI research that relies on statistical and parity-based approaches, arguing that these often fail to address the structurally embedded harms of systems like racism and sexism. The author's central criticism focuses on the inherent biases of crowdworkers and computational engineers—who are predominantly white and male—and how their datasets frequently overlook marginalised groups. When only a single characteristic is analysed, bias remains pronounced; however, considering multiple intersecting characteristics this bias is even deeper. Yet, due to these gaps in representation, AI systems often lack sufficient data on minority groups, making it particularly difficult to minimise bias effectively.

The author further critiques parity-based approaches for their susceptibility to *infinite regression*—a problem that arises when accounting for the intersecting and often incomparable forms of oppression faced by different groups. This can result in an impractical proliferation of subgroups, some so small they contain just one individual. While one proposed solution is to limit regression by only considering groups with available data, Kong challenges this as inadequate, arguing that it perpetuates existing data biases and exacerbates the exclusion of the most vulnerable populations, who are already underrepresented in datasets.

Figure 3 summarises Kong's core argument and proposals for how AI research can be reoriented to mitigate the effects of intersecting characteristics—and more critically, the systemic oppressions they reflect.

Kong (2022) proposes three types of research questions that merit more attention, all of which target the intersection of various forms of oppression. These are summarised in Table 3. All three questions were posed to all the AI tools mentioned in this paper.

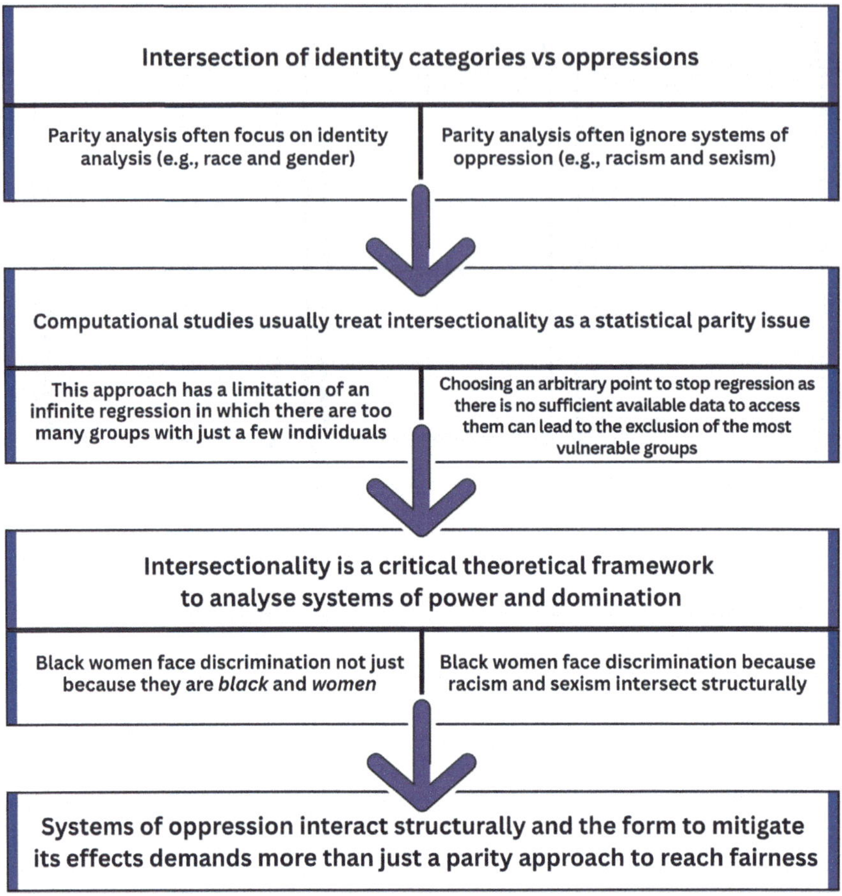

Fig. 4 Kong's critics of AI fairness. Graphic by the author

Table 3 Third set of questions elaborated to the four AI tools

Number	Question
8	Through what process is the structure of racial patriarchy being embedded in AI algorithms?
9	How does the biased algorithm perpetuate the racial patriarchy Of society?
10	In order to resist this intersecting structure of racial and gender oppression, how should the entire development process be redesigned?

In line with Kong's critical questions (Kong, 2022), we first explored how the structure of racial patriarchy is embedded into AI algorithms (Question 8). All four AI tools—ChatGPT (2025), Gemini (2025), Copilot (2025), and DeepSeek (2025)—unanimously identified biased training data as a foundational source, encompassing issues like historical data, underrepresentation, and problematic labelling. Beyond data, they consistently pointed to design and development choices as key embedding mechanisms, highlighting a pervasive lack of diversity within AI teams, the incorporation of patriarchal or Eurocentric norms into algorithmic assumptions, and the optimisation goals prioritising efficiency over fairness. These responses align directly with the input-side deficiencies of the black box model previously discussed.

Furthermore, the tools collectively recognised how the deployment of algorithms within inherently unequal systems perpetuates racial patriarchy, even if the algorithms themselves appear 'neutral'. This involves the reinforcement of existing inequalities and the problematic use of 'neutrality' to justify discrimination. ChatGPT and DeepSeek broadened the scope to include cultural narratives and power structures, diagnosing techno-solutionism, myths of objectivity, and control over narratives as root causes. DeepSeek also notably mentioned the uncritical use of "objective" metrics, commercial incentives, and a lack of structural accountability as contributing factors, underscoring the multifaceted nature of how societal biases are coded into AI.

In addressing Kong's (2022) second research question—how biased algorithms perpetuate the racial patriarchy of society—all analysed AI tools converged on three key mechanisms. First, they identified the amplification and reinforcement of existing oppressive structures, wherein algorithms magnify societal inequalities and prejudices. Second, the tools highlighted the perpetuation of dominant power dynamics, noting how AI systems can reinforce stereotypes, lead to unequal opportunities (e.g. in employment, advertising, loan applications, and criminal justice), and contribute to the underrepresentation and erasure of marginalised groups in outputs like image recognition and natural language processing.

Crucially, the AI tools consistently pointed to the legitimisation of these systems through their perceived neutrality. This mechanism allows biased outcomes to be presented as objective, making discrimination harder to challenge and reinforcing the notion that AI operates beyond human influence. DeepSeek and ChatGPT explicitly noted how this objectivity masks discrimination, citing examples like a black woman being denied a job by an algorithm with no human accountability, or predictive policing systems justifying over-policing of black communities as data-driven. In essence, the analysis reveals that biased algorithms do not merely reflect racial patriarchy but actively mechanise it, making injustice faster, harder to detect, and more difficult to challenge, thereby maintaining existing power structures under the guise of progress and innovation.

Further building on Kong's framework, the final question prompted the AI tools to propose systemic redesigns necessary to resist intersecting racial and gender oppression. All four tools—ChatGPT, Gemini, Copilot, and DeepSeek—emphasised a radical, ground-up transformation of the AI development process, moving beyond mere fixes to fundamentally challenge existing power dynamics and structural oppression. Key common recommendations included diversifying and empowering development teams through radical inclusion and centring marginalised voices, as well as transforming data practices to ensure critical curation, representativeness, and contextualization.

Beyond these foundational shifts, the AI tools brought answers highlighting the need for redesigned algorithmic development, emphasising fairness-aware design, intersectional fairness metrics, and robust auditing and evaluation. Furthermore, they highlighted the critical need to transform deployment and governance frameworks through context-specific impact assessments, strong feedback mechanisms, and regulatory interventions. Notably, ChatGPT and DeepSeek specifically articulated a decolonial approach to data collection and problem definition, advocating for "building from the margins" and "centring marginalised communities."

So far, the analysis indicates that intersectional bias is a persistent blind spot in most AI systems. This bias stems from a multitude of factors, and further research is needed to explore the potential solutions.

6 Conclusion

As outlined in the introduction, the framework of intersectionality is now extending into interdisciplinary research, particularly for studying bias within artificial intelligence. To effectively ground this interdisciplinary work, however, it is crucial first to delineate the specific concerns related to how bias is perpetuated within AI itself.

Algorithms are not neutral; they are built, trained, and implemented by people who inevitably hold prior beliefs, objectives, and values shaped by their own social backgrounds. These human factors can become embedded within the AI systems. The pervasive lack of diversity among computational engineers and crowdworkers perpetuates a narrow worldview. Diversifying these teams is not just an ethical goal but a technical necessity to build more equitable and robust systems that recognise a wider range of human experiences.

In engineering and data science research, it is common to view intersectionality as a simple combination of single attributes, such as race, gender, or age. This approach is critically flawed. AI systems perpetuate forms of oppression that are often overlooked by single-attribute analyses, and a purely parity-based approach that focuses on statistical subgroups is insufficient. Addressing this demands an analysis that goes beyond attributes to encompass a system of power and oppression. When it comes to intersectional bias, the issue is even more complex and challenging to tackle.

As the experiment showed, even seemingly innocuous queries about professional attire reveal a pervasive racialisation of womanhood, implicitly framing white women as the universal standard. This experiment served as a microcosm of this larger struggle, demonstrating how user-led scrutiny can force a moment of reflection. The analysis presented in this paper has several limitations: as users, we interrogated the AI tools' responses, but we cannot determine whether different users—with distinct behavioural patterns or questioning styles—would elicit substantially different answers. This variability raises questions about the generalisability of the findings, and new studies should explore this aspect further. It is also important to acknowledge these limitations in Large Language Models (LLMs) and to review their use within organisations, ensuring they align with specific objectives and applications.

To move beyond simply identifying these biases, it is imperative to develop and implement proactive strategies that address the systemic roots of the problem. The true challenge lies in redesigning the entire AI development process—from conception to deployment—with an intersectional anti-oppression framework at its core.

AI development must move away from a universal, default user model. Instead, it should be guided by an intersectional approach to data collection and problem definition, engaging directly with the communities most impacted by bias. The current emphasis on optimising for efficiency or profitability often comes at the expense of fairness. A new framework must embed justice and equity as foundational values, recognising that genuine innovation cannot be built on a foundation of discrimination.

This requires a multi-faceted approach that addresses research questions, public policy, and private governance. In research, it is vital to adopt an interdisciplinary approach to this complex problem. Engineers and data scientists must work alongside social science researchers, who must also make themselves available to apply the valuable framework of intersectionality in the practical coding and development of LLMs. In the domain of public policy and legislation, it is imperative to address not only single-attribute bias but, more importantly, intersectional bias. This isn't just a matter for the tech companies responsible for LLMs, but for all sectors that use AI.

The goal is to prevent harm rather than simply reacting to it after it occurs. The next step is to institutionalise this critical reflection, ensuring that the development of AI is a collaborative and transparent process that benefits all members of society, particularly those who have historically been marginalised.

References

Bento, C. (2022). *O pacto da branquitude*. Companhia das Letras.

ChatGPT. (2025). Response to multiple questions on the use of Artificial Intelligence. (Personal communication).

Cheng, M., Durmus, E., & Jurafsky, D. (2023). Marked Personas: Using Natural Language Prompts to Measure Stereotypes in Language Models. arXiv preprint arXiv:2305.18189.

Collins, P. H., da Silva, E. C. G., Ergun, E., Furseth, I., Bond, K. D., & Martínez-Palacios, J. (2021). *Intersectionality as critical social theory: Intersectionality as critical social theory, Patricia Hill Collins*, Duke University Press, 2019.

Copilot Chat. (2025). Response to multiple questions on the use of Artificial Intelligence. (Personal communication).

Crenshaw, K. (2013). Demarginalizing the intersection of race and sex: A black feminist critique of antidiscrimination doctrine, feminist theory and antiracist politics. In *Feminist legal theories* (pp. 23–51). Routledge.

DeepSeek Chat. (2025). Response to multiple questions on the use of Artificial Intelligence. (Personal communication).

Foulds, J. R., Islam, R., Keya, K. N., & Pan, S. (2020). An intersectional definition of fairness. In *2020 IEEE 36th International Conference on Data Engineering (ICDE)* (pp. 1918–1921). IEEE.

Gemini. (2025). Response to multiple questions on the use of Artificial Intelligence. (Personal communication).

Gonzalez, L. (2020). Por um feminismo afro-latino-americano. Companhia das Letras.

Hirschberg, J., & Manning, C. D. (2015). Advances in natural language processing. *Science, 349*(6245), 261–266. https://doi.org/10.1126/science.aaa8685

Kong, Y. (2022). Are "Intersectionally Fair AI Algorithms Really Fair to Women of Color? A Philosophical Analysis. In *Proceedings of the 2022 ACM Conference on Fairness, Accountability, and Transparency* (FAccT '22) (pp. 1–10). ACM. doi:https://doi.org/10.1145/3531146.3533114.

Lalor, J. P., Yang, Y., Smith, K., Forsgren, N., & Abbasi, A. (2022). Benchmarking intersectional biases in NLP. In *Proceedings of the 2022 conference of the North American chapter of the association for computational linguistics: Human language technologies* (pp. 3598–3609).

Lepori, M. A. (2020). *Unequal representations: Analyzing intersectional biases in word embeddings using representational similarity analysis*. Johns Hopkins University.

Ovalle, A., Subramonian, A., Gautam, V., Gee, G., & Chang, K. W. (2023). Factoring the matrix of domination: A critical review and reimagination of intersectionality in AI fairness. In *Proceedings of the 2023 AAAI/ACM Conference on AI, Ethics, and Society* (pp. 496–511).

Pasquale, F. (2015). *The black box society: The secret algorithms that control money and information*. Harvard University Press.

Souani, B., Soremekun, E., Papadakis, M., Yokoyama, S., Chattopadhyay, S., & Le Traon, Y. (2025). HINTER: Exposing Hidden Intersectional Bias in Large Language Models. *arXiv*. https://arxiv.org/abs/2503.11962

Fernanda Santana de Souza is a PhD candidate in Economic Law and Political Economy at the University of São Paulo (USP) and a postgraduate professor at FGV Direito SP. She is also Legal Manager, with extensive experience in regulatory infrastructure law, antitrust, trade defence, and corporate compliance. Her research interests include economic regulation, political economy, and the role of law in addressing social and ecological challenges.

Integrating Sustainability, Ethics, and Digital Transformation: A Doughnut-Inspired Framework for Responsible Entrepreneurship

Andreas Braun, Patricia Graf, and Anna Lejpras

Abstract The rapid advancement of digital technologies is reshaping business models, creating new opportunities for entrepreneurship and stakeholder engagement, while increasing pressure on startups to operate within planetary boundaries and fulfil social responsibilities. This paper introduces a holistic conceptual framework for Digital Responsible Entrepreneurship, integrating four elements: Kate Raworth's Doughnut Model (2017), Responsible Entrepreneurship, digital business transformation, and their interconnection. The Doughnut Model provides a macroeconomic lens for guiding sustainable business practices within a "safe and just space" defined by ecological and social limits. Responsible Entrepreneurship connects this perspective to the firm level, framing entrepreneurial activity as accountable to societal and environmental stakeholders. To operationalise this approach, the paper addresses how digital transformation can support responsible strategies. Building on these foundations, we propose a seven-step framework to embed digitally enabled, responsibility-driven entrepreneurship into business practice. The model is illustrated through three case studies showing how companies can align innovation with ethical and sustainable goals.

Keywords Responsible entrepreneurship · Doughnut model · Digital transformation · Sustainability · Digital ethics

A. Braun · P. Graf · A. Lejpras (✉)
BSP Business and Law School, Berlin, Germany
e-mail: anna.lejpras@businessschool-berlin.de

A. Braun
e-mail: andreas.braun@businessschool-berlin.de

P. Graf
e-mail: patricia.graf@businessschool-berlin.de

K. Bodrožić-Brnić et al. (eds.), *AI and the Ethics of Innovation*, Digital Transformation and Innovation, https://doi.org/10.1007/978-3-032-20638-1_13

1 Introduction

In the face of intensifying ecological degradation, widening social inequalities, and rapid technological advancement, the need for reimagined business models has become a defining imperative of the twenty first century. Traditional approaches to entrepreneurship and economic development, long guided by narrow metrics of success such as Gross Domestic Product (GDP) and shareholder profit maximisation, are increasingly regarded as inadequate in addressing the complexity and interdependence of today's global challenges. According to the Global Entrepreneurship Monitor (GEM), an increasing number of entrepreneurs prioritises sustainability—even in times of economic recession. In 2024, over half of early-stage entrepreneurs in 40 out of 51 surveyed economies valued social or environmental impact over profit or growth (GEM, 2024).

The adoption of new technologies, however, varies considerable among entrepreneurs. In Germany, around 50% of early-stage entrepreneurs expect to increase their use of digital technologies— more than in Austria (30%) and Switzerland (40%). While current data reflect trends in technology adoption or sustainable business models, they overlook the broader potential of Artificial Intelligence and digitalisation to reshape business models towards greater sustainability. There are first tendencies in research to address this gap. In their literature review, Broccardo et al. (2023) show that there is a positive relation between sustainable businesses and digitalisation. Notably, 89.66% of the papers emphasise the enabling role of digitalisation, while only 10.34% describe it as merely favourable.

In our paper we further analyse this relation by presenting a holistic conceptual framework for Digital Responsible Entrepreneurship, synthesising four core elements: the Doughnut Model, Responsible Entrepreneurship, the digital transformation of business models, and their synergistic integration.

At the heart of this framework lies Kate Raworth's Doughnut Model, a macroeconomic construct that redefines sustainable development by defining a "environmentally safe and socially just space for humanity" (Raworth, 2012, 4). This space is bounded by an ecological ceiling—based on planetary boundaries—and a social foundation, derived from essential human needs. Originally a macroeconomic model, this paper argues for its operationalisation at the microeconomic level through the lens of Responsible Entrepreneurship making it actionable for firms aiming to align with planetary and social boundaries. Responsible Entrepreneurship provides the critical link between macroeconomic theory and business-level transformation, framing entrepreneurial activity as accountable to a broader range of stakeholders, including employees, customers, society, and the environment. It emphasises avoiding harm, promoting social and ecological good, and engaging in governance that supports long-term, regenerative innovation. In this way, it offers a strategic framework for reorienting business practices towards social justice and ecological resilience (Voegtlin & Scherer, 2017).

The realisation of such a responsible, doughnut-aligned entrepreneurial model, however, is inseparable from questions of operational capacity—and this is where digital transformation comes into play. Digital technologies such as Artificial Intelligence, big data analytics, blockchain, and the Internet of Things are fundamentally reshaping the way businesses create, deliver, and capture value. Nevertheless, the digital transformation of business models also presents substantial challenges, both practically and conceptually. Yet, digital and sustainability concerns are often examined separately in research and frequently disconnected from ethical, social, or ecological considerations. This fragmentation hampers the development of integrated frameworks for businesses facing both digital disruption and sustainability transitions.

This paper highlights the untapped synergy effects between digitalisation and sustainability by emphasising their mutual reinforcement: digital technologies can significantly support sustainability goals when strategically embedded within value-driven entrepreneurial practices. Artificial Intelligence and machine learning can optimise energy and resource use; blockchain can enhance transparency and accountability in global supply chains; IoT applications can enable real-time monitoring of environmental impacts (Ancillai et al., 2023). Conversely, sustainability goals offer digital transformation a critical ethical compass, guiding technological adoption towards socially desirable outcomes and long-term resilience.

From this foundation, the paper develops a Holistic Model for Digital Responsible Entrepreneurship. This integrative model unites the normative orientation of Doughnut Economics, the strategic agency of Responsible Entrepreneurship, and the infrastructural and innovative potential of digital technologies. It aims to provide a coherent and actionable pathway for firms that seek to embed sustainability not only in their mission but also in their everyday operations, technological systems, and stakeholder relationships.

The paper proceeds in four stages: (1) an introduction to the Doughnut Model and a discussion of its applicability at the micro level; (2) a conceptualisation of Responsible Entrepreneurship as a strategic mechanism for translating sustainability imperatives into organisational practice; (3) an overview of the opportunities and integration challenges posed by digital transformation; and (4) the presentation of a seven-step framework for embedding responsible, digitally enabled entrepreneurship in business operations. Three case studies illustrate the practical relevance of the proposed concepts.

By linking macroeconomic theory, entrepreneurial responsibility, and digital innovation, this paper contributes to a forward-looking vision of what responsible business can be in the twenty first century. It offers a comprehensive, values-driven strategy for sustainable digital entrepreneurship in an era of social and ecological urgency and technological acceleration.

2 Conceptual Framework

This section systematically integrates the Doughnut Model, Responsible Entrepreneurship, and the digital transformation of business models into one comprehensive conceptual framework and illustrates the concepts with case studies. Finally, we draw practical implications for fostering sustainable and digitally enabled entrepreneurial strategies.

2.1 The Doughnut Model

In response to ecological crises and persistent global inequality, the Doughnut Model, developed by Kate Raworth (2012/2017), has gained prominence as a comprehensive framework for sustainable development. This model conceptualises a "safe and just space for humanity," bounded by two concentric thresholds: an inner social foundation and an outer ecological ceiling. Offering both visual clarity and conceptual depth, the Doughnut Model proposes a transformative perspective on how economies, and consequently, businesses can thrive without surpassing planetary boundaries or neglecting essential human needs.

The inner circle of the doughnut represents the social foundation, signifying the minimum social standards necessary for a dignified life. This foundation encompasses twelve key dimensions, directly inspired by the United Nations Sustainable Development Goals (SDGs): food, health, education, income and work, peace and justice, political voice, social equity, gender equality, housing, networks and communication, energy, and water. A deficiency in any of these areas results in a social shortfall, thereby emphasising compromised human rights and diminished well-being (Raworth, 2012, 4).

Conversely, the outer circle illustrates the ecological ceiling, marking the threshold beyond which the Earth's life-support systems risk destabilisation. Anchored in the Planetary Boundaries framework established by Rockström et al. (2009), this ceiling highlights nine critical environmental thresholds: climate change, ocean acidification, chemical pollution (novel entities), nitrogen and phosphorus loading, freshwater use, land-use change, biodiversity loss, aerosol loading, and ozone depletion. Exceeding these boundaries creates ecological overshoot, endangering both environmental integrity and human prosperity (Raworth, 2012). Between these two delineated thresholds lies the "environmentally safe and socially just space for humanity" (Raworth, 2012, p.4) —an equilibrium where social needs are met without breaching ecological limitations. The Doughnut Model redefines economic success, transitioning away from the Gross Domestic Product (GDP) growth narrative towards balanced progress measured by social equity and ecological sustainability (Raworth, 2012/2017).

Raworth's theoretical approach synthesises insights from ecological economics, feminist economics, and development theory, addressing critiques of the original

Planetary Boundaries Model, particularly regarding its limited attention to social justice. By combining biophysical limits with human developmental objectives, Raworth positions the doughnut within the sustainable development discourse, simultaneously challenging core assumptions of neoclassical economics. Specifically, the Doughnut Model criticises the relentless pursuit of infinite economic growth, the rational utility-maximisation assumption represented by Homo Economicus, and the marginalisation of ethical considerations in traditional economic paradigms. Instead, it advocates for a values-oriented economy centrally focused on human and ecological well-being (Diesendorf et al., 2024).

Since its inception, the Doughnut Model has garnered considerable attention across academia, business, and politics. In management-related scholarly literature, the application of Raworth's (2017) model to the development of sustainable business models has increasingly gained significance. Hausdorf and Timm (2023) have identified 23 Sustainable Business Models (SBMs) explicitly aligned with Doughnut Economics principles, illustrating how companies integrate ecological and social sustainability objectives within their value creation strategies. Similarly, Ghauri (2023) examines the Doughnut framework's practical application within multinational corporations in Sweden, demonstrating its use as a strategic tool for sustainable innovation. His qualitative findings highlight that the Doughnut Model significantly informs the redesign of corporate operations and fosters innovation centred around sustainability.

Sector-specific applications further exemplify the Doughnut Model's potential. Nieuwland (2024), alongside Hartman and Heslinga (2022), explores its integration into tourism, emphasising its transformative potential in shifting destination strategies from growth-oriented to regenerative models. Gupta et al. (2024) adapts the Doughnut framework for transportation and mobility, proposing six strategic principles aimed at achieving a "safe and just operating space." In construction, Francart et al. (2024) introduce the Doughnut Biotool, designed to quantify biodiversity impacts throughout building project lifecycles. Ortega et al. (2024) extend the model to fisheries in the Mediterranean, identifying crucial ecological and social deficits necessitating transformative actions.

Despite widespread recognition and diverse applications, practical implementation of the Doughnut Model faces significant challenges. Demastus and Landrum (2024) highlight that most corporate sustainability practices adopt a "weak sustainability" approach, typically focusing only on reducing harm without fundamentally altering growth- and resource-intensive business logic. Consequently, prevailing sustainability frameworks often inadequately address the Doughnut Economy's comprehensive requirements, posing substantial barriers to effective real-world business implementation.

While the Doughnut Model primarily operates as a macroeconomic construct, embedding it within the context of Responsible Entrepreneurship allows for a more precise and actionable operationalisation at the business level.

2.2 *Responsible Entrepreneurship*

Responsible Entrepreneurship refers to entrepreneurial action combining economic objectives with social and environmental responsibility. From this perspective, entrepreneurs transcend their conventional roles as mere drivers of economic growth to become key actors in sustainable development (Schaltegger & Wagner, 2011). Voegtlin and Scherer (2017) outline three critical dimensions through which responsible entrepreneurship contributes to sustainable development: (1) the duty to avoid harm, (2) the duty to do good, and (3) the need for governance structures fostering responsible innovation.

The first dimension focuses on risk management, standards, and certifications. Entrepreneurs should include their suppliers, employees, and consumers in their strategy. Clear indicators can help to prevent social, economic, or environmental harm. This entails adopting a new perspective on stakeholders. It involves expanding the stakeholder spectrum to include society and the environment. Additionally, it calls for shaping stakeholder relationships in line with the values of the Doughnut Model. Finally, it requires all stakeholders to consider how shared value can be maximised for the benefit of all (Jayashree et al., 2022).

The second dimension, *doing good*, involves concepts such as social entrepreneurship, shared value, social innovations, and eco innovations. Here, the value proposition and resource management should not be guided solely by the pursuit of maximum profit. Instead, products and services should be aligned with social, ethical, and ecological values (Zbuchea & Nikolaidis, 2016) and, through the principle of *creative destruction*, replace existing products and processes with more socially and environmentally responsible alternatives (Schaltegger & Wagner, 2011).

The third dimension—*governance*—is located at the global level, according to Voegtlin and Scherer, as individual companies alone cannot tackle global challenges such as climate change. This implies that on the level of policies for sustainability, the support of responsible entrepreneurship should be key.

Halberstadt et al. (2024) emphasise that responsible entrepreneurs do not form a homogeneous group of idealistic "do-gooders." Rather, they can be categorised into different types based on their motivation, objectives, and modes of opportunity recognition.

Quartiermeister: Enjoying beer with social impact

Founded in 2010, Quartiermeister is a social enterprise that supports local social and cultural projects through the sale of beer. A fixed amount from each bottle sold is donated directly to initiatives that promote community engagement and social participation (Quartiermeister, n.d.).

The organisation is structured as a hybrid model, consisting of a limited liability company (GmbH), a nonprofit association, and a foundation. The GmbH is responsible for the production and distribution of the beer, while the foundation safeguards the company's social mission and manages the funding. The association allows consumers to participate in the decision-making process by voting online for which local projects receive funding (Deutscher Social Entrepreneurship Monitor, 2019).

"We chose this hybrid structure because there is no legal form that combines both components—the entrepreneurial and the social—within a single framework" states David Griedelbach, one of the founders of Quartiermeister (cited in Deutscher Social Entrepreneurship Monitor, 2019, 21). He thereby points out that at least in German tax law social businesses have still difficulties to combine community engagement with business profit.

Quartiermeister does not brew the beer but collaborates with independent breweries, such as the Stadtbrauerei Wittichenau in Lusatia, to produce a range of craft organic beers, including pilsner, Helles, red beer, alcohol-free Kellerbier, and wheat beer (VG Dresden, n.d.). for distribution, it works together with organisations like the consumer cooperative Dresden, which is focused on sustainable, regional products.

Since its founding, the enterprise has invested over €250,000 in more than 200 grassroots projects. Quartiermeister demonstrates how consumption can be successfully combined with a commitment to the common good and community development (VG Dresden, n.d.).

2.3 Digital Transformation of Business Models

As responsible entrepreneurship increasingly intersects with technological advancement, we introduce digital transformation as a critical factor for changing business models: The digitalisation of businesses refers to the systematic integration of information and communication technologies into corporate activities and processes (Ancillai et al., 2023). Information and communication technologies encompasses a wide array of digital technologies, commonly referred to as new-age technologies, including artificial intelligence, cloud computing, big data analytics, machine learning, robotics, blockchain, virtual and augmented reality, and automation via software. These technologies form the foundational elements of the Industry 4.0 concept and the Internet of Things paradigm, significantly driving the contemporary shift towards digital transformation (Akter et al., 2022; Kagermann et al., 2013).

Digital transformation enables companies not only to adapt but fundamentally reshape their business models, significantly altering the underlying firm's logic and rationale for value sensing. Specifically, the transformation affects four critical aspects: value proposition, value creation, value capturing, and delivery (Ancillai et al., 2023; Foss & Saebi, 2017; Osterwalder & Pigneur, 2010; Teece, 2010). Digital technologies have demonstrated profound impacts at three distinctive levels: externally, internally, and holistically.

Externally, digital transformation enhances customer experience and value proposition through advanced personalisation and improved customer interaction. Internally, these technologies reshape value creation by transforming operational workflows and organisational structures. Holistically, digital technologies often lead to comprehensive transformations resulting in entirely novel business models (Ancillai et al., 2023; Foss & Saebi, 2017). Notably, the degree to which digital technologies impact business models varies significantly among companies and industries (Arnold et al., 2016; Rachinger et al., 2019). It ranges from incremental (marginal) improvements to radical (fundamental) transformations, depending on an organisation's digital maturity and strategic orientation (Habtay & Holmén, 2014).

Role of Digital Technologies in Reshaping Business Models

Digital technologies drive business model innovations, offering a wide range of opportunities and giving rise to various trends, as summarised below.

Changes in value proposition: By providing new and accurate information on consumer behaviour, digital technologies enable firms to better sense customer needs and reconfigure existing solutions—products and services—or develop novel ones tailored to customers' preferences. This capability allows companies to significantly improve customer experience and well-being (Ancillai et al., 2023; Rachinger et al., 2019; Shen et al., 2024).

Automation and personalisation: Leveraging data analytics and cloud computing enables automation in customer segmentation and personalisation of marketing strategies. This results in more targeted marketing approaches—personalised advertising and optimised price personalisation—profoundly enhancing customer engagement and altering the customer relationship management landscape (Ancillai et al., 2023; Kumar et al., 2019). These capabilities also enable companies to introduce new revenue models such as dynamic pricing, pay-per-use, or freemium offerings (Dasí et al., 2017). The integration of these technologies not only improves customer experiences but also allows businesses to capture value more effectively through innovative pricing and revenue strategies.

Servitisation: The shift from traditional product-centric offerings to a model that integrates services into the core value proposition of manufacturing companies represents a significant facet of digital transformation. By leveraging digital technologies, companies can collect and analyse real-time data from their products, enabling predictive maintenance, remote monitoring, and performance optimisation (Vendrell-Herrero et al., 2017). Furthermore, IoT technologies have paved the way for the creation of smart, connected products that can be delivered as services, effectively blurring the lines between products and services (Kohtamäki et al., 2019). This transition not only allows companies to develop new revenue streams but also to foster stronger, long-term relationships with their customers (Bustinza et al., 2017).

Process transformation and optimisation: Technologies such as robotics, cloud services, big data analytics, AI, additive manufacturing, and blockchain enable comprehensive process transformations. These transformative capabilities allow businesses not only to optimise existing processes and infrastructure management but also to fundamentally redefine operational strategies, realising higher efficiency, flexibility, and innovation potential (Björkdahl, 2020; Rachinger et al., 2019). The integration of these technologies facilitates the creation of smart factories and digital supply chains, enhancing operational agility and responsiveness to market changes (Schneider et al., 2020).

Data-driven decision-making and strategic renewal: Digital transformation promotes data-driven decision-making by leveraging advanced analytics and AI to deliver insights that significantly enhance strategic and operational decision-making (McAfee & Brynjolfsson, 2012). This shift from intuition-based to evidence-based management profoundly reshapes managerial practices (Provost & Fawcett, 2013). The integration of big data analytics and machine learning algorithms supports strategic renewal processes, uncovering previously invisible patterns and trends (Günther et al., 2017). This empowers businesses to continuously adapt and evolve their business models in alignment with changing market dynamics, thus ensuring long-term competitiveness and agility (Ancillai et al., 2023; Trischler & Li-Ying, 2023).

Challenges of Employing Digital Technologies for Businesses

While digital technologies offer numerous opportunities to reshape business models, implementing digital transformation in companies is associated with many challenges that organisations must navigate (e.g. Ancillai et al., 2023; Jorzik et al., 2024). These challenges can be broadly categorised into business challenges, skill gaps, and ethical considerations.

Business challenges: The digital transformation of business models confronts firms with significant changes across various operational areas, including procurement and production processes, promotion and communication, customer interaction, and financing. Beyond the financial difficulties associated with IT investments (Arnold et al., 2016), these challenges encompass understanding industry transformations, adapting to new technologies, managing the transition of work systems, and rethinking the division of labour between machines and humans. Additionally, companies must address the implications of these changes on existing business models (Spencer, 2023; Tahiri, 2022).

Skills gaps: A significant challenge hindering the full realisation of digitalisation's potential, widely discussed in the literature, is the skills gap (Ancillai et al., 2023; Jorzik et al., 2024; Tahiri, 2022). This gap often leads to employee prejudice, distrust, and resistance towards digital technologies (Fülöp et al., 2024; Jorzik et al., 2024). There is a pressing need for ongoing training and education to develop new skills and core competencies, including data analysis and human intervention during machine failures, to ensure employability in the rapidly evolving digital landscape. Scholars argue that current training structures may inadequately prepare individuals for the skills required in the digital economy, exacerbating potential skills gaps (Fülöp et al., 2024). This mismatch between available skills and industry demands poses a significant obstacle to effective digital transformation and business model innovation.

Ethical challenges: The application of digital technologies raises significant ethical concerns that require attention. These challenges include determining responsibilities associated with digital tools and recognising the inherent lack of morality in technologies like robots. Multilayered ethical issues emerge, such as algorithmic bias leading to discrimination and unintended unethical consequences in business models, exemplified by the creation of social media bubbles (Jorzik et al., 2024). The potential misuse of AI for malicious purposes further compounds these concerns. Addressing these challenges necessitates the development of specific ethical codes across various fields and professions (Fülöp et al., 2024). As businesses integrate advanced digital technologies, they must navigate these ethical complexities to ensure responsible innovation and maintain public trust.

Case study: Platform-based placement of freelance physicians in German hospitals

German hospitals are increasingly facing a shortage of medical specialists, particularly for night and weekend shifts. To bridge these gaps, many institutions rely on freelance physicians (Honorarärzte), who are placed via digital platforms such as *Nurse-to-rent*, *SeDiDoc*, or *Notarztbörse*. These platforms automate the matching process and handle administrative tasks like automatic invoicing, making the integration of freelance staff much easier for hospitals (Wissing & Trenkmann, 2020).

At the core of these platforms lies an algorithm-driven matching system, which benefits from positive network effects: the more users on both sides, the more efficient the matching process becomes (Wissing & Trenkmann, 2020). For doctors, the platforms offer personalised job suggestions, easy access via mobile devices, and reduced effort for job searching and administration. They also allow for flexible working schedules, provide insight into different clinical environments, and offer higher pay rates.

However, there are risks: freelance doctors are often not well integrated into existing teams, may lack knowledge of internal procedures, and typically avoid structural responsibilities. This can lead to tension among permanently employed staff, especially due to the significant pay gap (Wissing & Trenkmann, 2020).

Legally, the German Federal Social Court ruled in 2019 that freelance doctors are subject to mandatory social insurance contributions, as they are bound by instructions and do not assume entrepreneurial risk. As a result, some platforms such as *doc to rent* have modified or ceased their operations. A shift towards temporary employment and leasing models is anticipated.

2.4 Doughnut Economics & Responsible Entrepreneurship & Digital Technologies

Having discussed the theoretical foundations of Doughnut Economics, the principles of Responsible Entrepreneurship, and the transformative potential of digital technologies, this section now offers a practical framework comprising seven strategic steps that businesses can implement to effectively integrate these concepts into their core operations.

Transitioning to a business model that integrates the principles of Doughnut Economics with the values of Responsible Entrepreneurship demands a comprehensive, strategic and digital transformation. This transformation must be rooted not only in theoretical alignment with sustainability objectives but also in the practical redesign of core business functions. It requires firms to fundamentally reimagine their governance, ownership, finance, networks, and purpose to align with ecological ceilings and social foundations. The framework proposed herein outlines seven interrelated steps designed to support businesses in navigating this complex transformational process.

Define & Embed a Regenerative and Ethical Purpose

The first foundational step is to clearly define and embed a regenerative and ethical purpose within the organisation. A mission-driven purpose ensures long-term social and environmental well-being, aligning with Doughnut Economics by emphasising human needs within planetary boundaries (Hollensbe et al., 2014). Organisations should revise their mission statements accordingly and operationalize this purpose through sustainability and social responsibility KPIs across all departments (Raworth, 2017). Purpose-lock mechanisms, such as steward ownership structures or B Corp certifications, can legally safeguard this alignment. Furthermore, through targeted workshops and training programs, businesses must engage employees to embed these shared values into the organisational culture, ensuring consistency between strategic intentions and daily practices (Glavas, 2016). Staff in leadership positions play a key role in translating a responsible organisational culture into everyday business practices. Leaders act as role models, clearly articulating and promoting long-term sustainability goals to motivate employees. Ethical leaders do not only act according to moral principles on an individual level— they also serve as key actors in establishing and maintaining a culture that prioritises integrity, transparency, fairness, and accountability. In doing so, they ensure that ethical considerations are embedded in everyday decision-making processes and organisational structures.

Sustainability leaders foster a cohesive organisational culture grounded in transparency, integrity, and collaboration, building trust and enabling collective action towards sustainability objectives (Jayashree et al., 2022). Leadership development programs that emphasise sustainability competencies further align leaders' behaviours with strategic sustainability targets. Ethical leadership, a key dimension of sustainability leadership, stresses moral integrity, fairness, and accountability. Ethical leaders embed ethical standards throughout the organisation, influencing employees by consistently demonstrating high ethical behaviour. Classified within transformational leadership approaches, ethical leadership strengthens employees' ethical awareness and supports alignment with broader social and ecological goals. By establishing clear ethical guidelines and ensuring consistent compliance, ethical leadership fosters a responsible organisational culture essential for integrating sustainability into business strategies.

Redesign Business Networks for Ethics, Sustainability, and Ecosystem Integration

The second step involves restructuring business networks to prioritise ethics, sustainability, and responsible ecosystems. Businesses operate within interdependent networks; thus, supply chains, partnerships, and stakeholder relationships must reflect ethical standards. Organizations should cultivate long-term partnerships with responsible suppliers committed to fair trade practices and environmental sustainability. Implementing stakeholder inclusion mechanisms, such as community consultations and supplier feedback loops, promotes shared accountability (Jayashree et al., 2022). Obtaining certifications such as Fair Trade, Rainforest Alliance, or B Corp can validate ethical commitments. Additionally, responsible advocacy practices should replace traditional lobbying, with businesses proactively supporting public policies that enhance labour rights, environmental protection, and market ethics. Managers must explicitly acknowledge and address the challenges associated with integrating digital transformation and sustainability to ensure informed, strategic adoption of digital technologies.

Restructure Governance for Multi-Stakeholder Decision-Making

The third strategic step is restructuring governance frameworks to enable multi-stakeholder decision-making. As outlined in the Responsible Entrepreneurship principles, effective governance requires distributing decision-making authority beyond a narrow shareholder focus. Companies should adopt governance models that include representatives from employees, customers, communities, and environmental stakeholders, thus democratising strategic influence (Glavas, 2016; Jayashree et al., 2022). Transparency is critical, necessitating regular reporting of social and environmental performance alongside financial disclosures. Independent sustainability boards or mission-aligned foundations can provide additional oversight, ensuring accountability to societal objectives. Encouraging internal debate and flexibility within organisational decision-making processes facilitates responsiveness to evolving challenges and business model innovations. Digital platforms can support governance by enabling real-time collaboration and resource-sharing among stakeholders (Jayashree et al., 2022).

Shift to Mission-Locked or Shared Ownership Models

The fourth strategic step emphasises transitioning towards mission-locked or shared ownership models. Ownership structures profoundly influence organisational priorities, determining who benefits from and steers company actions. Traditional shareholder-focused models often conflict with long-term sustainability. Businesses should adopt steward ownership models that legally bind organisational missions to corporate governance, ensuring alignment with sustainability goals. Alternative structures, such as employee cooperatives, equity-sharing schemes, or community and supplier ownership, democratise economic benefits and decision-making. Companies must intentionally attract long-term investors aligned with responsible entrepreneurship to counteract short-term profit-driven pressures (Shepherd & Patzelt, 2011).

Restructure Finance for Sustainable Growth

The fifth strategic area involves restructuring financial mechanisms to prioritise sustainable growth over profit maximisation. Conventional finance models typically favour short-term returns, undermining investments in sustainability. Doughnut-aligned businesses should cap shareholder dividends, reinvesting retained earnings into regenerative initiatives, innovation, and employee well-being (Raworth, 2017). Patient capital from impact investors can shift financial incentives towards sustainable long-term value creation. Companies may also establish internal reinvestment funds dedicated explicitly to ecological restoration and social equity projects. Alternative finance models, such as profit-sharing and community-supported funding, further align financial strategies with mission-driven outcomes (Sullivan et al., 2015).

Implement Circular & Regenerative Business Models Supported by Digital Technologies

The sixth step involves implementing circular and regenerative business models, ensuring comprehensive product lifecycle sustainability. Businesses should transition from linear to circular systems, employing biomimicry principles, minimising waste, and designing products for reuse or recycling. Sustainability should be integrated as a core business activity, driving revenue through ecosystem-restoring innovations (Geissdoerfer et al., 2017).

Digital technologies act as critical enablers of this transformation. Artificial Intelligence and machine learning can optimise resource efficiency, reduce waste, and predict environmental impacts throughout supply chains. Internet of Things sensors embedded in production equipment and logistics can provide detailed data on resource usage, emissions, and material flows, enabling precise sustainability management. Blockchain technology ensures supply chain transparency and verifies ethical sourcing and environmental certifications via decentralised, tamper-proof ledgers. Additive manufacturing (3D printing) minimises material waste by producing items on-demand (Saberi et al., 2019). Digital platforms enhance stakeholder participation and accountability through real-time feedback and transparency regarding sustainability performance.

Actively Engage Employees & Customers in the Sustainability Mission

Finally, the seventh step focuses on actively engaging employees and customers as central actors in driving social and ecological transformation. Internally, companies must ensure fair wages, ethical working conditions, and meaningful professional development opportunities to integrate sustainability into organisational culture comprehensively (Glavas, 2016).

Externally, businesses should empower customers to make sustainable choices through transparent communication and educational campaigns highlighting product impacts. Digital solutions, such as mobile applications providing real-time sustainability data and online sustainability dashboards, foster informed consumer decisions. Interactive digital tools, including gamified loyalty programs and eco-incentive schemes, further incentivise sustainable behaviours like product recycling or reduced packaging.

Internally, digital platforms facilitate comprehensive employee engagement through targeted sustainability training, collaborative knowledge sharing, and feedback mechanisms. Training programs focused on digital competencies reduce resistance and cultivate innovation. Anonymous surveys and internal communication tools can systematically identify and address areas requiring improvement in working conditions, equity, or environmental initiatives.

By embracing inclusive digital solutions, businesses can foster participatory, transparent, and accountable stakeholder relationships. This digital and ethical alignment reinforces stakeholder trust and operationalises the core principle of Doughnut Economics: meeting human needs equitably within planetary boundaries (Raworth, 2017).

Case study: Digital platforms as drivers of sustainability in the real estate industry
Digitalisation plays a key role in promoting the circular economy within the construction sector. One of the leading platforms in this field is *Restado*, Europe's largest online marketplace for reusable building materials. By facilitating the trade of used components such as bricks, windows, or parquet flooring, Restado helps reduce raw material consumption, energy use, and CO_2 emissions (Gebäudeforum, 2026). To

specifically meet the needs of large-scale buyers, the *Concular* platform was launched in 2020. This software solution optimises material flows by digitally recording materials, planning deconstruction, and ensuring the availability of construction materials in the required quantity and quality (Lucks, 2023). In addition, *Bauteilnetz* offers a platform for regional building component exchanges, enabling direct interaction between suppliers and buyers. These digital marketplaces not only simplify the reuse of construction materials but also significantly reduce the need for new production and resource-intensive recycling. As a result, they make a substantial contribution to environmental sustainability in the real estate industry (Russ, 2024).

Klein (2025), however, reveals that in practice, these business models often fall short of their potential. One reason is that documentation efforts—such as those required by platforms like Madaster—are not financially compensated. Additionally, the platforms do not cover storage costs for unused materials or reclaimed building components. Furthermore, recycled components are often more expensive than new ones. For these digital business models to fulfil their promise, further structural and economic incentives are necessary.

3 Conclusion

In light of the pressing ecological, social, and technological challenges of the twenty first century, this paper has proposed a comprehensive conceptual framework for Digital Responsible Entrepreneurship that integrates the normative vision of Doughnut Economics, the strategic orientation of Responsible Entrepreneurship, and the transformative potential of digital technologies. We argue that sustainable transformation in business requires more than isolated technological or ethical interventions—it demands the deliberate synthesis of values, structures, and innovation.

By operationalising the Doughnut Model at the microeconomic level, we emphasise that enterprises can and must play an active role in aligning business activities with both planetary boundaries and social foundations. This shift necessitates a fundamental rethinking of purpose, ownership, governance, financial logic, and stakeholder relationships. Responsible Entrepreneurship serves as the crucial agentic bridge, facilitating this transformation through moral accountability, inclusive governance, and a commitment to doing no harm and generating positive impact.

At the same time, the integration of digital technologies is not merely a question of competitiveness or efficiency but a strategic enabler of sustainability-oriented business model innovation. From data-driven decision-making to servitisation and circular economy models, digital tools offer powerful means to implement and scale responsible practices. However, as our analysis and case studies have shown, digital transformation is not inherently ethical or sustainable. It must be guided by clear normative commitments, strategic foresight, and active reflection on social and environmental consequences.

To bridge the current conceptual and empirical gaps in the literature, we have proposed a seven-step framework that outlines how organisations can embed sustainability and ethics into their core operations by leveraging digital transformation. These steps—ranging from defining a regenerative purpose to stakeholder engagement and digital circularity—illustrate how the abstract principles of Doughnut Economics can be translated into actionable business strategies.

Moreover, our findings underscore that organisational culture and leadership ethics are pivotal in sustaining this transformation. Ethical leaders play a central role in institutionalising responsible values, ensuring that they are not confined to mission statements but embedded in daily practices, decision-making processes, and innovation agendas.

While the framework is theoretically grounded and illustrated through selected case studies, its full potential calls for further empirical research. Future studies should examine the effectiveness of these strategies across diverse industries, cultural contexts, and organisational types. Equally, policymakers and business support institutions must consider how to create enabling environments—through regulation, incentives, and education—that support responsible digital entrepreneurship.

In conclusion, navigating the complex interplay between sustainability, ethics, and digitalisation is one of the defining challenges—and opportunities—of contemporary entrepreneurship. This paper contributes to this endeavour by offering a holistic, future-oriented model that seeks not only to understand but to reshape the conditions under which business contributes to a safe and just space for humanity.

References

Akter, S., Michael, K., Uddin, M. R., McCarthy, G., & Rahman, M. (2022). Transforming business using digital innovations: The application of AI, blockchain, cloud and data analytics. *Annals of Operations Research, 308*(1), 7–39. https://doi.org/10.1007/s10479-020-03620-w

Ancillai, C., Sabatini, A., Gatti, M., & Perna, A. (2023). Digital technology and business model innovation: A systematic literature review and future research agenda. *Technological Forecasting and Social Change, 188*, 122307.

Arnold, C., Kiel, D., & Voigt, K.-I. (2016). How the industrial internet of things changes business models in different manufacturing industries. *International Journal of Innovation Management, 20*(08), 1640015. https://doi.org/10.1142/s1363919616400156

Björkdahl, J. (2020). Strategies for digitalisation in manufacturing firms. *California Management Review, 62*(4), 17–36. https://doi.org/10.1177/0008125620920349

Broccardo, L., Zicari, A., Jabeen, F., & Bhatti, Z. A. (2023). How digitalisation supports a sustainable business model: A literature review. *Technological Forecasting and Social Change, 187*, 122146.

Bustinza, O. F., Vendrell-Herrero, F., & Baines, T. (2017). Service implementation in manufacturing: An organisational transformation perspective. *International Journal of Production Economics, 192*, 1–8. https://doi.org/10.1016/j.ijpe.2017.08.017

Dasí, À., Elter, F., Gooderham, P. N., & Pedersen, T. (2017). New business models in-the-making in extant MNCs: Digital transformation in a telco. In *Breaking up the global value chain* (Vol. 30, pp. 29–53). Emerald Publishing Limited.

Demastus, J., & Landrum, N. E. (2024). Organizational sustainability schemes align with weak sustainability. *Business Strategy and the Environment, 33*(2), 707–725. https://doi.org/10.1002/bse.3432

Deutscher Social Entrepreneurship Monitor 2019. https://www.send-ev.de/wp-content/uploads/2021/03/DSEM2019.pdf (27.3.2025).

Diesendorf, M., Davies, G., Wiedmann, T., Spangenberg, J. H., & Hail, S. (2024). Sustainability scientists' critique of neoclassical economics. Global Sustainability, 7, e33. https://doi.org/10.1017/sus.2024.36

Foss, N. J., & Saebi, T. (2017). Fifteen years of research on business model innovation: How far have we come, and where should we go? *Journal of Management, 43*(1), 200–227. https://doi.org/10.1177/0149206316675927

Francart, N., Levasseur, A., Sala, S., Lasvaux, S., Morel, J. C., & Peuportier, B. (2024). The doughnut biotool: A tool to assess life-cycle biodiversity impacts from building projects. IOP Conference Series: Earth and Environmental Science, 1402(1), 012049. https://doi.org/10.1088/1755-1315/1402/1/012049

Fülöp, M. T., Ionescu, C. A., & Topor, D. I. (2024). Digital business world and ethical dilemmas: A systematic literature review. *Digital Finance.* https://doi.org/10.1007/s42521-024-00119-y

Gebäudeforum. (2026). Urban-Mining-Marktplätze: Recycling-Baustoffe und gebrauchte Bauteile. https://www.gebaeudeforum.de/wissen/nachhaltiges-bauen-und-sanieren/kreislaufwirtschaft-und-zirkulaeres-bauen/urban-mining-marktplaetze/ (24.03.2026).

Geissdoerfer, M., Savaget, P., Bocken, N. M. P., & Hultink, E. J. (2017). The circular economy—A new sustainability paradigm? *Journal of Cleaner Production, 143*, 757–768.

Ghauri, S. (2023). Swedish multinationals and sustainable innovations for transformation: The doughnut model. In P. N. Ghauri, U. Elg, & S. M. Hånell (Eds.), Creating a sustainable competitive position: Ethical challenges for international firms (international business and management, Vol. 37, pp. 129–152). Emerald Publishing Limited. https://doi.org/10.1108/S1876-066X20230000037008

Glavas, A. (2016). Corporate social responsibility and employee engagement: Enabling employees to employ more of their whole selves at work. *Frontiers in Psychology, 7*, 796.

Günther, W. A., Rezazade Mehrizi, M. H., Huysman, M., & Feldberg, F. (2017). Debating big data: A literature review on realizing value from big data. *The Journal of Strategic Information Systems, 26*(3), 191–209. https://doi.org/10.1016/j.jsis.2017.07.003

Gupta, J., van der Voorn, T., & Kharrazi, A. (2024). Transport within earth system boundaries. *npj Sustainable Mobility and Transport, 1*(1), 1–4. https://doi.org/10.1038/s44184-024-00006-z

Habtay, S. R., & Holmén, M. (2014). Incumbents' responses to disruptive business model innovation: The moderating role of technology vs. market-driven innovation. International Journal of Entrepreneurship and Innovation Management *11, 18*(4), 289–309.

Halberstadt, J., Schwab, A.-K., & Kraus, S. (2024). Cleaning the window of opportunity: Towards a typology of sustainability entrepreneurs. *Journal of Business Research, 171*, 114386. https://doi.org/10.1016/j.jbusres.2023.114386

Hartman, S., & Heslinga, J. H. (2022). The doughnut destination: Applying Kate Raworth's doughnut economy perspective to rethink tourism destination management. *Journal of Tourism Futures. Advance online publication.* https://doi.org/10.1108/JTF-06-2022-0123

Hausdorf, M., & Timm, J. M. (2023). Business research for sustainable development: How does sustainable business model research reflect doughnut economics? *Business Strategy and the Environment, 32*(6), 3398–3416. https://doi.org/10.1002/bse.3307

Hollensbe, E., Wookey, C., Hickey, L., George, G., & Nichols, C. V. (2014). Organizations with purpose. *Academy of Management Journal, 57*(5), 1227–1234.

Jayashree, P., El Barachi, M., & Hamza, F. (2022). Practice of sustainability leadership: A multi-stakeholder inclusive framework. *Sustainability, 14*(10), 6346. https://doi.org/10.3390/su14106346

Jorzik, P., Klein, S. P., Kanbach, D. K., & Kraus, S. (2024). AI-driven business model innovation: A systematic review and research agenda. *Journal of Business Research, 182*, 114764. https://doi.org/10.1016/j.jbusres.2024.114764

Kagermann, H., Wahlster, W., & Helbig, J. (2013). Recommendations for implementing the strategic initiative Industrie 4.0: Final report of the Industrie 4.0 working group. *Forschungsunion*, 12–25.

Klein, A. (2025). Herausforderungen bei der Implementierung der Circular Economy im Bau- und Immobiliensektor: Untersuchung der Hemmnisse und der Machbarkeit entlang des Immobilienlebenszyklus. Masterthesis.

Kohtamäki, M., Parida, V., Oghazi, P., Gebauer, H., & Baines, T. (2019). Digital servitization business models in ecosystems: A theory of the firm. *Journal of Business Research, 104*, 380–392. https://doi.org/10.1016/j.jbusres.2019.06.027

Kumar, V., Rajan, B., Venkatesan, R., & Lecinski, J. (2019). Understanding the role of artificial intelligence in personalized engagement marketing. *California Management Review, 61*(4), 135–155. https://doi.org/10.1177/0008125619859317

Lucks, B. (2023). Alt wird neu: Wie Concular zirkuläres Bauen digitalisieren will. Reset. Abgerufen am 16.01.2025 von https://reset.org/alt-wird-neu-wie-concular-zirkulaeres-bauen-digitalisieren-will/.

McAfee, A., & Brynjolfsson, E. (2012). Big Data: The Management Revolution. *Harvard Business Review, October 2012.*

Nieuwland, S. (2024). Urban tourism transitions: Doughnut economics applied to sustainable tourism development. *Tourism Geographies, 26*(2), 255–273. https://doi.org/10.1080/14616688.2024.2291431

Ortega, M., Smith, L., Delgado, P., & Torres, R. (2024). Can a doughnut economic framework be useful to monitor the blue economy success? A fisheries example. *Ecology and Society, 29*(1). https://doi.org/10.5751/ES-14326-290105

Osterwalder, A., & Pigneur, Y. (2010). Business Model Generation: A Handbook for Visionaries, Game Changers, and Challengers: Wiley.

Provost, F., & Fawcett, T. (2013). Data science and its relationship to big data and data-driven decision making. *Big Data, 1*(1), 51–59. https://doi.org/10.1089/big.2013.1508

Quartiermeister (n.d.). Über uns. https://quartiermeister.org/ueber-uns/ (27.3.2025).

Rachinger, M., Rauter, R., Müller, C., Vorraber, W., & Schirgi, E. (2019). Digitalisation and its influence on business model innovation. *Journal of Manufacturing Technology Management, 30*(8), 1143–1160. https://doi.org/10.1108/JMTM-01-2018-0020

Raworth, K. (2012). A safe and just space for humanity: Can we live within the doughnut? Oxfam Discussion Paper. Oxfam International. https://www-cdn.oxfam.org/s3fs-public/file_attachments/dp-a-safe-and-just-space-for-humanity-130212-en_5.pdf

Raworth, K. (2017). Doughnut economics: Seven ways to think like a 21st-century economist. Chelsea Green Publishing.

Rockström, J., Steffen, W., Noone, K., Persson, Å., Chapin, F. S., Lambin, E. F., Lenton, T. M., Scheffer, M., Folke, C., Schellnhuber, H. J., Nykvist, B., De Wit, C. A., Hughes, T., van der Leeuw, S., Rodhe, H., Sörlin, S., Snyder, P. K., Costanza, R., Svedin, U., et al. (2009). A safe operating space for humanity. *Nature, 461*(7263), 472–475. https://doi.org/10.1038/461472a

Russ, A. (2024). Gebrauchte Bauteile: Engagiert für zirkuläres Bauen. Deutsches Architektenblatt. Abgerufen am 16.01.2025 von https://www.dabonline.de/architektur/gebrauchte-bauteile-zirkulaeres-bauen/.

Saberi, S., Kouhizadeh, M., Sarkis, J., & Shen, L. (2019). Blockchain technology and its relationships to sustainable supply chain management. *International Journal of Production Research, 57*(7), 2117–2135.

Schaltegger, S., & Wagner, M. (2011). Sustainable entrepreneurship and sustainability innovation: Categories and interactions. *Business Strategy and the Environment, 20*(4), 222–237. https://doi.org/10.1002/bse.682

Schneider, S., Leyer, M., & Tate, M. (2020). The transformational impact of blockchain technology on business models and ecosystems: A Symbiosis of human and technology agents. *IEEE*

Transactions on Engineering Management, 67(4), 1184–1195. https://doi.org/10.1109/TEM.2020.2972037
Shen, P., Wan, D., & Zhu, A. (2024). Investigating the effect of AI service quality on consumer Well-being in retail context. *Service Business, 19*(1), 5. https://doi.org/10.1007/s11628-024-00575-x
Shepherd, D. A., & Patzelt, H. (2011). The new field of sustainable entrepreneurship: Studying entrepreneurial action linking what is to be sustained with what is to be developed. *Entrepreneurship Theory and Practice, 35*(1), 137–163.
Spencer, D. A. (2023). Automation and Well-being: Bridging the gap between economics and business ethics. *Journal of Business Ethics, 187*(2), 271–281. https://doi.org/10.1007/s10551-022-05258-z
Sullivan, R., Martindale, W., Feller, E., & Bordon, A. (2015). Fiduciary duty in the 21st century. UNEP FI, PRI, UN Global Compact.
Tahiri, S. (2022). The impact of digitalisation on firms' business models: Opportunities and limitations for digital leader. *Journal of Advanced Research in Leadership, 1*(1), 13–32.
Teece, D. J. (2010). Business models, business strategy and innovation. *Long Range Planning, 43*(2), 172–194. https://doi.org/10.1016/j.lrp.2009.07.003
Trischler, M. F. G., & Li-Ying, J. (2023). Digital business model innovation: Toward construct clarity and future research directions. *Review of Managerial Science, 17*(1), 3–32. https://doi.org/10.1007/s11846-021-00508-2
Vendrell-Herrero, F., Bustinza, O. F., Parry, G., & Georgantzis, N. (2017). Servitization, digitization and supply chain interdependency. *Industrial Marketing Management, 60*, 69–81. https://doi.org/10.1016/j.indmarman.2016.06.013
VG Dresden (n.d.). Quartiermeister. https://www.vg-dresden.de/bio-regional/regionallieferanten/portrait/quartiermeister (27.3.2025).
Voegtlin, C., & Scherer, A. G. (2017). Responsible innovation and the innovation of responsibility: Governing sustainable development in a globalized world. *Journal of Business Ethics, 143*(2), 227–243. https://doi.org/10.1007/s10551-015-2769-z
Wissing, C. & Trenkmann, J. (2020). Automatisierte Services im Gesundheitswesen—Eine explorative Studie zu den Effekten digitaler Plattformen. In M. Bruhn & K. Hadwich (Hrsg.), Forum Dienstleistungsmanagement. Automatisierung und Personalisierung von Dienstleistungen (S. 367–396). Springer Fachmedien Wiesbaden. https://doi.org/10.1007/978-3-658-30168-2_15
Zbuchea, A., & Nikolaidis, D. (Hrsg.). (2016). Responsible entrepreneurship: Vision, development and ethics. Proceedings of the 9th International Conference for Entrepreneurship, Innovation and Regional Development (ICEIRD), 23–24 June 2016, Bucharest, Romania. Comunicare.ro.

Andreas Braun is a professor of Business Administration specialising in Innovation Management, Sustainability, and Entrepreneurship at BSP Business and Law School Berlin. He holds a PhD in Innovation Management from the University of Potsdam, an MBA in General Management from CEU Business School Budapest, and both a B.Sc. and M.Sc. in Business Administration from the Technical University of Freiberg. With an extensive academic and professional background, Prof. Braun has led research and strategic initiatives, particularly in the fields of Open Innovation Management and Entrepreneurial Ecosystems. He seamlessly combines theoretical insights with practical applications, shaping how innovation and entrepreneurship contribute to organisational success and societal progress.

Patricia Graf is a Professor of Research Methods at the BSP Business and Law School, where she teaches modules such as Innovative Ecosystems and Scientific Thinking. As the head of the BMBF-ESF-funded project "Women and their Career Development in Scientific Research Teams," she has gained extensive expertise in addressing gender-specific barriers in academia and innovation contexts. Her research focuses on science and technology transfer, inclusive innovative ecosystems, and the role of stereotypes in the entrepreneurial financing process. At BSP, she contributes to the development of practice-oriented, interdisciplinary teaching and research, particularly in the areas of innovation policy, organisational transformation, and gender in science and entrepreneurship.

Anna Lejpras has been a professor of General Business Administration at the BSP Business and Law School since 2013. Before that, she worked as a research associate at the German Institute for Economic Research (DIW Berlin) in the Department of Innovation, Industry, and Services starting in 2007. In 2009, she completed her PhD at the European University Viadrina in Frankfurt (Oder) with a dissertation titled Essays on the Determinants of Firm Innovativeness, Performance, and Internationalisation (summa cum laude). She also worked there as a research associate between 2006 and 2008. In addition to her academic work, Anna Lejpras has contributed to several research-based policy advisory projects—primarily in the field of research and technology policy evaluation—for public institutions, including the German Federal Ministry of Economic Affairs and Technology (BMWi), as well as for foundations promoting scientific research.

From Digital Laggard to Responsible Leader? Why the German Mittelstand Turns out to be an Unexpected Role-Model for the Digital Age.

Philip Garra and Ninette Florschütz

Abstract In an era where digital transformation often prioritises speed over substance, the German Mittelstand offers a surprising counterintuitive alternative: value-driven leadership rooted in trust, long-term orientation, and communicative alignment. This article explores how these firms navigate the juxtaposition of transformation without losing identity—and why their approach holds lessons for responsible leadership in the digital age that are often overlooked by large corporations and academia.

Keywords German mittelstand · Value-driven leadership · Digital transformation · Responsible leadership

1 Introduction and Approach

The German Mittelstand is often portrayed as slow to embrace digital innovation—dare we say irresponsible in the face of a constant stream of seemingly groundbreaking technological innovations (Pahnke & Welter, 2019). It is easy to assume that a lack of resources relative to larger corporations is to blame. This view, however, underestimates the distinctive business logic that guides these companies: long-term planning, social cohesion, value-driven leadership, and an ingrained sense of generational stewardship allow Mittelstand firms operate with a fundamentally different perspective from large corporations or high-growth start-ups (Soluk & Kammerlander, 2021). Their guiding principle is not how to scale fast, but how to build something that lasts. In other words: the Mittelstand is responsible to its core.

P. Garra
SAMtoa GmbH, Hamburg, Germany
e-mail: philipp.garra@samtoa.de

N. Florschütz (✉)
Ilmenau University of Technology, Ilmenau, Germany
e-mail: florschuetz@mittkom.de

K. Bodrožić-Brnić et al. (eds.), *AI and the Ethics of Innovation*, Digital Transformation and Innovation, https://doi.org/10.1007/978-3-032-20638-1_14

This way of doing business has never been challenged more forcefully than it is today. As digital transformation accelerates across industries, the Mittelstand faces growing pressures to change everything from an ageing product line to its supposedly outdated company culture. Branded as "digital laggards" these companies have received their fair share of ridicule for a seemingly dismissive approach when it comes to integrating digital tools into their existing business models. In today's discourse, the Mittelstand is often hastily dismissed as a fading star — a relic of a bygone era, clinging to the past while grumbling about the future.

And yet the Mittelstand's approach toward digital transformation tells a different story. It does not seem to fit the mould of fast-paced start-up-success or large-scale corporate dominance: For one reason or another the Mittelstand seems to find its way through the storm of digital innovation and, in some instances, even seems to expand its hidden champions positioning. Against all odds, these companies fiercely defend their commitment to quality—even when digital products change rapidly. They sustain their commitment to in-house expertise and long-term employment in a world where value chains dissolve and communication is ubiquitous. And remarkably, these companies even manage to experiment, or rather "tinker," with their traditional products into the future. Here transformation is not imposed from the top down—but emerges through dialogue, experimentation, and alignment with core values.

What underpins this entire approach is the distinctive cultural identity of the Mittelstand — a trait most clearly reflected in its communication style: value-driven and communal. It is more than a leadership tactic—it is a cultural practice that enables operational alignment, builds legitimacy, and fosters participation across all levels of the organisation. It is the antithesis of the KPI driven corporate world with its focus on quarterly earnings. Mittelstand leaders communicate not just to inform, but to create purpose and a shared understanding of the company's goals. This approach that can become a source of stability and resilience—especially in an ever-changing digital environment.

By highlighting the Mittelstand's unique approach, this article offers a new lens on responsible leadership. It asks whether the Mittelstand—often overlooked and misunderstood—might offer a compelling blueprint for responsible transformation in a world facing both technological disruption and uncertainty. In doing so, we want to help close the distinct research gap between the obvious old-economy image of the Mittelstand and its surprising resilience in the face of digital change. It is certainly easier to analyse large corporations or fast-scaling start-ups — organisations that thrive on visibility, data, and bold narratives of success. In contrast, the Mittelstand's quiet, incremental approach to change often goes unnoticed (Simon, 2007). They are, after all, called hidden champions for a reason. But we believe it is time to step out of the shadows and take a closer look at what the rest of the economy might learn from these companies.

In this article we explore how Mittelstand firms apply value-driven communication to navigate the complexity of digital transformation and examine how firms manage coordination, trust, and accountability in increasingly fluid ecosystems. Thus, this article analyses the underlying mechanisms that reinforce the Mittelstand's approach to value communication: e.g. emergent strategy and network-based innovation which help align technology with long-term purpose (e.g. for ethical AI Implementation).

While this article presents a more optimistic view of the Mittelstand's future than current discourse suggests, it does not imply that the sector is immune to risk or turmoil. It is undergoing a profound transformation. This article argues that Mittelstand-specific mechanisms exist to actively and successfully navigate this change—mechanisms that many companies may not even realise they possess. We aim to demonstrate how Mittelstand enterprises can harness their strengths in a digital economy, and we hope that this article will help shine a spotlight on the academic gap concerning the Mittelstand as part of the digital economy.

Thus, the structure of this article is as follows: first, we provide a conceptual grounding of the Mittelstand and its distinctive leadership culture; second, we embed the question of responsible corporate orientation within a theoretical framework — in particular, by drawing on the principal-agent perspective in the context of digital transformation; and finally, we examine the mechanisms that enable sustainable, technology-driven management. This analysis draws on findings from our own study (Florschütz, 2024) and is being consolidated with insights from current empirical research.

2 Mittel-Management

To understand why the Mittelstand might defy its reputation as a digital laggard, we must first unpack the cultural, organisational, and strategic foundations that shape its unique mode of leadership and decision-making.

2.1 Cultural Foundations

The German Mittelstand is the sum of small and medium-sized enterprises (SMEs); it represents a distinctive economic and cultural model deeply embedded in the historical, social, and regional fabric of the country. Although often classified statistically—as firms with fewer than 5000 employees and less than €3 billion (Simon, 2007) pin annual turnover—the defining characteristics of the Mittelstand go well beyond metrics. They include ownership structure, governance style, long-term orientation, and a strong sense of responsibility towards employees, communities, and the broader society (Welter et al., 2014).

> Growth for the sake of growth or just chasing arbitrary numbers — that's not really something that gets you out of bed in the morning. There has to be a deeper sense of purpose. That's why we've moved away from goals like 'we want to have this many employees by 2025,' and instead focus on having a positive impact — by being sustainable in every sense. That means creating secure, long-term jobs and doing as much good for the environment as possible. (Florschütz, 2024, p. 275)

To clarify this point, it is helpful to distinguish between SMEs and the Mittelstand. While many Mittelstand firms meet the size criteria of SMEs, not all SMEs exhibit the core values and organisational structures that define the Mittelstand. A Mittelstand firm is characterised by the unity of ownership and management, with owners typically being personally liable and deeply involved in operational and strategic decisions. Here, size really does not matter. What unites these companies is a shared philosophy of responsibility and stewardship.

This structural coupling of ownership and leadership has profound implications. (Khadjavi & Volery, 2009). The entrepreneur's private wealth, family standing, and long-term legacy are tightly linked to the company's fate (Renker, 2012). Decisions are made not in abstraction, but in full awareness of their personal and societal consequences. The owner is fully accountable—for employees, for local communities, and for the firm's reputation (Florschütz, 2024).

Additionally, Mittelstand firms are frequently multi-generational and regionally anchored. They have grown in close dialogue with their environment, often playing a stabilising role in times of crisis. Their conservative financing, strong equity base, and aversion to short-term speculation enable them to weather downturns more robustly than many publicly traded corporations. For example: During the 2008 financial crisis, many Mittelstand companies retained staff and recovered faster than larger firms, thanks to leaner structures and a deeply embedded sense of duty towards employees and the region (Welter et al., 2020).

In this context, social norms become a powerful organising principle. The Mittelstand operates according to a logic that blends economic rationality with social expectations. Employees are not only seen as human capital but as co-stewards of the company's mission. An extension of informal trust replaces formal control systems, and proximity—both organisational and geographic—enables decentralised decision-making based on consensus and responsibility (Welter & Gröschl, 2016).

This approach extends to corporate social responsibility (CSR). Unlike the standardised, strategic CSR efforts found in large corporations, CSR in the Mittelstand follows a different logic: implicit, informal, and intrinsically motivated. Responsibility is lived rather than declared, rooted in the daily actions of owners and managers (Looser, 2017). The guiding principle is not one of image cultivation, but of moral obligation—CSR as a form of moral economy, embedded in the business's identity and social function (Looser, 2017; Schatilow, 2014). In fact, communication usually occurs through informal channels—personal conversations, town hall meetings, or local partnerships—and is guided by value-driven action (Schatilow, 2014).

Public communication of CSR is cautious and modest. As Looser observes, if one were to measure CSR through channels such as social media, websites, or reports, one might mistakenly assume that Mittelstand firms are disengaged from their social responsibilities (Looser, 2017). Many of these companies adhere to a high ethical standard but hardly communicate it. CSR is not a publicity tool, but an extension of the firm's culture and local embeddedness. Employees are involved in CSR activities not as a strategic gesture, but as part of a shared responsibility culture (Bader, 2011). The value system is based on reciprocity: what the region gives, the company returns (Schatilow, 2014).

Both aspects—the informal way of communication and its lack of publicity—already give a first glimpse into why the Mittelstand is both considered a laggard in the rapidly changing digital economy and why, so far—only few companies seem to mind their underdog positioning. The goal is not grandstanding for shareholders, but rather a grounded reputation management based on maintaining trusting relationships with stakeholders and fulfilling their commitment to the community.

2.2 Social Norms in Leadership

Even at this point, it is obvious that social norms are not abstract ideals in the Mittelstand; they are actively lived and embodied in everyday business practices and communication. The same local networks that support business continuity also define expected behaviours, ethical standards, and unwritten rules of interaction. Leadership, in this context, is less about formal hierarchy and more about personal integrity, consistency, and mutual respect.

Or to describe this fact with a little more colour and fanfare: Regional and local events like fairs, sports clubs, or volunteer firefighting units serve as informal arenas where business leaders and employees engage not as employer and employee, but as neighbours and peers. This constant proximity reinforces a norm-based leadership model built on trust rather than control. Agreements are often verbal, loyalty is mutual, and decisions carry social repercussions beyond the balance sheet. Something we like to call the "Schützenfest-Effect."

These social norms manifest clearly in the way communication is practised within Mittelstand firms:

- Low-Power Distance Communication: Despite clear hierarchies, leaders are approachable and expected to maintain a direct dialogue with staff. Open-door policies are common, and decisions are often discussed in town-hall-style meetings or informal settings.
- Value-Based Messaging: Communication from leadership frequently emphasises stability, shared responsibility, and craftsmanship over aggressive expansion or cost-cutting. This narrative builds collective commitment and long-term identification with the company mission.
- Relational Communication with Stakeholders: Customers and suppliers are treated as partners, not transactional entities. Trust-based communication minimises the need for legal safeguards and lowers friction in negotiations.
- Embedded Accountability: Because the community is both audience and stakeholder, leaders must communicate with a high degree of authenticity. Misalignment between words and actions—such as laying off staff while sponsoring high-profile events—can lead to reputational damage not just for the company, but for the individual leader (Florschütz, 2024).

In this context, communication serves not only an operational function but a normative one. It signals alignment with shared values and reinforces organisational culture. And as Mittelstand companies adopt digital tools—from collaborative platforms to AI-driven decision-making—they must ensure that these tools do not disrupt these deeply ingrained norms but ideally enhance them. Instead, digital communication should be tailored to strengthen transparency, reinforce personal accountability, and preserve the trust-based culture that has sustained these companies for generations. It should enable niche expertise to become even more niche and thus more valuable to the market—both in terms of the company and in terms of personal expertise. Sharing this expertise—thus communicating—becomes the essential skill for staying relevant in a digital world.

2.3 Long-Term Planning as a Competitive Advantage

The culmination of these social norms and cultural characteristics reveals a single, defining trait—one that fundamentally contradicts the logic of most prevailing digital strategies: long-term planning. For the Mittelstand, this is not a strategic choice; it is an existential principle. Mittelstand firms operate according to the philosophy of being *enkelfähig*—literally "fit for grandchildren"—which implies that business decisions are consistently guided by a long-term orientation aimed at safeguarding the company, its normative foundations, and its material assets for future generations. This orientation is institutionally embedded within the ownership structure and closely tied to a governance logic in which decision-making authority and responsibility remain inseparable, as "the person who puts their neck on the line must also make the final decision—reuniting decision-making and responsibility at the very top" (Florschütz, 2024, p. 286).

This contrasts starkly with the managerial logic of the corporate world, where performance is measured quarterly, often leading to optimisation strategies that prioritise immediate shareholder returns over structural resilience or community impact. In such environments, decisions around headcount, outsourcing, and R&D can be volatile, driven by analyst expectations or shareholder interest. Mittelstand leaders, in contrast, often forgo short-term profitability to reinvest in long-term capabilities—whether in employee training, local supplier networks, or energy-efficient production systems.

This long-term horizon influences business practices in multiple ways:

- Capital Structure: Mittelstand firms typically avoid high leverage and rely on retained earnings and conservative financing, making them less vulnerable in crises and more capable of weathering downturns without immediate layoffs or cost-cutting.
- Product Strategy: Instead of competing on price or hype cycles, these firms aim to create technically superior products with long lifespans, often in highly specialised

industrial niches. Their focus on durability and reliability directly appeals to quality-sensitive B2B customers worldwide.
- Workforce Development: The willingness to train and retain skilled labour over decades reflects a commitment to institutional knowledge and workforce stability, rather than short-term labour cost optimisation.

Nevertheless, this cautious approach has posed challenges in the digital age. The culture of rapid iteration and disruption in digital environments often contrasts with the Mittelstand's emphasis on precision and risk mitigation. A 2023 study by the Technical University of Munich (Fördere et al., 2023), conducted in the Heilbronn-Franken region, found that nearly two-thirds (62%) of SMEs lack a digital transformation strategy, and over half of those have no intention of developing one. The study identified core barriers to digitalisation: underdeveloped digital infrastructure, a shortage of skilled workers, and excessive bureaucracy. This aligns with a 2018 whitepaper by the Bertelsmann Stiftung, which emphasised that while some Mittelstand firms have made progress in digital transformation, the pace remains slow. A key obstacle is a cultural adherence to "old industry" logic, which clashes with the fast-paced demands of the digital age. The authors argue that a shift toward a new "digital logic"—embracing data-driven experimentation and agile structures—is necessary for long-term competitiveness.

All of this might lead to the conclusion that the Mittelstand's strength can turn sour in highly volatile markets or industries undergoing rapid disruption. The reluctance to abandon proven processes or long-standing supplier relationships can slow the pace of transformation. Mittelstand leaders express scepticism toward tech trends that contradict their incremental innovation model. As a result, some firms risk becoming reactive rather than leading the way. We propose that with the right planning mechanisms and foresight, this long-term orientation can become a competitive asset in digital transformation. Instead of impulsively introducing technologies, medium-sised companies use their resource-oriented approach to integrate digital tools in a way that strengthens their core competencies and deepens their value proposition—especially in areas such as predictive maintenance, supply chain transparency and smart manufacturing.

The key challenge is not to sacrifice long-term thinking, but to reconcile it with digital agility: making experimentation and iterative learning part of the culture, without compromising on values like product excellence, workforce stability, and responsibility. Then, just maybe, the Mittelstand might have what it takes to not only to survive but to strive in a digital world.

3 Value-Driven Communication as a Leadership Tool

In the face of increasing complexity and strategic uncertainty, value-driven communication emerges not only as a leadership instrument but as a core mechanism through which Mittelstand firms persevere.

3.1 Business Communication for Leadership and Legitimation

In the Mittelstand, communication is not an accessory to leadership—it is its most essential tool, given that its strategy, size and social norms do not allow leaders to fall back on organisational hierarchies or the rigidity and anonymity of the corporate world. Especially in times of strategic change or digital transformation, communication serves as the mechanism through which trust is maintained, legitimacy is earned, and alignment is achieved. Building on insights from organisational communication theory, we can understand leadership communication as both constitutive and instrumental: it shapes reality for employees while steering collective action.

Leadership communication in the Mittelstand typically fulfils three interdependent functions:

- Legitimation: By openly articulating vision, purpose, and decisions, leaders earn credibility and foster stakeholder buy-in. This is particularly vital in family-owned businesses, where legitimacy is not derived from position alone but also from a leader's perceived integrity, social embeddedness, and alignment with shared values.
- Operational Alignment: Communication ensures that strategic goals are translated into actionable tasks. In Mittelstand firms, this often occurs through direct, interpersonal channels rather than formalised reporting systems. Because of flat hierarchies and high relational proximity, alignment relies more on shared understanding than on KPIs alone.
- Participation Mechanism: In many Mittelstand companies, leadership is dialogical. Decision-making is often preceded by consultation with internal and external stakeholders. This reflects a normative leadership model in which dialogue is not merely informative but co-creative. Communication creates a sense of ownership among employees and suppliers, reinforcing the social fabric of the organisation.

Drawing on frameworks of communicative leadership, we can further understand this approach as value-driven communication, namely:

- Narrative-based, using storytelling to embed organisational change within a broader historical and ethical context.
- Dialogical, allowing feedback loops that strengthen identification and reduce resistance.
- Symbolic, recognising that leadership acts (e.g. a personal message, a visit to the factory floor, public acknowledgment) carry meaning beyond content.

In the context of digital transformation, these communication functions become more urgent. Leaders must articulate not only the what (new tools, platforms, or processes), but also the why—explaining how digital initiatives align with core values like quality, sustainability, or regional responsibility. Without this contextualisation, employees may perceive digitalisation as an externally imposed threat rather than an evolution of the company's identity.

Moreover, effective communication must manage emotional undercurrents: fears of job loss, uncertainty about competence in digital systems, or scepticism toward agile working models. Studies show that transformation processes fail not because of technical deficiencies, but because of a lack of emotional alignment and trust in leadership. Mittelstand firms, with their direct communication cultures and value orientation, have a distinct advantage here—provided their leaders actively cultivate transparent and participative dialogue.

In short, leadership communication in the Mittelstand is both a cultural artifact and a strategic capability. It translates long-term vision into daily reality, preserves trust in uncertain times, and allows for adaptive change without eroding the organisation's normative foundations. It also provides an explanation of and guidance on a successful leadership approach in changing time. It helps to understand why, despite all the negative press and predictions of its demise, the Mittelstands is able to continue to reinvent itself and seem to hold on: As it turns out: the rumours of the Mittelstands death have been greatly exaggerated.

3.2 *Navigating Digital Transformation*

All this talk about communication presents a paradox for Mittelstand leadership: digital transformation demands speed, flexibility, and experimentation—traits often at odds with the traditional strengths of continuity, precision, and stability. Nowhere is this tension more visible than in leadership communication.

First, the rise of remote work and distributed teams alters the spatial and social dynamics of leadership. The informal, proximity-based communication style common in Mittelstand firms—"management by walking around"—becomes harder to maintain. Leaders must now find new channels to remain visible and approachable, while ensuring accountability in teams that no longer share the same physical space. This change especially plays to the strengths of the hidden champions of the Mittelstand who tend to be used to organising and communicating across boundaries and large spatial differences as most of them have experience with worldwide production and distribution.

Second, increased digital collaboration blurs the distinction between internal and external actors. Mittelstand firms increasingly rely on ecosystems of freelancers, platform providers, and international suppliers. Communication must therefore extend beyond the traditional boundaries of the organisation and become more modular, layered, and scalable—without losing its personal touch.

Third, data-driven decision-making and AI tools can risk eroding the normative leadership culture if not introduced thoughtfully. Employees may feel reduced to data points, especially if performance is measured by dashboards rather than relational feedback. Leaders must put technology into context and emphasise that digital tools serve to support and complement human decisions and long-standing structures of trust—not replace them.

Practical examples illustrate both the risk and potential: an engineering firm in North Rhine-Westphalia integrated a digital platform for customer feedback and service ticketing. However, implementing such a system is a high-risk strategy when the business model relies on personal—not digital—interaction. Initially met with resistance by long-tenured service staff, the platform gained acceptance only after leadership engaged in a series of dialogue sessions, linked the platform's KPIs to customer satisfaction values, and emphasised how it would preserve—rather than undermine—their long-standing relationships.

Thus, the communication challenge in digital transformation is not simply about delivering information. It is about reframing the narrative of change, anchoring new technologies in the existing value system, and maintaining relational integrity in an increasingly virtual environment.

Mittelstand leaders must master what can be called hybrid communication leadership: blending digital fluency with analogue trust-building, agile language with stable values, and global coordination with local resonance. Only through such integrated communication can the Mittelstand maintain its unique identity while evolving its business model for a digital economy. This communicative balancing act reflects a deeper organisational logic prioritising long-term continuity: "The profits generated are primarily used for refinancing and achieving individual goals. They are therefore seen more as a means to a long-term, unchanging purpose: securing or maintaining the necessary resources to ensure the organisation remains stable and independent." (Florschütz, 2024, p. 275).

Thus, Mittelstand leadership finds itself caught in a paradox. While its core values—sustainability, trust, and stability—have long been sources of strength, these same principles are now being challenged by a digital economy defined by volatility, uncertainty, and the rapid dissolution of established value chains. As Schauf (2009) notes, one of the greatest management problems lies in the fundamental unpredictability of future developments: shifting technologies, new markets, changing consumer behaviours, and regulatory interventions all undermine the ability to make reliable forecasts. In this context, strategic leadership becomes an act of navigating the tension between responsibility for the future and the impossibility of fully anticipating it.

This paradox raises the next question in this article: is the Mittelstand's response merely anecdotal or idiosyncratic—or can it be understood within a broader theoretical framework? Can its value-driven, communication-based approach to leadership be situated in established organisational theory, thereby gaining legitimacy? Might it even be possible to find a model that reconciles this paradox and not only explains its resilience in the face of digital disruption, but also offers actionable insights for other economic actors? In other words, could SMEs, with their traditional orientation, serve not only as a cultural curiosity, but also as a model for responsible leadership in the digital age? In short: yes.

4 Principles and Agents

To understand how Mittelstand firms preserve trust, alignment, and strategic continuity in the face of digital complexity, the Principal-Agent model offers a valuable lens—highlighting how leadership must evolve when control gives way to coordination, and contracts are replaced by communication.

4.1 Why a Model-Based Perspective Is Useful

To meaningfully assess how Mittelstand firms communicate and thus navigate through digital transformation while preserving their core values, the Principal-Agent (P-A) model presents a fitting analytical lens. Originally developed to explain contractual relationships under conditions of asymmetric information, the P-A model provides insight into how principals (owners, leaders) guide agents (employees, partners, subsidiaries) toward common objectives, even when incentives or access to information differ (Jensen & Meckling, 1976).

Although the P-A model is not without its limitations—it remains useful in the context of value-preserving transformation. In Mittelstand firms, principal-agent relationships are frequently governed not through explicit contracts or formalised oversight, but through implicit norms, shared purpose, and trust. Personal proximity between owners and employees, flat hierarchies, and long tenures often reduce the perceived need for extensive monitoring systems. However, the increasing complexity of digitalisation introduces new challenges to this model. As firms adopt more distributed structures, the physical and informational distance between principals and agents grows. The resulting opacity weakens informal coordination mechanisms, making questions of alignment and accountability harder to answer. The P-A model helps clarify how incentive structures and information flows must evolve to sustain coherence and strategic direction.

In contrast to large corporations that heavily rely on data-driven control systems and a standardized, interchangeable managerial class, the Mittelstand mitigates information asymmetries through close-knit relationships, direct communication, and value-based leadership. Where these corporations often fall short—particularly from a principal-agent perspective—is in the separation of ownership and control, which undermines alignment of interests and weakens long-term accountability. Simply put: When the principal is also the managing director—or embedded in close relational networks with those who are—the risk of opportunistic behaviour by agents is reduced, and trust-based coordination can flourish. Suddenly, long-term decision-making and a sustained focus on employees become possible. And, from our point of view, emerge as best practice strategy in a fast-paced digital world.

4.2 Strategy and Plummeting Transaction Cost

Classic, and somewhat universal models of business strategy, such as Porter's value chain or Henderson's BCG matrix, for example, assume that firms create internal structures to overcome information scarcity and coordination inefficiencies Evans & Wurster, 1997). A company, and thus its strategy, is valid, where and when the internal cost of coordination (communicating information) is lower than its external alternative. Digital technologies, of course, shift these assumptions fundamentally. Real-time analytics, cloud collaboration, and AI-driven monitoring collapse informational hierarchies, allowing for greater decentralisation and transparency.

Imagine, for instance, a medium-sized industrial pumps manufacturer in Thuringia has adopted IoT-enabled sensors to monitor equipment performance globally. Where previously, performance feedback from service teams might have taken weeks to reach leadership, executives can now review usage and maintenance patterns in real-time dashboards. As a result, decisions around product improvements, spare parts logistics, and service scheduling are now data-informed and decentralised—reshaping the traditional principal-agent relationship. But this transparency also introduces new challenges. More data does not automatically translate into better alignment. As Jiang et al. (2025) argue, digital transparency can create "data noise" and erode trust if not contextualised. Mittelstand leaders therefore act as *sense-makers*, not just data consumers, by providing context, translating insights into decisions that align with long-term strategic intent and cultural expectation. Contextual communication somewhat counterintuitively, defines the boundaries of a firm in a world where information and noise are ubiquitous, and coordination is otherwise impossible.

The theoretical foundation for this changing logic of firm boundaries was laid long before the digital revolution—most notably by economist Ronald Coase. In his seminal work *The problem of Social Cost (1960)* he argued that firms exist primarily to reduce transaction costs—the costs of negotiating, coordinating, and enforcing contracts in the open market. Notably the cost of communication. When these costs are high, firms internalise functions; when they fall, outsourcing and market-based coordination become more attractive.

Digital infrastructures have dramatically lowered transaction costs in communication, coordination, and knowledge sharing. This development is a key reason why firms now outsource specialised functions or co-innovate through ecosystems instead of keeping everything in-house. For the Mittelstand—long rooted in vertical integration and deep in-house expertise—the shift toward outsourcing was mainly believed to be a disruptive challenge.

But there is a second, more subtle way to apply Coase's thinking—one that goes beyond the cost-focused logic of externalities. The Coase Theorem is often invoked in discussions of negative externalities—pollution, social harm, health risks—and how they can be internalised through regulation or pricing mechanisms. (Kahneman et al., 1990). Yet, the Mittelstand presents a rare case where positive externalities—such as workforce stability, regional cohesion, and vocational training—are internalised, even when they are not monetised (in the short term) or easily quantifiable.

A family-run manufacturer in Baden-Württemberg may not calculate the external social benefit of retaining ageing technicians through AI-enhanced work design—but the result may very well be a stronger community, preserved expertise, and lower systemic risk. These are unintended positive externalities—and Mittelstand firms tend to internalise them not because they are measured, but because they are embedded in the logic of long-term value creation.

In this sense, the Mittelstand subtly defies Coasean assumptions: it internalises not only what is cost-efficient, but what is ethically consistent with its purpose. And paradoxically, this may enhance competitive advantage in the digital age. By grounding technological change in values and communication, Mittelstand firms maintain stakeholder trust, reduce resistance, and align distributed ecosystems—precisely the coordination challenges digital transformation often fails to solve in purely rationalist models.

Thus, revisiting Coase in a Mittelstand context reveals a new perspective: digital transformation is not just a question of lowering transaction costs, but of choosing which externalities to internalise—and how communication, trust, and purpose can be used to do so.

4.3 Getting Coas(e)Y

This theoretical discussion comes alive once we understand how digital technologies are dissolving vertical value chains across all industries—emerging as a central force behind today's economic upheaval. As Baldwin (2016) notes, global value creation increasingly occurs through modular, distributed networks rather than vertically integrated pipelines. This affects Mittelstand firms profoundly: their historical advantage lay in mastering entire production flows; now, they must integrate seamlessly into ecosystems.

Consider a real-world example: a mid-sized supplier of medical imaging components has shifted from providing hardware alone to co-developing embedded AI applications with hospitals and startups. This requires flexible contracts, interoperable standards, and strategic realignment—far beyond traditional procurement models. The firm now sees itself less as a manufacturer and more as a *platform node* within a network of data producers, regulators, and solution developers.

Principal-agent dynamics in such constellations are fluid. Accountability is shared, and authority rotates, and communication emerges as the central tool for coordination. To succeed, Mittelstand firms use technology to shift from controlling to *coordinating*, thereby building greater relational trust and understanding.

- Establishing shared understanding among distributed agents (e.g., cross-functional project teams, joint ventures).
- Legitimiseing strategy shifts (e.g., integrating AI in production).

- Maintaining coherence of purpose (e.g., across sustainability reports, internal dashboards, and supplier onboarding).

As Weick and Weick (1995) notes, organisations don't discover meaning, they construct it. Mittelstand leaders must use communication to narrate continuity amid disruption.

Example: Premium Pricing through Sustainability: A manufacturer of precision glass instruments in Lower Saxony integrates recycled materials and low-emission processes, commanding a 15–20% price premium in EU markets sensitive to environmental standards.

Supply Chain Resilience through Social Standards: A Mittelstand textile firm in North Rhine-Westphalia retained its Turkish suppliers through the pandemic by offering prepayments and guaranteeing minimum volumes—earning long-term loyalty and ensuring stability even during supply chain disruptions.

Talent Attraction through Purpose: A Black Forest-based engineering firm recruits young engineers by offering flexible schedules, strong vocational mentorship, and community engagement programs—positioning itself as a high-integrity employer in an ageing region.

These firms don't need external regulation in the Coasian-Sense to force internalisation; they do it proactively because the *non-economic benefits*—reputation, employee retention, brand capital—are tightly linked to long-term returns. In doing so, they model a richer interpretation of the Principal-Agent model—one that incorporates social capital alongside economic incentives.

4.4 Actions Speaks Louder than Words

Historically, Mittelstand firms relied on in-house expertise, vertical integration, and local embeddedness. As digitization reconfigures cost structures and value creation, firms must adapt by engaging in networks—without losing their core identity.

This means developing new capabilities:

- Platform Competence: The ability to collaborate via digital ecosystems, APIs, and shared data environments.
- Modular Strategy Execution: Allowing smaller units or partners to experiment and scale solutions autonomously.
- Cultural Continuity: Ensuring that shared norms, such as responsibility, trust, and quality, remain intact—even when parts of the business are externalised.

All of this requires reframing communication as action: Leaders are now tasked with guiding distributed, digitally augmented teams while preserving clarity of purpose and coherence in execution. Digital tools should serve to amplify, and not replace, the relational dynamics at the heart of effective leadership. Finally, the Mittelstand may view digitalisation not as a threat to its identity, but as an opportunity to scale its values. In an increasingly networked economy, this values-based leadership, rooted in responsibility, stewardship, and long-term orientation, becomes a competitive advantage. Rather than reject the P-A model as outdated, we should adapt it to Mittelstand realities:

Traditional P-A logic	Mittelstand reality
Formal contracts	Implicit norms and social ties
Information asymmetry	Data transparency, tacit knowledge
Incentive alignment through pay	Alignment through values, trust, reputation
Centralised control	Distributed coordination via platforms

This reimagined model helps explain how Mittelstand firms can remain competitive, not by mimicking Silicon Valley speed, but by blending relational strength with digital adaptability. It shows how digital transformation challenges Mittelstand firms to revise—not abandon—their core strengths. Principal-agent dynamics are shifting from control to collaboration, from hierarchy to networks, and from cost minimisation to purpose maximisation.

Success will depend on the Mittelstand's ability to:

- Use digital tools not just for efficiency, but for strategic alignment and value communication.
- Redefine principal-agent relationships across organisational boundaries.
- Reinforce trust, responsibility, and long-term logic—now in a platform-mediated, data-rich environment.

5 All that Talk

The final question remains: what does this communication look like in practice? This section outlines four key mechanisms through which Mittelstand firms maintain alignment between digital innovation and long-term success, alongside areas for future research.

5.1 Navigating Complexity with Incremental and Recursive Strategy

Unlike large corporations that formulate strategy through rigid annual planning cycles, Mittelstand firms rely on an incremental and recursive approach shaped through continuous learning, stakeholder input, and iterative experimentation. This idea, conceptualized by Mintzberg as *emergent strategy* (Mintzberg, 1978), was once seen as unfolding spontaneously—deus ex machina—is now increasingly understood as something that can be actively shaped and influenced. Communication is

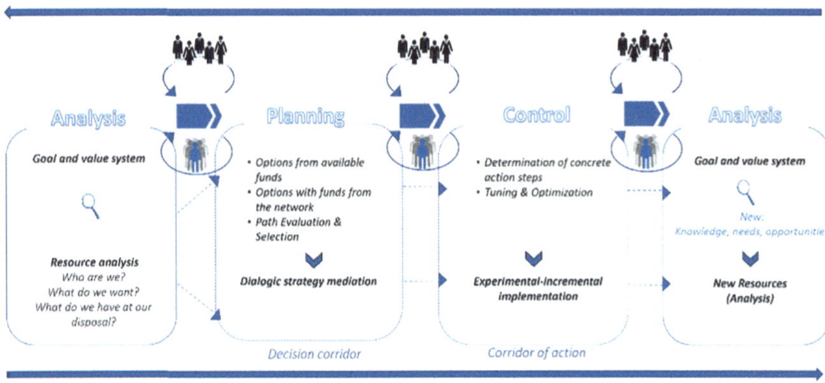

Fig. 1 Iterative communication and decision cycles in value-oriented management. Adapted from Florschütz (2024, p. 309)

not simply a tool for cascading decisions, but a medium through which strategy itself is co-created (Florschütz, 2024).

Leaders engage in ongoing, dialogic exchanges with employees, customers, and suppliers—transforming informal conversations into strategic insight. This becomes particularly valuable in digital transformation contexts, where complexity is high, and planning horizons are short. Rather than overcommitting to top-down digital roadmaps, Mittelstand firms often explore new technologies through small-scale pilots, guided by feedback rather than fixed KPIs.

This strategic approach requires leaders to communicate uncertainty constructively. By openly acknowledging that not all answers are known—and that learning is both expected and valued—Mittelstand leadership fosters psychological safety and encourages initiative. This open communication culture allows strategy to unfold organically, without losing alignment with long-term purpose (Florschütz, 2024). This approach that can be depicted as follows Fig. 1:

5.2 *Purpose-Driven Leadership: Shared Values over Shareholder Value*

For Mittelstand firms, purpose is not a branding exercise, it is the normative compass that informs all major decisions. Leadership is judged not only by financial performance but by its alignment with the company's long-term responsibilities to employees, customers, and the broader community. This sense of purpose reflects the values of founding families and defines the company's identity over time. In this context, purpose functions as a filter. Digital initiatives are not pursued for the sake of innovation, but for their contribution to enduring value, whether that means safeguarding local jobs, enhancing product quality, or strengthening customer relationships.

Purpose also fosters internal cohesion. Especially in periods of change—such as automation or restructuring—employees are more likely to support transformation when they see how it aligns with the firm's deeper mission. This is particularly important as digitalisation brings new tensions: efficiency versus. resilience, scale versus personalisation, automation versus. human contribution.

Mittelstand leaders navigate these tensions by re-anchoring digital change in purpose. The guiding questions are not: Is this the latest tool? But rather: Does this technology support our craft? Reinforce our customer bonds? Sustain our regional roots? As Simon Sinek famously put it: "People don't buy what you do; they buy why you do it." (Sinek, 2009, p. 46). Mittelstand firms apply this principle internally: when employees understand the "why" behind digital change, alignment follows more naturally (Sinek, 2009).

In this way, medium-sized enterprises are redefining digital tools and structures—not as transformative ends in themselves, but as means to safeguard their strategic autonomy and operational continuity. Digitalisation thus becomes instrumental in preserving enduring values such as craftsmanship, reliability, and trust. Purpose, in this context, serves as a bridge between tradition and innovation. In the Mittelstand, there is no technology for technology's sake.

5.3 Iterative Experimentation: Building Trust through Small Wins

Mittelstand firms, though traditionally rooted in manufacturing precision, have always drawn from agile principles, favouring incremental transformation over disruptive change. Rather than large-scale digital overhauls, they favour a step-by-step approach: launching small pilots, gathering structured feedback, and refining based on both technical performance and human response.

Crucially, these feedback loops go beyond metrics. They include relational insights: how customers react, how processes adapt, and how employees experience the change. Communication is central—informal, frequent, and grounded in respect for operational expertise (Florschütz, 2024).

This approach aligns with Amy Edmondson's (1999) research on psychological safety, which indicates that teams are more willing to take risks and learn from mistakes when they feel their input is valued and failure does not carry social penalties. In the Mittelstand, iterative experimentation is not only a method—it's a leadership culture built on mutual trust and continuous dialogue.

5.4 *Network-Based Innovation: Coordinating Expertise through Communication*

Mittelstand innovation seldom ever emerges from siloed R&D departments, but from open, trust-based networks. Firms co-develop solutions with suppliers, universities, startups, and industry consortia—leveraging external expertise while maintaining strategic focus. What began as informal collaboration is now scaled through digital tools: shared platforms, collaborative software, and virtual coordination mechanisms. Perfect for digital solutions. This dynamic of continuous alignment is vividly reflected in practitioners' accounts, as illustrated in the following excerpt:

> The mutual, mostly informal communication among Mittelstand companies within their networks serves to continuously align their own goals and values with the demands and opportunities of both the organisational and external environment. This requires constant readjustment — because the market doesn't sleep, it evolves. You have to make sure you're not hiding in your cave thinking you're always right. For us, the most important thing is to stay close to the market, to the end customer, but also to our partners — and that means communication in both directions." (Florschütz, 2024, p.276)

This collaborative model reflects Chesbrough's (2003) theory of open innovation: in fast-changing environments, firms gain competitive advantage by integrating external knowledge flows. What holds these networks together is not just shared infrastructure, but shared understanding. Communication aligns expectations, manages boundaries, and ensures accountability across organisational lines. In these ecosystems, communication is not a coordination afterthought—it is the architecture that holds the network together.

6 Gazing into the Future

This article has argued that the German Mittelstand, frequently overlooked in digital discourse, warrants renewed attention. Far from trailing behind, these companies embody a form of transformation that is both deliberate and deeply rooted in normative commitments. Their strength lies not in technological flamboyance, but in the alignment of strategy and identity through communication.

Rather than adopting digital tools as a means to an end, Mittelstand firms use them to preserve autonomy, strengthen stakeholder relationships, and reinforce longstanding values such as craftsmanship, trust, and continuity. Communication emerges as the critical enabler, and as a constitutive force that gives purpose in uncertain times.

As for practical implications: small and medium-sized enterprises (SMEs), appear to be on the right track by not mimicking large corporations or start-ups, but rather by scaling what already makes them resilient. This may include: choosing digital solutions that are resource-appropriate and interoperable, to support both internal alignment and external collaboration and implementing feedback-driven tools that maintain flexibility and inclusivity across stakeholder networks.

Emerging use cases already demonstrate this path: AI-supported quality control that preserves tacit knowledge; in-house AI academies that reinforce employee retention; or purpose-driven recommendation systems that adapt communication across different stakeholder groups. These are not acts of digital catch-up, they are examples of context-aware innovation rooted in a moral economy. Rather than adopting AI as a black-box efficiency machine to replace employees, Mittelstand firms treat it as a contextual, value-aligned instrument, enhancing human expertise rather than replacing it.

All of this leaves much research to be done: The Mittelstand not only deserves more empirical attention—it may also push the boundaries of existing theoretical models. Future research should explore how digital tools—particularly AI—can support this communicative alignment. Can AI help encode informal knowledge, maintain relational trust, and tailor communication without diluting authenticity? Can SMEs become laboratories for *ethical AI* that balances efficiency with responsibility?

This is not only a practical question for Mittelstand leaders, but a theoretical opportunity for organisational scholars: to study transformation where it happens quietly, incrementally, and meaningfully. In a time when leadership is often mistaken for visibility and speed, the Mittelstand offers a subtler—but perhaps more sustainable—model for navigating complexity in the digital age.

Glossary

Mittelstand A term used to describe a unique category of small and medium-sized enterprises (SMEs) in Germany, characterised not merely by size, but by ownership structure, long-term orientation, regional embeddedness, and a strong sense of social responsibility. Mittelstand firms are often owner- or family-owned, emphasise continuity overgrowth, and prioritise stakeholder relationships over shareholder value.

Value-Driven Communication A leadership practice in which communication is used not only to disseminate information, but to foster alignment, legitimacy, and shared purpose. In the Mittelstand context, it replaces formal control mechanisms and anchors organisational change in deeply held values such as trust, craftsmanship, and responsibility.

Principal-Agent Model An economic and organisational theory describing relationships where one party (the principal) delegates tasks to another (the agent), often under conditions of information asymmetry. Mittelstand firms challenge the traditional model by relying on relational trust, shared values, and informal communication to align interests, rather than on contracts and control systems.

Transaction Costs The costs associated with negotiating, coordinating, and enforcing exchanges between economic actors. Ronald Coase (1960) argued that firms exist to reduce such costs. The article suggests that Mittelstand firms internalise not only economic functions, but also positive social externalities—such as community stability and vocational training—thus redefining the logic of firm boundaries.

Responsible Digital Transformation A process of integrating digital technologies in a way that maintains ethical standards, social responsibility, and long-term viability. Rather than adopting technology for its own sake, Mittelstand firms pursue digitalisation that supports human expertise, preserves identity, and aligns with the firm's purpose.

Network-Based Innovation An innovation model where firms collaborate with external partners—such as suppliers, startups, or universities—through trust-based networks rather than closed R&D departments. In the Mittelstand, this is often facilitated by informal communication, shared values, and digital platforms that enable distributed coordination.

Enkelfähigkeit A German term meaning "fit for grandchildren," reflecting a core principle of Mittelstand leadership: decisions are made with the goal of preserving the company's integrity, independence, and value for future generations. This long-term orientation shapes strategic planning, employee relationships, and investment decisions.

References

Bader, N. (2011). Fallstudie: CSR-Kommunikation von kleinen und mittleren Unternehmen. In J. Raupp, S. Jarolimek, & F. Schultz (Eds.), *Handbuch CSR. Kommunikationswissenschaftliche Grundlagen, disziplinäre Zugänge und methodische Herausforderungen* (pp. 356–372). Springer VS.

Chesbrough, H. (2003). The logic of open innovation: Managing intellectual property. *California Management Review, 45*(3), 33–58.

Evans, P. B., & Wurster, T. S. (1997). Strategy and the new economics of information. *Harvard Business Review, 75*(5), 70–83.

Florschütz, N. (2024). *Zwischen Ad Hoc Kommunikation und Strategischer Planung.* Springer Gabler.

Fördere, J., Geier, C., & Lindenmayr, M. (2023). *Fortschrittbarometer Digitale Transformation Mittelstand 2023.* Technische Universität München.

Jensen, M., Meckling, W. (1976). Theory of the firm: Managerial Behavior, Agency Costs and Ownership Structure, In: *The Journal of Financial Economics*, 3.Jg. 1976, Nr. 4.

Jiang, K., Chen, L., Li, J., & Du, X. (2025). The risk effects of corporate digitalization: Exacerbate or mitigate? *Humanities and Social Sciences Communications, 12*(1), 1–19.

Kahneman, D., Knetsch, J. L., & Thaler, R. H. (1990). Experimental tests of the endowment effect and the Coase theorem. *Journal of Political Economy, 98*(6), 1325–1348.

Khadjavi, K., & Volery, T. (2009). Wertmanagement in mittelständischen Unternehmen. *ZfKE–Zeitschrift für KMU und Entrepreneurship, 1*, 27–52.

Looser, S. (2017). *Schweizer KMU und interne CSR-Kommunikation: Ergebnisse einer Interview-studie.* Springer Verlag.

Mintzberg, H. (1978). Patterns in strategy formation. *Management Science, 24*(9), 934–948.

Pahnke, A., & Welter, F. (2019). The German mittelstand: Antithesis to silicon valley entrepreneurship? *Small Business Economics, 52*(2), 345–358.

Renker, C. (2012). Marketing im Mittelstand. Anforderungen, Strategien, Maßnahmen, 4. Aufl., Berlin: Erich Schmidt.

Schatilow, L. C. (2014). Politische Kommunikation deutscher Familienunternehmen. In *Pilotstudie zur Differenzierung von Unternehmenstypen in der politischen Interessenvertretung*. Springer VS.
Schauf, M. (Ed.). (2009). *Unternehmensführung im Mittelstand: Rollenwandel kleiner und mittlerer Unternehmen in der Globalisierung* (2. Aufl.). Hampp.
Simon, H. (2007). *Hidden Champions des 21.* Die Erfolgsstrategien unbekannter Weltmarktführer. Campus Verlag.
Sinek, S. (2009). *Start with why: How great leaders inspire everyone to take action.* Penguin.
Soluk, J., & Kammerlander, N. (2021). Digital transformation in family-owned Mittelstand firms: A dynamic capabilities perspective. *European Journal of Information Systems, 30*(6), 676–711.
Weick, K. E., & Weick, K. E. (1995). *Sensemaking in organizations* (Vol. 3, pp. 1–231). Sage publications.
Welter, F., Gröschl, J. (2016). Unternehmer und Unternehmerinnen in Deutschland. In: *Unternehmertum, Reihe Politik und Zeitgeschichte*, 66. Jhg., 2016, 16–17.
Welter, F., May-Strobl, E., Wolter, H.-J. & Günterberg, B. (2014). Mittelstand im Wandel. Mittelstand Companion and Promotor of Structural Change. *IfM-Materialien* Nr. 232, Institut für Mittelstandsforschung Bonn.
Welter, F., Schlepphorst, S., Schneck, S. & Holz, M. (2020). Der gesellschaftliche Beitrag des Mittelstands: Konzeptionelle Überlegungen, *IfM-Materialien* Nr. 283, Institut für Mittelstandsforschung Bonn.

Philipp Garra completed his studies at the Westfälische Wilhelms-Universität Münster (B.Sc.) and his master's degree at Maastricht University, where he wrote his thesis on the subject of social entrepreneurship. He went on to found two start-ups and most recently led cloud sales for some of Germany's leading enterprises at Microsoft. As Managing Director of SAMtoa GmbH he supports Mittelstand companies to reduce their software expenditures. He is the author of Das neue Wirtschaftswunder: Wie der Mittelstand unseren Wohlstand rettet (The New Economic Miracle—How medium-sized businesses are saving our prosperity), published by Rowohlt in 2024.

Ninette Florschütz holds a diploma in Business Administration and a master's degree in Communication Research. Since 2018, she has worked as a research assistant at the Mittelstand-Digital Zentrum Ilmenau at the Technical University of Ilmenau. In addition, she teaches as a lecturer at the Institute for Media and Communication Studies (IfMK) at the Technical University of Ilmenau and in the Department of Business Administration at the Gera-Eisenach Cooperative State University. She earned her PhD in 2023 from the University of Erfurt with a dissertation on the influence of owner management on strategic communication management. Her academic work focuses on strategic communication management as well as on the impact of digital transformation on the design of related structures and processes in medium-sized companies.

Legal and Ethical Implications of AI in Urban Transportation: A Case Study from São Paulo

Cristina Godoy Bernardo de Oliveira, Otavio de Paula Albuquerque, Emily Liene Belotti, Isabella Ferreira Lopes, Tiago Augustini de Lima, and João Victor Palermo Gianecchini

Abstract This paper examines the legal, ethical, and social implications of using artificial intelligence (AI) technologies in urban transportation context, focusing on São Paulo's metro issue. The study employs a web scraping approach to collect and analyse judicial decisions from the São Paulo Court of Appeal (TJSP) related to AI. The research identifies decisions related to biometric data collection by ViaQuatro, the concessionaire of São Paulo Metro Line 4. ViaQuatro's implementation of Digital Interactive Doors (DID) captures users' biometric data for advertising purposes without performing facial recognition. This practice has raised significant privacy concerns, prompting the Brazilian Institute for Consumer Defense (IDEC) to file a lawsuit. The paper presents a detailed case study of this dispute, highlighting the legal arguments, court decisions, and broader implications for privacy and data protection. The findings emphasise the need for explicit user consent and transparency in AI applications, as mandated by Brazil's General Data Protection Law (LGPD). The analysis reveals that, despite anonymisation claims, the data collection practices potentially violate users' privacy rights. This study underscores the importance of robust legal frameworks to govern the use of AI in public services, ensuring that technological advances do not compromise individual privacy and societal trust. Future

C. G. B. de Oliveira (✉) · O. de P. Albuquerque · E. L. Belotti · I. F. Lopes · T. A. de Lima · J. V. P. Gianecchini
University of São Paulo (USP), São Paulo, Brazil
e-mail: cristinagodoy@usp.bcr

O. de P. Albuquerque
e-mail: otavioalbuquerque@usp.br

E. L. Belotti
e-mail: emilybelotti@usp.br

I. F. Lopes
e-mail: isabella.lopes6@usp.br

T. A. de Lima
e-mail: tiagoaugustini@usp.br

J. V. P. Gianecchini
e-mail: joaovictorpgianecchini@usp.br

K. Bodrožić-Brnić et al. (eds.), *AI and the Ethics of Innovation*, Digital Transformation and Innovation, https://doi.org/10.1007/978-3-032-20638-1_15

research should continue to explore the intersection of AI, law, and ethics to guide the development of fair and transparent AI systems.

Keywords Artificial Intelligence · Biometrics · Data protection · Facial recognition · Privacy · Transparency

1 Introduction

Rapid advancement of technology has caused unprecedented changes in various sectors, including the public ones. The integration of emerging artificial intelligence (AI) technologies and tools into public services has raised significant privacy and security concerns from society and scientists. These concerns could involve the improper or unclear collection and use of personal data by public sectors or even from private companies that have a public-private partnership concession. Such practices often include the sharing of the data with third-party services, which could represent, in a major scale, privacy and security bigger issues for individuals.

To investigate how these issues have been treated at the legal level, we performed a web scraping approach using an open-source API to extract decisions data from the São Paulo Court of Appeal (TJSP). Using 103 terms related to artificial intelligence, 10,892 decisions were collected and categorised according to the relevant term. In a qualitative analysis approach, the decisions were individually analysed considering the following research question: How do judicial decisions from the São Paulo Court of Appeal reflect the legal and ethical challenges of AI implementation in public services?

Based on an analysis of four decisions from the portal of TJSP, we carry out a case study on the dispute between the Brazilian Institute for Consumer Defense (IDEC) and the Concessionaire of Line 4 of the São Paulo S.A. Metro (ViaQuatro S.A.), regarding the mandatory collection of data from urban rail system users through the "Digital Interactive Doors" installed at ViaQuatro stations. The contract with the State Government of São Paulo, signed on 29 November 2006, was the first public-private partnership contract in the country relating to underground railway systems. It grants the concessionaire the right to operate and maintain the Line 4-Yellow for a period of 30 years. On 10 January 2018, ViaQuatro entered into a service and materials supply agreement with "Dual Midia OOH Publicidade LTDA." to install, execute and maintain the digital panels (VideoWalls) that make up the Line 4 digital media system (interactive digital doors). In general terms, this system would only capture users' biometric data, without performing facial recognition, in order to assess consumers' emotions in relation to the advertisements displayed just below the cameras mounted on the metro doors. The data would be anonymised and subsequently discarded.

Initially, the analysis was limited to the judgements scraped from the portal, which dealt with different decisions on the same case. However, a more in-depth analysis reveals that the dispute involves not only AI technology but also important ethical, consumer, and social implications of a digital system that had previously been used on a pioneering and large-scale basis in the country. Therefore, to better develop the case study, the complete list of the case files in question was accessed to deepen the analysis of the related judgements and understand both parties' arguments and any attached documents and reports.

As we shall discuss, regardless of whether facial recognition is used or whether or not it is anonymised, the matter concerns the collection of sensitive biometric data from the population of one of Brazil's most populous cities, in a transport system where each train can carry up to 1500 passengers, and which operates with a fleet of 29 trains under the management of ViaQuatro. Therefore, discovering and understanding how digital interactive doors work, what arguments are advanced by each party, how the judges are deciding the matter, and how the case relates with AI in a smart city context is essential not only for this pioneering case, but also for those that may follow.

The remainder of this article is structured as follows: Section 2 introduces a description of key concepts. Section 3 outlines the methodology used to scrape data on the judgements of TJSP, and the qualitative method of the research. Section 4 presents the case study under investigation. Section 5 discusses legal, ethical, and social implications of the decision analysed. Section 6 offers the concluding remarks.

2 Background

2.1 Biometric Processing

Biometric data is defined by the US National Institute of Standards and Technology (NIST) as a digital or analogue representation of a behavioural or physical characteristic of an individual that can be used by an automated system to distinguish an individual as belonging to a subgroup of the entire population or, in many cases, can be used to uniquely establish or verify the identity of a person (compared to a claimed or referenced identity) (NIST, 2015). On the other hand, "WP193" from Opinion 3/2012 on developments in biometric technologies distinguishes "biometric data" from "sources of biometric data," i.e. "the sources of biometric data (e.g. human tissue samples) cannot be considered as biometric data themselves but can be used for the collection of biometric data (through the extraction of information from them)" (Data Protection Working Party, 2012). Thus, the extraction of biometric information from samples constitutes the collection of personal data and must be subject to consent. Biometric processing corresponds to the processing of biometric data and can be referred to "interchangeably as recognition, identification, authentication, detection or other related terms, as well as (often opaque) ways of collecting and storing biometric data, even if the data is not processed immediately" (Montag et al., 2021).

This process consists of two phases (Data Protection Working Party, 2012; Stallings & Brown, 2014): *enrolment*, which involves storing two types of information—"template," which is the information obtained from the biometric reading, such as facial anthropometric points, and "associated data," which can such as name, address, age range, biological sex, etc.). The second phase corresponds to *matching*, where biometric reading is carried out, relevant and available characteristics are extracted, and the data obtained is compared with that previously recorded in the enrolment phase. The first phase requires the consent of the individuals to be carried out. However, it is possible to enrol individuals without their consent or knowledge in surveillance camera systems with built-in facial recognition functionalities (Data Protection Working Party, 2012). From a technical point of view, facial recognition technology (FRT) is a subcategory of Artificial Intelligence because it identifies the characteristics of an individual's face and compares them to a database (matching) (Zhao et al., 2023).

2.2 *Anonymised Data*

While personal data relating to an identified or identifiable natural person is protected by Article 2 of the General Data Protection Law (LGPD), anonymised data is not, according to Article 12 of the LGPD: "anonymised data shall not be considered personal data for this Law, except when the anonymisation process to which it has been subjected is reversed, using its means exclusively, or when, with reasonable efforts, it can be reversed." The Information Commissioner's Office (2015)—the UK authority with a role similar to that of the National Data Protection Authority in Brazil (ANPD)—defines this distinction between personal data and anonymised data as Information that enables a group of people to be identified, but not any particular individual within the group is not personal data (Information Commissioner's Office, 2015).

3 Materials and Methods

Exploratory research was conducted to investigate the factors that influence the decision-making by the TJSP on matters related to Artificial Intelligence (Gil, 2002). The study was based on data collected from the decisions stored in the portal of services (E-SAJ) of the Court of Appeal portal using a Web Scraping technique, which consists of extracting online data to obtain content of interest in a systematic and structured manner (Glez-Penã et al., 2014).

In this research, most of the data collection and treatment procedures were automated using computer programmes. The technologies used can be defined into two categories: (1) web scraping tools and (2) data treatment coding.

3.1 Web Scraping Tools and Frameworks

To scrape the data from the Court of Appeal, an Application Programming Interface (API) named "TJSP" was used. It is a community open-source application published on GitHub (de Jesus Filho, 2020). The main goals of the TJSP tool are to collect, organise, and structure data from first- and second-instance judgements issued by the TJSP, using different methods for various data extraction proposals. This tool was developed using the programming language R, and the language's native integrated development environment (IDE), called RGUI, was used to manipulate the code and instantiate the API for the purposes of our research, defining the terms and authenticity properties.

The API was used to extract data from proceedings available on the Court of Appeal web portal by searching for all decision documents containing the term "Artificial Intelligence" and 102 other related terms. These terms were selected by examining two lists associated with the subject: a compilation published by the Organization for Economic Cooperation and Development (OECD) (Baruffaldi et al., 2020), comprising 226 English terms, and the ISO/IEC 22989:2022 standard (ISO/IEC, 2024), which includes 115 English terms. The translations to Portuguese of all the selected terms were incorporated when they exist. Additional terms reflecting the latest advances in AI and terms identified in documents extracted from legal portals in Brazil were also included. Exclusion criteria were adopted to avoid scraping decision documents considered out of scope. Some of the analysed terms were grouped under comprehensive categories; too general terms that deviated from the AI scope were also excluded.

The functions available in the API were improved to deliver the data in structured and organised files. After defining the search terms, the following steps were taken: (1) Download the corresponding HTML pages, which contain summaries for all the decision documents from the TJSP web portal that include at least one of the selected terms; (2) Based on the obtained HTML files, identify the most relevant information about the proceedings, returning data such as class, subject, rapporteur, court district, judging body, date of judgement, date of publication, case, summary, and code of the decision; (3) Structure the retrieved information in a data frame, where each column represents specific information and each row represents a decision document; (4) Convert the data frame into a spreadsheet for qualitative and quantitative analysis.

3.2 Data Treatment

Among the information retrieved from the decisions, there are different types of data, including integers, date-time, and character strings. Given the goal of our study and to facilitate the qualitative analysis, we applied different data treatment techniques, divided into pre- and post-processing approaches. The complete code used for scraping and data processing can be accessed at the public GitHub (https://github.com/anonymous-code-repo-1/tjsp). These approaches were applied to the "Jurisprudence" column, which contains the decision text. Data-cleaning techniques were developed using the Python programming language and deployed in the Google Colab IDE, to leverage the platform's performance advantages and make them available to the research team.

Data Pre-Processing

The pre-processing and cleaning of data are the most critical and time-consuming stages of any web scraping project. To obtain a good visualisation of the dataset, it usually requires multiple iterations of cleaning, transforming, and visualising the data before it is in a suitable form (VanderPlas, 2023). There are different techniques, ranging from the simplest to the most advanced, to pre-process a data collection, i.e. prepare, clean, and transform data from an initial form to a structured and context-specific form. In our research, we applied data mining techniques to clean and search for repetitive or redundant content in the "Jurisprudence" column, to improve the qualitative analysis.

The text of each decision follows a standard structure containing repetitive or redundant sections. These sections include: (1) titles, headers, references, and terms that are identical for all documents, such as "Judiciary Power," "Court of Appeal of the State of São Paulo," "Electronic Signature," "Decision," among others; (2) appeal and vote numbers, which differ for each decision but will not be used in the analysis. These numbers are identified by being preceded by terms such as "appeal n," "civil appeal n," "appeal.," "record:," "vote n," and others; and (3) document page identifiers, such as current page numbers, referenced section page numbers, or total page numbers of the decisions. These identifiers are preceded by sections such as "*(fls.,*" or "*(fl..*" Using the previously mentioned cleaning techniques, these elements were removed from the resulting spreadsheets.

Data Post-Processing

After data cleaning, the post-processing stage involves organising the data into an analysable format to derive insights (Lan et al., 2021). This step ensures the data is structured according to the research context, highlighting and grouping key parts of each decision to assist manual analysis. Automated procedures were developed to enhance qualitative analysis by identifying relevant terms and content. Key steps include: (1) selecting paragraphs containing searched terms and adding them to a new column, (2) identifying references to other decisions by process number and storing this information, and (3) grouping decisions by rapporteurs using Python modules for efficient analysis.

To ensure the data remained up to date and analytically useful, scraping procedures were repeated periodically. The methods developed include: (1) a results-counting mechanism to compare term matches across scraping iterations, with updates performed on a monthly basis, and (2) a highlighting function to flag new cases in the results spreadsheet, in order to help analysts easily identify new results and avoid redundancies.

3.3 Exploratory Approach

Of the 103 terms researched in the scraping process, only 45 returned at least one result, and then the decision data extracted were split into their respective related terms. To create a systematisation in the decision's content qualitative analyses and ensure that only decisions that truly fall within the scope of AI were retained, the authors selected and alphabetically organised the relevant terms, proceeding to analyse each decision associated with them individually. A cross-search data-mining validation was applied to improve the qualitative analysis, that is, to verify whether a decision contained more than one of the 103 terms used in the scraping process. The aim was to exclude false positives, where the terms are employed in contexts unrelated to the AI subject, such as in names of companies related to the case, which proved to be very common.

To ensure that the cross-search validation did not have the opposite effect—i.e. removal of important results for the search—, each of the first five terms was individually analysed, following the order of appearance among the terms that yielded results: agente de ia" ("ai agent"), "agente de aprendizado" ("learning agent"), "agente móvel" ("mobile agent"), "ai agent" and "algorithm." None of the results for these terms fell within the intended scope, as the expressions were used in contexts unrelated to artificial intelligence. The sixth term "algoritmo" ("algorithm") returned 65 results, which were manually analysed as well. Among the judgements that did fall within the scope, four (4) decisions regarding the same case (No. 1090663–42.2018.8.26.0100) were identified. Considering the relevance of the subject matter, these decisions were selected for deep analysis and adopted as a case study.

3.4 Qualitative Analysis Method

In this article, a case study was developed on the litigation involving the IDEC and the ViaQuatro metro concessionaire. The former filed a public civil lawsuit against the latter on 30 August 2018, seeking to halt the mandatory collection of consumer data through the "Interactive Digital Doors" installed at ViaQuatro stations. The claim aimed to protect the right not to have biometric data processed without consumer consent, and to challenge the imposition of excessive obligations on the users of the public transport service, i.e. the violation of the right to protection of their personal information (Article 6, IV, of the Consumer Protection Code, hereinafter CDC), which constitutes an abusive practice (Article 39, V, CDC) (Case No. 1090663–42.2018.8.26.0100, p. 3).

The study focuses on the discussion between the facial detection mechanism and the facial recognition mechanism of the digital interactive doors on Line 4, and their ethical, social and legal implications. To this end, four judgements were analysed from the public portal of the São Paulo State Court TJ/SP, as obtained through the scraping described in the quantitative methodology, along with the corresponding case files, also accessed via the same portal using login credentials—available to any lawyer duly registered with the São Paulo chapter of the Brazilian Bar Association (OAB). As of the writing of this text (July 2025), the case was still ongoing and comprised 4137 pages.

It should be noted that the case study method is a qualitative research approach that involves a contextual and in-depth analysis of a specific instance, event, individual, or group (Ginor & Becker, 2017). It aims to provide a comprehensive understanding of complex issues in real-life settings by examining the intricate details and interactions within a case. This method is precious for exploring phenomena where the boundaries between the context and the phenomenon itself are not evident, allowing researchers to capture the richness and diversity of the subject. Using multiple sources of evidence, such as interviews, observations or documents, case studies offer a differentiated perspective that can reveal underlying patterns and generate insights that may not be apparent through other research methods (Yin, 2018).

The analysis of various documents from the case file can provide a more plural view of the subject matter, whether through the allegations of the plaintiffs and the defendant, the decisions of the TJSP and higher courts, such as the Superior Court of Justice (STJ), or even the reports of technical experts and annexes of contracts and news from journalistic outlets.

4 Case Study

Case No. 1090663–42.2018.8.26.0100, currently pending final judgement before the TJSP, concerns the public civil lawsuit filed by IDEC challenging the mandatory collection of biometric data by the "Digital Interactive Doors" at ViaQuatro stations. Figures 1 and 2 illustrate the physical infrastructure of the Digital Interactive Doors (DID) system installed at ViaQuatro stations, highlighting both the scale of passenger exposure and the discreet embedding of facial data capture devices, as well as the subsequent judicially ordered deactivation of such equipment. The dispute centres on the protection against the processing of biometric data without consent and the imposition of excessive obligations on public transport users.

IDEC argues that the conduct of the defendant: (i) violates the right of public service users to the protection of their personal information (Law No. 12.527/2011 and Article 6, IV, of the CDC); (ii) fails to comply with the requirements of Article 10 of Law No. 13.709/2018; (iii) violates the basic consumer right against abusive

Fig. 1 Train platform with platform screen doors on São Paulo Metro Lines 8–Diamante and 9–Esmeralda. The photograph shows a high-density passenger platform equipped with platform screen doors (automatic glass barriers separating the platform from the train). This infrastructure is used on Lines 8–Diamante and 9–Esmeralda of the São Paulo railway system, operated by ViaMobilidade. These lines were subject to judicial scrutiny due to the installation of facial data capture technologies without transparency or a valid legal basis under Brazilian data protection law. Maps and directional signage typical of metropolitan transport environments are visible above the doors. *Source* Authors' photograph

Fig. 2 Detail of platform screen doors with operator branding and covered facial data capture point. The photograph shows a close-up of the platform screen doors displaying the operator's logo on the glass structure. In installations on São Paulo Metro Lines 8–Diamante and 9–Esmeralda, facial data capture devices were discreetly embedded within similar structures, rendering them difficult for passengers to detect. The image shows the physical measures adopted following a decision by the São Paulo Court of Appeal (TJSP), which ordered the deactivation of such devices, including the covering of camera points with adhesive material. *Source* Authors' photograph

practices (Article 6, IV, and Article 39, V, of the CDC); (iv) fails to clearly inform about the prices of products and services (Articles 6 and 31 of the CDC); (v) imposes onerous obligations on consumers (Articles 6, V, 39, V, and 51, §1, I to III, of the CDC); (vi) violates the constitutional right to image protection (Article 5 of the Constitution and Article 20 of the Civil Code); and (vii) infringes the rights of children and adolescents by collecting their personal data. The plaintiff alleges that the defendant conducts an "automated market research" by collecting consumers' emotions in reaction to advertisements in the metro, without authorisation. This allows the generation of revenue through the sale of such data to third parties, who then use the reactions to guide their advertising strategies.

The defendant argues that IDEC incorrectly describes the image recognition system and fails to understand its legality. The ViaQuatro concessionaire claims that: (i) the system only detects possible faces, without recognising people; (ii) it does not use images or personal data of users; (iii) the data are anonymised, preventing the identification of individuals; (iv) the granting authority (the State of São Paulo) approves the generation of complementary revenues through advertising, including this project. Finally, it asserts that (v) there is no illegality in the technology used, nor any causal link or proven damage, therefore, there is no duty to indemnify.

5 Discussion

The discussion regarding the imputation of civil liability to the concessionaire company ViaQuatro is based on the use of an artificial intelligence tool, namely facial recognition, as an instrument to capture sensitive personal data and its subsequent commercialisation without the consent of the users of the Line 4-Yellow metro service in São Paulo. In the academic sphere, the discussion has gained prominence (McClurg, 2007).

5.1 Civil Liability

According to the judgement, the liability of the defendant company arises from the use of equipment to record images of users at ViaQuatro stations, intended for advertising and statistical purposes. The facial recognition system stored users' personal data without their consent, for the commercial and advertising benefit of ViaQuatro and the contracted company, collecting information such as gender, age group, and emotional reactions to enhance further advertising.

By subsuming the concrete facts into the legal framework applicable to the provision of services by the defendant, it is possible to understand that the issue hinges on the application of Law No. 13.709/2018 (the Brazilian General Data Protection Act). This is because facial recognition—or even mere facial detection—may enable the concrete identification of individuals by accessing their facial images and therefore falls within the legal definition of biometric data. Such data is classified as sensitive personal data and is subject to special protection under Law No. 13.709/2018.

Therefore, the use of sensitive personal data by ViaQuatro and its exploitation without the consent of the users of the Line 4-Yellow metro service would, at least in theory, give rise to the civil liability of the responsible companies, namely, the service concessionaire company and the company contracted for the provision of services related to advertising through the capture of biometric data of public transport users (Capanema, 2020).

5.2 *The Data Subject's Consent*

In the context of this case, although the legal institute of consent has been invoked, a deeper understanding is required due to its complexity. According to the Brazilian General Data Protection Law (LGPD) (Brazil, 2018), Article 5, Item XII, consent is the "free, informed, and unequivocal expression by which the data subject agrees to the processing of their personal data for a specific purpose." Consent, therefore, is closely linked to informational self-determination, which means "personal control over the flow of data related to the data subject themselves—and thus an extension of individual freedoms" (Melo Nogueira & da Fonseca, 2020). This principle reinforces that the data subject is the "main protagonist," meaning that only they have the power to amend, erase, rectify, and supplement their data, ensuring that they maintain control over their personal information throughout the entire data processing cycle (Bioni, 2020).

In the case of data concerning children or adolescents, Article 14 of the LGPD requires the consent of parents or guardians and mandates that the use of the data must always serve the best interest of the child or adolescent. Even with parental consent, "if it eventually contradicts the best interest of the child, it will not be upheld as a legal basis, and the data processing practice may be considered abusive" (Bioni et al., 2020). Therefore, in the case under analysis, the consent of the metro user cannot be considered in a generic manner. The collection, processing, and storage of sensitive personal data are only permitted without the user's consent in the specific cases provided for in Article 11, Item II, of the LGPD, which includes the security of the location and the users, as emphasised by the judge in his ruling. Therefore, for commercial purposes, the use of sensitive data requires the explicit consent of the data subject at each stage of processing. Moreover, the terms of data collection must be clear and specific, to be understandable to the average citizen (de Lima, 2014).

The word "unequivocal" in the LGPD regarding consent is crucial, as it requires that the will of the data subject be specific. Consent must be explicit and directed to each stage of the collection, storage, and processing of personal data, ensuring that the data subject is fully aware of and agrees with each step of the processing (de Lima, 2019). Furthermore, facial recognition systems that collect facial biometrics or biometric patterns involve the processing of sensitive personal data. As such, their use is subject to the legal requirements in Article 11 of the LGPD concerning the lawful collection and processing of such data.

According to the Brazilian National Data Protection Authority (ANPD) (Brazil, 2023), there is a difference between consent and the individual's awareness/knowledge of the collection of their data. Awareness, therefore, is an essential and indispensable condition for data collection. Regardless of the legal basis invoked for processing, the data subject must be informed about who is processing their data, for what purposes, and for how long (Bioni, 2020). Transparency in consumer relations, defined as "clear and correct information about the product to be sold and the contract to be signed, meaning loyalty and respect between supplier and consumer" (Marques, 2002), is essential for the data subject to exercise their right to informational self-determination, as provided for in Articles 9, 18, 19, and others of the LGPD. Without such clarity, the mechanisms of protection and balance between controllers and data subjects are compromised, affecting the privacy, intimacy, honour, and image of the data subject.

Accordingly, despite ViaQuatro's argument that the technology does not identify individual metro users, the concessionaire should inform about the collection of personal data through facial biometrics, in accordance with Article 6, Items I and II, of the LGPD, which require transparency and clear information, ensuring that data subjects are aware of the collection, processing, and storage of their personal information.

5.3 Digital Interactive Doors (DID System) Issue

The distinction between biometric personal data and anonymised data is the main subject of discussion between the parties to the lawsuit. Three technical expert reports on the video surveillance technology of the digital interactive doors used in Line 4 metro were attached to the case file. The expert report IBP 20045 (Case No. 1090663–42.2018.8.26.0100, p. 2115.) comments that the digital interactive door system (AdMobilize Digital Interactive Doors, henceforth DID), despite containing elements in common with biometric recognition systems, is not intended to identify individuals, but only to classify them, by direct inference from the facial features captured, into the following categories: (i) Biological sex: male or female; (ii) Age group: youth, young adult, adult or senior; (iii) Emotion: "angry," "happy," "calm," "sad," "neutral," "surprised," "disgusted," (iv) Visualisation: indicates whether the detected face is looking at the camera. The first two categories can be considered semi-identifiers, while the third and fourth are not identifiers, because the third is extremely changeable, and the fourth is an ephemeral circumstance, which is also changeable.

Then, according to forensics, the image is captured by sensors (cameras), then extracted and undergo the process of summarisation and suppression. The expert comments that, even after going through these stages, the remaining data may still enable the identification a specific individual, requiring their consent. It is later argued that ViaQuatro does not use the "registration phase," using static pre-stored models of the client software called "Matrix," which is not updated with the users' faces. The expert points out that the AdMobilize documentation did not contain the database used to create these models, and it was impossible to identify how difficult this anonymisation would be. Subsequently, comparisons are made between the characteristics derived from capture and anonymisation (which are not necessarily completely anonymous) and the AdMobilize database. Finally, the expert's conclusions, reiterated by ViaQuatro in its defence, reveal that the DID System does not process personal data or facial recognition, only face identification, and thus does not violate the LGPD by not requiring the consent of users of ViaQuatro's metro system for its operation, since it is impossible to identify an individual's reaction when faced with a specific advertisement (Case No. 1090663–42.2018.8.26.0100, p. 2091).

Specifically in terms of how it works, the DID mechanism can be summarised as follows: phases 1 and 2 involve the processing of personal data from metro users and the consequent development of a mathematical model of the face in order to detect the emotions expressed when the AdMobilize AI algorithm displays the advertisement. At this stage, users' rights have been violated for two reasons: (i) the duty to inform users about data processing was not fulfilled and (ii) users have not consented to the use of their images. This violation in itself compromises the entire processing chain due to the initial illegality (theory of the fruit of the poisoned tree, Superior Tribunal de Justiça, 2023). In phase 3, the "anonymised" data is sent via aggregation to ViaQuatro. ViaQuatro, however, did not meet its burden of proof, failing to demonstrate how it carries out the anonymisation process—a serious fault, since this process is not absolute, and as mentioned above, anonymisation is characterised by gradations and the more sensitive the data collected, such as users' faces, the more robust, transparent, and effective this process must be, in order to avoid attack by external (hackers) and internal (insiders who sell such information for their own benefit) agents. Although AdMobilize claims that it does not store personal data, but only processes it and then deletes it, it is undisputed that this data remains in its databases for a certain period, and as the process of disposal and processing has not been detailed, there can be numerous failures at these stages.

The plaintiff argues that such expert reports should be dismissed due to the phenomenon of "borrowed evidence" being used without proper observance of the adversarial principle—specifically, an indirect expert report without having examined the real and specific equipment and respective of the ViaQuatro urban rail operating systems. This argument was upheld by the reporting judge, who noted that the defendant had:

> on more than one occasion, failed to request an expert report on the equipment and operating systems linked to them, essential evidence to prove its allegations, requesting only and in a generic way the use of borrowed evidence in the form of the expert report produced in case file No. 1003122-02.2018.8.26.0704 (Case No. 1003122-02.2018.8.26.0704, subsidiary to Case No. 1090663-42.2018.8.26.0100, concerning borrowed evidence), an inadmissible measure, as already addressed. (Case No. 1090663-42.2018.8.26.0100, p. 3800)

Specifically in relation to the DID system, IDEC argues that the claim that "data is anonymous from the outset" is untrue, as it refers only to the output of a data processing operation executed by a software programme. There was a sequence of steps taken to achieve this result: (i) image collection; (ii) detection and analysis of reference points in the image of a human face to generate data such as gender, age group and consumer emotion; (iii) modification (anonymisation process) and (iv) comparison with the database. The face of a human being is intrinsically biometric and sensitive. In short, it is biometric data processing, so it is impossible to carry out facial detection without first collecting and processing personal data.

In fact, the expert report notes that, should an attacker (hacker or insider) gain access to the information collected by DID, the chances of damage to privacy are low, as only two semi-identifying characteristics are collected (age range and biological sex)—less than systems with fully identifying aspects (address, exact age, etc.) (Case No. 1090663–42.2018.8.26.0100, p. 2110). However, no matter how small, the risks arising from possible security breaches not only cause harm to the individual, but also to the community and to individual' civil liberties, violating not only the principle of freedom of choice, but also the principle of informational self-determination, in which each individual has the right to know, consent to and choose the processing of their personal—or even sensitive—data.

Finally, the defendant argues that there is no excessive advantage for the company over the users of public transport since it only uses statistical data for advertising purposes, and that this data, even if anonymised, roughly compiles characteristics about the public: "number of people, gender, age group and receptiveness to the [advertising] campaign (by recognising emotions)." The defendant itself acknowledges that forced market research was carried out, without the users' knowledge, since the advertising panel is located just below the sensor (camera). Article 12, §2, of the LGPD states that "those [anonymised data] used to form the behavioural profile of a specific natural person, if identified, may also be considered personal data for the purposes of this Law," i.e. identified anonymised data can become personal data if it is used to form behavioural profiles. The Brazilian Federal Constitution, also known as the "Citizen's Constitution," protects diffuse and collective rights, and is concerned not only with the individual, but also with their insertion into the social corpus and its effects. Therefore, even the group profiling used by DID to analyse the effects of an advertising campaign also violates the right to freedom of choice and computer self-determination of groups profiled without their express consent, as it involves sensitive data such as their faces.

Meanwhile, various aspects of the individual and the community within it have been violated (Case No. 1090663–42.2018.8.26.0100, p. 3992): the limitation of the user's freedom of choice (art. 6, II); absence of adequate and precise information, which is necessary to enable free and informed consent (art. 6, III, Consumer Protection Code—CDC, which is also applicable to users of public services); the right to quality public services and the adequacy between means and ends when imposing obligations on users of public services (Federal Law 13. 460/2017, art. 5 and State Law 10.29/1999, art. 7, V) and protection against unfair commercial methods (art. 6, III, CDC; Federal Law 13.460/2017, art. 5 and State Law 10.294/1999, art. 7, V) and protection against unfair commercial methods (art. 6, IV); and the imposition of excessive advantage of the company over the consumer, characterising an actual abusive practice).

5.4 Comparative Perspective: Legal and Regulatory Responses to Facial Recognition in Brazil and the European Union

To deepen the normative assessment of the São Paulo Metro case and contextualise it within global regulatory debates, this section presents a comparative analysis between the Brazilian legislative landscape and the recently adopted EU Artificial Intelligence Act (Regulation 2024/1689) (European Parliament and Council of the European Union 2024). It also contrasts these provisions of the substitute text of Bill No. 2.338/2023, approved by the Brazilian Senate, which proposes a national framework for AI governance (Senado Federal do Brasil, 2024a). The comparative lens underscores both regulatory divergences and normative convergences, particularly concerning biometric surveillance, risk categorisation, and safeguarding fundamental rights.

In the European Union, the AI Act introduces a horizontal, risk-based regulatory architecture, classifying AI systems according to four risk levels—unacceptable, high, limited, and minimal (Zulehner, 2024). Within this framework, real-time remote biometric identification (RBI) systems used by law enforcement in publicly accessible spaces are generally categorised as "prohibited AI practices" under Article 5 (EY Greece, 2025), subject only to tightly constrained derogations such as narrowly defined public security threats and prior judicial or administrative authorisation (EDRi, 2024). The internal market harmonisation logic embedded in the AI Act seeks to balance innovation with a high level of protection of fundamental rights, drawing its legal basis from Article 16 of the TFEU (data protection and privacy) (Paolucci, 2024).

By contrast, the Brazilian legislative framework remains at an incipient stage. The substitute text of Bill No. 2.338/2023, recently approved by the Federal Senate, adopts a risk-based structure that echoes elements of the AI Act but lacks the same degree of institutional granularity and enforcement infrastructure. It introduces foundational principles—such as non-discrimination, human oversight, transparency, and algorithmic accountability (Senado Federal do Brasil, 2024b)—and defines high-risk systems, including those with significant impact on fundamental rights (EPRS, 2021). However, unlike the AI Act, the Brazilian bill does not categorically prohibit real-time facial recognition systems by public or private actors in open spaces.

From a doctrinal standpoint, this difference is pivotal. The AI Act's approach to biometric surveillance is grounded in a theory of ex-ante governance, leveraging compliance-by-design, fundamental rights impact assessments (FRAIAs), and mandatory documentation before deployment (EYGreece, 2025; Paolucci, 2024). Although robust in its guiding principles, the Brazilian bill lacks enforceable tools for ex-ante supervision and relies on generalist enforcement by multiple existing agencies. This Brazilian scenario raises significant concerns regarding regulatory fragmentation, uneven accountability, and the potential for function creep—i.e. the expansion of technologies beyond their initially intended scope, as evidenced in the ViaQuatro case.

Applied to the São Paulo Metro case, the AI Act's prohibitions and procedural safeguards would likely render the installation and operation of interactive digital doors with facial data collection unlawful under European law (EYGreece, 2025; Paolucci, 2024), particularly if deployed without explicit consent, legitimate public interest justification, or a prior fundamental rights impact assessment. Conversely, under current Brazilian law, enforcement depends on post-hoc judicial review and diffuse institutional oversight—a markedly weaker framework in practice. This comparison can be observed through the Table 1.

This comparative exercise reveals that while both jurisdictions share a normative commitment to fundamental rights and human dignity, the EU adopts a hard-law, institutionalised, and precautionary regulatory model. In contrast, Brazil relies on in a principle-based, decentralised, and aspirational framework. Bridging this gap will be essential for Brazil to meet international AI governance standards and ensure adequate protection against biometric mass surveillance.

Against this backdrop and informed by the empirical dimensions of the São Paulo Metro case, we now move towards a broader synthesis. The concluding reflections that follow are situated at the confluence of normative theory, institutional imaginaries, and regulatory strategy—not merely as a summation but as a forward-looking provocation. They aim to illuminate how evolving legal architectures, both in Brazil and the European Union, may reshape the ethical boundaries and democratic legitimacy of artificial intelligence in the governance of public life.

6 Conclusion

There has been a lot of debate about the reason for analysing a process that is still in progress and studying a technology that will develop into more complex forms in a few years' time. This question is fundamental to understanding the importance of this case study. It is known that digital data is never a tabula rasa but must be experienced by socio-political-cultural structures and layers (Lupton, 2016; Mol, 2008) and that artificial intelligence does not project itself, but through certain conditioning factors that shape it. Therefore, the characteristics of the agents who shape these technologies merge with them, so that they can reproduce stereotypes, ways of thinking and projections of certain groups that materialise them. Thus, ethical-legal notions such as consent, informational self-determination, constitutional principles, and agent responsibility, for example, tend to metamorphose less frequently than technologies, which is why their study in this case is relevant as a precedent for future ones. The case involving DIDs in São Paulo's ViaQuatro (metro concessionaire) is the first of its kind in Brazil and could become a leading case for any future similar cases—both because of the parties' arguments and because of the modus

Table 1 Comparative: EU AI Act vs. Brazilian AI Bill (PL 2.338/2023)

Dimension	EU Artificial Intelligence Act (2024)	Brazilian AI Bill (PL 2.338/2023)
Regulatory model	Hard-law, centralised, institutionalised	Principle-based, decentralised, aspirational
Risk classification	Four-tier system: Unacceptable, high, limited, minimal	Echoes risk-based logic but lacks clear institutional detail or layered categorization
Biometric surveillance	Real-time facial recognition by public authorities in open spaces is prohibited (art. 54), with very limited exceptions	Facial recognition in public spaces is not categorically prohibited
Ex-ante controls	Mandatory fundamental rights impact assessments (FRAIA), compliance-by-design, documentation (arts. 16–29)	No mandatory ex-ante assessments: Oversight left to general existing agencies
Institutional infrastructure	Specific governance bodies and coordination mechanisms at EU level	No dedicated institutional body; potential for regulatory fragmentation
Foundational principles	Emphasises fundamental rights, data protection (TFEU art. 16), transparency, accountability	Principles include transparency, non-discrimination, human oversight, algorithmic accountability (art. 3°, Ch. I)
Enforcement mechanism	Strong enforcement via supervisory authorities and harmonisation logic across member states	Post-hoc judicial review and diffuse enforcement across multiple agencies
Legal basis for data protection	Anchored in the charter of fundamental rights and GDPR	Informed by LGPD (lei Geral de Proteção de dados), but not integrated with AI-specific mandates
Example—São Paulo metro case	Likely illegal without consent, public interest justification, or FRAIA	Informed by LGPD (lei Geral de Proteção de dados), but not integrated with AI-specific mandates
Normative approach	Ex-ante, precautionary, rights-centred	Reactive, principle-driven, and reliant on aspirational norms

operandi of the TJSP's decisions, which could act as "caselaw." The growing popularisation of new AI technologies is very likely to give rise to future litigation, so this case study can indirectly outline how such cases might be discussed and decided in the future.

As already mentioned, this case is still in progress. On September 14, 2018, the judge who reported the first TJ/SP ruling on this case argued that even without any expert document proving that facial recognition images had actually been captured, he decided to oblige ViaQuatro to cease capturing images through the digital door cameras, as well as turning them off, based on the argument that there is no guarantee of a contractual nature, between the concessionaire and passengers, that the processing of data, as well as any storage, meets digital security standards (Case No. 1090663–42.2018.8.26.0100, p.358). The latest court ruling dated November 29, 2023, and entered into the case files on March 18, 2024, upheld the same position, stating that there was no full proof of the purpose of the information collected by the company. In addition, capturing images of users without their knowledge or consent, for commercial purposes that benefit the defendant and the contracted company, already justifies turning off the cameras in the urban rail system. (Case No. 1090663–42.2018.8.26.0100, p. 3802).

In summary, the legal dispute centres on use the biometric processing technology of the interactive digital doors to identify the faces of passengers. However, from a technical point of view, it has so far been proven that the DID system is very controversial because the data processing stages and anonymisation techniques have not been described in detail to the point of resolving any doubts regarding security in relation to data leakage by insiders and outsiders, the ethical use of biometric data, and the disposal of users' identifiable data.

Therefore, it is appropriate for judges to require new expert analysis and to restrict its use due to the suspicions and uncertainties raised by DID. Just the fact that AdMobilize's technology has an AI algorithm that can identify people's faces (if this data is later deleted) is sufficient justification for its problematisation and investigation, since sensitive data from a large part of the population is being captured without their consent. In this era in which technologies are evolving, constitutional guarantees, social rights, and principles must be solidified, protected, and expanded, thus avoiding a socio-scientific collapse.

Acknowledgements This work was carried out at the *Center for Artificial Intelligence* (C4AI-USP), with support by the São Paulo Research Foundation (FAPESP grant \#2019/07665-4) and by the IBM Corporation. This study was financed in part by the Coordenação de Aperfeiçoamento de Pessoal de Nível Superior—Brasil (CAPES)—Finance Code 001.

References

Baruffaldi, S., Beuzekom, B., Dernis, H., Harhoff, D., Rao, N., Rosenfeld, D., & Squicciarini, M. (2020). *Identifying and measuring developments in artificial intelligence: Making the impossible possible.* https://doi.org/10.1787/5f65ff7e-en

Bioni, B. R. (2020). *Proteção de dados pessoais: A função e os limites do consentimento* (2nd ed.).

Bioni, B., Favaro, I., & Rielli, M. (2020). O tratamento de dados de crianças e adolescentes pode ser legal? *Observatório Privacidade.*. https://observatorioprivacidade.com.br/o-tratamento-de-dados-de-criancas-e-adolescentes-pode-ser-legal/

Brasil. (2018). *Lei Geral de Proteção de Dados Pessoais—LGPD, Lei n° 13.709. de 14 de agosto de 2018.* http://www.planalto.gov.br/ccivil_03/_ato2015-2018/2018/lei/l13709.htm

Brasil. (2023). Nota Técnica n° 175/2023 CGF/ANPD: Acordo de Cooperação MJSP e CBF. https://www.gov.br/anpd/pt-br/documentos-e-publicacoes/documentos-de-publicacoes/nota-tecnica-no-175-2023-cgf-anpd-acordo-de-cooperacao-mjsp-e-cbf.pdf

Capanema, W. A. (2020). A responsabilidade civil na lei geral de proteção de dados. *Cadernos Jurídicos, 21*(53), 163–170.
Data Protection Working Party. (2012). *Opinion 3/2012 on developments in biometric technologies*. Article 29 working Party.
de Lima, C. R. P. (2014). O Ônus de Ler o Contrato no Contexto da "Ditadura" dos Contratos de Adesão Eletrônicos. In Rover, Aires José; Cella, José Renato Gaziero; Ayuda, Fernando Galindo (Org.). Direito e Novas Tecnologias I. Conpedi UFPB. Florianópolis: 2014, p. 343–365 (p, 350). Disponível em: http://publicadireito.com.br/artigos/?cod=981322808aba8a03. Acesso em: 05 de junho de 2014.
de Lima, C. R. P. (2019, Nov). Consentimento Inequívoco versus Expresso: o que muda com a LGPD? In Lei Geral de Proteção de Dados Pessoais – Revista do Advogado, nº 144, nov. 2019, p. 60–67 (p. 62). Disponível em: https://aplicacao.aasp.org.br/aasp/servicos/revista_advogado/paginaveis/144/. Acesso em: 05 de junho de 2024.
EDRi. (2024). How to fight biometric mass surveillance after the AI Act: A legal and practical guide. https://edri.org/our-work/how-to-fight-biometric-mass-surveillance-after-the-ai-act-a-legal-and-practical-guide/
European Parliament and Council of the European Union. (2024). Regulation (EU) 2024/1689 of the European Parliament and of the council of 13 June 2024 on harmonised rules on artificial intelligence (artificial intelligence act). http://data.europa.eu/eli/reg/2024/1689/oj
European Parliamentary Research Service (EPRS). (2021). Regulating facial recognition in the EU (PE 698.021). https://www.europarl.europa.eu/RegData/etudes/IDAN/2021/698021/EPRS_IDA(2021)698021_EN.pdf
EY Greece. (2025). AI act: Prohibited AI practices become applicable. https://www.ey.com/content/dam/ey-unified-site/ey-com/en-gr/technical/tax/tax-alerts/2025/02/ai-act-en-v3.pdf
Filho, J. de J. (2020). Pacote TJSP: Coleta e Organização de dados do Tribunal de Justiça de São Paulo. https://github.com/jjesusfilho/tjsp
Gil, A. C. (2002). *Como elaborar projetos de pesquisa* (4ª ed.). Editora Atlas.
Ginor, F., & Becker, H. S. (2017). *Sociological work: Method and substance* (1ª ed.). Routledge.
Glez-Peña, D., Lourenço, A., López-Fernández, H., Reboiro-Jato, M., & Fdez-Riverola, F. (2014). Web scraping technologies in an API world. *Briefings in Bioinformatics, 15*(5), 788–797. https://doi.org/10.1093/bib/bbt026
Information Commissioner's Office. (2015). Anonymisation: Managing data protection risk code of practice. https://ico.org.uk/media/fororganisations/documents/1061/anonymisation-code.pdf
ISO/IEC. (2022). ISO/IEC 22989:2022 Artificial intelligence concepts and terminology. https://www.iso.org/standard/74296.html
Lan, H., Sha, D., Malarvizhi, A. S., Liu, Y., Li, Y., Meister, N., Liu, Q., Wang, Z., Yang, J., & Yang, C. P. (2021). Covid-scraper: An open-source toolset for automatically scraping and processing global multi-scale spatiotemporal COVID-19 records. *IEEE Access, 9*, 84783–84798. https://doi.org/10.1109/ACCESS.2021.3085682
Lima, C. R. P. (2014). O ônus de ler o contrato no contexto da "ditadura" dos contratos de adesão eletrônicos. In A. J. Rover, J. R. G. Cella, & F. G. Ayuda (Eds.), *Direito e novas tecnologias I* (pp. 343–365). Conpedi UFPB. http://publicadireito.com.br/artigos/?cod=981322808aba8a03
Lima, C. R. P. (2019). Consentimento inequívoco versus expresso: O que muda com a LGPD? *Lei Geral de Proteção de dados Pessoais– Revista do Advogado, 144*, 60–67.
Lupton, D. (2016). Digital companion species and eating data: Implications for theorising digital data–human assemblages. *Big Data & Society, 3*(1), 1–5. https://doi.org/10.1177/2053951715619947
Marques, C. L. (2002). Contratos no Código de Defesa do Consumidor: O novo regime das relações contratuais (4ª ed.). RT.
McClurg, A. J. (2007). In the face of danger: Facial recognition and the limits of privacy law. *Harvard Law Review, 120*(7), 1870–1891.
Melo Nogueira, F. A. C., & Fonseca, M. L. (2020). O consentimento na lei Geral de Proteção de dados: Autonomia privada e o consentimento livre, informado, específico e expresso. In B. M.

Grossi (Ed.), *Lei Geral de Proteção de dados: Uma análise preliminar da lei 13.709/2018 e da experiência de sua implantação no contexto empresarial* (pp. 15–44). Editora Fi.
Mol, A. (2008). I eat an apple. *On theorizing subjectivities. Subjectivity*, 28–37.
Montag, L., McLeod, R., Mets, L. D., Gauld, M., Rodger, F., & Pelka, M. (2021). *The rise and rise of biometric mass surveillance in the EU*. EDRi & EIJI.
National Institute of Standards and Technology. (2015). Special publication 500–290: Data format for the interchange of fingerprint, facial & other biometric information. https://doi.org/10.6028/NIST.SP.500-290e3
Paolucci, F. (2024). *From global standards to local safeguards: The AI act, biometrics, and fundamental rights*. Springer.
Senado Federal do Brasil. (2024a). Projeto de Lei n° 2.338, de 2023. https://www25.senado.leg.br/web/atividade/materias/-/materia/157233
Senado Federal do Brasil. (2024b). Projeto de Lei n° 2.338, de 2023. Retrieved from https://www25.senado.leg.br/web/atividade/materias/-/materia/157233 (Texto aprovado em Comissão e parecer final do Senador Eduardo Gomes).
Stallings, W., & Brown, L. (2014). *Segurança de computadores: Princípios e práticas* (2ª ed.). Elsevier.
Superior Tribunal de Justiça. (2023). STJ no Seu Dia fala sobre a validade da colheita de provas em inquérito policial. https://www.stj.jus.br/sites/portalp/Paginas/Comunicacao/Noticias/2023/19052023-STJ-No-Seu-Dia-fala-sobre-a-validade-da-colheita-de-provas-em-inquerito-policial.aspx
VanderPlas, J. (2023). *Python data science handbook: Essential tools for working with data*. O'Reilly Media.
Yin, R. K. (2018). *Case study research and applications: Design and methods*. Sage Publications.
Zhao, W., Chellappa, R., Phillips, P. J., & Rosenfeld, A. (2003). Face recognition: A literature survey. *ACM Computing Surveys, 35*(4), 399–458.
Zhao, W. X., Zhou, K., Li, J., Tang, T., Wang, X., Hou, Y., Min, Y., Zhang, B., Zhang, J., Dong, Z., Du, Y., Yang, C., Chen, Y., Chen, Z., Jiang, J., Ren, R., Li, Y., Tang, X., Liu, Z.,... Wen, J.-R. (2023). A survey of large language models [Preprint]. arXiv. https://doi.org/10.48550/arXiv.2303.18223
Zulehner, B. (2024). *EU artificial intelligence act: Regulating the use of facial recognition technologies in publicly accessible spaces*. Stanford-Vienna European Union Law Working Paper No. 91 (TTLF). https://law.stanford.edu/wp-content/uploads/2024/06/EU-Law-WP-91-Zulehner.pdf

Cristina Godoy Bernardo de Oliveira is a Professor of Law at the University of São Paulo (USP), with a PhD and LL.B. from USP. Post-doctoral degree at Université Paris I and the University of Oxford. Fellow Researcher at IRCAI UNESCO and Co-chair at Columbia University. PI at the Centre for Artificial Intelligence USP-IBM-FAPESP (C4AI). Member of the Executive Committee at the Centre of AI and Machine Learning at USP (CIAAM). Coordinator of the Regulatory Sandbox on AI and Data Protection of the Brazilian National Authority (ANPD).

Otavio de Paula Albuquerque holds a B.S. degree in Information Systems from the Federal Rural University of the Amazon, Brazil, which included an exchange program at the University of Porto, Portugal. He received his M.S. degree in Information Systems from the University of São Paulo, Brazil, in 2020, where he is currently pursuing his PhD degree in Information Systems. Since 2021, he has been an AI Researcher at the Centre for Artificial Intelligence (USP/IBM/Fapesp).

Emily Liene Belotti is a lawyer pursuing a Master's degree in Law at the University of São Paulo (USP), focusing on the regulation of artificial intelligence. She is a researcher at the Centre for

Artificial Intelligence and Machine Learning at the University of São Paulo (C4AI/USP / CIAAM/ USP).

Isabella Ferreira Lopes is a Computer Engineer and AI ethics researcher at the Centre for Artificial Intelligence and Machine Learning in Brazil, pursuing a Master's degree in Artificial Intelligence at the University of São Paulo, with a focus on data mining, machine learning, AI ethics, and regulation.

Tiago Augustini de Lima is a PhD. Candidate in Law at the University of São Paulo, Ribeirão Preto Law School (FDRP/USP). Master's in Law from the University of São Paulo, Ribeirão Preto Law School (FDRP/USP). Researcher at the Centre for Artificial Intelligence of the University of São Paulo (C4AI/USP / CIAAM/USP).

João Victor Palermo Gianecchini is a PhD candidate in Law at Goethe University Frankfurt. He holds a scholarship from the Friedrich-Ebert-Stiftung. He holds a Master's degree in Law from the University of São Paulo, where he was a research fellow at the Centre for Artificial Intelligence (C4AI/USP / CIAAM/USP) and the Goethe Research Experience Program (GREP).

Civil Liability of Digital Platforms: The Imaginary Conflict Between Freedom of Expression and Protection of Democracy—Brazilian Experiences and Guidelines

Anderson Schreiber

Abstract This article examines the civil liability regime applicable to digital platforms in Brazil, in light of ongoing constitutional review proceedings before the Brazilian Supreme Federal Court. At issue is Article 19 of the so-called Civil Rights Framework for the Internet (Law No. 12.965/2014), which shields platforms from liability for third-party content unless a court order for removal has been issued. While intended to protect freedom of expression, this provision has been criticised for excessively limiting platform accountability, particularly in cases involving disinformation and online attacks against democratic institutions. By analysing the Court's emerging stance, the article explores the broader implications for freedom of expression and democratic resilience in the digital age, offering insights into the evolving relationship between technology, law and constitutional rights in Brazil.

Keywords Civil liability · Platform regulation · Freedom of expression · Disinformation · Constitutional law

1 Introduction

Iracema Cristina, a psychologist working for a large corporation, was featured on a romantic dating platform. Alongside her full name and actual work telephone number, the website displayed the following description: "*person proposing to engage in affective and sexual activities in exchange for money*." This case was examined by the Brazilian Superior Court of Justice (STJ) in Special Appeal No. 566468/2004 (Relator: Justice Jorge Scartezzini, decided on November 23, 2004). Please note that all plaintiffs' names mentioned in this text have been changed to ensure anonymity.

A. Schreiber (✉)
State University of Rio de Janeiro (UERJ), Rio de Janeiro, Brazil
e-mail: schreiber@schreiber.adv.br

K. Bodrožić-Brnić et al. (eds.), *AI and the Ethics of Innovation*, Digital Transformation and Innovation, https://doi.org/10.1007/978-3-032-20638-1_16

To have her name removed, Iracema had to file a lawsuit, in which she stated, in a personal deposition, that she feared losing her job due to the humiliating public exposure she had suffered.

False profiles and other forms of spreading false information may cause irreparable harm to those targeted by such practices. The publication of false or defamatory content in the digital environment produces tangible effects, ranging from mere mistrust to the deterioration of professional and personal relationships, and at times leading to more concrete consequences—such as being overlooked for a promotion, excluded from a job interview, dismissed from employment, or even experiencing the breakdown of close relationships. Victims are frequently impacted by such incidents and begin to be perceived as careless or disinterested individuals, even when they have played no part in causing the situation. The notion that "*there is some truth to it*"—so common in Brazilian society—is not easily dispelled. The removal of false or defamatory content from the internet thus proves to be only the first step in a long journey towards restoring the victim's reputation.

As if that were not enough, this initial step often encounters significant resistance. The removal of damaging information—even when it is clearly false—is a measure that companies operating in social media and online dating platforms frequently avoid. The case of Adriana Valença is emblematic. Genuine photographs taken for a modelling portfolio circulated online on a false Facebook profile that, alongside her mobile phone number, claimed Adriana was a "call girl." She began receiving phone calls from "clients" seeking her alleged services, and those who knew her began to view her with suspicion. She made every effort to have the false content removed, sending multiple emails to the platform, but claims that she did not even receive a reply. Her last resort was to take the matter to court, with all the associated costs and burdens. This case was examined by the Court of Justice of the State of São Paulo (TJSP) in *Civil Appeal No. 0173842–95.2012.8.26.0100/2014* (Relator: Associate Justice Beretta da Silveira, decided on January 21, 2014).

Such lawsuits, which may appear simple or even unnecessary at first glance, often escalate into protracted legal battles. The need to defend one's honour frequently encounters a significant obstacle, one that has come to symbolise a central issue in contemporary society: the scope of freedom of expression in the digital realm.

This discussion is directly related to a major concern in the regulation of digital platforms in Brazil. The Federal Supreme Court has recently concluded its judgement regarding Article 19 of the Brazilian Civil Rights Framework for the Internet, Law No. 12.965/2014. In this judgement (Extraordinary Appeal No. 1.037.396/SP) the Court addressed the constitutionality of Article 19 under the Brazilian legal framework. This judgement was connected to an earlier leading case, *Extraordinary Appeal No. 1.057.258/MG*, which predates the enactment of the Framework and raised the question of whether companies hosting websites have a duty to monitor published content and remove it from the internet when deemed offensive, even without prior judicial intervention. But what is the context behind this judgement and why is this so relevant for the future of the internet in Brazil?

2 The Background for Civil Liability in Cyberspace in Brazil Prior to the Civil Rights Framework for the Internet

Before the enactment of the Civil Rights Framework for the Internet in 2014, Brazilian Courts adopted varying approaches to platforms' liability for third-party content that violated rights on the Internet. Civil liability arising from the online dissemination of content generated by third parties was a subject of intense debate in Brazilian courts before 2014. While victims of false or defamatory content sought compensation, businesses and owners of social networks and dating platforms maintained that they could not be held liable for content uploaded by users, as it would be impossible for them to monitor all content uploaded to their sites.

Although case law remained highly fragmented, and no unanimous or consolidated position had yet emerged, an examination of the Brazilian court judgements revealed a straight path to overcoming the theory of no-liability of business companies that owned social networks and dating platforms. Such owners—which, in an effort to remove their liability, prefer to call themselves mere "*administrators,*" but which, actually, are true owners of the brand, of the web domain, the advertising space, and all other components that makes up the social network—had been suffering, throughout Brazil, convictions for damages resulting from content posted by users of their sites.

Such rulings were based on two different legal grounds. On the one hand, they relied on the notion of a defective service (Article 14 of the Consumer Defence Code)—a basis which presupposes the classification of the relationship between users and social networks as a consumer relationship.

Such rulings were based on two different legal grounds. On the one hand, they relied on the notion of a defective service (Article 14 of the Consumer Defence Code)—a basis which presupposes the classification of the relationship between users and social networks as a consumer relationship. As stated by the Brazilian Superior Court of Justice (STJ) in *Special Appeal No. 1308830/2012* (Relator: Justice Nancy Andrighi, decided on May 8, 2012):

> The fact that the service provided by the internet service provider is free does not exclude the existence of a consumer relationship, since the term "by remuneration," contained in Article 3, paragraph 2, of the Consumer Defence Code, must be interpreted broadly to include the indirect gain of the supplier. (Brazilian Superior Court of Justice [STJ], *Special Appeal No. 1308830/2012*, May 8, 2012)

On the other hand, such rulings invoked the characterisation of social networks as involving a high-risk activity (Civil Code, Article 927, sole paragraph), given the high potential for harm inherent in the creation of a space where the content inserted acquires a public dimension without any kind of prior moderation. This interpretation was illustrated by the Court of Justice of the State of Rio de Janeiro (TJRJ) in *Civil Appeal No. 0006047–50.2009.8.19.0040/2009* (Relator: Associate Justice Benedicto Abicair, decided on December 1, 2009).

In this scenario, prior to the enactment of the Civil Rights Framework for the Internet, Brazilian courts began to informally adopt a version of the notice and takedown mechanism, borrowed from United States copyright law, which shields platforms from liability if they promptly remove harmful content upon notification. This approach was influenced by the Digital Millennium Copyright Act (Public Law No. 105–304/1998), which, in its Title II—known as *Online Copyright Infringement Liability Limitation*—sets out detailed procedures for notification and counter-notification, as well as the measures that service providers must follow to qualify for limitation of liability, particularly those established in Sect. 202, which substantially amended § 512 of Chap. 5 of Title 17 of the United States Code, compilation of federal rules of a general and permanent nature.

However, this transplant was both incomplete and unregulated in Brazil, lacking clear procedures and safeguards. As a result, it was applied inconsistently and offered limited protection to victims. The prevailing vote in a decision by the Court of Justice of the State of Rio de Janeiro illustrates this point, affirming that the *notice and takedown* doctrine diverges from Brazilian legal tradition:

> Damage happens at the time of publication; therefore, the theory that the plaintiff should first request the removal of the page is not valid, as this mere step does not eliminate the loss already sustained. There is not in our law an offense which is not subject to indemnification. (Court of Justice of the State of Rio de Janeiro [TJRJ], *Civil Appeal No. 2008.001.56760/2008*, Relator: Associate Justice Otávio Rodrigues, decided on December 3, 2008)

In any case, the very mechanism of *notice and takedown*, when adopted by a legal system, must contain safeguards to prevent its abusive use and ensure its effective operation. In the United States, for instance, the notification must contain minimum requirements (such as identification of the infringing content and contact information of the complainant), and there are express provisions for counter-notification by the alleged violator of copyrights, along with specific timeframes for action by the platform owner (United States Code, 2018, Title 17, § 512).

The danger of the Brazilian judiciary's incorporation of the notice-and-takedown model lay precisely in its partial adoption. As often occurs in the Brazilian context—particularly in matters of civil liability—the "idea" of the institution was embraced without prior understanding or acceptance of its multiple dimensions (Schreiber, 2014).

The limited scope available to a judge in an individual case did not allow for the detailed development of the institution. As a result, the notion of *notice and takedown* began to find its way into Brazilian case law—always with the best of intentions, but in a somewhat precarious and risky fashion. An essentially procedural mechanism started to appear in judicial decisions without any formal regulation, without provision for counter-notification, and lacking the other safeguards that had originally accompanied it. This led to a distorted version of the original doctrine, supported more by deference to the authority of the U.S. experience than by a proper understanding of that model and its adaptation to the inherently diverse and particular Brazilian legal context.

The impending discussion of the Bill that would become the Civil Rights Framework for the Internet promised, however, to eliminate these risks. At that moment, it was expected that the Legislative Branch would act impartially and effectively, providing detailed regulation of the *notice and takedown* procedure to establish an efficient mechanism for resolving internet-related disputes in Brazil. Unfortunately, the outcome was precisely the opposite.

3 Article 19 and the Enactment of a Questionable Regime for Civil Liability on the Internet

Instead of regulating the *notice and takedown* procedure by establishing reciprocal safeguards and ensuring its effective operation, the Civil Rights Framework for the Internet introduced an extremely rigid mechanism. This framework offers strong protection to companies operating social media platforms, while simultaneously weakening the level of protection that had already been developed through Brazilian case law in favour of internet users. Consider the wording of Article 19 of Law No. 12.965:

> Art. 19. In order to ensure freedom of expression and prevent censorship, the provider of internet applications may only be subject to civil liability for damages resulting from content generated by third parties if, following a specific court order, they fail to take action, within the scope of their service and within the time stated in the order, to make unavailable the content that was identified as being unlawful, unless otherwise provided by law. (Brazil, 2014)

The wording of the provision makes clear from the outset which side of the scale it seeks to favour. In a section entitled "*Civil Liability for Damages Arising from Content Generated by Third Parties*" Article 19 begins with an unusual statement of purpose, invoking the values of freedom of expression and the prohibition of censorship—principles which, in the abstract, would appear to argue against the very notion of liability. Yet the entire debate on liability arises precisely when the exercise of freedom of expression infringes upon the fundamental rights of others, becoming either abusive—in contradiction with the purpose of free expression—or illegitimate, insofar as it violates, through reasoned consideration, the protected sphere of other rights of equal constitutional rank in the specific context. Fundamental rights such as honour, privacy, and image are also protected under the Brazilian Constitution and possess an axiological status no lower than that of freedom of expression. The decision to highlight only "*one side of the coin*" at the beginning of Article 19 reflects poor legislative technique and offers an early—and troubling—indication of what was to follow.

After its unusual introduction, Article 19 states that the "*provider of internet applications*"—a term defined in Article 5, VII of the Civil Rights Framework for the Internet as any entity offering a "*set of functionalities that can be accessed through a terminal connected to the internet*" thereby adopting a technical terminology that conceals the proprietary and commercial nature of these services—"*can only be subject to civil liability*"—with the word *only* already signalling a restrictive view of such liability—for "*damages resulting from content generated by third parties following a specific court order,*" it does not take any steps to remove the unlawful content designated in the judicial order, "*within the scope of their service and within the time stated in the order,*" unless otherwise determined by law (Brazil, 2014).

The reference to a "*court order*" delivers a fatal blow to the very logic of the *notice and takedown* model. As previously noted, the legal limitation of civil liability for so-called "*application providers*" could only be justified as an incentive for proactive conduct—one capable of preventing the dissemination of harm regardless of the time and expense required to initiate legal proceedings. If the victim of a violation of fundamental rights must turn to the judiciary and obtain a formal court order to compel the platform to act, then Article 19 becomes essentially redundant. This is because the option to seek judicial relief has always existed under Brazilian law, and the failure to comply with a court order, independently of any civil liability considerations, already constitutes the criminal offence of disobedience (Article 330 of the Brazilian Criminal Code).

Even more troubling is the fact that, according to the literal wording of Article 19, non-compliance with a court order becomes a necessary condition for holding providers liable. In this context, initiating legal proceedings ceases to be merely a means of protecting the victim's rights or obtaining redress for their violation, and instead becomes a *sine qua non* requirement for the recognition of civil liability. The victim—who once turned to the courts as a last resort in seeking to establish the defendant's responsibility—must now first file a lawsuit and secure a specific court order, such that only in the event of the provider's failure to comply with that order may the operator of the website or social media platform be held liable. In a legal reality increasingly aware of the overburdening of the judiciary, the Civil Rights Framework for the Internet diverges from virtually every international trend by making the judicialisation of online disputes a prerequisite for protecting the victim's rights. Yet in the online environment—marked by speed and dynamism—judicial remedies are often less effective and, accordingly, more open to criticism.

In truth, rather than providing the victim with a more effective system for the protection of fundamental rights, Article 19 ends up safeguarding the interests of the companies that operate web-based platforms. It does so by imposing the requirement that the court order be "*specific*"—thus allowing room for arguments about a lack of specificity that might justify non-compliance—and by limiting the obligation to comply to actions taken "*within the framework of their service.*" This opens yet another avenue for contesting compliance, particularly through technical arguments. Such arguments often place the claimant at a disadvantage since defendants—by virtue of their in-depth knowledge of the very operations they manage—typically possess far greater expertise in these matters than members of the judiciary. This asymmetry is particularly acute in legal proceedings that deal with the technical infrastructure of digital services.

Perhaps to soften the evident regression, paragraph 3 of Article 19 provides that: "*Claims for compensation for damages arising from internet content affecting honour, reputation or personality rights, as well as requests for its removal by internet application providers, may be brought before small claims courts.*" However, this so-called consolation prize does little to mitigate the inconvenience of requiring victims to resort to the judiciary to trigger the civil liability of internet companies. Nor does it represent a meaningful benefit, insofar as this procedural option was already available to victims prior to the enactment of Law No. 12.965. At that time, victims could bring claims before small claims courts provided, they did not assign a specific monetary value to non-pecuniary damages or if the total amount claimed did not exceed the jurisdictional ceiling of such courts. In practice, however, this condition proves largely irrelevant. Most lawyers in Brazil typically refrain from specifying the amount of non-material damages, leaving it to the judge's discretion, to avoid the impact that the amount claimed would have on court fees and, ultimately, on potential liability for the opposing party's legal costs. For this reason, paragraph 3 of Article 19 introduces no meaningful improvement for victims that was not already part of the pre-existing legal landscape.

In short, for individual internet users whose fundamental rights may be harmed by online content, Article 19 offers no meaningful benefit. On the contrary, it represents a clear setback when compared to the developments previously established by Brazilian case law on the matter. It is a provision that protects companies operating internet services—particularly social media platforms and virtual communication spaces.

When compared with regulatory frameworks outside Brazil, this rule provides significantly greater protection to the internet industry than the regulatory frameworks of countries traditionally known for safeguarding business interests online, such as the United States. From a legal-technical standpoint, the mechanism of *notice and takedown* is profoundly distorted. The rule redirects disputes to an already overburdened judiciary, straying so far from the original model that it becomes difficult to understand how legal scholars can continue to claim that the Civil Rights Framework for the Internet incorporates the *notice and takedown* procedure. Under Article 19, a notice is neither sufficient nor likely to result in the takedown of unlawful content. Instead, the provision imposes conditions and obstacles that hinder effective compliance with legal orders. Far from improving the situation of victims, the rule fails to even preserve the level of protection guaranteed under general civil liability rules, ultimately weakening the protection of fundamental rights and undoing progress previously achieved through judicial interpretation in this field.

The remaining question is this: despite its many shortcomings, is Article 19 of the Civil Rights Framework for the Internet merely a poorly drafted provision, or is it in fact unconstitutional? From a legal-technical perspective, the issue was complex. Yet a thorough constitutional analysis led to the conclusion that the rule violates fundamental rights. This interpretation was ultimately confirmed by the Brazilian Federal Supreme Court, which, in its final judgement in June 2025 *Extraordinary Appeal No. 1.037.396*, held Article 19 to be unconstitutional. The Court's decision aligns with the understanding developed in this article and represents a significant step towards restoring adequate protection for individual rights in the digital sphere. Let's delve into it.

4 The Supreme Federal Court´s Ruling on the (Un)Constitutionality of Article 19

What options were available to the Supreme Court? In the trial that began in November 2024, the Brazilian Federal Supreme Court faced three possible courses of action: (a) upholding the constitutionality of Article 19 of the Civil Rights Framework for the Internet, thereby preserving the *status quo*; (b) declaring it unconstitutional, which would result in the application of the general civil liability rules set out in the Civil Code; or (c) interpreting Article 19 in conformity with the Federal Constitution, by establishing that platform liability should not be contingent upon prior non-compliance with a specific court order, but rather require extrajudicial notice—either through physical means or via an electronic channel provided by the platform itself.

Overall, the majority of the Supreme Court Justices converged on several key points—chief among them, the conclusion that Article 19 is ineffective in protecting fundamental rights. The Justices also recognised that, in certain circumstances, internet companies may incur strict civil liability for failing to remove third-party content, regardless of whether they have received an extrajudicial notification or a specific judicial order. These situations include the following objectively defined cases:

> (i) crimes against the democratic rule of law; (ii) acts of terrorism or preparations for terrorism; (iii) offences involving the incitement, inducement, or assistance of suicide or self-harm; (iv) racism; (v) violence against children, adolescents, or vulnerable individuals; (vi) any form of violence against women; (vii) violations of public health rules, including failure to implement, obstruction of, or resistance to public health measures during a health emergency; (viii) human trafficking; (ix) incitement to or threats of physical or sexual violence; (x) dissemination of blatantly false or severely decontextualised information leading to incitement to physical violence, threats to life, or acts of violence against socially vulnerable groups or individuals; and (xi) dissemination of demonstrably false or severely misrepresented information that may compromise the fairness of elections or the integrity of the electoral process. (Brazilian Federal Supreme Court [STF], Extraordinary Appeal No. 1.037.396, decided on June 26, 2025)

According to Rapporteur Justice Dias Toffoli, "Article 19, along with its paragraphs, is unconstitutional." Dias Toffoli suggested adopting the system outlined in Article 21 of the Civil Rights Framework for the Internet:

> which must, however, be interpreted in accordance with the Constitution to make it clear that the protection ensured by this rule is not restricted to the rights to privacy and sexual dignity that may be offended by the non-consensual dissemination of images, videos, or other materials containing scenes of nudity or sexual acts, but concerns the protection of all fundamental rights in the digital environment, such as the rights to privacy, private life, honour, and image, since, ultimately, all these rights emanate from the dignity of the human person as a founding value of the Brazilian State (Brazilian Constitution, art. 1, III) and, therefore, have the same legal-constitutional status. (Brazilian Federal Supreme Court, 2025)

Currently, Article 21 of the Civil Rights Framework for the Internet addresses a specific issue: the publication of material containing "nudity or sexual activities of a private nature."

> Art. 21. The internet application provider that makes third party generated content available shall be held secondarily liable for the breach of privacy arising from the disclosure of images, videos and other materials containing nudity or sexual activities of a private nature, without the authorisation of the participants, when, after receipt of notice by the participant or his/hers legal representative, refrains from removing, in a diligent manner, within its own technical limitations, such content. (Brazil, 2014)

Scholars have been studying this provision under the nomenclature of "*revenge pornography,*" borrowing terminology from U.S. sources. The labelling is improper, as the literal text of the rule alludes to scenes of nudity and sex regardless of the motive behind their disclosure. The use of the American expression can be accepted, provided that it does not lead to a restrictive interpretation of the rule. Strictly speaking, Article 21 is not the epitome of legislative technique, containing its own share of inaccuracies—most notably the equivocal use of the expression "secondarily." In fact, civil liability in this context is not secondary but rather direct and proper, since it derives from the inaction of the provider once it becomes aware of the infringing content. The term "secondary" should thus be understood merely as reinforcing the idea that the provider is held responsible for third-party content; technically, however, the liability is direct, not subsidiary. Consequently, there is no need for the victim to bring any claim against the original author of the content—who frequently cannot even be identified—as the action may be filed directly against the provider, either to compel removal or to obtain compensation for damages resulting from the exposure of the material between notification and effective removal.

Nevertheless, Article 21 has the great advantage of preserving the essential element of the *notice-and-takedown* system: the extrajudicial nature of the notification. Although the legislator did not explicitly refer to its extrajudicial character, the wording of the provision mentions merely a "notification." The interpreter, therefore, should not restrict this expression to judicial notifications, particularly when comparing the language of Article 21 with that of Article 19 of the same statute (Law No. 12.965/2014).

The reasoning put forward by Justice Dias Toffoli is eminently rational. If the protection of an individual's sexual privacy—and the corresponding liability of an internet application provider for damages arising from the unauthorised disclosure of nudity or sexual activity—can be triggered by a simple extrajudicial notification, it is difficult to comprehend why the protection of other attributes of human personality, which enjoy the same constitutional status under the Brazilian Constitution, should depend—under Article 19—on the issuance of a specific court order.

This inconsistency becomes especially apparent when comparing Articles 19 and 21 of the Civil Rights Framework for the Internet. While Article 21 permits extrajudicial notification to protect sexual privacy, Article 19 imposes the significantly heavier burden of requiring a judicial order to safeguard other fundamental rights, such as honour and image—an imbalance that lacks constitutional justification. In his vote, Justice Dias Toffoli also established a series of responsibilities that digital platforms must address, such as:

> (i) continuously updating Terms and Conditions; (ii) the requirement to have a legal representative in Brazil; (iii) creating mechanisms to ensure the authenticity of user accounts; (iv) rules

> for the standardised moderation of content; (v) combating disinformation and fake news; (vi) monitoring systemic risks in the digital environment, in addition to producing transparency reports; (vii) providing specific notification channels; (viii) and generating biannual transparency reports regarding the management and resolution of complaints through their internal systems. (Brazilian Federal Supreme Court, 2025)

Finally, the judge urged the Legislative and Executive Branches "to establish and implement a public policy within 18 months to combat digital violence and misinformation." (Brazilian Federal Supreme Court, 2025).

Following Rapporteur Justice Dias Toffoli, Justice Luis Fux argued that Article 19 creates a *comfort zone* for technology companies. Beyond their duty to remove harmful content generated by third parties, companies must promptly remove offensive material upon receiving an extrajudicial notification, without any prior deadline. In this context, Justice Fux advocated for a so-called "*reversal of the burden of judicialisation.*" In other words, once a notification has been received, the content should be removed; and if the company believes the material should be reinstated, it must seek judicial authorisation to do so.

Justice Luis Roberto Barroso argued that technology companies should be held accountable for third-party content, particularly if they do not take necessary actions to remove posts with criminal material. In his view, rather than being required to actively monitor and assume responsibility for each individual item of content, these companies should be subject to a general *duty of care*. Therefore, platforms must take proactive measures to ensure their environments are free from seriously harmful content and strive to mitigate the systemic risks created or worsened by their services. He believes that the measures should reduce these risks and their adverse effects on individual and collective rights, security, and democratic stability.

5 A Balance between Constitutionality and Unconstitutionality: An Analysis of the Partial Unconstitutionality of Article 19 of the Civil Rights Framework for The Internet Declared by the Brazilian Federal Supreme Court

In light of these circumstances, on 26 June 2025, the Brazilian Federal Supreme Court held, by eight votes to three, that Article 19 is "partially unconstitutional." The decision was consolidated in a thesis comprising fourteen items, which is transcribed below in full, as set forth in the official judgement of the Court (Brazilian Federal Supreme Court [STF], *Extraordinary Appeal No. 1.037.396*, 2025):

1. *Article 19 of Law No. 12,965/2014 (Civil Rights Framework for the Internet), which requires a specific court order for the civil liability of internet application providers for damages resulting from content generated by third parties, is partially unconstitutional. There is a state of partial omission arising from the fact that the general rule of Article 19 does not provide sufficient protection for*

constitutional legal rights of high relevance (protection of fundamental rights and democracy).

2. *Until new legislation is enacted, Article 19 should be interpreted to mean that internet application providers are subject to civil liability, except for the application of specific provisions of electoral legislation and normative acts issued by the Brazilian Superior Electoral Court.*
3. *The internet application provider shall be held civilly liable, pursuant to Article 21, for damages resulting from content generated by third parties in cases of crime or illegal acts, without prejudice to the duty to remove the content. The same rule applies in cases of accounts reported as inauthentic.*

   3.1. In Cases of Crimes Against Honour, Article 19 of the MCI Applies, Without Prejudice to the Possibility of Removal by Extrajudicial Notification.

   3.2. In the case of successive replications of the offensive act already recognised by a court decision, all social network providers shall remove publications with identical content, regardless of new court decisions, upon judicial or extrajudicial notification.
4. *Providers are presumed liable for illegal content in the case of (a) paid advertisements and boosts; or (b) artificial distribution networks (chatbots or robots). In these cases, liability may arise regardless of notification. Providers shall be exempt from liability if they prove that they acted diligently and within a reasonable time to make the content unavailable.*
5. *The internet application provider is liable when it fails to immediately remove content that constitutes serious crimes as defined in the following exhaustive list: (a) anti-democratic conduct and acts that fall within Articles 286, sole paragraph, 359-L, 359-M, 359-N, 359-P, and 359-R of the Brazilian Criminal Code; (b) crimes of terrorism or preparatory acts of terrorism, as defined by Law No. 13,260/2016; (c) crimes of inducing, instigating or assisting suicide or self-mutilation, under the terms of Article 122 of the Brazilian Criminal Code; (d) incitement to discrimination on the basis of race, colour, ethnicity, religion, national origin, sexuality or gender identity (homophobic and transphobic conduct), punishable under Articles 20, 20-A, 20-B and 20-C of Law No. 7,716 of 1989; (e) crimes committed against women on the basis of their female gender, including content that propagates hatred towards women (Law No. 11,340/06; Law No. 10,446/02; Law No. 14,192/21; Brazilian Criminal Code, Article 141, § 3; Article 146-A; Article 147, § 1; Article 147-A; and Article 147-B of the Brazilian Criminal Code); (f) sexual crimes against vulnerable persons, child pornography and serious crimes against children and adolescents, pursuant to Articles 217-A, 218, 218-A, 218-B, 218-C, of the Brazilian Criminal Code and Articles 240, 241-A, 241-C, 241-D of the Statute of Child and Adolescent; (g) human trafficking (Brazilian Criminal Code, Article 149-A).*

   5.1. The Responsibility of Internet Application Providers Provided for in This Item Concerns the Configuration of Systemic Failure.

5.2 Failure to adopt adequate measures to prevent or remove the illegal content listed above, constituting a breach of the duty to act responsibly, transparently, and cautiously, is considered a systemic failure attributable to the internet application provider.

5.3. Measures that, According to the State of the Art, Provide the Highest Levels of Security for the Type of Activity Performed by the Provider Are Considered Adequate.

5.4. The existence of illegal content in an isolated, fragmented form is not, in itself, sufficient to give rise to civil liability under this item. However, in this case, the liability regime provided for in Article 21 shall apply.

5.5. In the cases provided for in this item, the person responsible for publishing the content removed by the internet application provider may request its reinstatement in court, by demonstrating the absence of illegality. Even if the content is restored by court order, no compensation will be imposed on the provider.

6. *The civil liability regime set out in Article 19 remains applicable to (a) email service providers; (b) application providers whose primary purpose is to hold closed video or voice meetings; (c) instant messaging service providers (also known as private messaging service providers), exclusively with regard to interpersonal communications, protected by the confidentiality of communications (Article 5, item XII, of the Brazilian Constitution).*
7. *Internet application providers that operate as marketplaces are civilly liable under the Consumer Defence Code (Law No. 8,078/90).*
8. *Internet application providers shall issue self-regulation that necessarily covers notification systems, due process, and annual transparency reports regarding extrajudicial notifications, advertisements, and boosts.*
9. *They must also provide users and non-users with specific service channels, preferably electronic, that are accessible and widely publicised on their respective platforms on a permanent basis.*
10. *These rules must be published and reviewed periodically, in a transparent manner and accessible to the public.*
11. *Internet application providers operating in Brazil must establish and maintain headquarters and a representative in the country, whose identification and contact information must be made available and easily accessible on their respective websites. This representation must grant the representative, necessarily a legal entity with headquarters in the country, full powers to (a) respond to administrative and judicial authorities; (b) provide the competent authorities with information regarding the provider's operations, the rules and procedures used for content moderation and complaint management by internal systems; transparency reports, monitoring and systemic risk management; the rules for user profiling (where applicable), advertising and paid content promotion; (c) comply with court orders; and (d) respond to and comply with any penalties, fines and financial charges incurred by the represented party, especially for non-compliance with legal and judicial obligations.*
12. *There shall be no strict liability in the application of the thesis set forth herein.*

13. *The National Congress is requested to draft legislation capable of remedying the deficiencies of the current regime with regard to the protection of fundamental rights.*
14. *In order to preserve legal certainty, the effects of this decision are modulated and shall only apply prospectively, except for final and unappealable decisions."*

Despite constituting a significant advancement in redefining the civil liability of digital platforms, the Federal Supreme Court's thesis still faces criticisms. Firstly, the decision maintains the requirement of a judicial order in cases involving criminal offences against honour (item 3.1), without clarifying whether extrajudicial notice would suffice for civil offences of the same nature. Secondly, although the thesis introduces a presumption of liability in cases of serious crimes (item 5), concerns arise as to the practical feasibility of expecting individual judges to operationalise such complex systemic guidelines, such as viral replication control or cross-platform enforcement (item 3.2), tasks arguably better entrusted to specialised public bodies or autonomous regulatory authorities. Additionally, internal inconsistencies emerge in item 12, which excludes strict liability in general, whereas item 7 affirms that marketplace providers remain subject to the Consumer Defence Code, a regime grounded in strict liability. Finally, the modulation clause, by merely stating that the decision applies "*prospectively*" (item 14), does not clarify its reach over pending cases involving past damages, thereby generating some uncertainty in ongoing litigation and compromising the very legal certainty the Court sought to promote.

Nevertheless, it must be acknowledged that the thesis of the Federal Supreme Court represents a landmark decision to the Brazilian legal framework concerning digital platforms liability. The Court expressly recognised the systemic existing risks in digital environment, moving beyond the restrictive paradigm posed by Article 19. Moreover, by reassuring the limits of judicial intervention, the decision formally urged the Brazilian National Congress to enact a comprehensive legislation able to address the regulatory gaps identified, particularly with regard to transparency, content moderation, and the protection of fundamental rights in the digital sphere. In this sense, the decision not only settles past controversies but also inaugurates a new normative cycle. It is not clear, however, if this new normative cycle will be sufficient to operate a real transition from judicial protagonism to a legislative responsibility in shaping the future architecture of digital governance in Brazil.

6 Conclusion

Article 19 of Law 12.965/2014 addresses the issue of civil liability of companies for content published on their platforms with an extremely restrictive approach, representing a notable regression compared to the trajectory previously established by Brazilian case law on this matter. By conditioning civil liability on non-compliance with a "*specific court order,*" Article 19 fosters a troubling limitation on the protection of internet users' rights, which often include fundamental rights expressly safeguarded by the Brazilian Constitution, such as honour, image, and privacy. In doing so, the provision effectively creates a legal "*bubble*" of non-liability, shielding technology companies that operate platforms where harmful content is hosted. As a result, any claim for reparation is redirected towards third parties, who are typically anonymous and whose identity and location can usually only be ascertained by the very companies that the Civil Rights Framework for the Internet exempts from liability. Even when identified, third parties often lack the technical or economic means to mitigate the spread of the damage, leading to a scenario in which any theoretical liability becomes practically meaningless.

Beyond its technical shortcomings, Article 19 stands as an unconstitutional barrier to the protection of fundamental rights in Brazil's digital sphere. By prioritising platform immunity over individual dignity, it reverses the constitutional hierarchy that places personal rights at the core of the legal order. Therefore, it calls for an interpretation with the Constitution, as outlined above.

The Brazilian Federal Supreme Court recently achieved such goal, with a ruling of "*partial unconstitutionality*" of Article 19. The legal consequences cannot be framed as a simple reinstatement of the general civil liability regime, known as *notice and takedown*. Rather than suppressing Article 19 in its entirety, the Court preserved a residual framework while simultaneously recognising a constitutional duty of care applicable to digital platforms, especially in cases involving serious crimes or systemic risks. As a result, platform liability is no longer contingent solely on judicial orders and may arise from extrajudicial notice and even independently from notice in some specific situations. This inaugurates a new model that incentivises proactive measures by digital platforms to control content and prevent harm under Brazilian law. Time will show if it was an adequate response.

References

Brazil. (2014, April 24). Law No. 12.965 of April 23, 2014 (Marco Civil da Internet). *Diário Oficial da União*. http://www.planalto.gov.br/ccivil_03/_ato2011-2014/2014/lei/l12965.htm

Brazilian Federal Supreme Court (STF). (2025, June 26). *Extraordinary Appeal No. 1.037.396 (Relator: Justice Dias Toffoli)*. Brasília: Supremo Tribunal Federal. https://portal.stf.jus.br/processos/detalhe.asp?incidente=5256536

Superior Court of Justice (STJ). (2004, November 23). *Special Appeal No. 566468/2004 (Relator: Justice Jorge Scartezzini)*. Brasília: Superior Tribunal de Justiça.

Schreiber, A. (2014). *Novos Paradigmas da Responsabilidade Civil*. Atlas, São Paulo.

United States Code. (2018). *Title 17—Copyrights*. In *United States Code* (Vol. 17, §§ 512 et seq.). U.S. Government Publishing Office. https://uscode.house.gov/view.xhtml?req=granuleid:USC-prelim-title17-section512

Anderson Schreiber is a leading scholar in Civil and Comparative Private Law. He is a Professor of Civil Law at the State University of Rio de Janeiro (UERJ), where he is also a member of the permanent faculty of the Master's and PhD Programme. He also teaches Private Law at Fundação Getulio Vargas (FGV). He holds a PhD in Comparative Private Law from the Università degli Studi del Molise (Italy) and a Master's Degree in Civil Law from UERJ. He has been a Visiting Researcher at the Max Planck Institute for Comparative and International Private Law (Hamburg). He is also a member of the International Academy of Comparative Law, a state attorney in Rio de Janeiro, and the author of several books and articles published in Brazil and abroad.

The manufacturer's authorised representative in the EU is Springer Nature Customer Service Centre GmbH, Europaplatz 3, 69115 Heidelberg, Germany. If you have any concerns regarding our products, please contact ProductSafety@springernature.com

Printed and bound by CPI Group (UK) Ltd, Croydon, CR0 4YY
21/09/2026
02219991-0009